How to Build 50 Classic Furniture Reproductions

Monte Burch

 Sterling Publishing Co., Inc. New York

Photo credits:
The Metropolitan Museum of Art: Project Two—Tavern Table
    (10.125.110), Gift of Mrs. Russell Sage, 1909;
    Project Thirty-Seven—Round Tilt-Top Table (25.115.32),
    Rogers Fund, 1925.
The Nelson-Atkins Museum of Art, Kansas City, Missouri
    (Nelson Fund): Project Forty-One—Hepplewhite Serpentine
    Bureau, 32- 190/1; Project Forty-Two—Hepplewhite Toilet
    Mirror, 32-190/2; Project Forty-Eight—Chippendale Lowboy,
    34-201; Project Fifty—Philadelphia Highboy, 33-163.

Every effort has been made to ensure that all the information in this
book is accurate. However, due to differing conditions, tools, and
individual skills, the author and the publisher cannot be responsible
for any injuries, losses, or other damages that may result from the
use of the information in this book.

Library of Congress Cataloging-in-Publication Data
Burch, Monte.
        How to build 50 classic furniture reproductions / by
    Monte Burch.
            p.   cm.
        Includes index.
        ISBN 0-8069-0302-3
        1. Furniture making.   I. Title.   II. Title: How to build
    fifty classic furniture reproductions.
    TT197.B943   1993
    749'.1'0287—dc20   92–41776
                                                CIP

10   9   8   7   6   5   4   3   2   1

Published by Sterling Publishing Company, Inc.
387 Park Avenue South, New York, N.Y. 10016
© 1993 by Monte Burch
Distributed in Canada by Sterling Publishing
℅ Canadian Manda Group, P.O. Box 920, Station U
Toronto, Ontario, Canada M8Z 5P9
Distributed in Great Britain and Europe by Cassell PLC
Villiers House, 41/47 Strand, London WC2N 5JE, England
Distributed in Australia by Capricorn Link Ltd.
P.O. Box 665, Lane Cove, NSW 2066
Manufactured in the United States of America
All rights reserved

Sterling ISBN 0-8069-0302-3

Acknowledgments

Putting together a book of this kind simply isn't possible without help from a lot of people. First and foremost is my wife, Joan, who does my editing and who checks and rechecks facts, figures and measured drawings. In general, she manages to keep things organized, making it possible always for me to find my scale ruler, favorite pen or a photo I need.

Thanks go to our daughter, Jodi, who spent an entire summer entering the manuscript into a computer, and our son Michael, who did all the darkroom work, including producing prints. Thanks also to my editor, Hannah Steinmetz, who has handled an extremely complicated project with skill and good humor.

Edna Faith, Elvie Wilson and Arlene Lear were kind enough to allow us into their homes to measure some of the fine furniture they have collected. I am also grateful for the cooperation of the museums we visited: the Nelson-Atkins Museum of Art, Kansas City, and the Metropolitan Museum of Art, New York. A special thanks to Ms. Carol Collier at the Nelson-Atkins Museum of Art for taking so much time to help us.

A number of tool manufacturers helped a great deal by supplying unusual new tools to try out on reproduction techniques for this book. Thanks go to the Toolmart Company, makers of the lathe duplicator; to Jeff Laskowski of Laskowski Enterprises Inc., makers of the Dupli-Carver® and the Wood-Mizer®; and to Carlo Venditto and Freud USA, makers of fine, industrial-quality woodworking tools, such as shaper cutters, dado sets, and saw blades. A special thanks to Mike Mangan of Sears for all his help in so many areas, to Susan Kirias of United Gilsonite Laboratories, and to Vince Pax at Shopsmith.

Preface

As a young man, I worked in a custom cabinet and furniture shop. My first job was to disassemble and repair broken furniture. I found that building furniture was a lot like putting together a puzzle. Often, what seemed like a simple joint was really much more complicated. I also noticed that regardless of style, furniture made with "classic joints" and good craftsmanship was able to stand up to the test of time.

I think you will find that building reproductions of fine furniture pieces is exciting, challenging and very rewarding. After your first couple of reproductions, you will be able to appreciate fully the craftsmanship of pieces in museums and private collections.

The fifty projects in this book have been drawn from a wide range of furniture-making traditions. I have tried to pick furniture from as many of the major furniture styles as possible, including the Jacobean period in England and the classic styles of the Queen Anne period. Then there are some reproductions of furniture by one of the most famous and most copied cabinetmakers, Thomas Chippendale. Some projects have been patterned after Early American pieces that were made in Philadelphia, the great furniture-building center during the middle to late part of the 18th century. But this book covers many later American pieces as well, including reproductions of furniture made in the early 19th century, in the Victorian period, and even in the early 1900s.

This book has projects for almost every type of furniture, as well. It tells how to make beds, tables, chairs, chests, and rather more unusual pieces, such as a lowboy, highboy, and even an upholstered wing chair. While most craftsmen probably will not bother to do any upholstering themselves, the wing-chair project provides insight into how wood frames of "stuffed" chairs are made.

This book includes projects for every level of woodworking skill, ranging from simple projects, such as a clock shelf, to the extremely complicated and elaborate pieces, such as the Philadelphia highboy, which was patterned after an original in the Nelson-Atkins Museum of Art, in Kansas City. Tackling the highboy is definitely not for novice craftsmen. But this is not to discourage anyone from attempting the project. In furniture making, as in any other endeavor, skill comes with experience. And any craftsman who successfully completes the highboy project is no longer an amateur.

In addition to the satisfaction of using your woodworking skills to construct these reproductions, you will find an intrinsic pleasure in decorating your home with classic furniture pieces that cannot be purchased in stores. And, of course, a faithful reproduction of a classic—particularly a larger, more complicated one—can be quite a valuable addition to your home.

Each of the projects here will provide a chance to build an unusual piece of furniture that any craftsman would be proud to display. I hope you get as much enjoyment from building these projects as I did in preparing them for this book.

Contents

Basic Furniture-Reproducing Techniques

All the projects in this book have been measured from actual furniture pieces and are reproduced in scale drawings. I used either ½- or ¼-inch scale, which means ¼ inch to the foot, etc., for the original pencil drawings. But, because drawings had to be reduced to fit in the book, the scale (but not relative proportions) have been changed.

There are also a lot of squared drawings for carvings, turnings and scroll-shaped items. In fact, almost every project has some. All the squares in the drawings equal one inch. In other words, to create a full-size plan, make a grid of one-inch squares on a sheet of paper. Number both the grid on the squared drawings in the book and the full-size grid. Place dots at each point where a pattern line intersects a squared line. Then simply connect the dots to transfer the pattern to your sheet of paper with the full-size grid. To transfer this pattern to the stock, rub the back of the paper with charcoal or put carbon paper between the pattern and the stock.

Choosing the Correct Woods

Choosing the correct wood is one of the most important aspects of building classic reproduction furniture. For instance, Chippendale lowboys were traditionally made of walnut or mahogany and would be completely out of character in oak. This would affect both the appearance and value.

On the other hand, country furniture, though beautifully constructed, was quite often made of whatever wood happened to be available.

In most cases, however, knowledgeable craftsmen also tried to match the characteristics of the wood to the project. For instance, the earlier furniture pieces from England were quite often made of oak because it was available, but also because it was a strong and sturdy building material.

Much fine furniture today is made of oak, and it is an excellent choice for many of the projects shown in this book. But it should be noted that oak is hard to carve, especially on delicate undercut carvings. For this reason carving on oak furniture usually consists of simple chip carving, such as that on the English court cupboard. Fine carving on mirror frames and other items, especially those that were gilded, was frequently done in tulipwood or basswood, and that is still a good choice today. But if differences in types of wood will show up on a finished piece, you have no choice but to do carvings in the wood chosen for the rest of the piece. Thus, carving characteristics may well be a factor in selecting wood for a project. Walnut and mahogany both carve quite well. Walnut is a little softer and easier to carve than mahogany. Walnut, on the other hand, can be somewhat brittle across the grain, and you must watch that chips do not "pop out" during carving.

Walnut and mahogany were the primary woods used by the English furniture makers during the Georgian and Chippendale periods. The latter was the great furniture-building era of the middle 1700s. Americans often substituted wild cherry for these woods. Wild cherry has about the same workability as mahogany, and was often finished to resemble mahogany. To some degree it does. But with a natural finish, wild cherry is one of the most beautiful woods, and it's a shame so much cherry furniture has been stained dark.

Mahogany was used for the majority of the furniture made from the early 1700s to the late 1800s. It is still a treasured furniture wood, although true mahogany—not Honduras, Mexican or African mahogany—is quite rare and expensive. There are many reasons for the popularity of mahogany as a furniture wood. First, of course, is its beauty. But it is also easy to work and carve and not prone to insect infestation, warping, and shrinking. It's also a strong, long-lasting wood; this durability is an important consideration when great pains are to be taken to construct a fine piece of furniture.

The only wood that approaches mahogany in terms of use by Early American furniture builders is black walnut. English furniture builders did not use much black walnut because it was not native to England. But among American colonists and furniture builders it was a very popular wood from about 1690 to 1740, running through the Georgian and Queen

Anne periods. Although used to some extent during the Chippendale period, it was not nearly as popular.

Walnut is an extremely beautiful wood and has many configurations that are used in furniture making, including veneers from burls. It is easy to work and holds a cut quite well. The main problem with walnut is that it is subject to insect infestation, and many fine, museum-quality furniture pieces have been literally eaten to dust.

Walnut is usually classed into one of four basic varieties: French, English, California, and black walnut. French walnut holds a cut best. It is highly prized by gunstock builders, because it takes a fine checkering, and very little of it is available for furniture building.

Because of its abundance, maple was often used as a substitute for both mahogany and walnut by many Early American craftsmen. This was especially true throughout the New England area, where walnut was not as common.

There are two varieties of maple used for furniture: hard-rock maple and sugar maple. Both were used extensively throughout most of New England from about 1760 to the middle 1800s.

A beautiful hardwood, maple was used for everything from chairs to highboys, and fine examples of curly-maple work can still be seen in museums. But maple is hard to work, especially the figured kinds, such as curly or birds-eye. It will dull tools quickly and is extremely hard to carve. It is, however, an excellent choice for turnings, so furniture builders

Choosing the correct wood for a reproduction project is very important. Not only should the wood be similar to the type used in the original furniture piece, it should also be suited to the type of construction involved. For instance, walnut was extremely popular during the Queen Anne, early Georgian, and other periods. It can be turned and carved quite well, so it is well suited to this type of project. On the other hand, hickory would be a better choice for pieces that must be bent to shape.

tended to use more turnings on their furniture made of maple.

The softer woods, such as pine, were also used by Early American country craftsmen, again mostly because of their availability. But pine was also easy to work and had a beautiful appearance. Although yellow pine was sometimes used for furniture, the primary pine variety used was white, then called "pumpkin pine." There were very large trees then, and broad wooden surfaces on chests, tabletops, etc., were often made from a single wide board of white pine. In many instances the broad surfaces of a furniture piece were made from pine, while the legs were made of sturdier maple.

Fruitwoods, such as apple and pear, were also used for furniture. Apple, a favorite wood for turnings, was popular during both the early Georgian and Chippendale periods of furniture building. Apple wood resembles birch, which was also often substituted for mahogany.

Many other woods, of course, were used for building fine furniture. Exotic woods, such as teak or rosewood, were imported for cabinet pieces built to the particular desires of a customer. Other woods were used because they were available. During the Victorian period, a lot of furniture made of gum was passed off as mahogany.

One aspect of the early cabinetmakers that isn't seen as much these days is the use of different kinds of wood in a single piece. The idea is to take advantage of the characteristics of each type of wood. For example, a chair could be made with hickory bent pieces, maple turned pieces and a pine seatboard.

Naturally, all wood used by early furniture builders was air dried, and it often took several years to dry even a 1-inch-thick board. Even then, the wood was dried only to ambient humidity. As a result, early craftsmen had to be extremely careful to use joinery that allowed for the expansion and contraction of wood. This is one of the main reasons why many antiques are in better shape than more recently constructed pieces using weaker but less complicated joinery and kiln-dried woods. The use of frame-and-panel construction, with panels free to "float" in the frames, allows for normal day-to-day expansion and contraction caused by humidity changes. By the same token, large surfaces on antiques, such as tabletops, usually have been finished on both top and bottom surfaces to minimize warping.

Early craftsmen also knew that if you secured joints without any "give" they would eventually split the wood parts. For this reason, slotted dovetails and dado joints were used on many furniture pieces. Of course, with today's kiln-dried woods and hardwood-faced plywood, many of the problems faced by early craftsmen have been solved. But some of their tech-

Wood for the project will often be purchased, kiln-dried stock. When imported woods such as mahogany are called for, you will have little choice but to use kiln-dried stock. Recycled lumber can also be used. The walnut shown was salvaged from an old barn.

For those who have their own wood lot, a one-man sawmill, such as the Belsaw® unit, can often pay for itself in savings on hardwood stock.

This portable sawmill, the Wood-Mizer® by Laskowski Enterprises Inc., is also an excellent choice because you can easily move it from place to place. Since it is portable, you are able to saw logs that would normally be discarded or used for firewood.

One of the best investments you can make is a good surface planer. The unit shown will plane a 12-inch board. You can use it to plane salvaged lumber, home-sawn lumber, or rough-cut, kiln-dried lumber.

niques are still important for creating long-lasting furniture.

Although I purchase a lot of kiln-dried stock, I also like to use old, salvaged woods. I hunt especially for walnut and have found it in a variety of places, including discarded church pews and old barns. I have located the remnants of a barn that is over a hundred years old. Although the barn collapsed, I have salvaged a great deal of excellent walnut stock from it. The wood is extremely dry and, when planed, produces a fine powder. But it is very hard and cuts and finishes beautifully.

There is also a fairly large walnut grove on our farm, and I use a small, one-man Belsaw® saw mill to mill my own white oak and walnut lumber for furniture building. Any of the small saw mills, such as the Belsaw or portable band saw mill by Laskowski Enterprises Inc., are excellent for the purpose.

Although I air-dry wood, it is possible to build a solar air dryer that will speed up the process quite a bit. Plans and information are available from the Department of Forest Products, 210 Cheatham Hall, Virginia Tech, Blacksburg, Virginia 24061.

Tools

Naturally, all the period-style furniture pieces were built with hand tools alone, including treadle or foot-powered lathes for the turnings. Furniture can still be built that way. In fact, hand tools are enjoying something of a renaissance, and many fine ones are available from woodworking supply companies. Sears also has a full line of fine woodworking hand tools. For the projects in this book a set of moulding planes such as the Model 55, an old-timer produced by Stanley®, are a necessity. A number of other specialty planes can also help, including tongue-and-groove, dado and rabbeting planes.

Most craftsmen, however, will want to use modern tools or a combination of hand and power tools. Many modern tools can make recreating antique furniture much easier. These include the standard shop saws, drill presses, sanders, etc. But there are also specialty tools, such as shapers, routers and especially

To re-create some mouldings, you can use one of the old Stanley® 55 hand-moulding planes. These are no longer being made, but you may find one at an auction or through an antiques dealer. They work just as well today as they did a hundred years ago.

One of the many Stanley® 55 moulding plane cutters that can be used to duplicate old mouldings.

Another useful hand plane by Stanley® is the tongue-and-groove plane, here being used to cut a tongue on one side of a piece of stock.

With a quick adjustment, the plane also cuts the grooves in the opposite side of the stock.

The resulting tongue-and-groove joint will be smooth and snug-fitting.

A dado plane can also be used to cut dadoes or dovetail slots in stock by hand.

New tools make short work of re-creating antique mouldings, etc. Here, a router is being used to shape the edge of the frame for a Chippendale mirror project.

With the wide variety of accessories and cutter heads available, almost any type of old-style moulding can be duplicated by using a router and router table.

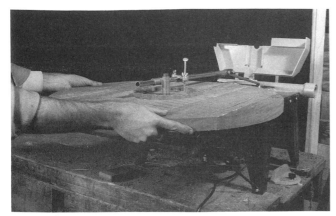

Fit the table with an edge-crafter accessory, and a piecrust tabletop is easy to make.

With the Sears® Router Crafter, a router can be used to cut reeding or fluting, depending on the router bit used.

the router accessories by Sears. These include the router table and Edge Crafter, which can be used to make the scalloped edges on Georgian-style tilt-top, piecrust tables. The Sears® Router Crafter can be used for fluting spiralling legs as well.

Another excellent modern-day tool is a lathe duplicator. You can't fully appreciate these duplicators until you make a full set of dining room furniture with turned legs, turned back splats, and turned arm supports. The tool shown here is from the Toolmart Corporation. It quickly and easily duplicates almost any turning. You can even keep your patterns to duplicate the part any time you wish. The pattern can be a round turning or simply a flat profile cut from ¼-inch hardboard. Incidentally, the latter is a great way of storing a number of furniture patterns for duplicating as needed.

Another tool that can really help is a carving duplicator, such as the Dupli-Carver® from Laskowski Enterprises, Inc. It can duplicate carved panels of cabinets, carved cabriole legs and even elaborately carved decorative pieces. In fact, you could even take

a finished cabriole leg and a chunk of wood and simply start right out duplicating the leg, without even blocking it out first. (However, rough-cutting the leg first on a band saw does save a great deal of time.) As you can see, this one tool makes creating the ornately carved cabriole legs on a piece such as the highboy much easier, taking a great deal of the effort out of the project.

Another excellent, modern-day tool that saves a lot of work is a lathe duplicator. The Toolmart Duplicator is shown here, mounted on a Shopsmith® lathe.

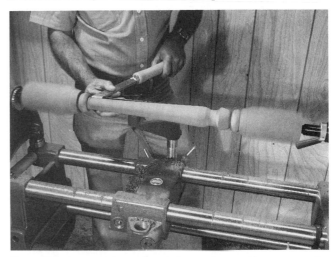

To reproduce a number of turnings, first turn the pattern piece on your lathe.

Then duplicate your turning with the lathe duplicator, which is guided by the shape of the original.

The rough-cut duplicate will look like this.

Some fine smoothing will clean up the duplicate. Then sand it smooth while it is still in the lathe.

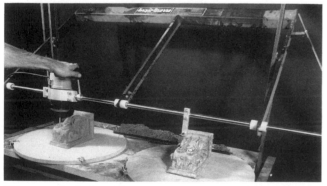

Most period furniture pieces have a lot of carving work and a carving duplicator can be a great time-saver. It can be used for reproducing flat carvings such as drawer fronts, pedestals, etc.

The carving duplicator also reproduces elaborate parts, such as cabriole legs. Just use the stylus of the machine to guide the router cutter over the block until it is shaped to the original.

Another way to re-create a turning is to make up a pattern. Here the center post for a tilt-top table is being traced. Trace the pattern onto a piece of hardboard and saw out the profile on a band saw. Then use this as the guide for the lathe duplicator when making turnings.

Joints

The types of joints used by early cabinetmakers depended a great deal on the type of materials they had on hand. In many cases, neither glue nor other fasteners, such as nails or screws, were used. For finer furniture pieces, such as the highboys, the primary joint was a type of mortise-and-tenon joint fastened with glue. Often these were also secured with wooden pegs set in offset holes. Once the tenons had been seated, the peg was driven in place to pull the pieces together firmly. Then the ends of the pegs were cut off and smoothed flush with the wood surface. This type of joint is used in both the lowboy and tavern table.

Another common type of joint was a dowel joint, although this was used much later, especially in the manufacturing period of American furniture making. It is also an excellent, strong joint and can be made quite easily using modern equipment.

One of the most popular methods of joining cabinet shelves to the sides was a slotted dovetail or dado joint. These joints often were stopped just short of the front facer of the cabinet and were thus concealed from view. This was a popular method of installing web dust frames, as well as shelves, on such pieces as highboys and chests.

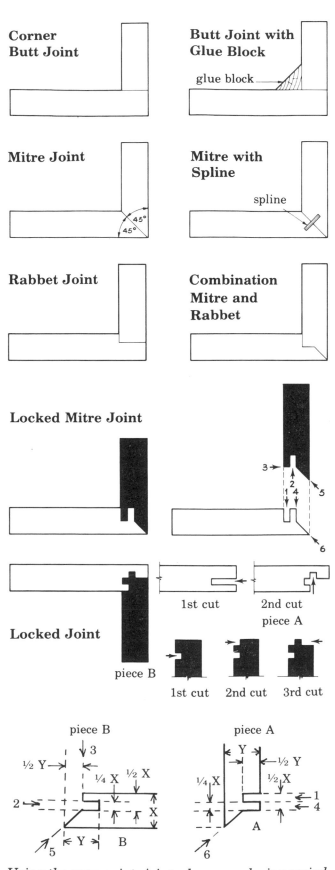

Corner Butt Joint

Butt Joint with Glue Block

glue block

Mitre Joint

45°
45°

Mitre with Spline

spline

Rabbet Joint

Combination Mitre and Rabbet

Locked Mitre Joint

3
2
1 4
5
6

Locked Joint

1st cut

2nd cut
piece A

piece B

1st cut   2nd cut   3rd cut

piece B
3
½ Y
¼ X   ½ X
2
X
5   Y   B

piece A
Y
½ Y
¼ X   ½ X
1
4
A
6

Using the appropriate joint when reproducing period furniture is extremely important, both for the strength of the piece and for authenticity. A number of joints used in furniture construction are shown here.

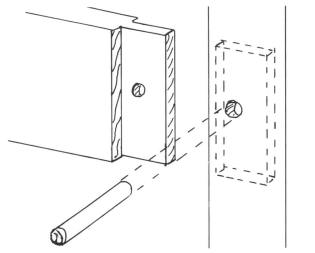

One of the most common joints used in early furniture is mortise-and-tenon. The joint was often held together with a peg inserted in holes that were drilled slightly offset from each other. This wedged the two parts tightly together when the peg was driven in place.

One of the simplest methods of cutting mortises is with a drill press. You must have a stop gauge on the drill bit or a stop marker on the press to assure all the holes are bored to the same depth. Use the bit to drill a line of overlapping holes to rough out the mortise.

Use a sharp chisel to remove the wood from between the holes and to smooth up the mortise sides and bottom.

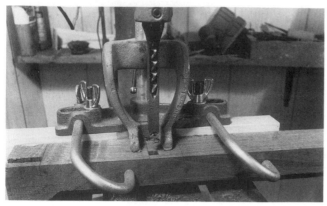

A mortising attachment for your drill press can make the job much easier and more accurate. It is especially helpful when deep mortises must be cut.

There are several different kinds and sizes of mortising attachments, including round mortisers and square-hole mortising attachments. Round mortisers can be attached in moments. The square-hole mortiser shown here is a semi-permanent attachment and if you do a lot of mortising work, a second drill press fitted with the mortising accessory can be a great help. Or you might be able to find an antique mortising machine that would be ideal!

The tenons for a mortise-and-tenon joint can be cut quite easily on a radial arm or table saw. Make sure tenons are snug in the mortises but not too tight. Although a single blade can be used to cut a few tenons, a dado head will speed up the job.

The dowel joint is very popular for joining together narrow pieces to make up wide stock.

The first step is to joint all edges of the stock to make them as smooth as possible. Lay out the pieces to be joined, alternating heartwood and sapwood facing up. This cuts down on warping problems. Then number or letter each piece and mark directly across each joint of the wood with a sharp pencil.

For precise alignment of the holes, use a Stanley dowelling jig to guide the bit. You can also use a stop gauge on the bit to make sure all holes are bored to the correct depth.

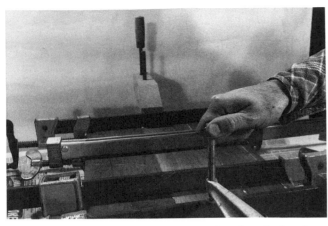

Then place glue in the holes, tap the dowels in place using a rubber mallet, and clamp the stock until the glue sets. Note that there are clamps at each end, in addition to a bar clamp running across the stock. These end clamps prevent the piece from buckling as a result of the pressure of the bar clamps.

Wipe away excess glue with a warm, damp cloth. There will still be some excess after it hardens, and that can be removed easily with a sharp chisel.

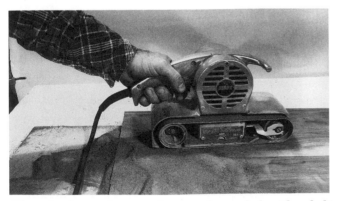

The glued-up piece can be rough-sanded with a belt sander, then finish-sanded or scraped with a cabinet scraper.

Dowelling is also an excellent method for joining rails and stiles to posts and furniture legs. Again lay out and carefully mark the pieces; then drill the holes using a dowelling jig for accuracy.

Keep the front edge of the jig the exact distance from the front face on both wood pieces, and the holes will be positioned exactly.

Place glue in the dowel holes and on the joining surfaces. Tap the dowels in place.

Sometimes nothing more than glue is used for joining pieces, especially when gluing up strips to make turning blocks. Make sure the glue is evenly distributed over both surfaces.

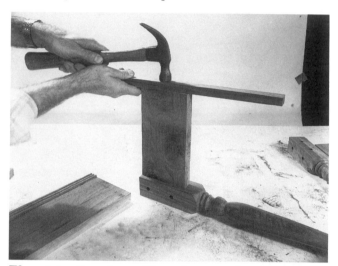

Then join the pieces. Note the use of a scrap block when tapping pieces together to prevent damage to the wood surface.

Then clamp securely overnight.

On a project such as this table, the two side sections are assembled first, then front and back pieces are put in place between them. Afterwards, turn the project upright on a smooth, flat surface. If all the legs rest evenly on the surface, clamp the parts securely together until the glue sets.

Edge Joint with Spline

spline

Edge Joint with Rabbetted Edges

Tongue-and-Groove Edge Joint

Shaped Edge Joint

Another method of joining stock to make wide boards is to shape the edges and use glue on the joints. Shown here are a few of the various configurations that can be used.

Edge Joint with Rabbet Edges

Tongue-and-groove joints are often used on antiques where rails and panels are joined to posts and legs.

Both the tongues and the grooves can be cut on a table saw or radial arm saw. Note that the saw guard has been removed for clarity.

A dado set can make cutting the grooves a fast and precise job. (The guard has been removed for clarity.)

Dado Joint **Combined Rabbet and Dado** **Dovetail Dado**

Dado or dovetailed dado joints were quite popular for joining shelves or web frames to the sides of cabinets.

Cutting the Dovetail Slot

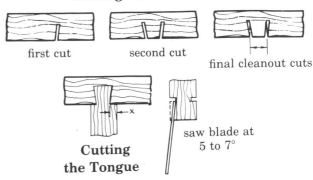

first cut second cut final cleanout cuts

Cutting the Tongue saw blade at 5 to 7°

The dado can be cut with a dado set in a radial arm or table saw. But cut a dovetail dado with a regular saw blade tilted to make the angle cuts for the dovetail groove; then cut between to remove the material. It makes both the tongue and dovetail groove.

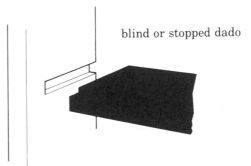

blind or stopped dado

Most of the dado or dovetail slot joints on period furniture are blind, or stopped back from the front edge of the side.

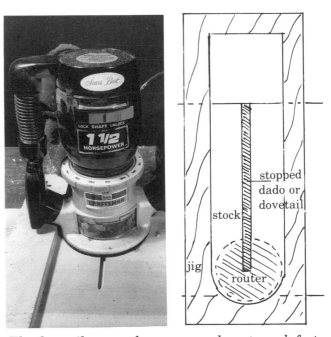

stopped dado or dovetail

stock

jig

router

The dovetail groove, however, can be cut much faster using a dovetail bit in a router. A special jig can be used to guide a router when making these stopped cuts (either a dado or dovetail dado joint).

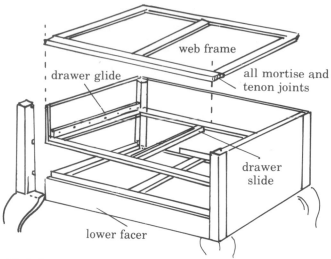

Web-frame construction is used on a great deal of period-style furniture. Shown is an exploded view of a typical web-frame construction, set in a case formed by leg posts and panelled sides and back.

In fact, a great deal of period furniture uses a standard web or dust frame construction. Web frames (see drawing) are drawer supports that also serve as anchors for the sides or other frame pieces. The side panels are left free to "float" in their frames and are not attached to the web frames. Corner posts in all cases are notched to receive the web frames, thus providing another joint to strengthen the assembly. Frames are assembled using cross-lap joints, mortise-and-tenon joints, or dowel joints. The fronts of the web frames are made of hardwood to match the rest of the case, while the back, sides and center sections are often made of more economical softwoods.

Drawer guides are fitted between the posts to guide the sides of the drawer and a small wooden drawer slide is often attached to the center web-frame member to guide the drawer in place. Drawer stop blocks may also be glued to the back web-frame member, so that when the drawer is closed, its front will be flush with the cabinet front.

Drawers

The proper construction and fitting of the drawers is extremely important. In most cases, the best method is first to make the cabinet or carcass, then measure and fit each individual drawer into its opening. With this method, you can be sure of the best possible fit for the drawer, and that it will work easily in the carcass. With a few exceptions, the drawers in period furniture are flush; that is, their fronts are flush with the front facers of the case. Some lowboys and highboys had overlapping drawer fronts, and in some cases only three edges were overlapped.

The drawer fronts are usually made of hardwood stock to match the carcass wood, while the drawer sides, back, and bottom are of softwood stock, often

planed down so that it is thinner than the fronts. This is still the best method, but some craftsmen use plywood or hardboard for the drawer bottoms.

Drawer sides are usually dovetailed into the drawer fronts, and the sides and back are dovetailed together. There is usually a dado cut into the inside face of the front, back and the sides about ¼ inch up from their bottom edge. The bottom piece is set in this dado. The back has a notch cut in its bottom edge to allow for a center drawer guide that slides through it.

Small drawers such as "cubbyhole" drawers in desks or secretaries are simply glued together.

You can also get special shaper heads that are used by cabinet and furniture makers to cut special drawer joints. These joints are cut using the appropriate cutters, or in the case of the Freud unit shown here, by merely positioning the board in different directions. The drawers are then joined with glue.

Frame-and-Panel

Frame-and-panel assemblies may be either for the sides, front, or back of a case, or they may be used for doors and sometimes even drawers. When frame-and-panel assemblies are used on the sides, the front and back legs usually act as the verticals or stiles of the frame. Horizontal pieces—stretchers or rails— are fastened to them with tenons cut to fit into grooves in the legs. There is also a groove cut into the inside edges of the rails. The edges of the panels fit into these grooves. The panels are not glued in place, but are allowed to "float" free. This allows for the shrinking and swelling that occurs with solid hardwoods.

Tenons can be cut quite easily with a radial arm or table saw, or even with hand tools. The grooves in the leg posts and the rails are cut using a router in a router table, a dado head in a radial arm or table saw, or with a hand dado plane.

The panels on door frame-and-panel assemblies are often dressed with a shaper, using a Safe-T-Planer®, or with a table saw tilted at a slight angle. This creates a raised panel effect.

Door frame-and-panel assemblies can be made in several ways and with several different types of joints. One very popular door joint used today by furniture builders is a cabinet joint. A modification is also used on some of the older furniture pieces. The cabinet joint is a shaped edge on the inside edges of the rails and stiles, providing a good glue-holding joint. The shaping is done on a shaper. Use a matching set of female and male cutters, as well as spacers, to make the different cuts.

Veneering

In many cases, the wood used in period furniture was veneered. Veneering can also be used to create truly beautiful, one-of-a-kind furniture pieces. With

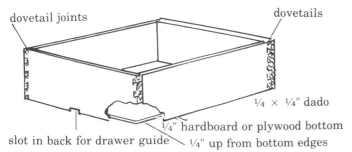

Basic drawer construction for antique furniture consists of dovetailed joints with the bottom inset in a dado in the sides, back and front. In most cases the drawer front is flush with the carcass facing.

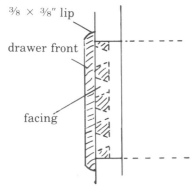

Quite often the front is lipped as shown here.

Laying out Dovetails

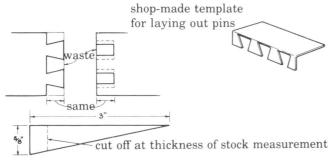

Common dovetail layout

Drawer dovetails can be cut with hand tools. The first step is to lay out the pins for the joint, using a bevel gauge or a homemade template.

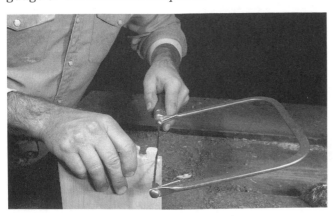

Cut the pins using a dovetail or coping saw.

Use the pins to mark the cuts on the mating board.

You can cut the dovetails quickly and easily with a dovetailing accessory for your router.

Installation of drawers begins with the drawer guide. The guide is first installed loose, or fastened only at the front end.

Then the drawer is inserted over the guide and moved around until the front fits perfectly and the drawer slides easily. The position of the drawer guide is marked and then it is fastened in place to the back of the case.

Drawer Glue Joints by Freud

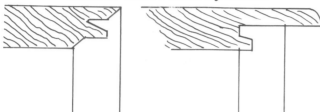

In addition to dovetails, special drawer glue joints can also be created.

They are made with special Freud cutter heads on your shaper. The head shown can be used to cut both pieces by cutting one piece on its edge and the other down flat.

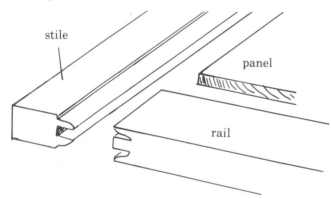

stile

panel

rail

Frame-and-panel assemblies, such as doors or cabinet sides, are often made using a cabinet joint.

Cabinet joints are made using special male and female cutters, such as those shown from Freud, on routers or shapers. The joints are then simply fastened together with glue.

Decorating Frame-and-Panel Doors

veneer
frame shaped
frame veneer covered

diamond matched

French Provincial frame design

French Provincial door design
raised panel

applied moulding
frame shaped on outer face

carved and stamped panel

shaped frame
applied moulding
¼" plywood veneer covered

raised panel
applied moulding

applied moulding

raised panel

Corner, Side and Arc Designs

Carbide Router Bits (¼" shafts)

Panels are usually left free to float in the frames, and are not glued in place. Panels may be flat, routed, shaped, or raised.

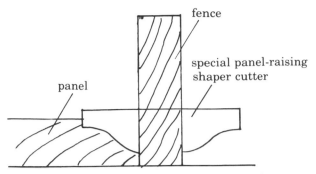

Shaped panels are cut using a shaper and a fence if they are square-sided, with a guide pin for curved panels.

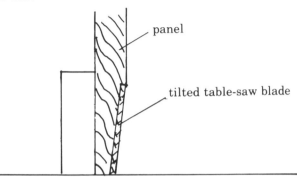

Cut raised panels on a table saw with the blade set at an angle.

Veneer can be used to create highly unusual and decorative furniture surfaces. It is available in a number of highly figured grains and unusual woods. With today's contact glue it is quick and easy to apply.

Veneer Press Frames (make as many as necessary to space 6–8″ length of stock)

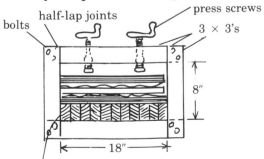

2 × 4's are edge-glued and surface-planed to form bed

Using a veneer press and animal glue was the old-fashioned way to make up veneered panels.

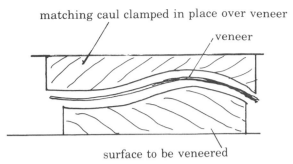

A veneer press is still one method of veneering angled and curved surfaces. Use carpenter's glue and special forms shaped to hold the veneer in place until the glue sets.

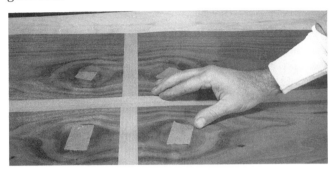

There are any number of ways the veneer pieces can be joined to form beautiful patterns. The first step in veneering a pattern is to make up the pattern. Do this by taping the front of the veneer sheets together with brown-paper tape.

Coat the veneer back and wood surface with veneer cement and allow it to dry until tacky. Place wooden strips on the tacky wood surface and put the veneer sheet over the strips. Remove one end strip and press the veneer in place at that point.

Remove the remaining strips one by one and roll the veneer solidly down in place, then scrape away the tape. Do not use a power sander as you can quickly cut through the veneer.

today's contact glue, it's much easier to make up a veneered surface than in the past, when a full set of clamp frames was needed to hold the veneer firmly to the panel until the glue set.

Mouldings

Re-creating appropriate mouldings for the various furniture-making periods is a large part of the work that goes into reproducing antiques. It is very important to match the moulding pattern as closely as possible.

Although all the moulding used on early pieces was hand-made, many shapes can be duplicated these days with shapers, routers, or shaper heads on radial arm or table saws. The equipment used depends on the individual mouldings. Carved mouldings are first shaped to the profile; then the carvings are cut into them. Larger mouldings are usually made up of several different pieces glued together to create the final shape. Old-fashioned moulding planes can also be used to recreate the exact shape of most moulding profiles.

Scratch stock was a very popular moulding method used on earlier furniture. Since the tools were hand-made, the moulding profile was very individual. The only way to duplicate this pattern is to build a scratch-stock tool for each profile you need.

The tool is made by cutting a block of stock into a handle to fit over the edge of the stock to be shaped (see drawing). Then tool steel is filed and sharpened to the profile desired. It is fastened to the wooden handle blank with wood screws. By pulling the steel edge over the moulding stock edge, it scratches the pattern into the edge, creating the "scratch stock" profile. Scratch-stock moulding is always shallow. Even so, it takes quite a bit of time to create a full, complicated profile with this method.

Moulding is shaped in some cases, such as for the pediment moulding on top of highboys. These mouldings are created by first roughing out the profile on a wide piece of stock. Then the moulding is cut on a shaper using a pin guide without the fence. Finally, the moulding piece is cut away from the wide stock.

Cock beading is a form of moulding that was used quite extensively, especially during the early to middle 1800s. It was used to help protect the edges of a veneered front as well as to provide a simple decoration. It is a tiny rounded bead of wood normally inset into a rabbet around the outside edge of the drawer front. In some instances it is simply glued in place over the veneer; however, it is also sometimes inset in from the edge of the door or drawer front.

Bending Wood

Some furniture, especially the later Victorian oak pieces, such as the oak dining chair and oak rocker, have some bent parts. The first step in creating these bent parts is to acquire unseasoned green wood. It

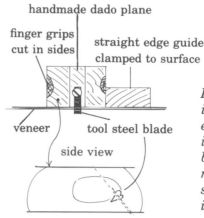

Inlays can be set in veneer quite easily. Straight inlay grooves can be cut with a router or with a special handmade inlay tool.

Use an oval matte cutter for cutting oval grooves for doors, such as on a Chippendale breakfront project. Then inlays are glued in place with contact cement.

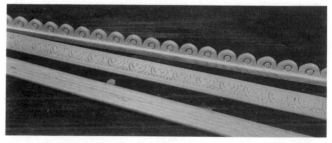

Carved mouldings are first cut to profile with power tools. Then the carving is done on the moulding strips. Sometimes you can buy carved mouldings, such as these from R & R Wood Products Corp.

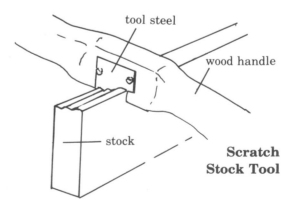

To make scratch-stock moulding, the tool is pulled along the edge of the stock to cut the moulding shape. You can make this cutter from a piece of wood and tool steel.

Moulded curved pieces, such as those on the top of a Philadelphia highboy pediment, are made by first cutting the curved shape on a band saw on wide stock.

Then cut the moulding on a shaper using a guide pin system.

And finally, cut the moulding away from the wide stock.

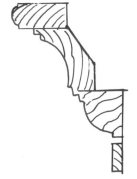

Complicated moulding is often made up of several different moulding profiles, cut separately and glued together.

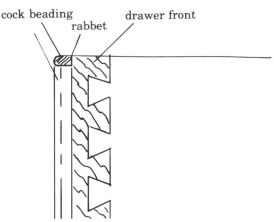

Cock beading is a form of moulding that is applied to drawer fronts and sometimes doors. It is usually glued in a rabbet around the drawer edge, but if inset from the sides it is mounted in a dado or groove. It is rounded on the top edge, mitred at the corners, and glued in place.

should be straight-grained, without any knots or weak spots. Preferably it should be hickory or white oak. The latter was used on both of the chairs shown. In the case of shaped or carved pieces, such as the back splat of the rocker, the pieces are first cut to shape and carved, then bent to shape. The primary method of bending wood is to use steam and then fasten it over a form.

There are several homemade shop steamers that can be made for steaming wood pieces. You can steam in the old-fashioned way with a simple fire outdoors, boiling water to create the steam. Or make a smaller kitchen-stove unit for steaming small parts. Regardless of the method used, the wood should be steamed for at least an hour for each inch of thickness. Then remove it from the steam using heavy rubber gloves, being careful not to burn yourself, and, as quickly as possible, clamp it to the form. Note that the form must be a bit more pronounced than the final curve you wish to attain with the wood stock.

Dry the wood as fast as possible with a heat lamp, but do not expose it to direct sunlight. It will take a bit of experimentation to find just the right curve to the form for each individual piece, species and size of stock.

Finishing

The amount of final smoothing and the quality of finish applied to your reproduction furniture piece will make or break your efforts. A fine, warm, mellow finish that reveals the true color and character of the wood, yet protects it from use and the elements, sometimes requires as much time as the construction of the project itself.

Early furniture makers used everything from shellac to varnish, lacquers, oil, and even paint.

Steamer

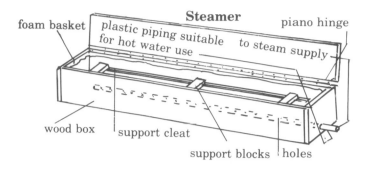

foam basket · plastic piping suitable for hot water use · piano hinge · to steam supply · wood box · support cleat · support blocks · holes

Clamping a Steamed Piece to Form

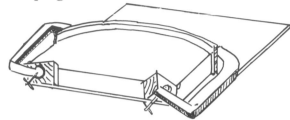

This homemade steamer helps when pieces must be bent to form special shapes, such as the back splats on chairs and arms or legs on some Victorian chairs. The wood must be green and should be an easily bent wood such as hickory or white oak. After the wood has been steamed, it is clamped to a special form until it dries.

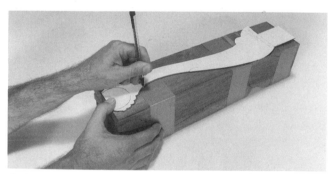

Cabriole legs can be made quite easily with a band saw. First, make up a pattern from stiff cardboard and mark it on the leg blank.

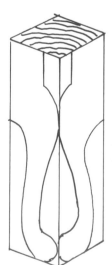 

It should be marked on two adjacent sides. Then cut one profile using a band saw.

Tape the cut-off pieces back together and re-mark across the tape using the paper pattern. Then cut away the outlines for the opposite side of the leg on a band saw.

Notice the beginning of a leg shape shown here.

Sand the leg to the shape desired, using a belt sander.

The foot on the leg can be carved in a traditional ball-and-claw shape.

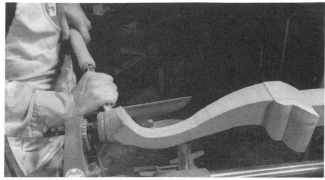

Or you can turn a Queen Anne slipper or similar style foot.

Tapered Legs

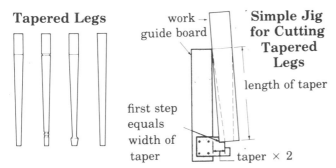

Simple Jig for Cutting Tapered Legs

work →
guide board
length of taper
first step equals width of taper
taper × 2

Quite often legs must be tapered. This can be done using the jig shown here on a table or radial arm saw.

Sometimes you may want to kerf stock to create a rounded or bent shape, such as on the curved frames of a china cabinet. This is done by making spaced saw kerfs using a table or radial arm saw.

Glue blocks anchored in place serve as guides for the kerfed piece.

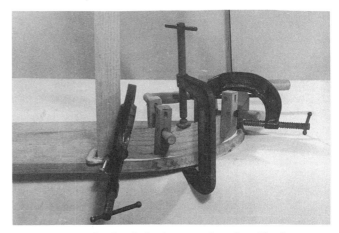

Then fasten the kerfed piece to the glue blocks.

Some carving, such as chip carving, is quite easy to do with the right tools. A straight-down cut is made first. Then a scoop cut breaks out the appropriate chip.

Relief carving is a bit more complicated. Again, the first step is to make a straight-down cut to outline the carving.

Then the chisel or gouge is turned and used to remove the background from around the carving.

Small chisels and rasps are then used to finish off the carving.

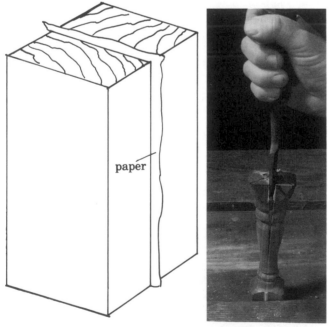

paper

Split turnings are also quite often used for decoration on many pieces. These are made by first gluing up a turning blank with a piece of newspaper between the pieces. Once you have turned the blank on a lathe, split the two halves apart with a wide chisel.

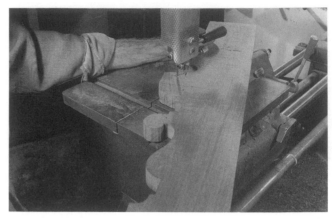

Because the Chippendale lowboy and mirror projects incorporate many of the techniques needed to reproduce period furniture, we will show in the following photographs the basic steps in constructing these two furniture pieces. (Full text and drawings are given in the chapters for these projects.) First, enlarge the squared drawings to make up all patterns. Then cut the curved pieces to shape on a band saw.

Because of the length of the lower apron, the cuts in the curves must be finished by hand with a coping saw.

The sides, back, and top pieces are constructed of small planks, planed and dowelled together.

A combination square is used to mark the chamfered outlines of the angled front faces of the front legs.

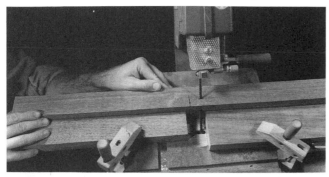

Cut the angled surfaces on the leg posts to shape using a band saw with the table set at an angle. Note the guide clamped to the tabletop.

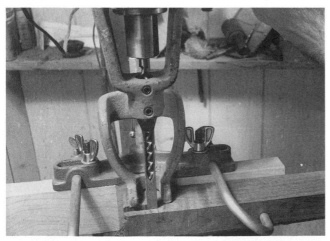

Next, cut all mortises and tenons in the leg posts, aprons, and sides.

Glue the wing blocks to the leg posts to make up the extra width needed for the cabriole legs.

Cut the cabriole legs to shape using a band saw.

This is the rough-cut leg post.

Rough in the ball-and-claw foot with a large gouge.

Then smooth it up with rasps and files.

Final smooth cutting is done with tiny chisels and knives. Keep them razor-sharp with a diamond-grit power hone.

Shape the drawer-front edges with a router in a router table.

Do the relief carving on the center drawer front and the apron.

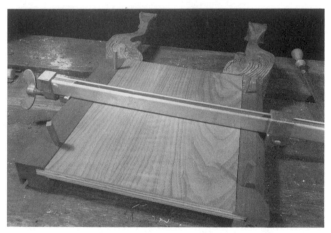

The sides and legs are assembled as one piece.

Then the carcass is assembled with glue and clamps, all four legs resting evenly on a smooth, flat surface.

Construct the drawers.

Fit the drawers in place.

The top is glued up, using a veneered plywood center and solid hardwood outside piece. Shape the top using a router.

Then fasten the top in place and glue the top mould-ing in place to the underside of the top.

Cut the mirror frame pieces to size and shape. Note the use of a guide strip clamped to the band saw to cut the straight part of the frame piece.

Use splines to join all corners.

Glue and clamp the frame together.

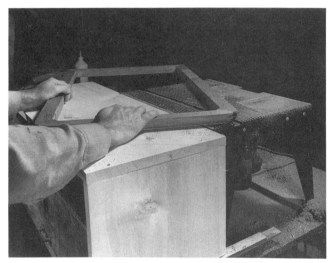

Shape the inside and outside of the front face with a router in a router table (and a pin-guide system). Then rout the back inside edge to make a groove for the mirror and mirror-holding panel.

Cut the top piece to shape on a band saw, do the relief carving, then install the back piece in the mortise in the top of the mirror frame.

Your choice of materials should complement the individual pieces.

A glossy, shiny finish is completely out of place on a recreation of a fine museum piece. Instead, the finish should have a satin-smooth, soft sheen. In fact, some of the earlier furniture pieces weren't finished at all; the appearance they have today is simply the patina from years of use.

Some earlier pieces were painted. The pie safe, painted and antiqued, will provide a focal point in any room setting. When a project is to be painted, it can be crafted of white pine, with shelving material cut from economical pine or spruce. Simply cut around the knots and blemishes to produce the stock needed.

The first step in finishing a piece is the final smoothing and sanding of the wood surfaces. Although less important when heavy-bodied, opaque materials are used, a smooth, finely sanded surface is critical when water stains and a light transparent finish are to be applied to a highly grained piece of wood.

All machine marks must be removed. This can be done with cabinet scrapers, which leave a shiny, glass-smooth surface, or you can use progressively finer grits of sandpaper and do it by hand or with power sanders. The final paper should be at least 1800 grit. After the last sanding step, dust or vacuum the surface and then carefully examine all surfaces. Use a small hand-held flood lamp for this inspection. Once the stain and finish has been applied, even the smallest blemish or tool mark will show glaringly. This is especially true when a dark stain is applied to a light wood.

Staining

Though you may want to finish some pieces without any stain, many of the projects in this book require staining to achieve an authentic appearance. Some stains can even enhance the grain of the wood. For instance, a golden-brown stain applied to oak will bring out the deep pores of the grain and produce a beautiful, mellow appearance.

There are basically two types of stains that are used today: water or dye stains; and oil-based stains. Water-based stains are a great deal more transparent and will reveal more of the grain of the wood. On the other hand, they raise the grain of the wood, require subsequent smoothing after application, and are sometimes complicated to apply. They can be mixed to the exact color needed by placing stain powder into the required amount of water.

Oil stains are more opaque but are much easier to apply. They are especially handy for wood surfaces that have areas with different coloration, such as a light sapwood streak that must be stained a bit darker to blend with the surrounding surface.

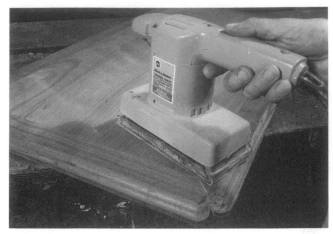

Proper finishing is as important as the construction itself. To make a beautiful piece of furniture, the best choice for wide surfaces is a cabinet scraper. Power sanders can be used in some places, if you're careful.

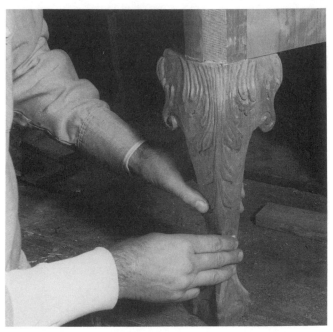

Carvings and other shaped areas will need lots of hand-sanding.

Staining is an important part of finishing the piece. Here an oil stain is being wiped on. Excess is wiped away.

Many of these stains, such as the Satin Zar® Stain by United Gilsonite Laboratories, also have a sealer in them. This helps provide a sealing surface, preventing the grain from raising, and making a smoother surface for the finish. Apply these stains by wiping them on with a cloth. A brush may be used to get the stain into the crevices of carvings. Then the excess is wiped away using a soft cloth. Allow the stain to dry for at least 12 hours.

Fillers

For open-grained woods, such as oak, a filler must also be applied. This is done in a separate step. Brush a thick layer of filler on the surface. Once it has dried to a dull sheen, wipe away the excess, across the grain.

In some cases you can also add the filler to the stain and apply the two together. To ensure that the two are compatible, mix a small portion together first to test them. (Apply the combination in the same manner as the filler.)

Finish

The finish will be determined by the type of project, the finishing equipment available, and personal preference. Today, there are basically three different types of finishes: wipe-on or rub-on oil; wipe-on or rub-on varnish or urethane; and lacquer. Lacquer is the easiest to apply if you have the equipment—namely, a good, heavy-duty compressor and a lacquer gun. Both are expensive, but a lacquer finish properly applied can provide one of the longest-lasting, most durable and most beautiful of all finishes. My technique is to apply at least a half-dozen light dusting coats. After the first two coats, to ensure that all stain is sealed off, rub down with extra-fine steel wool. Then rub down after each succeeding coat, including the last. Apply paste floor wax, buffing it thoroughly in place with extra-fine steel wool. An old, often-used alternative "polish" is beeswax dissolved in turpentine. Apply it with a soft cloth and buff it to a soft sheen.

For a varnish-like or polyurethane-like finish, I prefer the Satin Zar® in both the brush-on and wipe-on finishes. Again, after the second coat is applied, the finish should be rubbed down after each succeeding coat. Then apply a polish or paste wax.

Both the penetrating oil and wipe-on oil finishes are quite good for some furniture. These finishes are simply wiped on, allowed to dry partially according to the manufacturer's directions, and then the excess is wiped away. Additional coats are then applied until the desired depth and finish is achieved.

Use a wood filler on open-pored woods such as oak. Wipe it on, allow it to dry to a dull film, and then remove the excess with a coarse cloth.

Then apply the final finish. This can be sprayed-on lacquer, rubbed-on oil, or a wipe-on or brush-on polyurethane finish, such as the one being applied here.

Regardless of the type, several coats of finish should be applied. Smooth between coats with extra-fine steel wool. Then a last coat of wax or polish is applied and buffed to a soft sheen.

Early American Dressing Table

Circa 1780

This little dressing table is an interesting example of Early American "country-crafter" furniture. The design is uncluttered and somewhat unusual for the period. But the clean, elegant lines have an enduring appeal, and the table goes well with almost any decor.

Because this piece is small and fairly easy to build, it might make a nice starter project. The original table shown here was finished in pine veneer, but it would be especially beautiful in solid walnut, cherry, mahogany or pecan.

In making the patterns for this piece, I have departed slightly from the original. The bottom of the table shown is open, leaving the drawer glides exposed to view. To create a better-looking table, I added a solid bottom and sides.

The fact that the original table is covered with ⅛-inch pine veneer is unusual. I'm still not sure why anyone would build a table as elegant as this one and then veneer it with pine! But perhaps pine was the only material available at the time—a problem as enduring as the design of this table.

Construction

Construction of the table is fairly simple, and it has a standard web frame and drawer-slide construction.

Legs

Cut the legs (A) to shape. They are square blocks tapered on their two inside faces up to just below the junction with the bottom horizontal facers (F). The tapering can be done using a taper jig and a radial arm or table saw. Then cut mortises into the inside of the front legs for the facers (D,E,F). Cut the stopped grooves in the legs for the sides (B) and the back (C).

Sides

Make up the sides (B) from solid stock cut to size. Then cut tongues on their ends to fit into the grooves.

Back

Make up the back (C) from solid stock and cut the tongues on it.

Front

Cut all the front facers (D,G) to size from ¾ × 1½-inch-thick stock and cut the mitred spline joint for the corners where the bottom drawer facers (F,G) meet. Cut tenons on the outside ends of the two bottom horizontal facers (F) as well as on the top ends of the bottom vertical facers (G). Cut the bottom carved aprons (H) and carve them to shape. Bore holes for the holding dowels.

Web Frames

Make up the center web frame (M,O). The web frame is assembled with mortise-and-tenon joints. Note that it only protrudes partially into the front leg. This allows for the ¾-inch front facers that are fastened to the front of the web frame.

Inside Bottom and Sides

Cut the inside bottom boards (J) and side pieces (I) to size, and shape and cut the splined mitre joints along their inside bottom corners. Note that the bottoms will also have to be notched to fit around the front and back legs (A).

Top

Cut the top (S) from ½-inch-thick stock. Smooth and round all edges and sand both the bottom and top surfaces.

Assembly starts by placing glue on the tongues of the sides (B) and fitting them into the groove in the legs. Then assemble the inside bottom boards (J) and inside side pieces (I) with glue in the mitred spline joints. Fasten them in place to the underside of the assembled web frame (M,O) to make up the interior case section.

One unusual aspect of the assembly of this project is that the lower front facer unit is put together as a whole and then installed between the two leg units.

Start with the lower drawer facers (F,G), placing the spline in the grooves in the mitre joints and tapping these pieces together. Then insert dowels in the top of the bottom carved apron pieces (H) and attach this part to the lower drawer facers. Place dowels in the outside end holes as well. Then place vertical drawer-facer tenons up into the mortises of the horizontal center facer (E). Put this assembly into place between the side leg assemblies, fitting tenons on the sides of the facers into the leg mortises. At the same time, tap the bottom carved apron (H) dowels in place and insert the tenons of the top facer (D) in place between the two front legs.

Put in the inner case assembly—the web frame (M,O) and inner sides (I) and bottom (J). Before fastening in place, insert the tongues of the back (C)

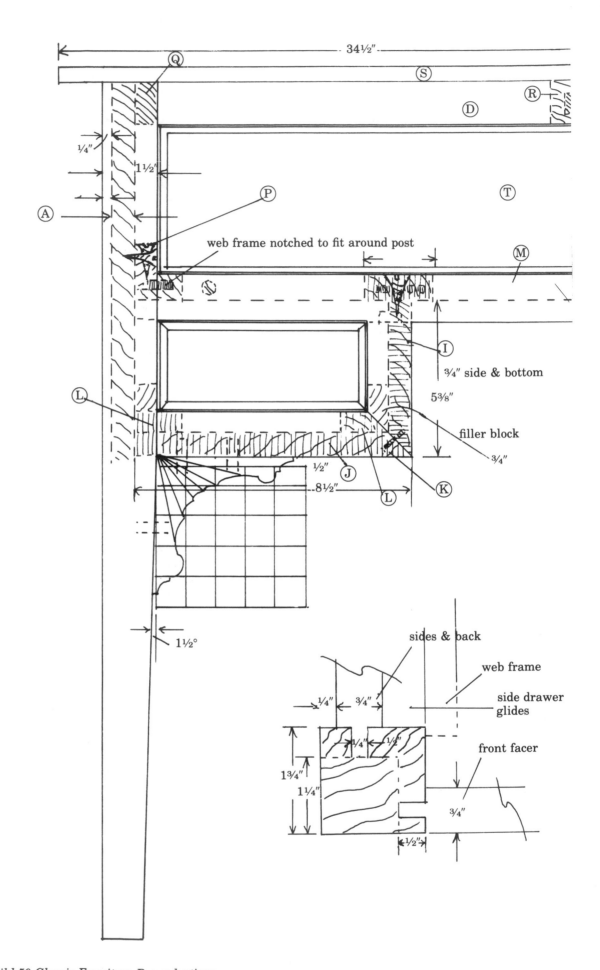

34½"

Q

S

R

D

¼"

1½'

A

P

T

web frame notched to fit around post

M

I

¾" side & bottom

L

5⅜"

filler block

J

½"

L

¾"

8½"

K

1½°

sides & back

web frame

¼"   ¾"

side drawer glides

¼"   ½"

front facer

1¾"

1¼"

¾"

½"

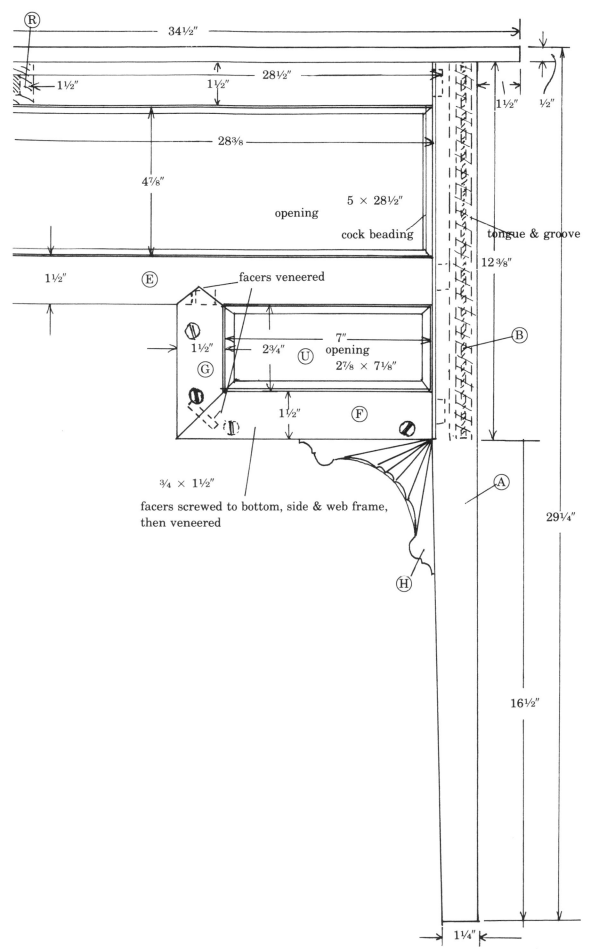

R

34½"

28½"

1½"

1½"

28⅜

4⅞"

opening

5 × 28½"

cock beading

tongue & groove

1½"

1½"

½"

12⅜"

1½"

E

facers veneered

1½"

2¾"

7"

opening

2⅞ × 7⅛"

U

G

B

1½"

F

D

H

¾ × 1½"

facers screwed to bottom, side & web frame,
then veneered

A

29¼"

16½"

1¼"

Early American Dressing Table • 35

into the grooves of the back legs. Then fasten the web frame and bottom assembly firmly in place to the sides, back, and front facers with counterbored wood screws. Cover over the holes with wood putty or wood plugs sanded smooth.

Fasten the inside drawer guides (L) to the inside of the inside bottom and sides. Put in the upper drawer slides (P), attaching them to the top sides of the web frames with glue and screws. Then install the top holding cleats (Q) and center top drawer tilt strip (R) with glue and screws.

Invert the top (S) on a smooth, flat surface and then position the table frame down on it. Fasten the frame to the top with glue and screws through the top holding cleats.

Drawers

Assemble the drawers (T,U) to fit the openings, making them with standard dovetail construction. Their fronts are covered with veneer, and cock beading is applied over the faces of the drawer fronts, as shown on page 23.

After the entire case is assembled, sand smooth, if desired, apply veneer if you want to the sides, front

facers, and back. Note that the front facer veneers are cut to provide an unusual "mitred" look where the lower drawer facers join.

Materials List

A—Legs—$1\frac{1}{2} \times 1\frac{1}{2} \times 28\frac{3}{4}$", 4 req'd.

B—Sides—$\frac{3}{4} \times 12\frac{1}{2} \times 16$", 2 req'd.

C—Back—$\frac{3}{4} \times 12\frac{1}{2} \times 29\frac{1}{2}$", 1 req'd.

Facers

D—Top—$\frac{3}{4} \times 1\frac{1}{2} \times 29\frac{1}{2}$", 1 req'd.

E—Center—$\frac{3}{4} \times 1\frac{1}{2} \times 29\frac{1}{2}$", 1 req'd.

F—Bottom horizontal—$\frac{3}{4} \times 1\frac{1}{2} \times 9\frac{1}{4}$", cut to length, 2 req'd.

G—Bottom vertical—$\frac{3}{4} \times 1\frac{1}{2} \times 5\frac{3}{4}$", cut to length, 2 req'd.

H—Bottom carved aprons—$\frac{3}{4} \times 5 \times 5$", 2 req'd.

I—Inside side pieces—$\frac{3}{4} \times 5\frac{1}{4} \times 16\frac{1}{4}$", 2 req'd.

J—Bottom boards—$\frac{3}{4} \times 9\frac{1}{4} \times 16\frac{1}{4}$", 2 req'd.

K—Bottom splines—$\frac{1}{8} \times 1 \times 16\frac{1}{4}$", 2 req'd.

L—Inside drawer guides—$1\frac{1}{2} \times 1\frac{1}{2} \times 16\frac{1}{4}$", cut to shape, 4 req'd.

Web Frame

M—Front—$\frac{3}{4} \times 2 \times 30$", 1 req'd.

N—Back—$\frac{3}{4} \times 2 \times 30$", 1 req'd.

O—Sides—$\frac{3}{4} \times 1\frac{1}{2} \times 15\frac{1}{2}$", 2 req'd.

P—Upper drawer slides—$\frac{3}{4} \times \frac{3}{4} \times 15$", 2 req'd.

Q—Side top cleats—$\frac{3}{4} \times 1\frac{1}{2} \times 15$", 2 req'd.

R—Top drawer tilt strip—$1\frac{1}{2} \times 1\frac{1}{2} \times 16\frac{1}{4}$", 1 req'd.

S—Top—$\frac{1}{2} \times 20 \times 34\frac{1}{2}$", 1 req'd.

T—Top drawer

Front—$\frac{3}{4} \times 4\frac{7}{8} \times 28\frac{3}{8}$", 1 req'd.

Sides—$\frac{1}{2} \times 4\frac{7}{8} \times 16\frac{1}{2}$", 2 req'd.

Back—$\frac{1}{2} \times 4\frac{7}{8} \times 28\frac{3}{8}$", 1 req'd.

Bottom—$\frac{1}{4} \times 16 \times 27\frac{7}{8}$", 1 req'd.

U—Lower drawers

Fronts—$\frac{3}{4} \times 2\frac{3}{4} \times 7$", 2 req'd.

Sides—$\frac{1}{2} \times 2\frac{3}{4} \times 16\frac{1}{2}$", 4 req'd.

Backs—$\frac{1}{2} \times 2\frac{3}{4} \times 7$", 2 req'd.

Bottoms—$\frac{1}{4} \times 6\frac{1}{2} \times 16$", 2 req'd.

Tavern Table

Circa 1700, New York State
The Metropolitan Museum of Art, Gift of Mrs. Russell Sage, 1909.

This table is a good example of the Colonial style of furniture made in America from the 1620s to around 1750. It is sturdily constructed with deep mortises and tenons that are further strengthened with pegs. The table shown is made of wild cherry. But almost any native American wood will do, including walnut, maple, oak, ash, birch, pecan, or even pine.

Construction

One unusual aspect of the construction of this table is the locking-peg method used with the mortise-and-tenon joints. The pegs were used in the original because glue was not readily available then.

The holes for the peg in the mortise and tenon were bored slightly off from each other. Then mortises and tenons were put together and an octagonal peg was driven through them. This wedged them solidly together. You can, of course, simply glue the pieces together, but putting pegs in the joints will add an extra touch of authenticity.

Legs

The first step is to enlarge the squared drawing and turn the legs (A) to size and shape. Then cut mor-tises in them for the side stretchers (F), aprons (B,C,D) and bottom drawer slides (H). Bore the holes for the holding pegs.

Stretchers

Turn the stretches (E,F) to size and shape. Cut the mortises and tenons on them and drill holes in each for the holding pegs.

Aprons

Cut the aprons (B,C) to size and make tenons on their ends to fit into the leg posts. Bore the peg holes. The lower front apron (D) must also be cut to size. It has tenons on its ends to fit in the front-leg mortises. Note that it has a simple ogee shape on the front edge. This is made with a shaper or router. Cut the L-shaped drawer slides (H) and make tenons on their ends to fit the leg mortises.

Top

Make up the top (G) from several pieces joined with glue and dowels or with tongue-and-groove joints. Then sand bottom and top surfaces smooth. Round the corners using a sabre saw or band saw. Round the top and bottom edges of the top piece with a router or shaper.

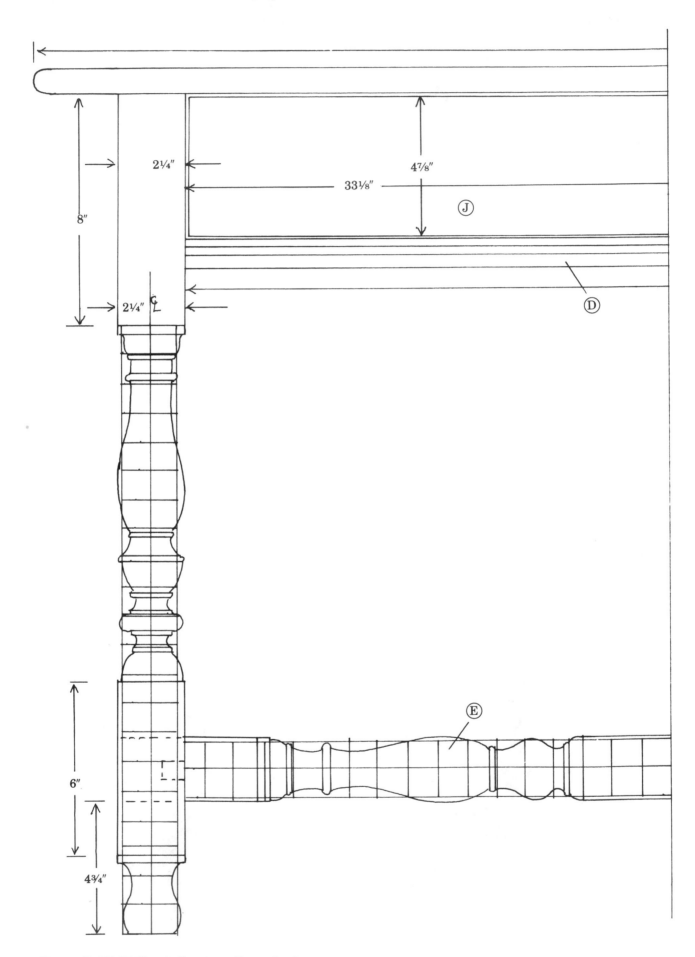

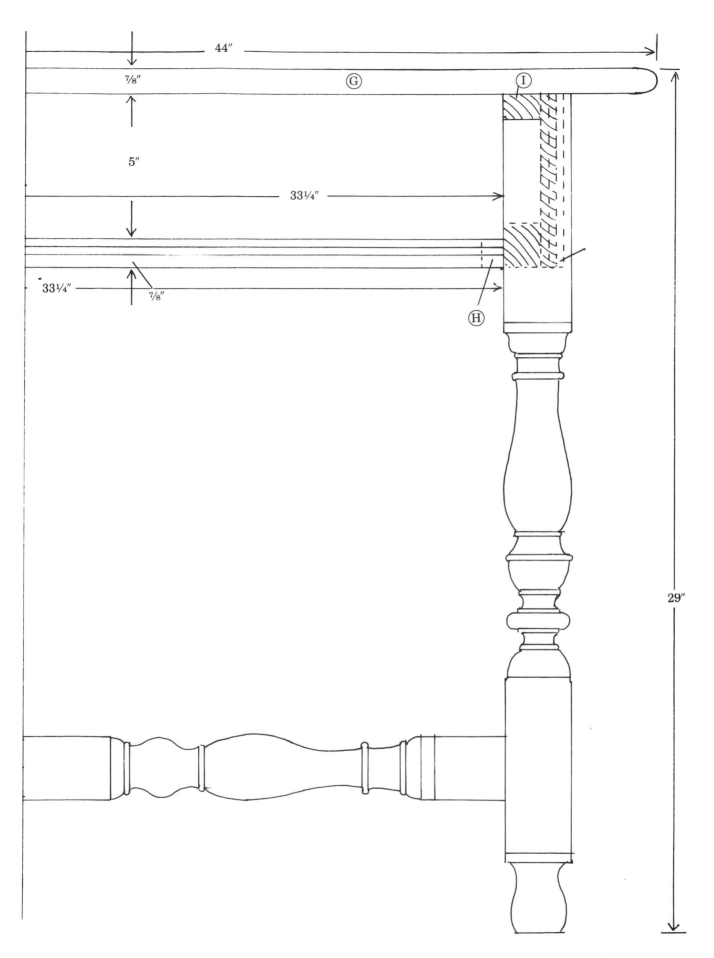

44"

7/8"

Ⓖ

Ⓘ

5"

33¼"

33¼"

7/8"

Ⓗ

29"

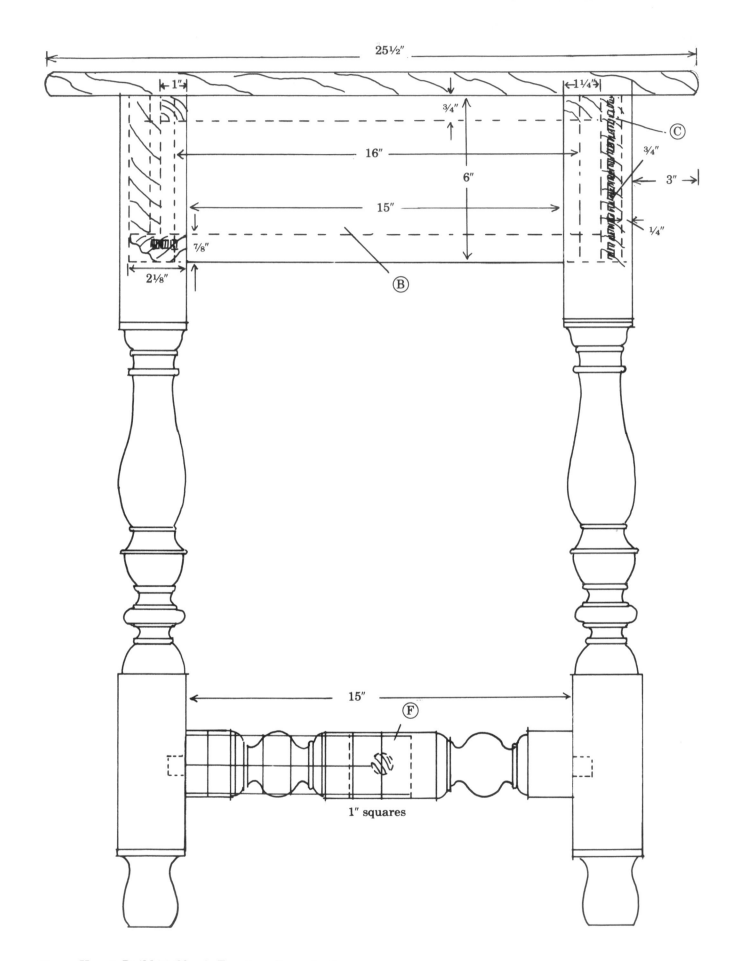

25½"

1"

1¼"

¾"

16"

6"

15"

¾"

3"

¼"

7⅛"

2⅛"

Ⓑ

Ⓒ

15"

Ⓕ

1" squares

Assembly

Place glue on each tenon of a side stretcher (F) and a side apron (B), then place them between the two legs (A). Position the drawer slides (H) between the two posts at the same time. Make sure the assembly is square; then clamp it solidly together and allow the glue to set. Fasten the drawer-slide supports to the side apron with screws from the inside of the drawer glide. Do the same for the other side unit.

After the glue on the two side assemblies has set, remove the sections from the clamps. Place glue on the tenons of the center stretcher (E) and place it between the side units. Do the same for the back apron (C) and the front apron (D). Stand the unit on a smooth, flat surface. Make sure it doesn't rock on its legs and that it is square. Then use bar clamps to clamp it together until the glue sets.

Turn the tabletop upside down on a smooth, flat surface; remove the table base assembly from the clamps, and place it upside down on the top. Fasten it to the top with counterbored screws driven in from the underside of the top side cleats (I) into the top. Make sure the screws don't go completely through the top piece. Turn the table upright.

Drawer

The drawer (J) is standard dovetail construction. First, cut the front to size and then cut the back and sides. Cut a 1/4 × 1/2-inch dado in their bottom edges to accommodate the drawer bottom. Then cut the dovetails on the front, back, and sides and assemble with glue.

Place the drawer in the table and make sure it works properly. Then turn the wood knobs. Sand, stain and finish the entire table. This table looks especially good with a hand-rubbed oil finish.

Materials List

A—Legs—2¼ × 2¼ × 28⅛″, 4 req'd.

B—Side aprons—¾ × 6 × 16″, 2 req'd.

C—Back apron—¾ × 6 × 34¼″, 1 req'd.

D—Lower front apron—⅞ × 2⅛ × 34¼″, 1 req'd.

E—Center stretcher—2¼ × 2¼ × 34¼″, 1 req'd.

F—Side stretchers—2¼ × 2¼ × 16″, 2 req'd.

G—Top—⅞ × 25½ × 44″, 1 req'd.

H—Bottom drawer slides—1¾ × 1¾ × 15″, cut to fit, 2 req'd.

I—Top side cleats—¾ × 1¼ × 15″, cut to fit, 2 req'd.

J—Drawer

  Front—¾ × 4⅞ × 33⅛″, 1 req'd.

  Sides—½ × 4⅛ × 16″, 2 req'd.

  Back—½ × 4⅛ × 33⅛″, 1 req'd.

  Bottom—¼ × 15¾ × 32⅜″, 1 req'd.

Tabletop Corner

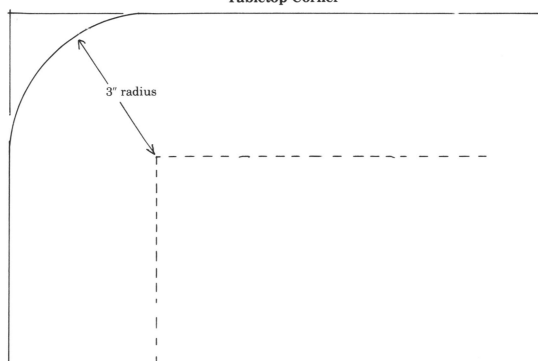

3″ radius

"Punkin" Pine Settee

Circa 1860

Made from the wide "punkin" pine, once plentiful in England, this settee is a typical example of "country" furniture that was popular both in England and New England during the early nineteenth century. The drawer under the seat was used for storing blankets and other items.

Although the settee could be made from almost any wood, including maple or cherry, it is traditionally made of pine. White pine is a good substitute for the original "punkin" pine.

Construction

Construction of the settee is fairly simple, the most complicated part being the decorative moulding on the posts and drawer front. The seat portion is constructed first, then the upper wings and back assembly are put together and installed in it.

Leg Posts

Construction starts by cutting the leg posts (A) to the proper size and shape, including running the decorative moulding cuts on the front and sides. This is done with a moulding head on a table saw or radial arm saw, or with an old-fashioned "moulding plane." First, cut the legs quite a bit longer than the finish size and run the moulding cuts. Then cut to the proper length.

There is also a groove on each of the two inside faces of the legs (see top view, leg post) for the side tongues and the bottom facer (C) tongue. Cut these using a dado head on a table saw or radial arm saw. Then cut the mortises for the drawer support piece (D) and the front seat support (E).

Bottom Sides

Enlarge the squared drawing and cut the bottom side pieces (B) to size and shape, including the tongues on their edges. Then cut the upper support cleats (K), upper drawer glides (J), side drawer supports (H), and drawer slides (I) to the correct size and shapes. Fasten them to the inside of the sides with glue and wood screws.

Bottom Back

Cut the bottom back (L) to size and shape. Its bottom contour matches the front and it can be cut from plywood, or make it with glue and dowelled stock.

Front Pieces

Enlarge the squared drawing and cut the bottom front facer (C) to size and shape. Cut the tongues on each end. Then cut the drawer support (D) to size and shape, including the tenons on each end to fit into the front-leg posts. Cut the top facer strip—(front seat support, (E)—to the same size and shape.

Assembly

Place glue on the ends of the tenons of the front pieces and position them in the mortises in the legs. Clamp in place, making sure they are all square with each other. Insert glue on the tongues of the side pieces, and insert these into the back mortises cut into the leg posts. Then position the back against the end of the sides, and fasten in place with glue and wood screws driven through the back into the ends of the sides. Place a couple of bar clamps across each side to hold the tongues in the mortise grooves of the leg posts. Make sure the assembly is square; then allow the glue to set overnight.

After removing the clamps, install the side drawer supports (H) to the side cleats with glue and screws, making sure they are perfectly aligned on a 90-degree angle with the front.

Install the back seat support cleat (G) and back seat support (F) to the inside edges of the back with glue and screws. Cut the front seat lip piece (Q) to size and shape and fasten it in place with glue and screws driven up from the underside of the front seat support (E).

Then cut the seatboards (R) to size and fasten them in place to the front and back seat supports with glue and screws, driven up from the underside. Note that the seatboards consist of a number of random-width boards running back to front. (See mating top and bottom assemblies drawing.) You could also make this from plywood or one large glued-up plank.

Drawer

Construct the drawer, first cutting the front (M) to size and shape from ¾-inch solid stock. Next cut the moulding on its front face using a moulding head on a radial arm or table saw. Then cut the sides, back and bottom (N,O,P) from ½-inch stock. Cut the da-

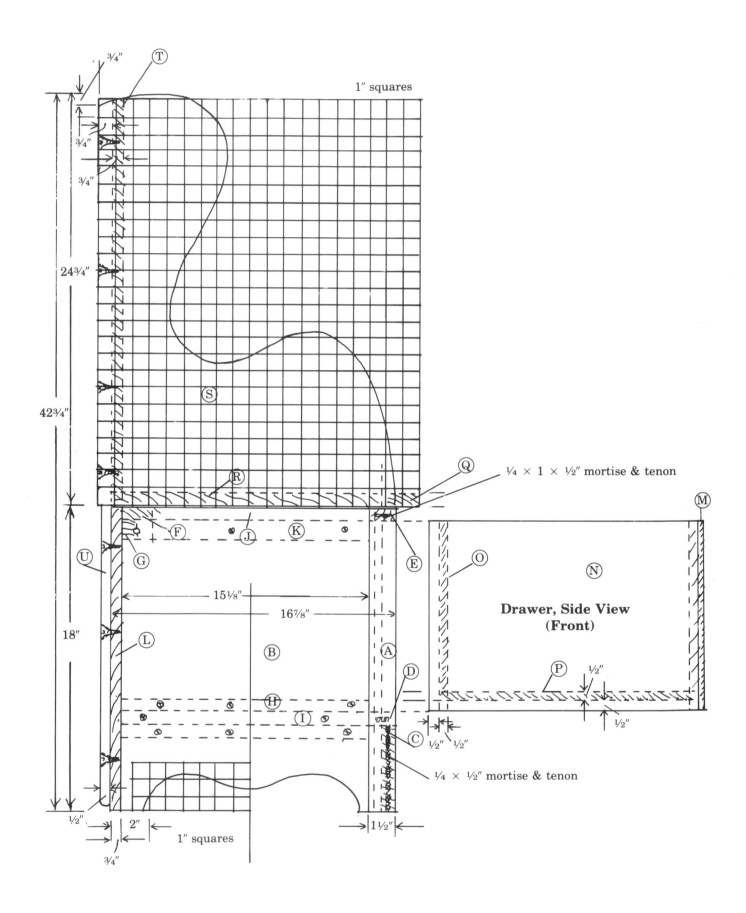

3/4"

T

1" squares

3/4"

3/4"

24 3/4"

42 3/4"

S

R

Q

1/4 × 1 × 1/2" mortise & tenon

M

F   J   K

E

O

N

U

G

15 1/8"

Drawer, Side View
(Front)

16 7/8"

18"

L

B

A

D

P   1/2"

H

C   1/2"   1/2"

1/2"

I

1/4 × 1/2" mortise & tenon

1/2"

2"

1" squares

3/4"

1 1/2"

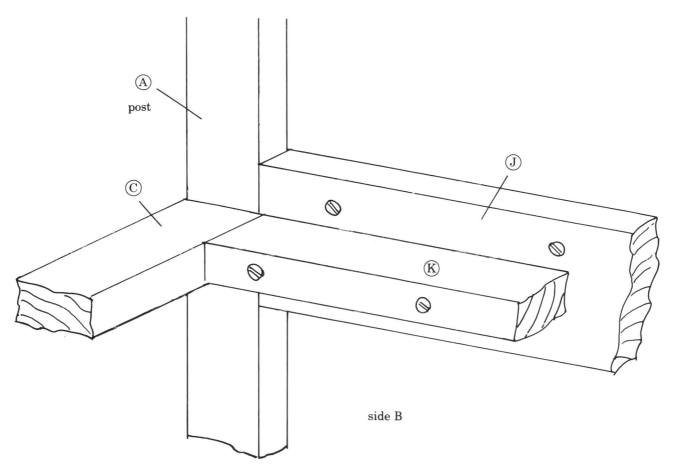

Ⓐ post

Ⓒ

Ⓙ

Ⓚ

side B

Top View, Leg Post, and Slide Assembly

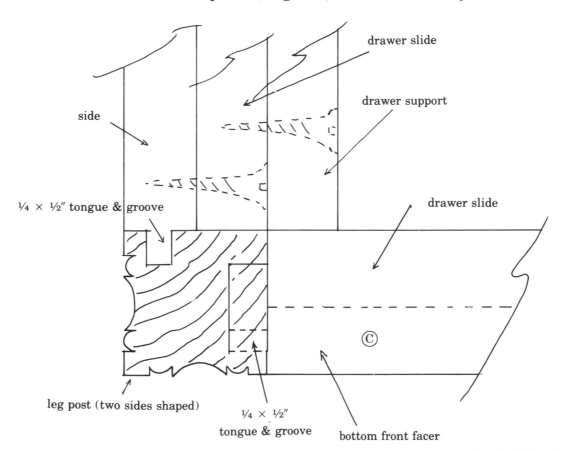

drawer slide

drawer support

side

¼ × ½" tongue & groove

drawer slide

Ⓒ

leg post (two sides shaped)

¼ × ½"
tongue & groove

bottom front facer

does in the sides, back and front for the bottom and then assemble with glue and nails. Note that the front joint is an overlap joint without nails.

Top Assembly

The sides and back on the original were made of ½-inch solid stock, but you could use plywood. You could make an even sturdier assembly using ¾-inch solid stock. Enlarge the squared drawing and create the patterns needed. Then cut to shape using a sabre saw or band saw.

Sand all edges smooth and join the side, or wing, pieces (S) to the back (T) with glue and countersunk wood screws or nails. Cover the holes with wood putty or wood plugs. The sides and back fit down over notches cut in the outside edge of the outside seatboards. (See drawing, mating top and bottom assemblies.) They are held in place with glue and screws or with finishing nails set below the surface. Cover with wood putty or wood plugs.

The back cleats (U) are cut from a piece of 1½-

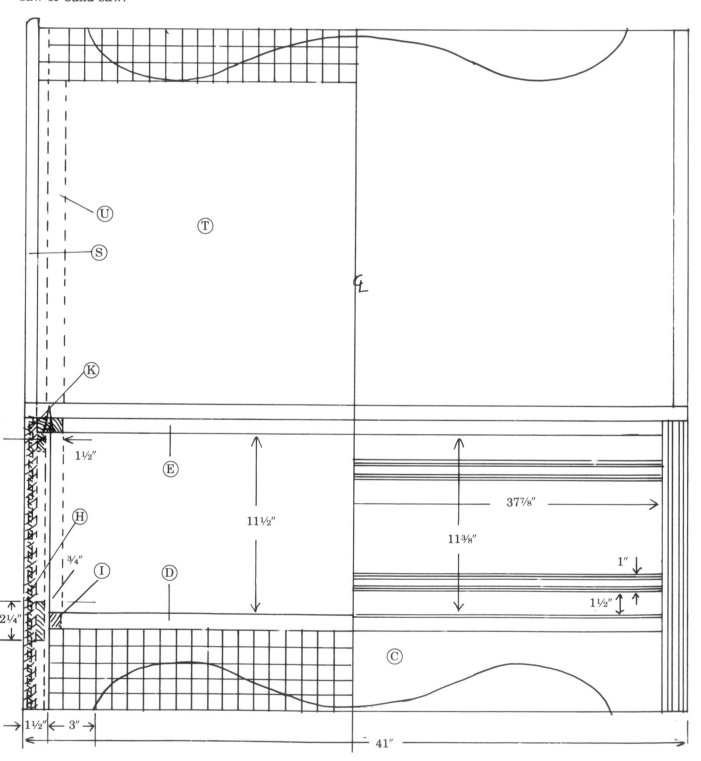

inch-thick stock with a taper from 1 inch to ½ inch at the bottom on their back edges. Install them on the back of the bottom and top back pieces (L,T) with glue and wood screws driven through the support pieces.

Sand, stain and finish and then install the hardware on the drawer.

Materials List

A—Leg posts—1½ × 1½ × 18″, 2 req'd.
B—Bottom sides—¾ × 15⅛ × 18″, 2 req'd.
C—Bottom front facer—¾ × 5 × 38⅛″, 1 req'd.
D—Drawer support—¾ × 1½ × 38⅛″, 1 req'd.
E—Front seat support—¾ × 1½ × 38⅛″, 1 req'd.
F—Back seat support—¾ × 1¾ × 36″, 1 req'd.
G—Back seat support cleat—¾ × 1¾ × 36″, 1 req'd.
H—Side drawer supports—¾ × 2¼ × 14⅞″, 2 req'd.
I—Drawer slides—¾ × ¾ × 14⅞″, 2 req'd.
J—Upper drawer glides—¾ × 1¾ × 14⅞″, 2 req'd.
K—Upper side support cleats—¾ × ¾ × 14⅞″, 2 req'd.
L—Bottom back—¾ × 18 × 41″, 2 req'd.

Drawer

M—Front—¾ × 11⅜ × 37⅞″, 1 req'd.
N—Sides—½ × 11⅜ × 15¾″, 2 req'd.
O—Back—½ × 10⅜ × 36⅞″, 1 req'd.
P—Bottom—½ × 14¾ × 37⅛″, 1 req'd.

Top Assembly

Q—Seat lip—¾ × 2¼ × 41″, 1 req'd.
R—Seat—¾ × 15½ × 40″, 1 req'd.
S—Top sides—½ × 17½ × 24¾″, 2 req'd.
T—Top back—½ × 24 × 40″, 1 req'd.
U—Back cleats—1 × 1½ × 42¾″, 2 req'd.

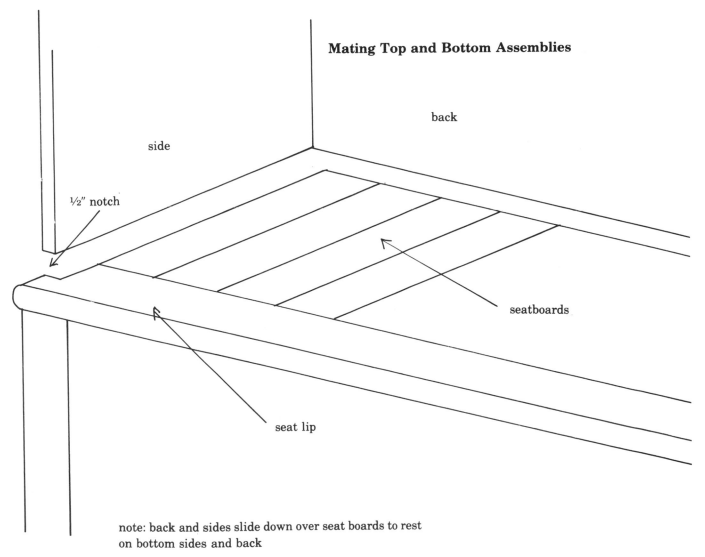

Mating Top and Bottom Assemblies

side

back

½″ notch

seatboards

seat lip

note: back and sides slide down over seat boards to rest on bottom sides and back

Open Washstand

Circa 1820

Until the introduction of indoor plumbing, wash-stands were a necessary piece of bedroom and kitchen furniture, and there were literally hundreds of thousands of them made. The open washstand chosen for this project features early Victorian styling and is just one of the many styles for this popular furniture piece.

Although originally made to hold a washbowl, pitcher, and hand towels, this open washstand makes a handy, good-looking table for many purposes. The workmanship on this particular piece is excellent. The project is also a good one for the intermediate craftsman. It offers some challenge without getting into the larger scale of other furniture pieces that are in this book.

The stand shown is made of beautifully grained walnut, although it would look good in almost any hardwood. White pine stained to either "punkin" pine coloring or a dark, antiqued look would also be effective.

Construction
There is a little of everything in constructing this washstand, making it one of the "fun" projects.

Legs
First, enlarge the squared drawing and make the pattern for the turned legs (A). Then turn the posts to shape and size on a lathe. A duplicator for the lathe can speed up this process.

Once the posts have been turned, cut mortises on their inside edges for the bottom shelf supports (G) and the back (C), sides (B) and front facers (D).

Aprons and Facer Strips
Cut the sides, back, front facer strips, and center drawer tilt strip (E) to size and make tenons on their ends to fit into the leg mortises. Carefully cut and fit these pieces by making several dry runs with each piece. Take only a little off the tenon at a time, until you get a snug and smooth fit with the mortise. Do the same for the bottom shelf supports.

Assembly
Glue and clamp together the leg and apron assembly, including the bottom shelf supports. Install the drawer tilt strip (E) at the same time, inserting its tenons in the front top facer and in the back piece. Make sure all four legs stand firmly and evenly on a smooth, flat surface. Allow the glue to set overnight.

Cut the drawer support slides (F) to shape, including the rabbet on their inside edges (to make the L-shape). Fasten in place to the sides with glue and screws driven from inside the case.

Saw the bottom shelf (H) to size and install with screws through the bottom shelf supports.

Top
Make the top to size and shape and cut the shaped edge with a router or shaper. Note that the shaped edge stops just short of the back, by about ½ inch. This provides an unusual and good-looking bit of craftsmanship.

Cut ¾ × ¾-inch notches 1⅜ inches from the front edge of the top piece for the front towel bar supports (K). Then turn the top upside down on a smooth, clean surface. Put the washstand frame assembly down on it. Fasten the bottom assembly to the top with screws driven through the drawer tilt strip (E) and screws countersunk deeply in the sides (B) and back (C). Make sure the screws don't go through the top.

If you prefer, you can add top holding cleats to the sides and back with glue and screws; then fasten the top to them. Or you can simply position glue blocks around the inside perimeter of the frame.

Top Back Piece
Enlarge the squared drawing for the top back piece (I) and cut it to size and shape using a band saw. Then rout or shape the outside edge, again stopping the shaped edge 1 inch from each lower end. Locate and bore holes for the towel bars (J) and fasten to the back (C) with glue and screws.

Towel Bar
Enlarge the squared drawing and turn the towel bar to size and shape, including tenons on each end. Make them to fit into the stopped holes in the top back (I) and front towel bar supports (K). Enlarge the squared drawing for the front holders and cut to shape on a band saw. Bore dowel holes in their lower ends to attach to the side posts. Place dowel locators in each hole and locate the dowel hole positions on each of the legs. Bore the dowel holes.

Towel Bar Assembly
Place glue on the tenons of each towel bar and insert into the holes in the back. Then fit them in the front support holes. Glue dowels in the front supports and,

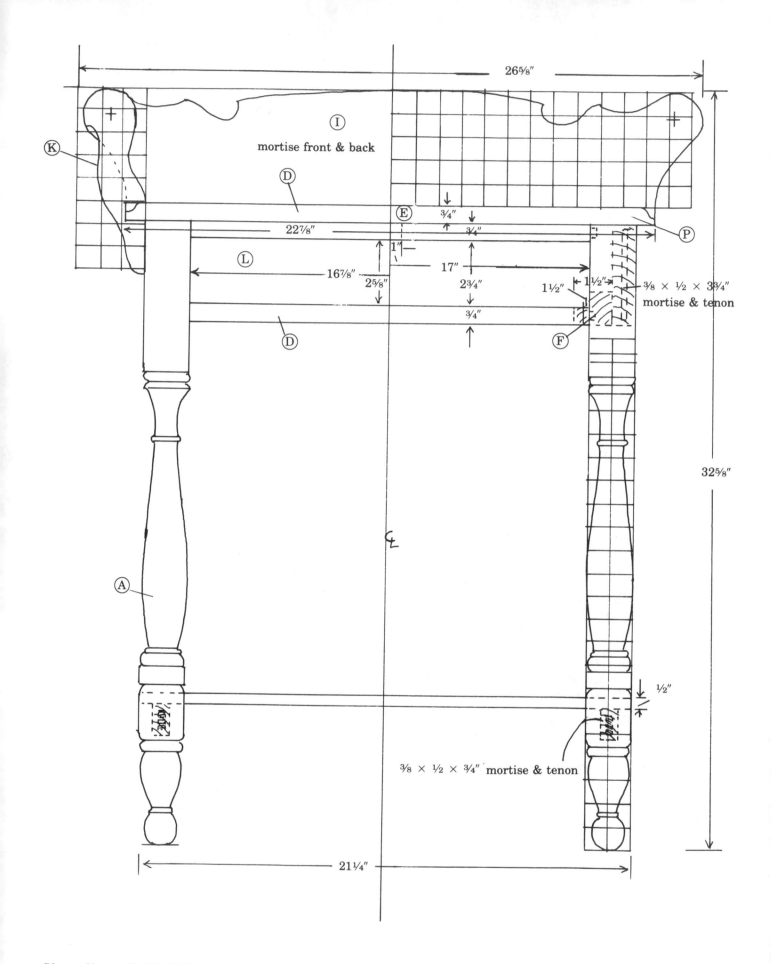

26⁵⁄₈″

Ⓘ
mortise front & back

Ⓚ

Ⓓ

Ⓔ
¾″
¾″
22⅞″
Ⓟ

1″

Ⓛ
17″
16⅞″
2⅝″
2¾″
1½″
1½″
³⁄₈ × ½ × 3¾″
mortise & tenon

Ⓓ
¾″
Ⓕ

32⅝″

Ⓐ

½″

³⁄₈ × ½ × ¾″ mortise & tenon

21¼″

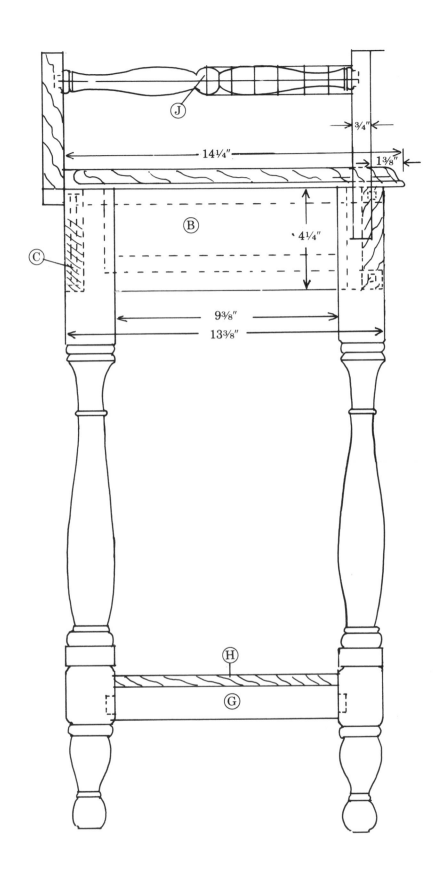

using a wood mallet or rubber-faced hammer, tap supports into place, seating them securely against the leg posts. Clamp securely and allow the glue to set overnight.

Drawer

The drawer (L-P) is made of ¾-inch stock for the front (L), ½-inch for the sides (N) and back (M), and ¼-inch for the bottom (O). The front and back edges of the sides are fastened to the front and back with dovetail joints and the bottom is fitted in a ¼ × ¼-inch dado cut in the front, back, and sides. Cut all the joints and assemble with glue.

Install the wooden knob, then sand, stain and finish.

Materials List

A—Legs—2 × 2 × 26⅞", 4 req'd.
B—Sides—¾ × 4¼ × 10⅜", 2 req'd.
C—Back—¾ × 4¼ × 18", 1 req'd.
D—Front facers—¾ × ¾ × 18", 2 req'd.

E—Drawer tilt strip—¾ × ¾ × 12", 1 req'd.
F—Drawer support slides—1½ × 1½ × 9⅜", 2 req'd.
G—Bottom shelf supports—¾ × 1¼ × 10⅜", 2 req'd.
H—Bottom shelf—½ × 9⅜" × 21¼", 1 req'd.
I—Top back—¾ × 6½ × 26⅝", 1 req'd.
J—Towel bars—1 × 1 × 13", 2 req'd.
K—Front towel bar supports—¾ × 3 × 8", 2 req'd.

Drawer

L—Front—¾ × 2⅝ × 16⅞", 1 req'd.
M—Back—½ × 2⅝ × 16⅞", 1 req'd.
N—Sides—½ × 2⅝ × 12³⁄₁₆", 2 req'd.
O—Bottom—¼ × 12 × 15⅞", 1 req'd.
P—Top—¾ × 14¼ × 22¾", 1 req'd.
Wooden knob—1 req'd.

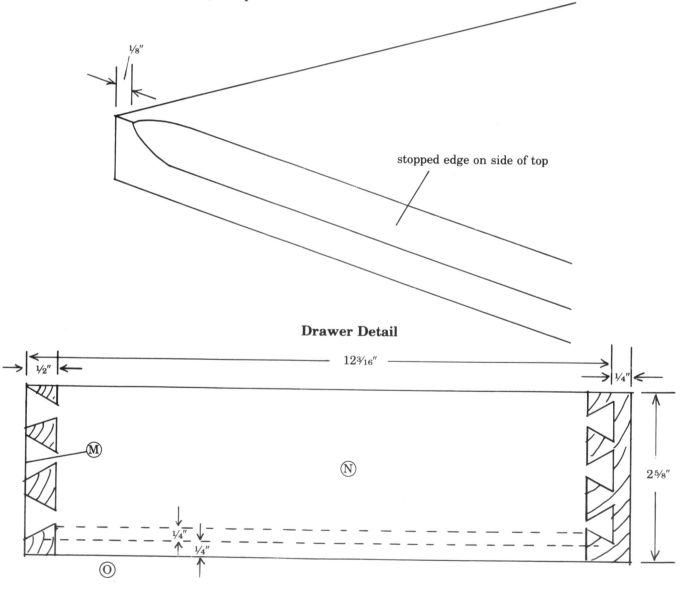

Drawer Detail

Three-Drawer Dressing Table

Circa 1780

Small dressing tables were fashionable through-out much of the 18th century and there were many varieties, including the one that served as the model for this project. Made in England, it has a relatively simple design and fluted, straight legs.

The table is made of oak, although almost any hardwood such as walnut, mahogany or pecan would serve just as well. Veneering is called for in this project, notably the decorative burl veneers used to cover the small drawer fronts. The top could also be veneered and inlaid; this would give the table a more elegant appearance. The drawer fronts also have cock beading, a small, decorative bead around the outside front edge that here protects the edges of the veneer.

Construction

First, enlarge the squared drawing and cut the lower front piece (E) and the entire back (D) to proper shape and size. The lower part of the back is cut to the same pattern as the lower front piece (E). Use a band saw to cut the curved parts. Then cut tenons on the ends of each piece. Cut mortises in the front piece (see detail A) for the center drawer slide supports and then cut the top front facer (O). Cut tenons on each end of the top facer, as well as mortises for the center drawer slide supports. Now make the center drawer slide supports (P) and cut tenons on each end. Cut the center front drawer facers (N) to size and make the mortise in it.

Front Assembly

Assemble the front piece, including lower facer (E), center drawer slide supports (P), center front drawer facers (N) and top front facer (O) with glue in the mortise-and-tenon joints; clamp overnight. Make sure all joints are flush and square.

If you plan to veneer the whole table front, you could make it up from one piece and simply cut out the drawer openings. The mortise for the center drawer slide support would be cut into the back of it.

Sides

Enlarge the squared drawings for the sides (C) and cut them to size and shape. Make the tenons on each end.

Legs

Cut the legs (A) to length, taper both inside faces of the lower portion of each leg using a taper jig on a

radial arm or table saw. The outside faces of each leg are decorated with fluting. This can be done with a router, shaper, or with a moulding head in a radial arm or table saw. You can also use homemade scratch stock to make the cut in the authentic way.

Top

Cut the top (B) to the correct size, and shape the edges. Note that the top on the original was also shaped using scratch stock.

Drawer Slides

Cut the drawer slides (Q,R) to the proper size and shape, and fasten the four inside drawer slides in place to the center drawer slide supports (P) with glue and screws.

Assembly

Work on a smooth, flat surface. Starting with the sides (C), smear glue on the tenons and insert them in the leg (A) mortises. Glue the center drawer slide support assembly (P) in its appropriate mortises in the assembled front piece and back (D). Then insert tenons of the front and back into the legs (A). Position bar clamps both ways to clamp the table frame assembly solidly together. Make sure the table stands square on all four legs. Allow the glue to set overnight.

Then install the outside drawer slides with glue and screws to the inside face of the sides. Fasten top support cleats to the upper sides with glue and screws.

With the tabletop upside down on a smooth, flat surface, mark the location of the table frame. Turn the table frame upside down and position it on the top. Fasten it securely in place with flathead wood screws, driven through the top support cleats into the upper side of the top. Be careful not to drive the screws all the way through the top.

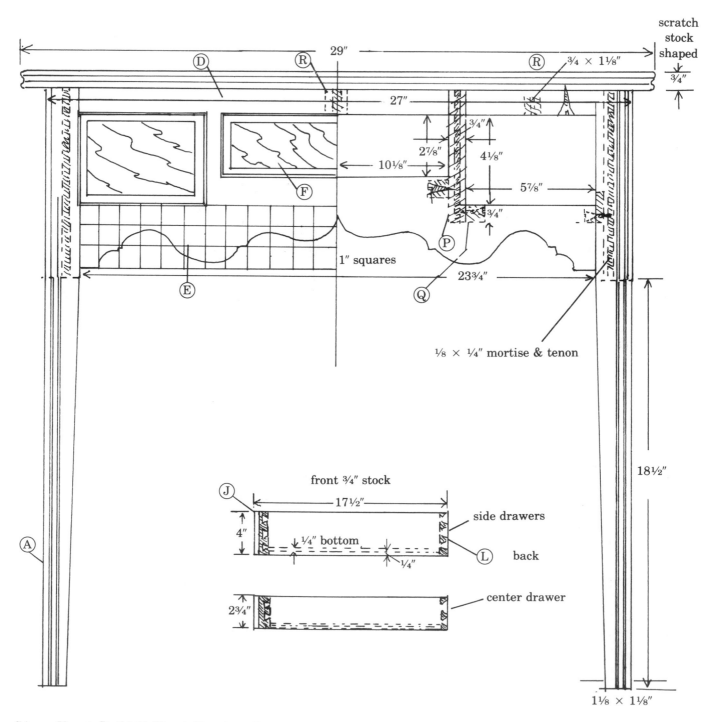

Install the upper drawer slides (R) on the underside of the top using glue and countersunk flathead wood screws.

Drawers

The drawer fronts (F,J) are made with ¾-inch solid stock, covered with veneer. They also have a small cock beading around their outside edges. This beading can be made using a shaper or moulding head on a table saw or radial arm saw. Run the bead on the edge of a piece of stock and then rip it off by using a resaw technique on a band saw or by using a table saw or radial arm saw equipped with an extra-fine-toothed plywood blade.

The drawer front and back are dovetailed to the sides, and the drawer bottom is inserted in a dado in

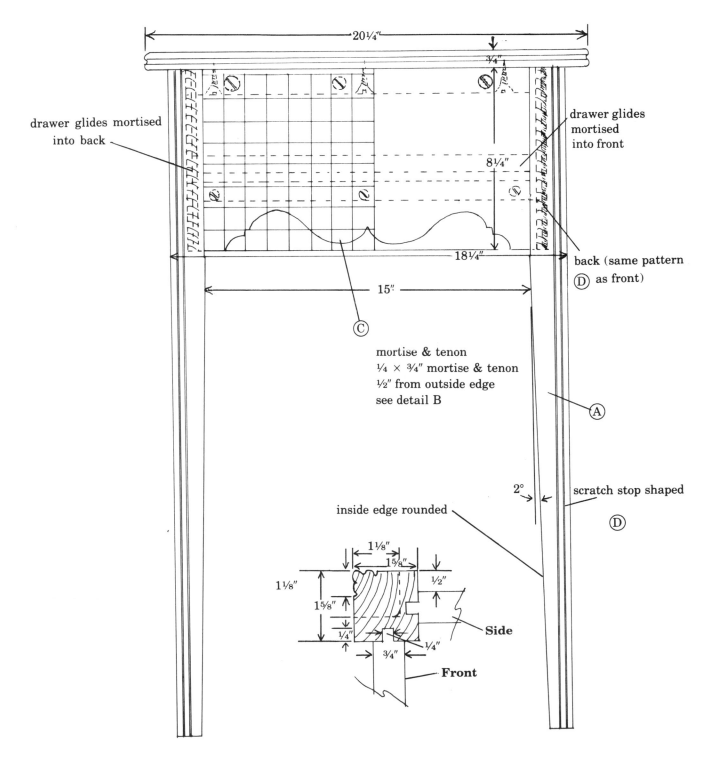

drawer glides mortised into back

drawer glides mortised into front

back (same pattern as front) Ⓓ

mortise & tenon
¼ × ¾" mortise & tenon
½" from outside edge
see detail B

Ⓐ

scratch stop shaped

Ⓓ

inside edge rounded

Side

Front

the front, back and sides. This technique is used on all three drawers.

Install the veneering as shown on page 21. Apply the cock beading over the veneer to hold it all securely in place and to protect the veneer edge on the drawer fronts.

Sand all wood surfaces smooth and stain and finish to suit. Install period-style hardware on the drawer fronts.

Materials List

A—Legs—$1\frac{5}{8}$ × $1\frac{5}{8}$ × 27″, 4 req'd.
B—Top—$\frac{3}{4}$ × 29 × $20\frac{1}{4}$″, 1 req'd.
C—Sides—$\frac{3}{4}$ × $8\frac{1}{4}$ × $15\frac{1}{2}$″, 2 req'd.
D—Back—$\frac{3}{4}$ × $8\frac{1}{4}$ × $24\frac{1}{4}$″, 1 req'd.
E—Front facer—$\frac{3}{4}$ × $4\frac{1}{2}$ × $24\frac{1}{4}$″, 1 req'd.

Center Drawer

F—Front—$\frac{3}{4}$ × $2\frac{3}{4}$ × 10″, 1 req'd.
G—Sides—$\frac{1}{2}$ × $2\frac{3}{4}$ × 17″, 2 req'd.

H—Back—$\frac{1}{2}$ × $2\frac{3}{4}$ × 10″, 1 req'd.
I—Bottom—$\frac{1}{4}$ × $9\frac{1}{2}$ × $16\frac{3}{4}$″, 1 req'd.

Side Drawers

J—Fronts—$\frac{3}{4}$ × 4 × $5\frac{3}{4}$″, 2 req'd.
K—Sides—$\frac{1}{2}$ × 4 × 17″, 4 req'd.
L—Backs—$\frac{1}{2}$ × 4 × $5\frac{3}{4}$″, 2 req'd.
M—Bottoms—$\frac{1}{4}$ × $5\frac{1}{4}$ × $16\frac{3}{4}$″, 2 req'd.
N—Center front drawer facers—$\frac{3}{4}$ × $\frac{3}{4}$ × $2\frac{7}{8}$″, 2 req'd.
O—Top front facer—$\frac{3}{4}$ × $1\frac{1}{8}$ × $24\frac{1}{4}$″, 1 req'd.

Drawer Slides

P—Center drawer slide supports—$\frac{3}{4}$ × 6 × $15\frac{1}{2}$″, 2 req'd.
Q—Slides—$\frac{3}{4}$ × $\frac{3}{4}$ × 15″, 6 req'd.
R—Upper drawer slides—$\frac{3}{4}$ × $1\frac{1}{8}$ × 15″, 3 req'd.

Drawer Detail

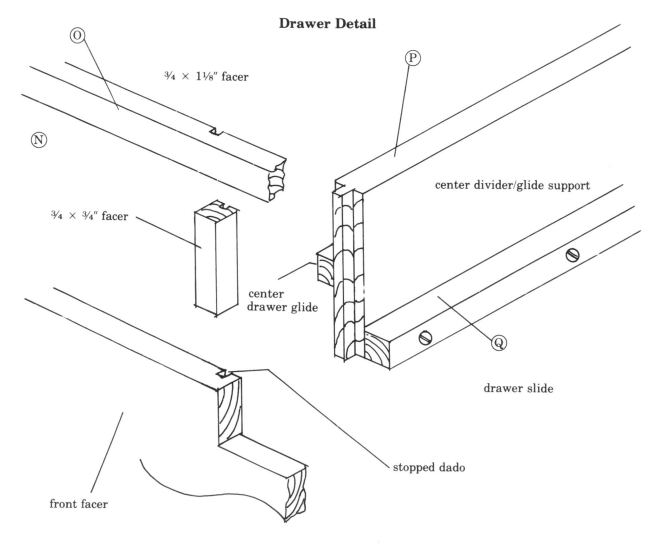

$\frac{3}{4}$ × $1\frac{1}{8}$″ facer

$\frac{3}{4}$ × $\frac{3}{4}$″ facer

center divider/glide support

center drawer glide

drawer slide

stopped dado

front facer

Detail A

Square Tilt-Top Table

Circa 1840

In almost all cases, tilt-top tables are round or oval; so this rectangular table is quite rare. It dates from about 1840 and is from England. The table is made of mahogany, but almost any hardwood will do, including walnut and rosewood.

Tilt-top tables, like many older furniture pieces, were designed to do double duty. With the top down, the table can be moved against a wall to be out of the way until needed. It was often used as a fire shield, to prevent glare from a fire while reading. Put the top up, and the table is ready instantly to hold a tea service or serve as a small reading table. The splayed-foot design of this particular table is typical of Chippendale styling, and the serpent's-head foot is quite simple in design.

Construction
The piece is fairly simple to construct yet provides a challenging and interesting project.

Support Post
The first step is to enlarge the squared drawing of the support post (A) and turn it to size and shape on a lathe. Bore the hole in the top for the top support holding dowel. Turn the support posts upside down and divide the end into three equal parts. Then cut the dovetail slots for the legs. They can be cut with hand chisels or with a router. When doing the work with a router, use the reeding or slotting jig to hold the router in position while the leg post is still in the lathe. Or use a Sears® Router Crafter. Make sure slots in the post and dovetails on the legs fit snugly. You want it tight enough that some tapping with a mallet is necessary. Otherwise the legs will be hard to glue in place.

Legs
Enlarge the squared drawing for the legs (B) and transfer it off onto the stock. But before cutting legs to shape, cut dovetails on the end of each using a table or radial arm saw to make the cuts. Then cut the legs to size and shape on a band saw. Round the edges on a shaper, or with a router in a router table. Then use a rasp to round the serpent's-head foot. Sand each leg as smooth as possible.

Smear some glue on the dovetails and drive the legs in place. Stand the assembly up on a smooth, flat surface, and make sure the support post is perfectly vertical. Use a large carpenter's square

against the side to check. If it is out of line, drive the legs up or down until the post is vertical.

Top
The top (E) of the original table is made of one solid piece and, as can be seen in the photos, it has warped. You may prefer to make up the top of smaller pieces of solid stock, glued and dowelled together. Or you could make the top of plywood and edge it with solid wood. In any case, cut the top to the correct size and shape, round the corners with a sabre saw, and shape the upper top edge using a shaper or router. Cut the table cleats (D,G) to size and shape, and drill counterbored holes for the screws, as shown. Bore the holes for the support dowel (F) through the cleats.

Assemble the cleat frame with wood screws. Fasten the cleat frame to the underside of the top with countersunk flat-head wood screws.

Cut the table support block (C) to size and shape and bore a hole through one side for the support dowel. See side view of tilt assembly. Drill a hole

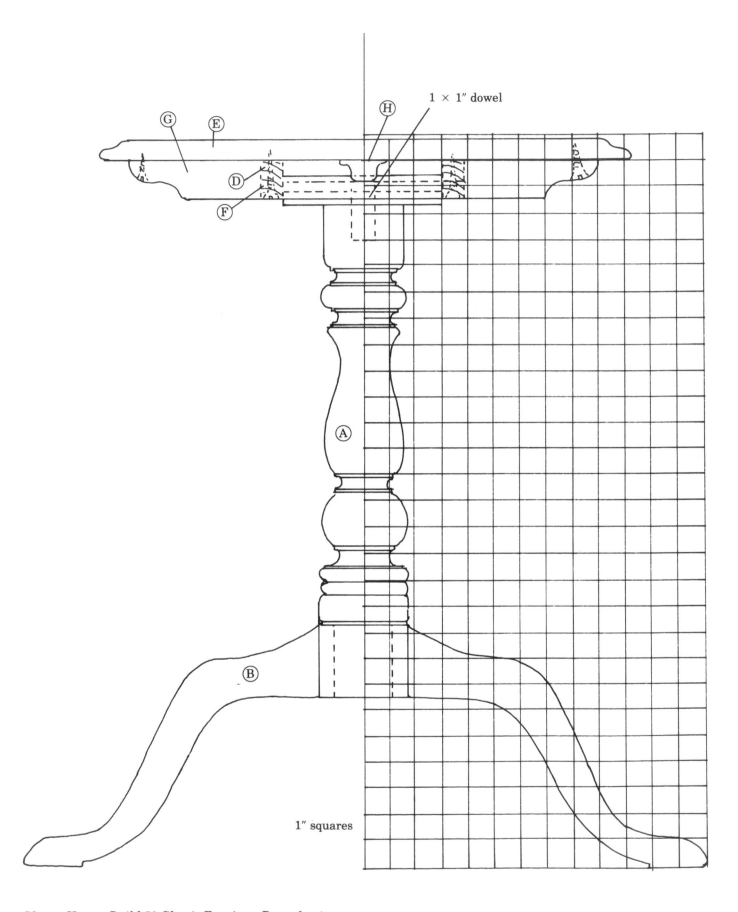

$1 \times 1''$ dowel

1" squares

(centered) through the top of the support block to accommodate the dowel on the support post (A). Place the support block down over the dowel on the support post and fasten it with glue and screws.

Position the tabletop over the support block, and put the support dowel through the aligned holes in the side cleats and support block. Fasten it in place with a small brad driven through the side of the support cleats. Install the tilt table fastener (H) (available from Horton Brasses).

Sand, stain, and finish.

Materials List

A—Support post—3½ × 3½ × 20″, 1 req'd.
B—Legs—1½ × 9½ × 12″, cut to shape, 3 req'd.
C—Table support block, 1 × 6 × 6″, 1 req'd.
D—Table cleats, side—¾ × 1½ × 18¼, 2 req'd.
E—Tabletop—¾ × 20½ × 28¾″, 1 req'd.
F—Support dowel—⅜ × 8″, 1 req'd.
G—Table cleats, end—¾ × 1½ × 18″, 2 req'd.
H—Tilt-top table fastener, 1 req'd.

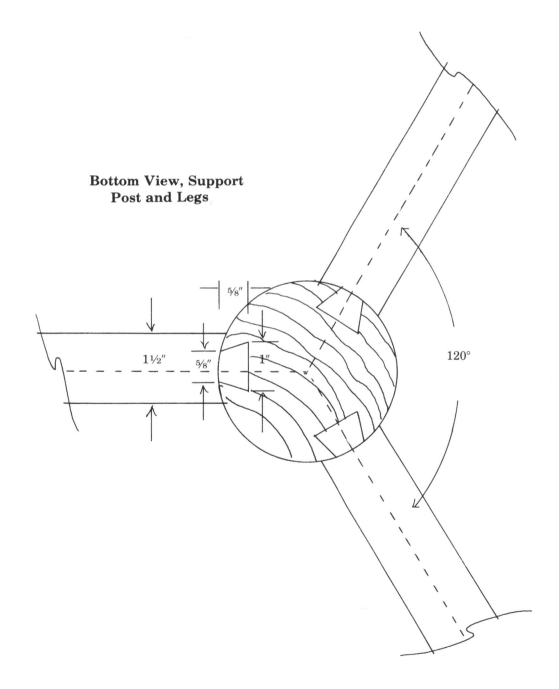

Bottom View, Support Post and Legs

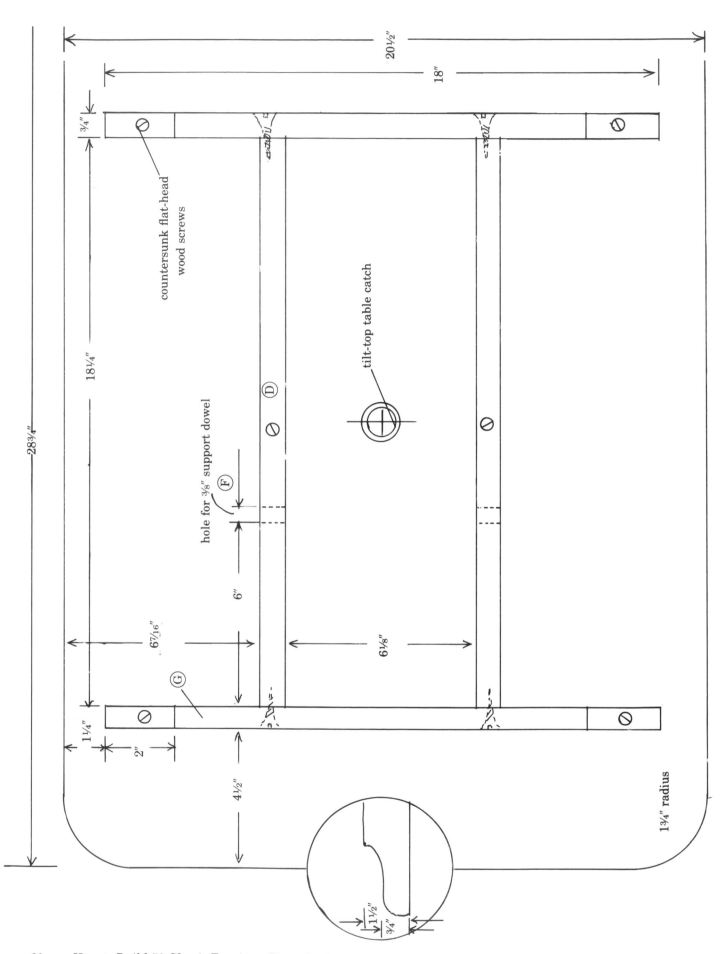

countersunk flat-head
wood screws

tilt-top table catch

hole for 3/8" support dowel

F

D

G

20½"

18"

¾"

18¼"

28¾"

6"

6⅞"

6⅞"

6⅞"

1¼"

2"

4½"

1¾" radius

1½"

¾"

Side View of Tilt Assembly

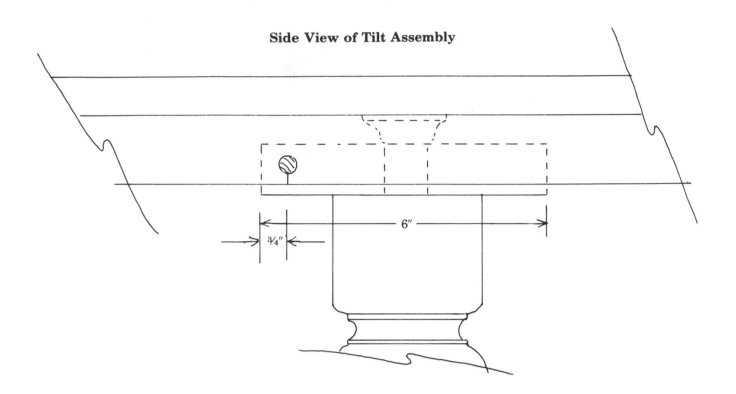

3/4"

6"

Gate-Leg Table

Circa 1810

Drop-leaf, gate-leg tables were a very popular item in early America. One reason was that they were so practical. One or both leaves of the tabletop could be lowered and the table pushed against a wall to save space.

The table shown here was carried into Missouri in a covered wagon, and its design reflects "country"-style craftsmanship. One very unusual feature of the table is that the top and both of the wide drop leaves are made of single pieces of solid stock. Amazingly, none of the pieces has warped. The original table is made of solid walnut, but it would look every bit as good in mahogany or even oak. Maple would also definitely give it an Early American flavor.

Construction
Construction is fairly simple and, except for the lathe work, the entire project can be made with hand tools. The legs and aprons are assembled with dowels and glue.

Legs
The first step is to enlarge the squared drawing for the legs (A). Cut the legs to the correct shape and length and then joint their sides. Turn them to shape

on a lathe. Note that there are six legs, and a lathe duplicator can really save a lot of work on this project. Cut the notches in the two swinging leg top posts to the correct size and shape.

Aprons
Cut the aprons (B,C) to size and shape, including the two outside swinging aprons (D) for the gate legs and the fixed aprons (E) that mate with them. Cut the hinge parts on the swinging aprons and outside fixed aprons with a band saw or coping saw. Round the edges of all fingers on hinge pieces. Fit mating hinge pieces together and bore the hole down through them for the dowel hinge pin.

Test-fit all aprons and legs together and mark dowel locations. Note that the end and outside aprons are set back from the front of the posts a bit. Bore all dowel holes in the leg posts and aprons. (See the Techniques Section for more on making dowel joints.)

Assembly
Fasten the end aprons (B) in place to the legs (A) with dowels and glue. Clamp these assemblies and allow the glue to set overnight. Then install the fixed

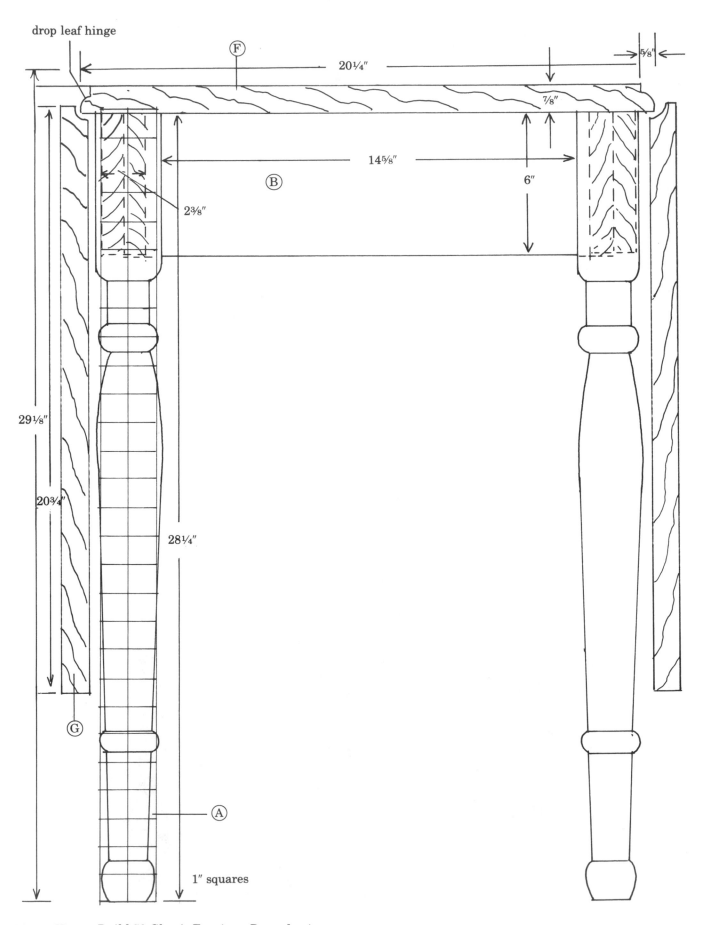

drop leaf hinge

F

20¼"

⅝"

7⁄8"

14⅝"

B

6"

2⅜"

29⅛"

20¾"

28¼"

G

A

1" squares

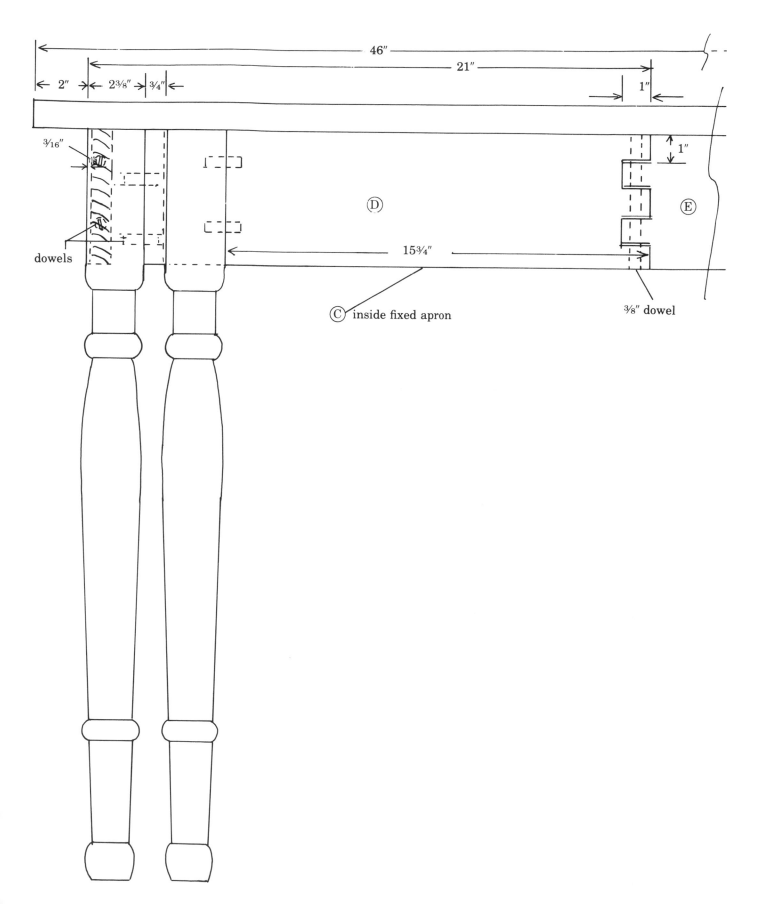

46″

21″

2″ 2⅜″ ¾″

1″

3/16″

1″

D

dowels

15¾″

C inside fixed apron

E

⅜″ dowel

aprons (C) on the front and back between the two end assemblies, again with dowels and glue.

Stand the table on a smooth, flat surface and make sure the table rests firmly and evenly on all four legs. Clamp and allow the glue to set overnight. Then install the two outside fixed aprons (E) with dowels and glue. Drive screws through the inside aprons into the outside fixed aprons.

Gate Legs

Fasten the swinging aprons (D) to the swinging legs with dowels and glue and clamp them securely until the glue sets. Then remove from the clamps and connect to the table frame using a wooden dowel run down through the hinge fingers. Anchor the dowel with a small brad driven through the top finger and into the dowel.

Cut to fit the small spacer apron blocks (H) between the swinging leg and the fixed leg (see top view) and fasten in place with glue and screws from the inside of the fixed apron.

Top

The table shown had full width, one piece stock for each of the top pieces (F,G). You will probably, however, have to make them up from glued-up widths of stock, alternating heartwood and sapwood to prevent warping. These pieces can be joined with tongue-and-groove joints or dowels and glue. You may also want to use hardwood-faced plywood edged with solid stock or veneer tape for the large top pieces.

Make the drop-leaf hinge joints on each piece. Position the center top (F) upside down on a smooth, flat surface. Fasten the table frame to it with screws deeply countersunk in the end aprons (B) and inside fixed aprons (C). You can also use glue blocks (or support cleats) and glue and screws.

Install the drop-leaf hinges on the center top section. Then, with the table upside down, position a drop leaf against the center section. Mortise and install the other half of the drop leaf hinge to it. Fasten the opposite top piece in place in the same manner. Install the small casters on the ends of each of the legs. Turn the table upright, sand, stain, and finish.

Materials List

A—Legs—2⅜ × 2⅜ × 28¼", 6 req'd.
B—End aprons—¾ × 6 × 14⅝", 2 req'd.
C—Inside fixed aprons—¾ × 6 × 37¼", 2 req'd.
D—Outside swinging aprons—¾ × 6 × 15¾", 2 req'd.
E—Outside fixed aprons—¾ × 6 × 18⅜", 2 req'd.
F—Center top—⅞ × 20¼ × 46", 1 req'd.
G—Drop leaves—⅞ × 20¾ × 46", 2 req'd.
H—Spacer apron blocks—¾ × ¾ × 6", 2 req'd.
Casters, 6 req'd.
Drop leaf hinges, 2 req'd.

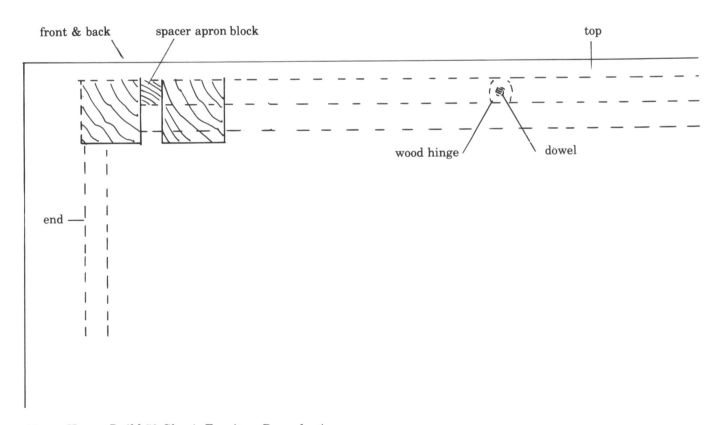

front & back   spacer apron block   top

wood hinge   dowel

end

Wine Table

Circa 1900

This dainty little table was made in America. It was often called a wine table, because it could be positioned at the host's side for serving wine. It was also called a candle table and could be used to hold a candle to light the corner of a room.

In any case, the table shown is made of walnut and features a faceplate-turned top that makes the project that much more interesting.

Top

The first step in construction is to create the turned top (A) for the table. This is made of ⅞-inch stock. You will probably have to glue and dowel together the stock needed to make it up. Make sure that you do not locate any dowels so that they will be exposed when the top is cut out from the glued-up stock. It's a good idea to make a rough outline of the top on the pieces of stock first, and then position the dowels accordingly.

The top is turned on a lathe using a faceplate. First locate the center of the glued-up stock. Mark its exact location, and then, using a large compass, mark the rough outline of the circle for the top. Use a band saw or sabre saw to rough-cut the top. Then fasten the faceplate to the top and place it on the lathe. Turn the outside profile first, creating the rounded edge. Then turn back the tiny bead or lip on the front of the turning and cut the recessed top.

Sand thoroughly and apply the finish while the piece is still in the lathe.

Cut the support block (C) from a piece of walnut and bore the center dowel hole in it. Then finish it and fasten it to the center of the underside of the tabletop with glue and wood screws.

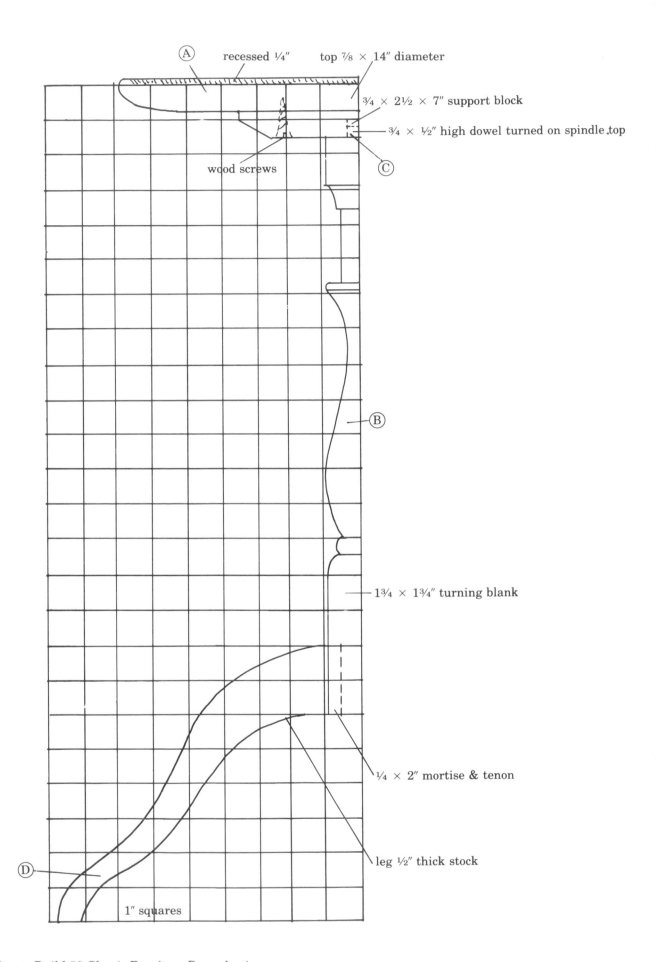

(A) recessed ¼″ top ⅞ × 14″ diameter

¾ × 2½ × 7″ support block

¾ × ½″ high dowel turned on spindle top

(C)

wood screws

(B)

1¾ × 1¾″ turning blank

¼ × 2″ mortise & tenon

leg ½″ thick stock

(D)

1″ squares

Support Post

The center support post (B) is a fairly simple turning project. A 1¾-inch turning block cut to length is used for the post. Enlarge the squared drawing and create the pattern to use as a guide for the turning.

Turn the dowel on the upper end and size it to fit snugly into the support block on the underside of the table.

Sand and finish this piece while it is still in the lathe.

The legs (D) are held in place with mortises cut into the bottom of the support post. To provide extra strength you could use dovetail slots. Either the dovetail slots or simple mortises may be cut while the post is still in the lathe. Use a router attachment for cutting beads and grooves. The router jig and technique is shown on page 17. Or you can use a Sears® Router Crafter for the job.

Legs

Enlarge the squared drawing for the legs and create a pattern for them. Trace the pattern onto ½-inch stock, and cut to shape. Sand the edges to remove any saw marks. Use a drum-sander attachment for a drill press or power saw, etc. Then round the edges using a shaper or router in a router table.

Assembly

Apply glue to the inside of the dovetail slots in the support post (B) and tap the legs into place. Make sure that none of the glue squeezes out. Turn the table upright as soon as possible and make sure it stands squarely and evenly on a smooth, flat surface. This won't be much of a problem because of the tripod effect of the three legs.

Place glue on the support post dowel and tap the top (A) in place. Check to make sure it is square and wipe away any glue that might have been squeezed out. Allow the glue to dry overnight, and that's all there is to it.

These little tables are so easy to build and go so well with any decor, you will probably want to build several as presents for friends and relatives.

Materials List

A—Top—⅞ × 14" diameter, 1 req'd.
B—Support post—1¾ × 1¾ × 16¾", 1 req'd.
C—Support block—¾ × 2½ × 7", 1 req'd.
D—Legs—½ × 4 × 12", cut to shape, 3 req'd.

Queen Anne Drop-Leaf Table
Circa 1840

This elegant Queen Anne table has a drop leaf and a swinging leg to support the table leaf in the "up" position. It was built in England about 1840 and is made of solid mahogany. Other good wood choices would be walnut, cherry or pecan. It features the classic Queen Anne style cabriole legs.

These tables were often used to serve tea, the drop leaf being raised to provide the extra space needed for the tea tray.

Construction

This is a fairly complicated table to build, although it doesn't appear so at first glance. Most of the difficulty is with the swinging leg. But the drawer is also something of a problem. Its front must be cut from the center of the solid-stock facing. Construction of the drawer is unusual as well; it is made of glued-up 3/16-inch solid stock with a 3/4-inch drawer front.

Legs

First enlarge the squared drawings for the cabriole legs (A) and then cut them to shape and size on a band saw. The bottom of the leg has a typical Queen Anne foot. This can be turned on the lathe after the leg has been cut, or you can carve it by hand if you prefer.

Sand and smooth the legs, using a drum sander to remove all saw marks and to clean up the cuts.

Aprons

The aprons (B-G) for the table frame are held to the legs with mortise-and-tenon joints. You could make slotted dovetails if you want to make the joints a bit stronger. The joint used on the original was mortise and tenon.

Cut the aprons to their correct lengths (allowing for tenons as needed), and cut the tenons on their ends to size and shape (see top view). Then cut matching mortises in the ends of the cabriole leg posts. Note that the one post on the front has two aprons (E,G) fastened to it. Be careful when marking and cutting these mortises and tenons because the aprons must fit properly against the post and against each other. In addition, the other aprons and outside edges of the cabriole legs must all be flush, so mark and cut these mortise-and-tenon joints carefully too.

The opposite corner on the same side of the table (the swinging leg corner) is a simple dovetail joint.

After cutting the dovetail for the back in each apron (G,D), make the recess so that the swinging leg will fit flush in place when it is pushed back against the aprons. Cut the side mortise in the swinging leg to fit around the table corner. Use a drill to bore holes in the cutout first, and then clean it up with a sharp, large chisel.

Cut the drawer front from the front apron (B). This is done by using a tiny drill bit that is large enough to allow a scroll saw blade to slide through the hole. Drill holes at each corner of the drawer opening. Then use a scroll saw to cut out the drawer front. Smooth up the inside of the opening in the apron using a wood rasp and file. Then smooth and sand all edges of the drawer front. Work carefully and don't remove too much material or the drawer will be too loose in the opening.

In addition, the other aprons and outside edges of the cabriole legs must all be flush. Mark and cut these mortise-and-tenon joints carefully too.

Cut the arms of the hinged apron (E,F) to the proper size and make the interlocking parts of the hinge joint. Fit the aprons together and bore a hole down through the top of the hinge joint for the wooden hinge pin.

Saw the drawer slides (K) and slide support (L) to the proper L-shape and size. Mark locations of tenons on their ends to fit into the side (C) and front aprons (B). Then cut matching mortises in the aprons.

Assembly

Assembly starts with the drawer slides (K) and slide support (L). Fasten the two slides to the back slide support (L) using glue in the mortise-and-tenon joints. Then put the front apron (B) in place over the tenons of the drawer slides and clamp this assembly overnight. Make sure it is square.

At the same time, you can also install the assembled swinging leg and apron (E). Glue the mortise and tenon of the apron and leg together and clamp. Place the opposite arm of the apron (E) into the other leg (the leg with the two mortises) and clamp it securely as well.

Now put the front apron and drawer glide assembly in between the two side aprons (C,G) and clamp them. At the same time, fit the two side apron ten-

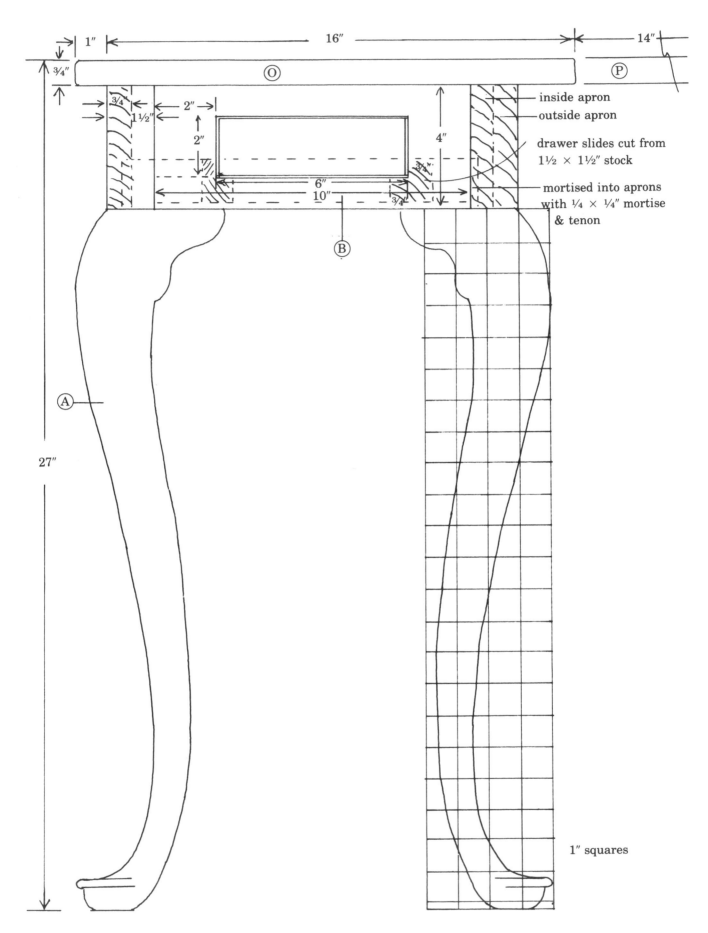

1"

16"

14"

3/4"

O

P

3/4"

1½"

2"

2"

inside apron

outside apron

drawer slides cut from
1½ × 1½" stock

4"

3/4"

6"

10"

3/4"

mortised into aprons
with ¼ × ¼" mortise
& tenon

B

A

27"

1" squares

ons into mortises of both front-leg posts and clamp this assembly securely.

The final step is to fit the back apron (D) into the dovetails in the side aprons. The last back-leg post is also installed at this time. Again make sure all joints are square and properly fitted, and clamp overnight.

During clamping of the final assembly, make sure the table is standing upright on a smooth, flat surface and that it is square and doesn't rock back and forth on the legs. If it does, remove from the clamps and rock the assembly a bit until it stands firmly on all four legs. Then replace the clamps.

Put the wooden dowel pin hinge in place and se-cure the dowel with a small brad through the top of one hinge finger. Fasten the two aprons (E,G) on the immobile side together with countersunk flat-head wood screws driven from the inside of the apron.

Tabletop

Cut the glue blocks (M,N), or top holding cleats, and fasten them in place to the underside edge of the apron. Note that on the original only glue was used to hold the top in place. But adding screws will pre-vent the top from being torn off when the table is moved around.

Cut the top pieces (O,P) to the correct size and

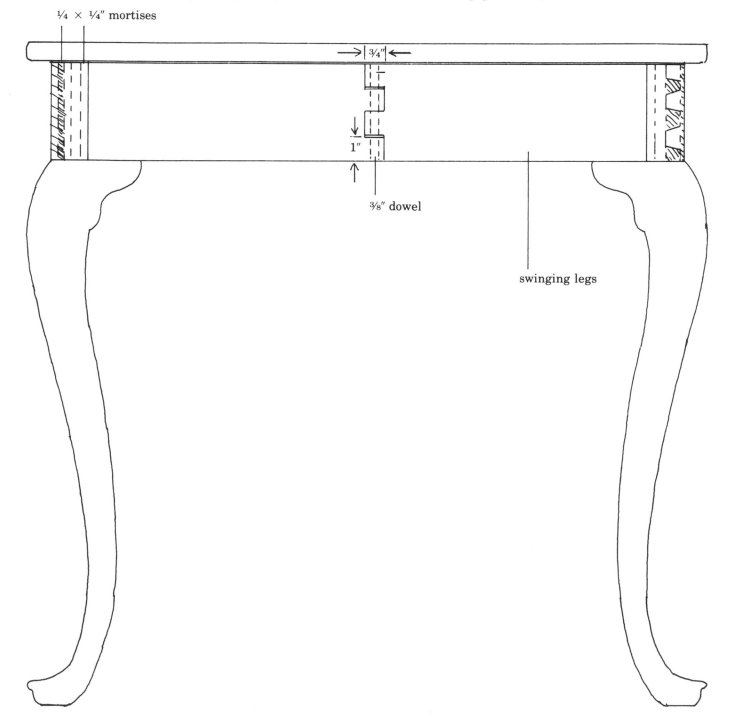

¼ × ¼″ mortises

¾″

1″

⅜″ dowel

swinging legs

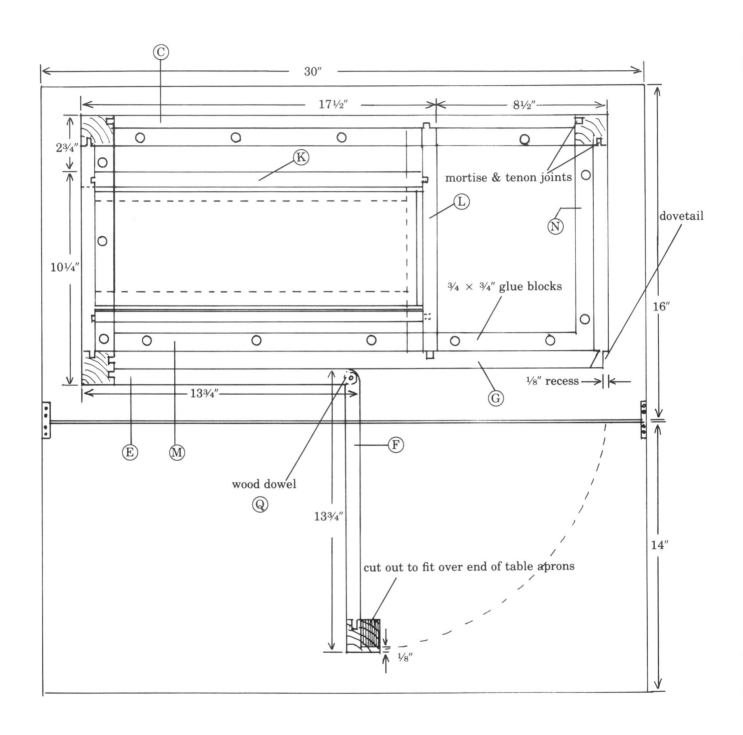

C

30"

17½"

8½"

2¾"

K

mortise & tenon joints

L

N

dovetail

10¼"

¾ × ¾" glue blocks

16"

G

⅛" recess

13¾"

E

M

F

wood dowel

Q

13¾"

cut out to fit over end of table aprons

⅛"

14"

round their edges up to the junction of the hinge joint. Then mark carefully and cut the mortises for the hinges. Install the hinges (R) on the top pieces; then position the top on the table frame and fasten in place with screws driven up through the glue blocks. Make sure the screws do not penetrate through the top.

Drawer

The drawer is constructed by simply cutting pieces of $\frac{3}{16}$-inch hardwood to size and gluing it up as shown in the drawer detail. The sides (H) and bottom (J) and back (I) are glued in $\frac{3}{16} \times \frac{1}{2}$-inch rabbets cut into the side and bottom edges of the back face of the drawer front. This makes for a flush-fitting drawer assembly.

There is a small finger recess cut in the underside of the bottom. To open the drawer, you simply reach under the table apron and insert your finger in the recess. Since the drawer bottom is thin, care must be taken when cutting this recess.

The traditional finish for this table is dark mahogany.

Materials List

A—Legs—5 × 5 × 26¼″, 4 req'd.

Aprons

B—Front—¾ × 4 × 10½″, 1 req'd.
C—Side—¾ × 4 × 23½″, 1 req'd.
D—Back—¾ × 4 × 11″, 1 req'd.
E—Outside fixed apron—¾ × 4 × 12½″, 1 req'd.
F—Outside swinging apron—¾ × 4 × 12½″, 1 req'd.
G—Inside fixed apron—¾ × 4 × 24¾″, 1 req'd.

Drawer

H—Sides—³⁄₁₆ × 1⅞ × 16¼″, 2 req'd.
I—Back—³⁄₁₆ × 1⅞ × 5⅝″, 1 req'd.
J—Bottom—³⁄₁₆ × 5⅝ × 15⁹⁄₁₆″, 1 req'd.
K—Slides—1½ × 1½ × 17″, 2 req'd.
L—Slide support—1½ × 1½ × 11¼″, 1 req'd.

Glue Blocks

M—Sides—¾ × ¾ × 23″, 2 req'd.
N—Front & back—¾ × ¾ × 10″, 2 req'd.

Tabletop

O—Tabletop—¾ × 16 × 30″, 1 req'd.
P—Drop leaf—¾ × 14 × 30″, 1 req'd.
Q—Dowel—⅜ × 4″, 1 req'd.
R—Hinge—card table or drop-leaf hinge, 1 req'd.

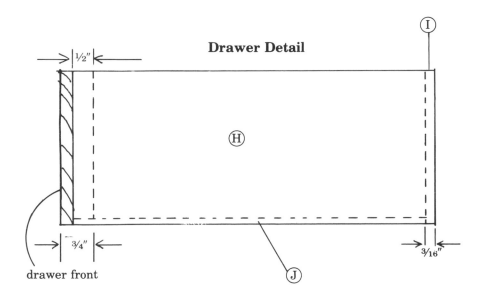

Drawer Detail

drawer front

Four-Poster Bed

Circa 1880

Bedsteads of this type were quite popular around the turn of the century, and many different styles can be found in antique shops across the country. The walnut bed shown here is typical of these beds in at least one design aspect. It is quite a bit higher from the floor than modern bedsteads. This was important in the days before central heating: It was warmer a foot or two above the floor. It was also easier to sweep under the higher beds with a broom, and in many cases off-season items were stored under the bed.

The post design in this particular bed is a refined and more elegant "cannonball" style than the heavier, full-rounded cannonball turnings quite often found on four-poster beds. The full-scrolled headboard provides an excellent opportunity to show off a beautifully grained piece of stock if you have a piece on hand. On this type of bed, the scrolled headboard was usually made of solid stock, rather than being veneered.

The bed shown is made of walnut, and this is the type of wood most often chosen for this style. You could, of course, use other hardwoods to match other bedroom pieces, and in this case mahogany would be the next choice. Lighter woods, such as ash, won't be as authentic in appearance, but if you wish to blend the bed in with more modern furniture, you could make it of pecan. For a truly unusual look, make the bed of oak or pine and stain it dark for the "antique pine" effect.

Construction

If you are proficient with a band saw and lathe, constructing a bed of this type is fairly easy. Also, there is less assembly time involved than in more complicated cabinets.

Patterns

The first step is to enlarge the squared drawings and create full-size patterns. Once you have built a four-poster bed, you'll probably get requests for others from friends and relatives. For this reason, make patterns on stiff paper and number, date and label them for future use. You can make half-patterns for the headboard, foot rails and head rails. The posts, however, require full-length patterns.

Gluing Up the Stock

Unless you have access to large walnut turning blocks, you will have to glue up the turning blocks for the posts (A,B) as shown on page 26. The headboard (J) should also be made of a glued-up section to prevent warping. Careful selection of the stock and alternating heartwood and sapwood pieces will result in a stable, strong piece. You may prefer to cut the headboard from hardwood-faced plywood or veneer the piece yourself, covering the cut plywood edges with veneer tape.

The old beds were the size shown here, but you can vary the sizes by simply adding more to the side rails (F) and the center section, including the turnings on the foot- and headboard. You should measure the size of your mattress before building the bed.

Turning the Posts

Because of the length of the posts, they are turned in two pieces and joined with glue and a large dowel. The foot spindle is made in three pieces, with holes bored in the center dowel to fasten on the end pieces. The top turning on the headboard is done in the same manner: turning the long dowel, boring holes in the ends, and joining the pediments with dowels turned on their ends.

After gluing up the turning blocks, turn the posts (A,B) to size and shape (again, the bottom and top sections of each post are turned separately). Create a turned dowel on the bottom of each of the upper posts (A), and bore a mating hole in each of the bottom posts (B). This can be done using a horizontal boring technique or with a portable electric drill and drill guide. It is very important, of course, to get the holes centered exactly in the posts.

Headboard and Footboard Turnings

The headboard and footboard turnings are made in the same manner. The headboard turning (H,I) is made in three parts, as is the footboard turning (C,D). Both of these, as well as all posts, must be sanded smooth and finished on the lathe. Use the same finish that will be applied to other parts.

Headboard

The next step is to cut the headboard (J) to size and shape. This can be done with a sabre saw or with a band saw, if you have one with a large throat. The outer end of the work should be well supported to prevent it from tipping down and causing cutting

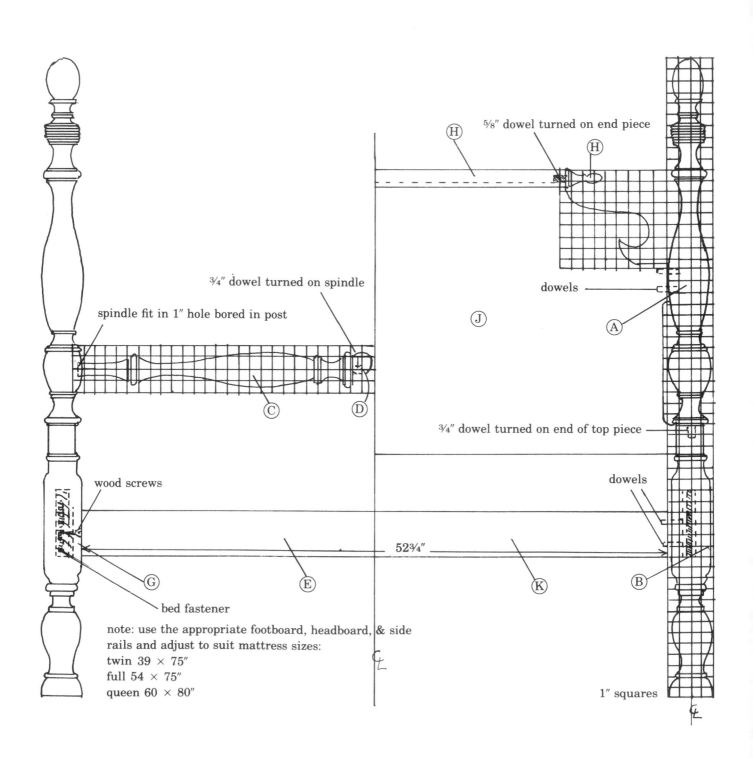

⁵⁄₈″ dowel turned on end piece

Ⓗ

Ⓗ

¾″ dowel turned on spindle

dowels

spindle fit in 1″ hole bored in post

Ⓙ

Ⓐ

Ⓒ   Ⓓ

¾″ dowel turned on end of top piece

wood screws

dowels

52¾″

Ⓖ   Ⓔ   Ⓚ   Ⓑ

bed fastener

note: use the appropriate footboard, headboard, & side
rails and adjust to suit mattress sizes:
twin 39 × 75″
full 54 × 75″
queen 60 × 80″

1″ squares

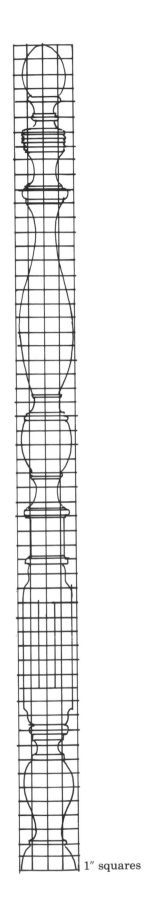

1″ squares

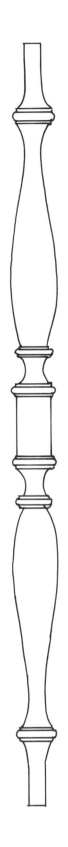

problems. The entire surface, including the edges, must be well sanded and smoothed.

Fit the scroll turning (H,I) onto the top of the headboard. There are two ways to do this. One way is to cut a flat on the underside of the turning and dowel it in place on the headboard top edge. The other way is to cut a mortise in the underside of the turning. Use a router and a jig to hold the router in place to the lathe bed and make the mortise before removing the turning from the lathe. Whatever the method, carefully cut and fit the turning in place. When you're sure it's perfectly mated, put glue in the slot and glue and clamp it in place. Make sure none of the glue oozes out of the joint, because it will stain the surface. It is especially hard to remove excess glue from the surface of the joint between the headboard and the turning.

Rails
Saw the lower headboard rail (K) and footboard rail (E) and the side rails (F) to size and plane their surfaces as smooth as possible. You will probably also want to round the upper edges of the side rails slightly.

Installing the Bed Fasteners
The side rails are held to the posts with purchased metal bed fasteners. Each set of these fasteners has a metal plate (with holes in it) that is mounted over a mortised slot cut into the bedposts. The other metal plate is fastened to the bed rails. It has hooks that fit down into the bedpost plate. To install them, first cut the mortise in the bedpost with a small chisel. Inset the bedpost plate so that it is flush with the surface of the bedpost. Then mount the side rail plate, insetting it as well.

Bed fasteners are available from various mail order woodworking supply houses.

Assembly
Both the headboard and footboard assemblies are put together using glue and dowels. Dowels for the holes in the rounded portion of the posts are located by first placing the posts on a flat, smooth surface. Mark a centerline on the headboard (J) and rail (K) using a pair of scribes or small block to hold the pencil. Then bore the holes in the headboard and rail ends.

Insert dowel center markers and press these in

Side Rail Detail

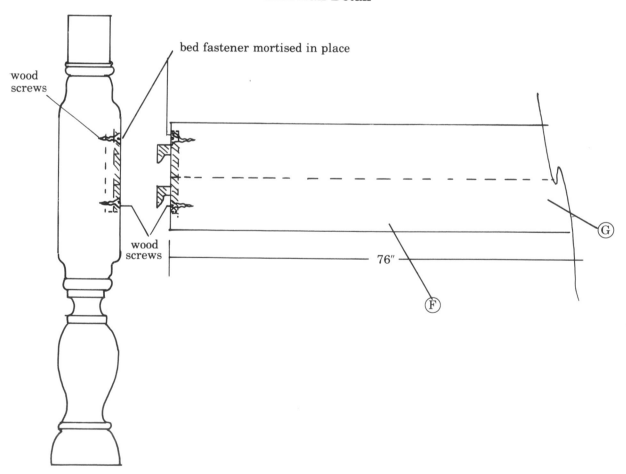

wood screws

bed fastener mortised in place

wood screws

76″

Ⓕ

Ⓖ

place against centerline marks on the posts. Or measure carefully and mark locations of the dowel holes in the posts. Use a drill press or portable electrical drill with drill guide to assure accurately bored dowel holes. Assemble with dowels and glue and clamp securely overnight. Make sure the assembly is flat, square, and not twisted.

Finishing

You may want to finish the headboard and rails before gluing and assembling, since the posts and turnings have already been finished on the lathe. A good wipe-on finish, such as tung oil by Zar, is a good choice for this type of project. It produces a finish that is a close match to the original.

Inside Support Cleats

You can adjust the height of the bed by the placement of the inside support cleats (G) as shown in the drawing. The cleats are fastened to the inside of the side rails (F) using glue and screws, and they must be firmly attached. Traditional four-poster beds used springs and wooden slats (L). But a box spring will fit in between the bed rails and rest on the support cleats, or bed rails may also be used for extra support for the box springs.

Materials List

A—Posts, upper—4 × 4 × 33″, 4 req'd.

B—Posts, bottom—4 × 4 × 25″, 4 req'd.

C—Footboard turnings—3 × 3 × 24½″, 2 req'd.

D—Footboard turning—2 × 2 × 4″, 1 req'd.

E—Footboard rail—1 × 4 × 52¾″, 1 req'd.

F—Side rails—1 × 6 × 76″, 2 req'd.

G—Inside support cleats—1 × 4 × 76″, 2 req'd.

H—Headboard turning—1½ × 1½ × 34½″, 1 req'd.

I—Headboard turning ends—1½ × 1½ × 3″, 2 req'd.

J—Headboard—¾ × 24½ × 53½″, 1 req'd.

K—Lower headboard rail—1 × 4 × 52¾″, 1 req'd.

L—Slats—¾ × 3 × 55, 3 req'd., cut to a tight fit.

Bed fasteners—2 pair.

Upholstered Settee

Circa 17th Century

This is an unusual piece of furniture for the period in which it was made. Most upholstered furniture of the time tended to be both uncomfortable and awkward in appearance. Upholstered pieces were also usually quite large in scale.

But the small settee for this project is the same size as today's popular "loveseats" and makes an interesting furniture piece that will fit with almost any decor. Although it is not an elaborate piece, it has sea-creature carvings that provide an unusual and decorative touch, as well as a challenge for carving enthusiasts. The original settee was made of walnut, though almost any of the more formal furniture woods, such as pecan, mahogany, or cherry, would do very nicely.

Construction

The settee is relatively easy to construct and dowelled joints are used for most of it. About the only problem is in getting the correct angles on the side aprons, which are fitted to the front and back legs. Also, the back of the arms must be cut on a compound angle to fit the back posts.

Legs

Start by enlarging the squared drawing and cutting the front legs (A) to shape and size. Then do the same for the back legs (B). Note that the back legs have wings (C) on their tops. It's easier and more practical to glue these pieces to the tops of the back legs, instead of cutting the entire back leg from a single, thicker piece of stock. Then create the carvings on the tops of the back legs.

Arms

Cut the arms (E) to size and shape as well, but leave the back ends long and do not cut the compound angle at this time. That should be done to fit the angle of the back, after it has been assembled.

Back Pieces

Cut the top back piece (J) to the squared drawing as shown. Then cut the center back stretcher (I) to size and shape. Cut the shaped beads on its front face using a router in a router table or a hand-held router plane. Note that the outside edges of the stretcher are notched to fit around the back side pieces (K). After cutting the side pieces to shape, make the notches in the stretcher to fit around them.

Bottom Aprons

Cut the side (D), back (H) and front (F) aprons to size and shape. Cut the side aprons to the angles shown in the top view drawing. Dress the outside surfaces of the front and side aprons with a router in a router table. There is a decorative trim piece (G) attached to the bottom edge of the front apron. Enlarge the squared drawing and cut this to shape. Cut the grooves in the front of the trim piece with a small veiner chisel. Then attach it to the bottom of the front apron with glue and screws driven from the bottom.

Carving the Back Pieces

Enlarge the squared drawings and make a pattern for the back side pieces (K). Note that they are fairly simple relief carvings, with the background stippled. Use various gouges and other chisels to outline the carving; then cut down the background around the figure. Next stipple the lowered surface. Finally, round and shape the figure.

Assembly

Begin the assembly of this and other dowelled-joint projects such as this one by laying out the section pieces together on a smooth, flat surface. In this case, begin with the back section. Align the pieces very carefully, then mark across them to locate the dowel holes. Mark each joining piece with a corresponding letter so you can find the right mating surfaces quickly once you start the final assembly.

Then bore the dowel holes, using a dowelling jig or similar tool to position each of the holes accurately. Remember to offset dowels in the leg posts, where the two aprons meet, so that you won't have one dowel hole bored into another. Once all dowel holes have been bored, sand each piece thoroughly.

Put the back-leg and side assemblies together with the dowels (but no glue) for a trial fit on a smooth, flat surface. Now you make the final, compound angle cuts on the back of the arms (E).

Assemble the side units with dowels and glue. Once both have been assembled, put the back pieces and front apron (F) between the two side assemblies and dowel and glue in place. Position the settee on a smooth, flat surface. Make sure it doesn't rock back and forth and that all four legs rest evenly on the surface. Then clamp it solidly together and allow the glue to set.

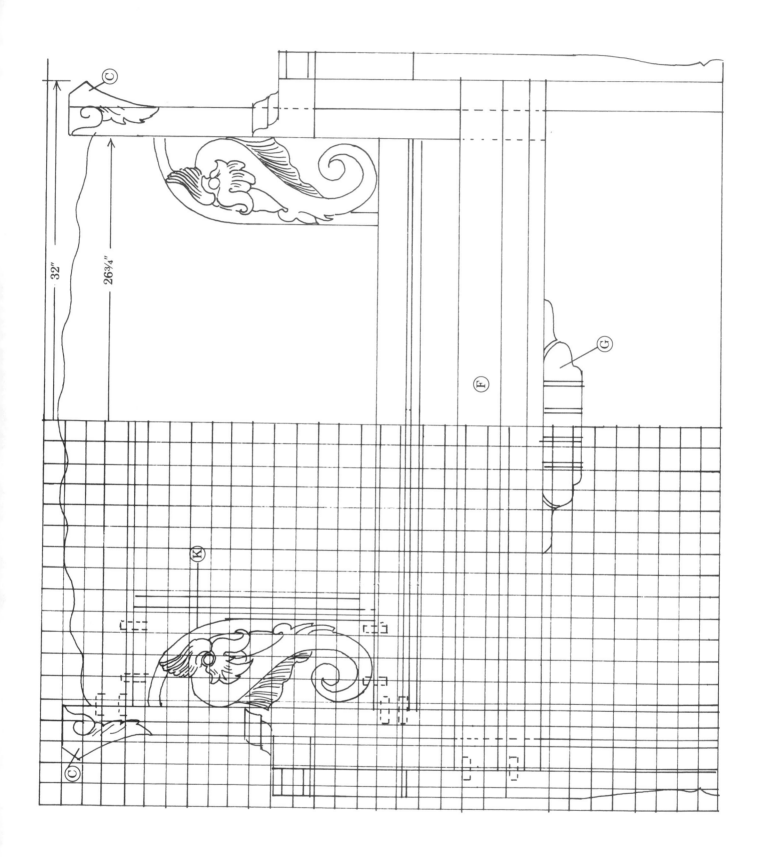

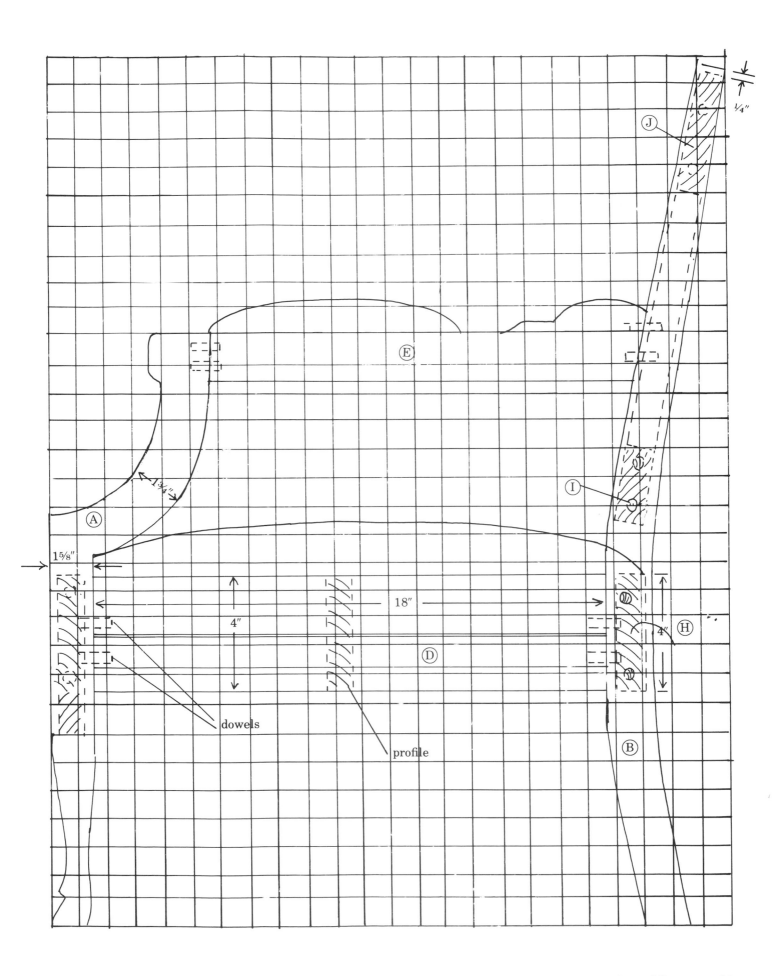

dowels

profile

Add the corner seat blocks (L) and center seat stretcher (M) with glue and screws. Note that the center seat stretcher is supported by and fastened to glue blocks (N) below its ends and fastened to front and back aprons. Sand, stain and finish, and then upholster.

Materials List

A—Front legs—1¼ × 6 × 21″, 2 req'd.
B—Back legs—1⅜ × 4½ × 31″, 2 req'd.
C—Back leg wings—1 × 1½ × 3½″, 2 req'd.
D—Side aprons—¾ × 4 × 18″, 2 req'd.
E—Arms—1⅜ × 3 × 16″, cut to fit, 2 req'd.

F—Front apron—¾ × 4 × 32⅛″, 1 req'd.
G—Front apron trim—¾ × 2 × 12″, 1 req'd.
H—Back apron—¾ × 4 × 26¾″, 1 req'd.
I—Center back stretcher—¾ × 2¾ × 26¾″, 1 req'd.
J—Top back piece—¾ × 4 × 26¾″, 1 req'd.
K—Back side pieces—¾ × 4¾ × 11¼″, 2 req'd.
L—Seat blocks—¾ × 3 × 3″, 4 req'd.
M—Center seat stretcher—¾ × 2 × 18¾″, 1 req'd.
N—Center seat stretcher glue blocks—¾ × ¾ × 2″, 2 req'd.

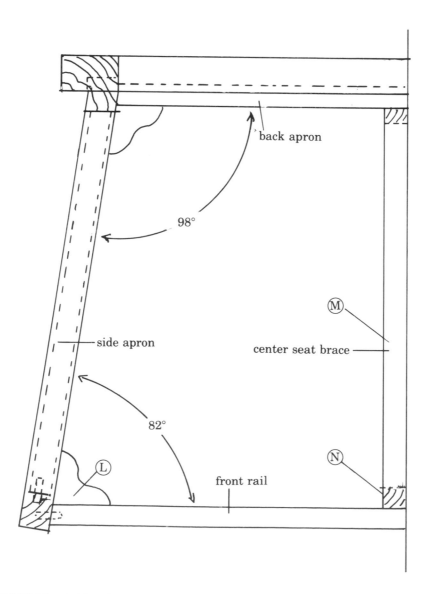

Armchair

Circa 1855

This is an extremely graceful and sturdy period-style armchair. It was made in England and is constructed of oak. The carving for the back is elegant, yet not overly detailed. The graceful Queen Anne-style legs show off the quarter-sawn oak grain beautifully, and the shell carving on the back adds a nice, decorative touch. Although this chair is especially suited to oak, it would also look good in walnut, mahogany, or even pecan.

Construction

Start construction by enlarging the squared drawings for all the pieces, including front and back legs (A,B), top back (C), back splat (D), arms (J), arm supports (K) and side aprons (G). Then transfer the patterns to the appropriate pieces.

Front Legs

The front cabriole legs (A) are cut to shape on a band saw. Shape their bottom ends on a lathe. The inside portion for the seatboard is cut away from the top of the leg posts using a chisel. (Note that wing pieces may be glued and dowelled to the sides if desired, rather than using one large piece for the entire leg.) Cut mortises into each side of the leg posts for apron tenons.

Back Legs

Cut the back legs (B) to size and shape on a band saw. Then cut mortises in their top ends for the top piece (C), in their front surfaces for the side aprons (G), and inside edges for the back apron tenons (F). Cut the mortise on the outside of each for arm tenons (J). Cut the decorative front moulding using a shaper with collars and spacers to properly guide the cuts.

Top Back

Before cutting the top back piece (C) to size and shape, rout a mortise in its underside for the back splat (D). Then cut mortises in each end for the back-leg tenons (B). After all mortises have been cut, cut the top back piece to the correct shape with a band saw. Carve to the patterns. Lightly round the upper part as shown in the side view drawing.

Back Splat

Cut the back splat (D) to size and shape according to the pattern. Carve the single decorative chip carving in the center.

Aprons

Cut the front (E) and back aprons (F) to size and shape and rout or shape the seatboard recess in the front and side aprons. Cut tenons on the apron ends to the proper size and shape. Then cut the mortise in the top center of the back apron for the back splat.

Arms

Make the arms (J) and arm supports (K) the correct size and shape, and carve grooves in both sides of the front of the arms. Cut mortises and tenons on the

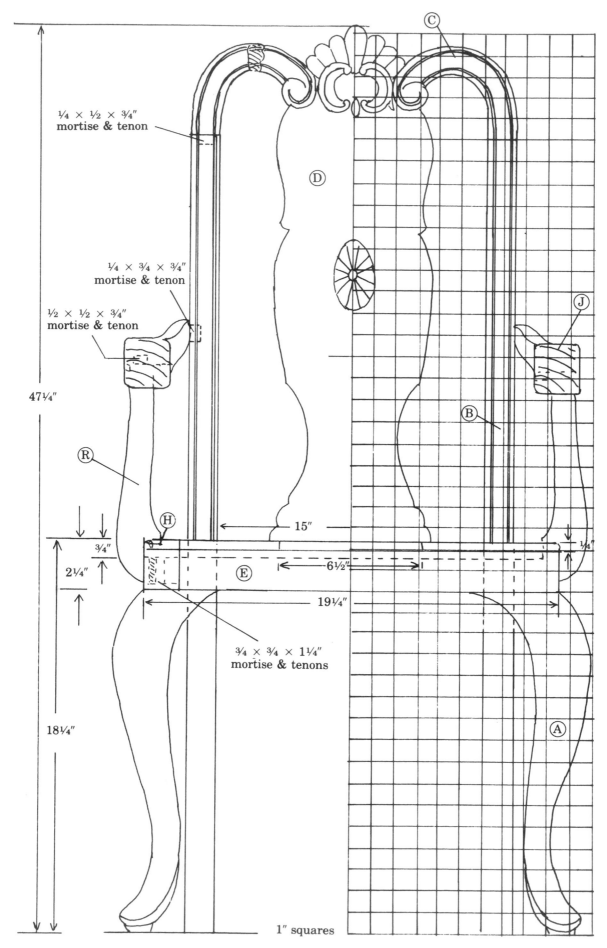

C

1/4 × 1/2 × 3/4"
mortise & tenon

1/4 × 3/4 × 3/4"
mortise & tenon

1/2 × 1/2 × 3/4"
mortise & tenon

D

J

B

47 1/4"

R

H

15"

1/4"

3/4"

E

6 1/2"

2 1/4"

3/4 × 3/4 × 1 1/4"
mortise & tenons

19 1/4"

A

18 1/4"

1" squares

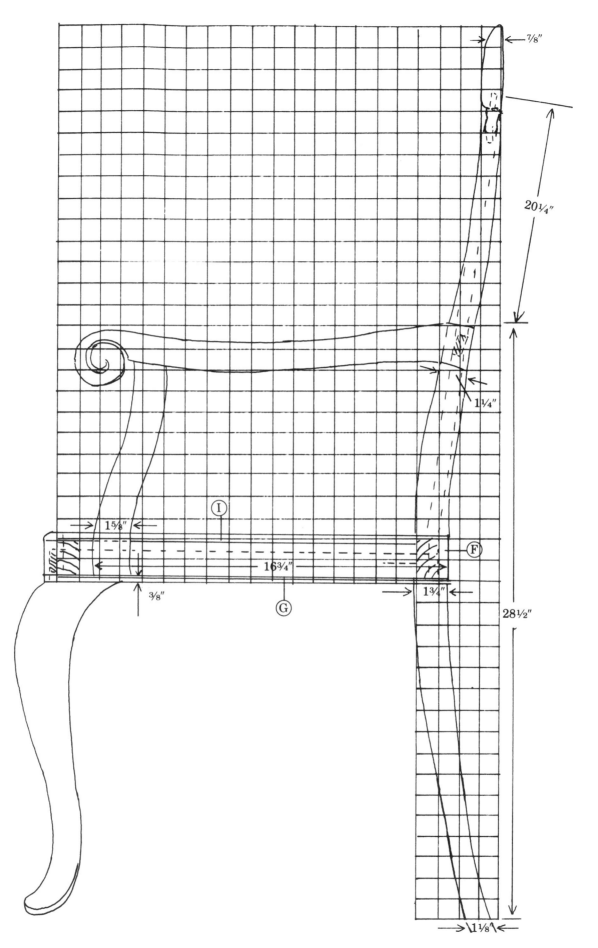

7/8"

20¼"

1¼"

1⅝"

Ⓘ

16¾"

Ⓕ

3/8"

Ⓖ

1¾"

28½"

1⅛"

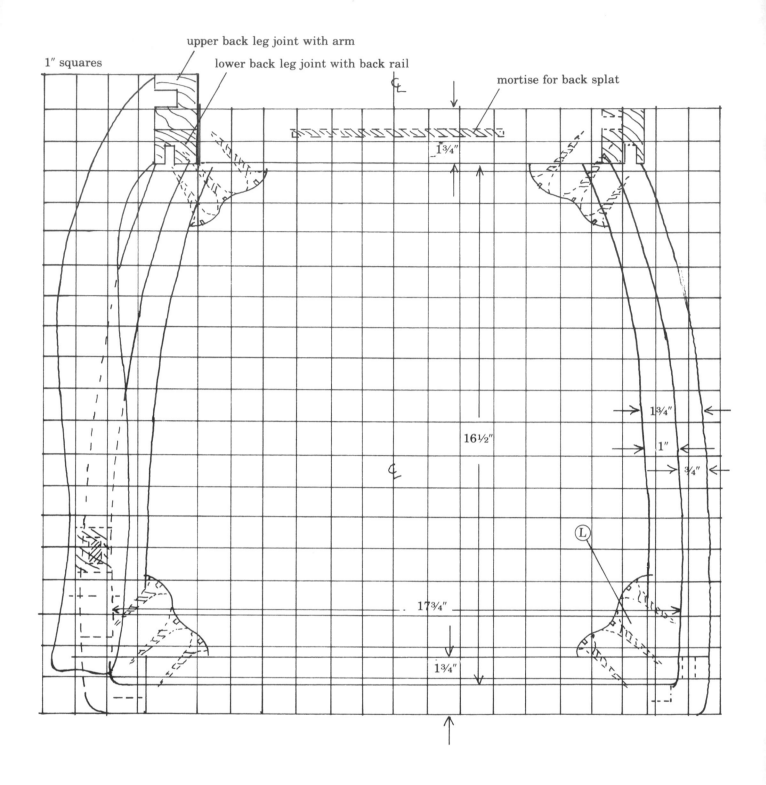

1" squares

upper back leg joint with arm

lower back leg joint with back rail

mortise for back splat

1¾"

16½"

1¾"

1"

¾"

Ⓛ

17¾"

1¾"

chair arm and arm support. Sand all pieces as smooth as possible.

Assembly

Chair assembly starts with the back legs (B). Place glue on the ends of the back apron tenons (F) and fit into mortises in the back legs. Then place glue on the bottom of the back splat (D) tenon and put it into the mortise in the back apron. Put glue in mortises of the top back piece (C), slide the piece carefully down over the tenons on the back chair legs and back splat. Make sure the entire assembly is square and all joints are tight. Then clamp securely in place and allow the glue to set.

While this is setting, you can fasten the front apron between the two cabriole front legs (A), again applying glue to the joints and then clamping in place. Countersunk screws driven from the underside of the leg wings and into the front apron will further strengthen the joint. Make sure all joints are as smooth as possible. They should be square and free of any openings.

The next step is to fasten the front and back assemblies together with the side aprons (G) between them. Glue the ends of side apron tenons and insert them in the mortises in the front- and back-leg assemblies. Make sure the chair is standing on a smooth, flat surface and that it doesn't rock or wobble. Then clamp securely and allow the glue to set. Drive countersunk wood screws up from the underside of the front-leg wings into the underside of the side aprons. Before the glue sets, add the seatboard supports (L) to the front and back with glue and three screws as shown in the drawing. Note that the top of the seatboard (M) should be flush with the top of the recess cut in the side and front aprons.

Arm Assemblies

Glue tenons of the arm supports (K) and insert into mortises on the underside of the arms (J). Place glue on tenons at the back of the arms, as well as on the lower edge of the arm support pieces. Put the arm assemblies in place. Clamp the back mortise-and-tenon joint in place. Temporarily clamp the lower front joint as well. Then drive countersunk wood screws from the inside of the side aprons (G) into the lower parts of the arm support to hold them securely in place. Now clamp all the arm pieces solidly until the glue sets.

Apron Trim

This chair has an unusual ¼-inch-thick rounded apron trim (H,I) glued to its top edge. It adds a decorative flair to the aprons.

Seat Board

Cut the seatboard (M) from one solid piece, or glue up smaller pieces to fit in the recess shown in the drawing. Then stain and finish the chair to suit. Cover the seatboard with the appropriate padding and upholstery material.

Materials List

A—Front legs—6 × 6 × 18″, 2 req'd.
B—Back legs—1½ × 4 × 37½″, 2 req'd.
C—Top back piece—1 × 6 × 15″, 1 req'd.
D—Back splat—½ × 8 × 21½″, 1 req'd.

Aprons

E—Front—1¾ × 2 × 17¼″, cut to length, 1 req'd.
F—Back—1¾ × 2¼ × 16½″, cut to length, 1 req'd.
G—Side—1¾ × 2 × 33¼″, cut to length, 2 req'd.
H—Front trim—¼ × ¾ × 19¼″, cut to length, 1 req'd.
I—Side trim—¼ × ¾ × 35″, cut to length, 2 req'd.
J—Arms—6¼ × 7 × 19¼″, 2 req'd.
K—Arm supports—2 × 3½ × 10⅜″, 2 req'd.
L—Seat supports—¾ × 2¼ × 2½″, 4 req'd.
M—Seat board—¾ × 16½ × 17¾″, 1 req'd.

Ladder-Back Chair

Circa 1880

A typical example of turn-of-the-century "country" furniture, this ladder-back chair was made in America and features a white oak split bottom. This type of chair has been quite popular in rural homes since Colonial times, and there are hundreds of varieties, sizes, and shapes.

The chair shown is made of oak, although ladder-chairs were also made of ash and hickory. Since the back legs and the ladder splats must be bent, these chairs were usually made of green or partially seasoned lumber.

Construction
Despite appearances, this project is actually one of the harder ones. Chairs tend to be more difficult to build, and this particular one requires a lot of bending. In addition, because of the compound angles and curves, it's harder to do an accurate job of cutting and fitting the pieces.

The wood used for the back legs and splats should be only green or partially cured. Use a wood that is easily bent, such as white oak, hickory, or ash.

Legs
The first step is to turn the back (A) and front (B) legs to the proper size and shape. You will need a lathe that will accept long pieces (at least 38 inches for the back legs). You could shorten them down to 36 inches to suit a smaller lathe.

Dowel Turnings & Rungs
Make the dowel turnings for the seat supports (C,D,E) and the rungs (F,G,H,I). Turn a shoulder on each of the dowel ends to fit holes bored in the front and back legs. Locate the position of the dowel holes in the front legs and bore them to the proper size and depth. Then locate the dowel holes in the back legs and bore them as well.

Ladder Splats
Finally, cut the mortises in the back legs for the back ladder pieces (splats). Use a mortising drill set in a drill press, or hand drill and then clean out the inside of the mortise with a chisel. Cut the splats (J,K,L) to size. Make tenons on each end to fit into the back-leg mortises.

Bending the Wood
The splats and the back legs are bent to shape, as shown in the drawing on page 24. Wood bending is discussed on pages 22–23.

Assembly
After the back pieces have been bent to the correct shape, assemble the chair. First, carefully sand all parts, including the top and bottom edges of the back splats (J-L). Then, starting with the back leg (A), place glue on the ends of the back rung (G), seat support dowel (E) and the splats. Put the parts in position, clamp the back assembly securely, and allow the glue to set.

Pay close attention to the clamping of the upper splats to the back legs. Splats have a tendency to twist out of the mortises unless properly clamped.

Remove the back assembly from the clamps. Assemble the front-leg (B) assembly in the same manner. Then continue with the side rungs (H,I) and side seat support dowels (D), until the entire chair is assembled.

Stand the chair on a smooth, flat surface and make sure that all four legs rest evenly on it. Then use band clamps on the bottom of the chair to hold the entire assembly securely in place until the glue sets. Wipe away any excess glue from the joints.

Sand, stain and finish.

Chair Bottoms
The split bottoms are made using splits of white oak. These can be cut in your shop using white oak saplings, or you can purchase the material. Splits are soaked in warm water until pliable and then woven around the tops of the seat rails in the pattern shown in the drawing. Fasten the weave in place with small tacks or staples in the bottom of the chair. Then finish the seat with a good grade of varnish or a polyurethane finish.

Materials List
A—Back legs—1¾ × 1¾ × 38", 2 req'd.
B—Front legs—1¾ × 1¾ × 17", 2 req'd.
C—Front seat support dowel—1 × 1 × 15", 1
   req'd.
D—Side seat support dowels—1 × 1 × 11½", 2
   req'd.
E—Back seat support dowel—1 × 1 × 11½", 1
   req'd.

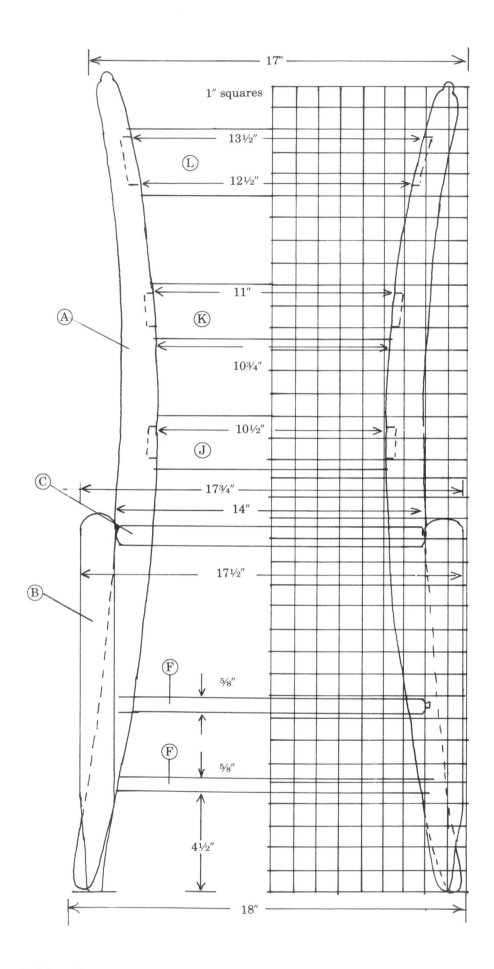

F—Front rungs—5/8 × 5/8 × 14¾″, 2 req'd.
G—Back rung—5/8 × 5/8 × 13½″, 1 req'd.
H—Bottom side rungs—5/8 × 5/8 × 13″, 2 req'd.
I—Top side rungs—5/8 × 5/8 × 12″, 2 req'd.
J—Bottom splat—½ × 2⅜ × 11″, 1 req'd.
K—Middle splat—½ × 2⅜ × 11½″, 1 req'd.
L—Top splat—½ × 3¼ × 14″, 1 req'd.
White oak splits

Bottom Herringbone Pattern

over 2
over 1
under 2
under 1
over 2
over 1
under 2

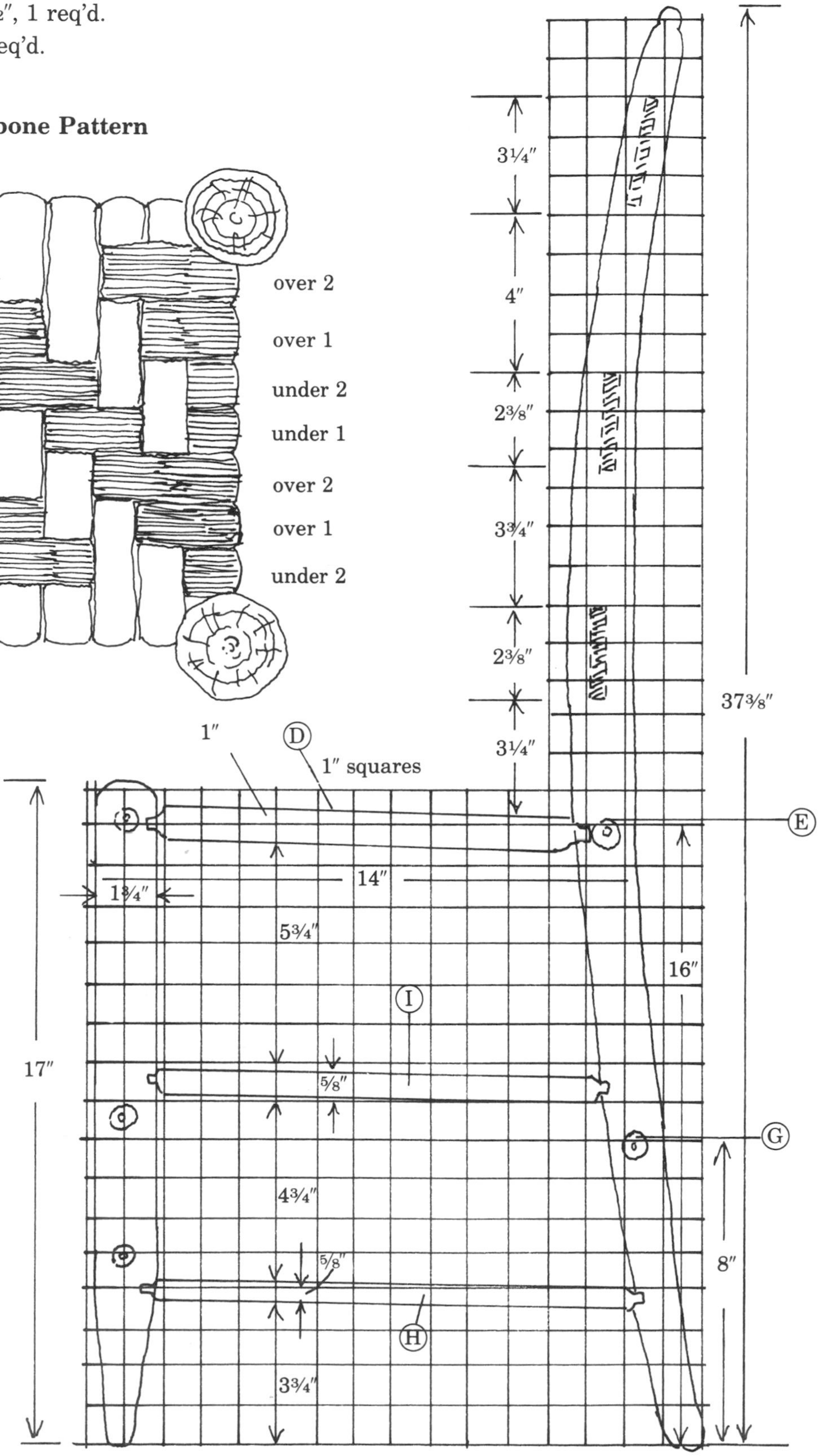
3¼″
4″
2⅜″
3¾″
2⅜″
3¼″
37⅜″
1″
D
1″ squares
E
14″
1¾″
5¾″
16″
I
17″
5/8″
G
4¾″
8″
5/8″
H
3¾″

Four-Drawer Bureau
1848

A family heirloom takes on special meaning when it has been hand-crafted by a family member. This unusual bureau was built in 1848 by Billy Fewell for my father's great-grandmother and is a prime example. It is made of walnut and is typical of "country" styling and construction.

The bureau was built to last, and last it has. The only flaw is a separation of a glued-up panel on one side. Much of the sturdiness of the piece can be traced to the massive side assembly and bottom support frame. The distinctive turnings are crisp and sharp with much fine detail and were, of course, turned on a foot-powered lathe.

Construction
The entire piece is made of solid wood, including the large back piece, and this is typical of construction in that period. Today, it would be much more economical (and feasible) to substitute plywood, using a hardwood-faced plywood for the side panels and drawer fronts.

Probably the most unusual feature is the method of insetting the drawer support frames into slots and notches cut in posts.

Back Posts
Start construction by cutting the back posts (A) to length; then cut rabbets in the back inside edge of each for the back (S). Use a table saw or radial arm saw.

Cut the cross dado in the back post for the web-frame drawer supports (see web frame detail). Use a dado head in a radial arm or table saw. Then rout a dado into the front inside face for the rail and panel side assemblies (see front post detail). Drill a hole in the bottom of the post for the dowel.

Front Post
Saw the front posts (B) to length and then make the long cutout in the front face; the turned section (Q) will be fitted in here. Incidentally, this massive post can be glued up to create the notch. Now make the dado for the side rail and panel assembly. Cut it into the back of the post. Cut the stopped mortises in the inside back corner of the post to accept the web frames. These can be cut using a mortising bit in a drill press or by boring holes and cleaning them out with a chisel. Accuracy is extremely important here, for the strength of the case, to ensure it will be square when assembled, and to make the flush drawers fit properly. Finally, bore holes in the post bottoms for the dowels.

Side Assemblies
Cut the side panels (E) to size. Again, these can be made with solid stock glued and dowelled together (¼-inch dowels), with plywood covered with veneer, or with hardwood-faced plywood. The latter could be ¼-inch plywood; this would make the project more economical. Saw the bottom and top side rails (C,D) to size and cut dadoes in their ends. Cut a groove in the edges that mate with the center panels to create tongue-and-groove joints. (See front-post detail.)

Assemble the side units by placing the upper and lower side pieces and center panel together. Then glue the rail tongues and slide the whole assembly into the front (B) and back (A) post grooves. Make sure everything is perfectly square and clamped solidly both crosswise and lengthwise. Also make sure the assembly doesn't buckle under clamping pressure; wipe away any glue runs and allow the glue to set overnight.

Turning Legs and Front Posts
Enlarge the squared drawings and turn the feet (P) and front-post turnings (Q). Because of the intricate shape of the turnings, a good solid hardwood, preferably heartwood, should be utilized. Bore holes in the cut-off ends of the turnings for the joining dowels.

Bottom Support Frame
The next step is to build the bottom support frame. Cut the bottom front and bottom side pieces (F,G) to size and plane or joint all these smooth. Cut the stopped half-laps to join the front piece to the two sides (see front-post detail). This can be done using a drill press or drill bit with a stop gauge, cutting to the depth desired on the side piece (F), and cleaning out with a chisel. The front piece joint is a simple half-lap. Cut notches on the inside back corners of the side pieces for the back (S).

Assemble and glue this section together, making sure it is absolutely square. After the glue has set, mark locations for the dowel holes for the feet (P) and front posts (B) to join the side assemblies in place. Bore these holes using a spur-type bit of the proper size.

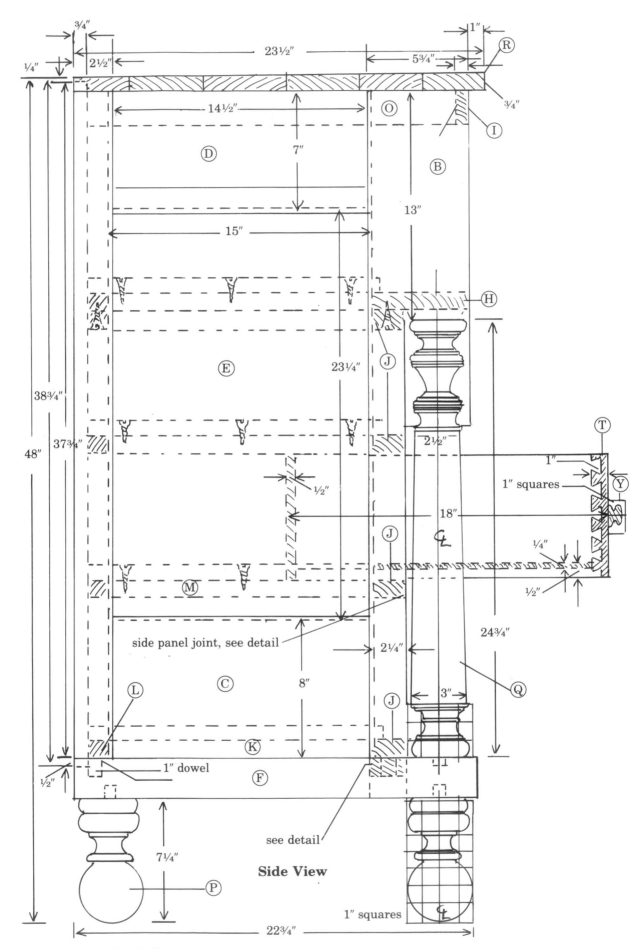

3/4"

1"

23½"

5¾"

2½"

1/4"

R

O

3/4"

14½"

I

D

7"

B

13"

15"

H

E

23¼"

J

38¾"

T

1" squares

Y

37¾"

½"

48"

18"

2½"

J

1/4"

CL

½"

24¾"

side panel joint, see detail

M

2¼"

8"

Q

C

3"

L

J

K

1" dowel

F

see detail

½"

7¼"

Side View

P

1" squares

22¾"

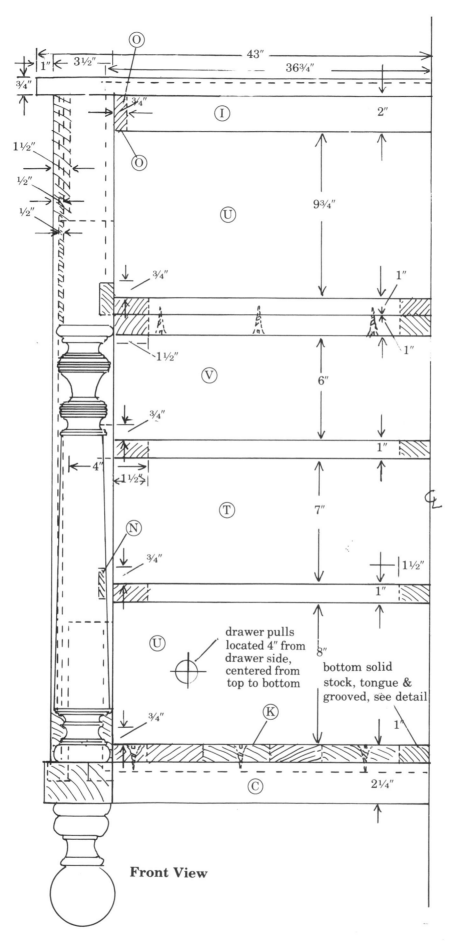

O

43″

3½″ 36¾″

1″
¾″

¾″
Ⓘ 2″

1½″
½″
½″

O

Ⓤ 9¾″

¾″ 1″

1½″ 1″

Ⓥ 6″

¾″

4″ 1″

1½″

Ⓣ 7″

Ⓝ

¾″ 1½″

1″

drawer pulls
located 4″ from
drawer side,
centered from
top to bottom

Ⓤ 8″

bottom solid
stock, tongue &
grooved, see detail

¾″ 1″

Ⓚ

Ⓒ 2¼″

Front View

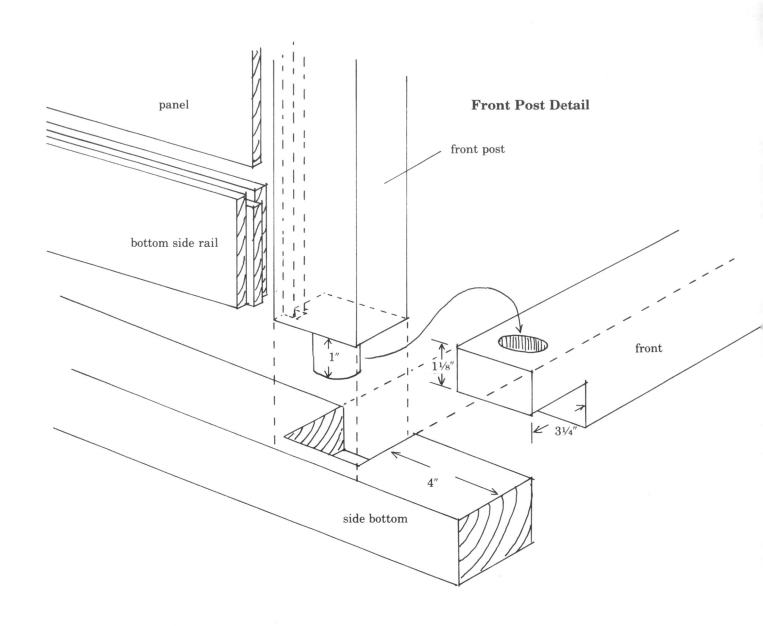

panel

Front Post Detail

front post

bottom side rail

1"

1⅛"

3¼"

front

4"

side bottom

Front Facers
Cut the top facer (I) to proper size and glue the top drawer tilt stripes (O) to the back edges of the facer using a slotted dovetail or tongue-and-groove joint. Make sure this is square and allow the glue to set.

Assembly
Now assemble the basic unit. Make sure the bottom and top edges of the side assemblies are smooth and flush. A belt sander does a fine job of this. Insert the dowels in the front post and in the bottom edges of the side assembly, place glue in the dowel holes of the bottom assembly, and put the sections together. (Note that the turned post sections must be put into place at this time.) Position the top facer (I) flush with the top edge and fasten its side pieces to the inside of the post with flat head wood screws. Use a stretcher piece, cut to the exact width of the front opening, between the corners of the back on both the

top and bottom. Install the top drawer support (H) and the bottom. Clamp the entire unit, wipe away glue runs, and allow the glue to dry.

Bottom Feet
Remove the assemblage from the clamps and install bottom feet, again with glue and dowels. The weight of the unit will firmly seat the feet in place, but make sure it is on a perfectly flat, smooth surface.

Drawer Supports
Next construct the web drawer supports. Each one of these will have to be individually measured and constructed to ensure that it fits exactly into its particular position. The time taken in this type of operation is what provides the quality of craftsmanship so lacking in many of today's furniture pieces.

The web frame consists of a front (J) and back (L) piece running between the posts as well as three web stretchers (M) between them (see web frame detail).

Tongues on the crosspieces fit into grooves on the front and back pieces. These are glued up and clamped individually. Make sure they are perfectly square and flat. Then a side support cleat (N) is fastened to their sides with glue and screws. It is sized exactly to fit the slots and notches cut in the end posts. As you can see, all units must be perfectly square and sized correctly before they will slide into place. Fasten them in place with screws driven from the side support pieces into the posts.

Note that the bottom is a solid tongue-and-groove assembly with the front piece tongue-and-groove to run at 90 degrees, as shown in the bottom detail. The upper drawer has a double web frame as shown.

Back and Top
Glue up the back (S) or cut it from plywood and fasten it in place with glue and wood screws. Glue up the top (R) from narrow strips of solid wood, alternating heartwood and sapwood to prevent warping. Fasten it in place with screws driven up from the underside of the top facer (I) and tilt strips (O) into the top. Make sure these do not break through the top. Counterbore screws in the front facing. Screws can also be driven through the back into the edge of the top as well.

Drawers
Because the drawers (T-W) are flush construction, all precautions must be taken to ensure they are correctly sized and square. Otherwise, even a carcass that is square will wind up looking shoddy.

First, cut the drawer fronts to size. Then cut the drawer backs and sides to size. Cut the bottom dado on the inside bottom edge of all pieces. The fronts of the drawers were dovetailed on the original and the backs fastened with nails. You could dovetail both backs and fronts into the sides.

The bottom on the original was also ½-inch solid stock. A better choice today would be ¼-inch hardboard.

After cutting all drawer pieces to size, assemble with glue and clamp solidly, making sure they are absolutely square.

Turn or purchase the wooden drawer pulls (X). The chest shown has a key lock for each drawer. These are available from fine hardware stores.

Sand the entire unit as smooth as possible, and finish. The finish on the chest shown was a hand-rubbed varnish finish.

Bottom Detail

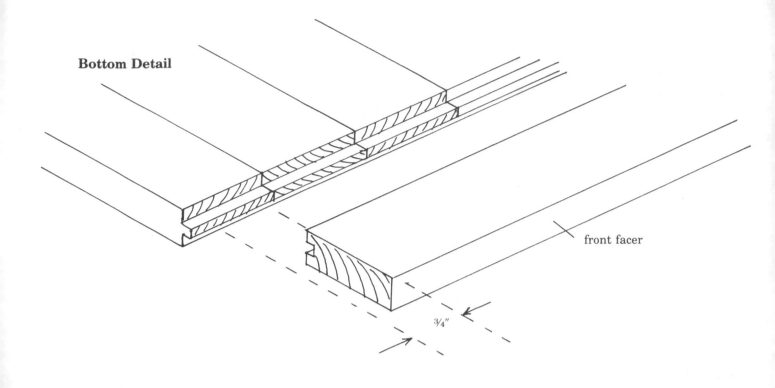

front facer

$\frac{3}{4}''$

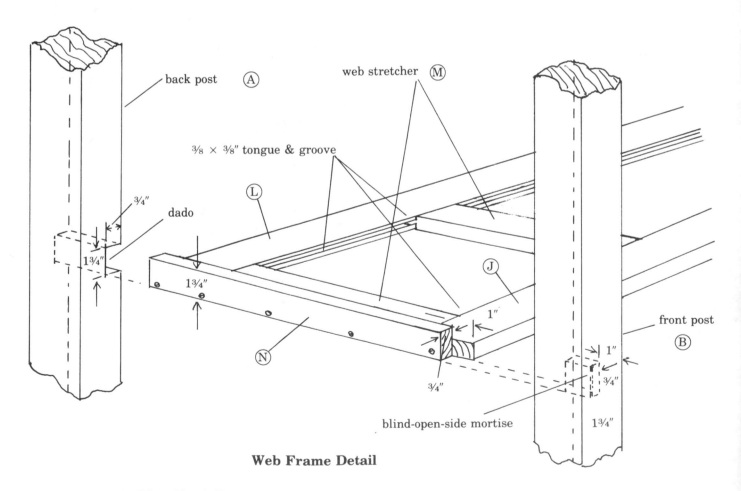

back post   Ⓐ

web stretcher   Ⓜ

$\frac{3}{8} \times \frac{3}{8}''$ tongue & groove

Ⓛ

$\frac{3}{4}''$

dado

$1\frac{3}{4}''$

$1\frac{3}{4}''$

Ⓙ

Ⓝ

$1''$

front post

Ⓑ

$\frac{3}{4}''$

$1''$

blind-open-side mortise

$\frac{3}{4}''$

$1\frac{3}{4}''$

Web Frame Detail

Materials List

A—Back post—2½ × 3½ × 37¾", 2 req'd.

B—Front post—3½ × 5¾ × 37¾", 2 req'd.

C—Bottom rails—1 × 8 × 15", 2 req'd.

D—Top rails—1 × 7 × 15", 2 req'd.

E—Side panels—⅜ × 15 × 23¼", 2 req'd.

F—Bottom side pieces—2¼ × 3¾ × 22¾", 2 req'd.

G—Bottom front piece—2¼ × 4¼ × 38½", 1 req'd.

H—Top drawer support—¾ × 5¾ × 36", 1 req'd.

I—Top facer—¾ × 2 × 36", 1 req'd.

J—Front drawer supports—¾ × 2¼ × 36", 4 req'd.

K—Bottom—¾ × 15¾ × 39", 1 req'd.

L—Back drawer supports—¾ × 1 × 36", 3 req'd.

M—Web stretchers—¾ × 1¾ × 14¾", 8 req'd.

N—Side support cleats—¾ × 1½ × 17½", 6 req'd.

O—Top drawer tilt strips—¾ × 2 × 21", 2 req'd.

P—Feet—4 × 4 × 8", 4 req'd.

Q—Front post turnings—4 × 4 × 26", 2 req'd.

R—Top—¾ × 23½ × 43", 1 req'd.

S—Back—¾ × 38¾ × 36¾", 1 req'd.

T—Drawer

    Front—¾ × 6⅞ × 35⅞", 1 req'd.

    Sides—½ × 6⅞ × 17¾", 2 req'd.

    Back—½ × 6⅞ × 34⅞", 1 req'd.

    Bottom—¼ × 17¼ × 34⅞", 1 req'd.

U—Drawer

    Front—¾ × 7⅞ × 35⅞", 1 req'd.

    Sides—½ × 7⅞ × 17¾", 2 req'd.

    Back—½ × 7⅞ × 34⅞", 1 req'd.

    Bottom—¼ × 17¼ × 34⅞", 1 req'd.

V—Drawer

    Front—¾ × 5⅞ × 35⅞", 1 req'd.

    Sides—½ × 5⅞ × 17¾", 2 req'd.

    Back—½ × 5⅞ × 34⅞", 1 req'd.

    Bottom—¼ × 17¼ × 34⅞", 1 req'd.

W—Drawer

    Front—¾ × 9½ × 35⅞", 1 req'd.

    Sides—½ × 9½ × 17¾", 2 req'd.

    Back—½ × 9½ × 34⅞", 1 req'd.

    Bottom—¼ × 17¼ × 34⅞", 1 req'd.

X—Knobs—¾ × 1½", 8 req'd.

Queen Anne Wing Chair

Circa 1875

Wing chairs are one of the most popular types of chairs. They have been built by furniture makers in a host of countries over the centuries and there are many different styles, shapes and sizes. Though some are awkward in appearance and others are uncomfortable to sit in, the chair shown here is a good one. It is fairly standard in size, and the plain lines of the Queen Anne leg help make it a simple yet elegant-looking chair.

This chair was built in England in the late 19th century and is made of mahogany. It has recently been restored and reupholstered. In fact, that is one of the prime reasons for the popularity of wing chairs with antique collectors. Because little of the wood is exposed, chairs are usually long lasting and can be restored quite easily with new fabric. This eliminates the problem of having to match up new wood pieces with the originals, as often happens when repairing other furniture types.

Since much of the construction of the chair is covered by the upholstery, a standard wing chair construction is shown in the drawings. The chair legs shown are made of mahogany and the interior parts are of soft wood. You could use almost any hardwood for the legs, including walnut, cherry, maple, rosewood or pecan. White pine or the similar softwoods are used for the upholstered portions.

Unless you're fairly experienced at upholstery you should probably leave that to a professional, because upholstering a wing chair can be quite a chore.

Construction

Because most of the chair frame will be covered with upholstery, you don't have to worry much about the wood finish. But shoddy craftsmanship will result in an unstable and short-lived chair. It will also be amplified by the upholstery, rather than concealed by it.

Legs

Construction of the chair starts with the front cabriole legs (A). Enlarge the squared drawing and make up the pattern. Then cut the legs to size and shape on a band saw. Enlarge the squared drawing for the back legs (B), transfer to the thick stock, and cut them to shape on a band saw. Sand the edges smooth.

Aprons and Stretchers

Cut the front (C), side (E) and back (D) aprons to size, as well as the lower back (M), vertical back (N) and side stretchers (P). Enlarge the squared drawing for the upper back shaped stretcher (L) and cut it to size and shape as well.

Side Turnings

The next step is to create the side turnings for the arms (G) and lower arm posts (F). These are done by turning softwood blanks to the size shown. Cut a half-lap notch in the inner side of each end of the arm turning blocks so they will fit over the back-leg posts and into the front arm support. Cut a half-lap notch on the bottom of each lower arm post block so it will fit over the side rails.

Arm Support

Cut the arm support pieces (H) and round their inside top edges to the circumference of the arm piece. Then cut the arm stretchers (Q) from 2-inch-thick stock to the shape shown, matching them to the arm support side posts. You will have to do some scribing and try-fitting to get a good smooth fit of the pieces. Make sure there is as much mating surface as possible for a good strong joint.

Wing Pieces

Enlarge the squared drawing and cut the wing pieces (I,J) to the correct size and shape, including the angled back edges of the front wings.

Assembly

Assembly starts with the bottom framework. This is assembled with glue and dowels. Refer to pages 14–17 for dowelling information. Dowel and glue the side aprons (E) and front (A) and back (B) legs together first. Clamp with bar clamps until the glue sets. Then dowel and glue in place the back vertical stretchers (N) between the upper (L) and lower back horizontal stretchers (M). Finally, dowel and glue this assembly and back apron (D) as well as front apron (C) between the two side assemblies. Make sure the chair is sitting on a smooth, flat surface and that it sits level. Then install the seat blocks (O) with glue and screws.

Install the side posts (F) in place with glue and screws. Fasten the arm support posts (H) in place and the arm stretchers (Q). Then fasten the arms (G) in place with glue and screws through the overlaps into the arm support post and back legs. Cut the wing pieces (I,J) to size and shape following the squared drawing and dowel together. Then fasten them to the arms and upper ends of the back legs with dowels and glue. Metal brackets or braces can also be used to help strengthen joints such as the wings to arms, etc.

Sand, stain and finish the exposed wood pieces.

Materials List

A—Front legs—5 × 5 × 14½", 2 req'd.

B—Back legs—1⅝ × 7½ × 46", 2 req'd.

Aprons

C—Front—1¾ × 4 × 27", 1 req'd.

D—Back—1⅝ × 4 × 22", 1 req'd.

E—Side—1⅝ × 4 × 21⅝", 2 req'd.

F—Lower arm posts—2½ × 2½ × 7¾", turned, 2 req'd.

G—Arms—3½ × 3½ × 20", turned, 2 req'd.

H—Arm support posts—2 × 2¼ × 12", 2 req'd.

I—Upper wing block—¾ × 2½ × 4", cut to length, 2 req'd.

J—Side wings—¾ × 6 × 20", cut to length, 2 req'd.

L—Upper back stretcher—¾ × 5½ × 23", 1 req'd.

M—Lower back stretcher—¾ × 2 × 23", 1 req'd.

N—Vertical back stretchers—¾ × 2 × 23½", 2 req'd.

O—Seat blocks—¾ × 2 × 2", 4 req'd.

P—Side stretchers—1½ × 2½ × 12", cut to fit, 2 req'd.

Q—Arm stretchers—2 × 2¼ × 6", cut to fit, 2 req'd.

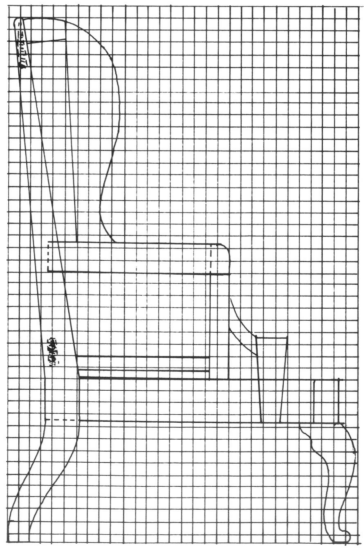

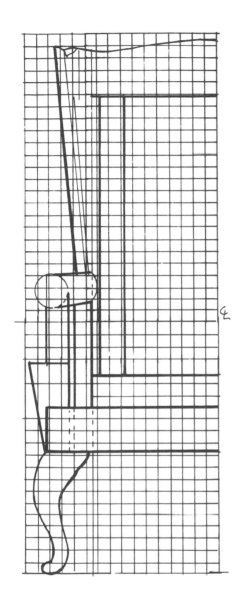

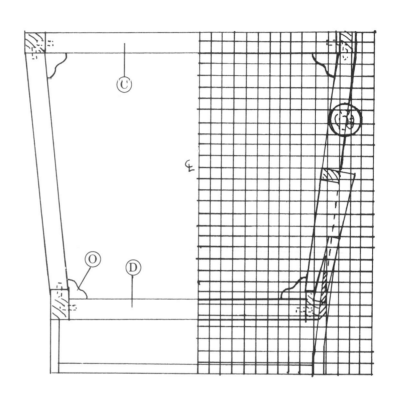

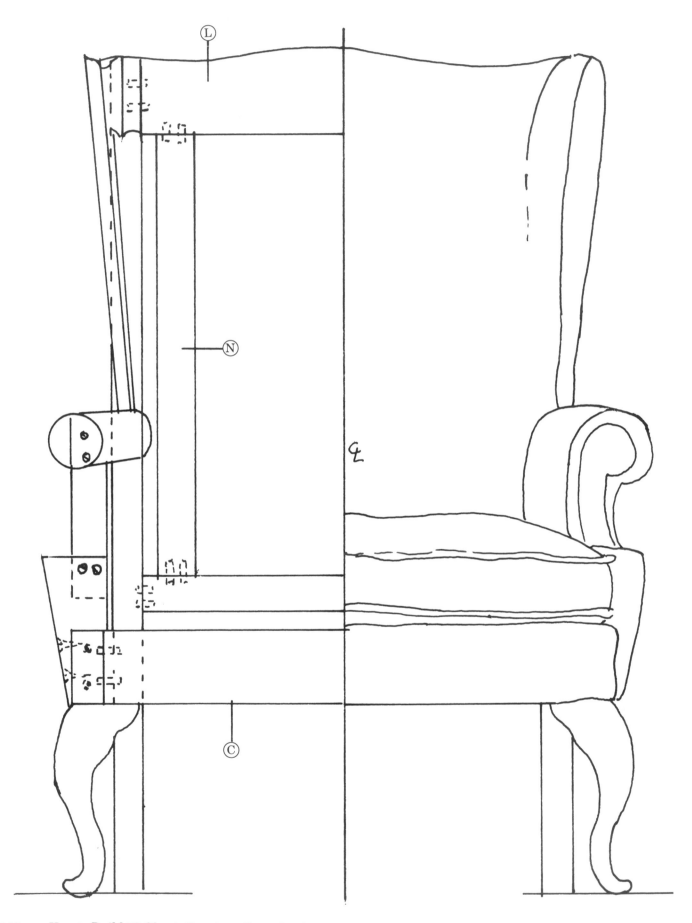

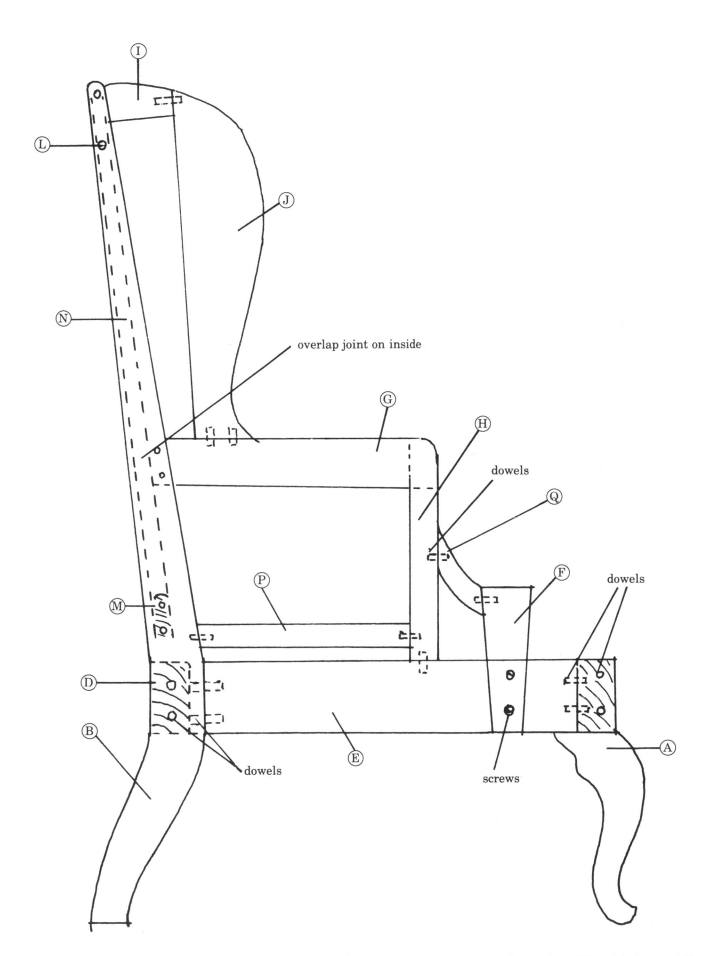

overlap joint on inside

dowels

dowels

dowels

screws

Secretary and Bookcase

Circa 1850

This beautifully constructed secretary was made in England from English oak cut in a quarter-sawn pattern to show off the beautiful grain. It features graceful Queen Anne-style legs and leaded glass in the upper bookcase section.

As with many pieces of this style, it is constructed in two sections and the upper and lower parts are joined with screws. Incidentally, you can make only the bottom drop-lid desk if you prefer, leaving off the upper bookcase section. Ageless in design, this secretary would look good in almost any hardwood, particularly cherry, mahogany, walnut or maple, as well as white or red oak.

Construction

Construction of the secretary is fairly simple. Parts of the case are joined with straightforward, standard period joinery. Half-lap joints are used at top and bottom, while slotted dovetails are used for the desk top and inside shelf-support frames. Stopped dovetail slots are used on the latter.

Legs

Start by creating the Queen Anne cabriole legs (E). First, enlarge the squared drawing to make up the pattern. Leg wings are glued to a smaller block to make up the size needed for the leg. Then transfer the pattern to the stock and cut it on a band saw to the shape required. (See page 24 for information on cabriole legs.) Turn the Queen Anne foot on the leg bottom with the stock in a lathe. This must be roughed in at a slow speed.

Sand smooth on a drum sander and bore the countersunk screw holes in each leg wing. Bore dowel holes in the top center of each leg for the center holding dowel.

Case Construction

To construct the case, cut the top piece (B) to size, joint its edge, and cut the rabbets on each end underside to create the overlapping joint. Cut the rabbet on the back edge to accept the back (I). Then cut the bevelled front edge to the correct bevel, as shown in the drawing. Make the upper bottom (C) to size and shape, cutting the rabbet on the upper back edge (for the back) with a hand plane or moulding head or router. Make the lower bottom (D) and shape the edges using a shaper or router or scratch stock tool.

These bottoms can be glued up from smaller pieces of solid stock. An alternative is to use plywood with a hardwood moulding frame glued in place around the outside exposed edges of the plywood. Use dowels or tongue-and-groove joints to hold the moulding in place and mitre it at the corners.

Make up the sides (A) to size and shape, seeing that their top slanted edges match the angle of the top piece. Cut the dovetail slots on their inside faces, using a pair of straightedges to guide a router in a straight line at the correct location. Be especially careful here to ensure an accurate job. You could also cut these slots the old-fashioned way using hand-held planes as shown on page 10.

The top dovetail is open because the inside desk top (H) also acts as a top facer between desk and drawers. The drawer support frames are held in the sides with slotted dovetails. These slots, however, are "stopped," ending just before you reach the front edge of the side, so that they will not be seen.

The next step is to cut the inside desk top (H) to size and shape. Again, this large piece may have to be made up of smaller stock dowelled and glued together. After it has been made up to size, cut dovetails on its side edges to fit into the dovetail slots in the sides (A).

Then make up the drawer support frames (F,G) as shown in the detail drawing, assembling them with mortise-and-tenon joints. Cut the pieces and try-fit them together. Then, before gluing them up, cut the dovetails on the outside edges of the stock. These dovetails can be cut with a radial arm or table saw. Make the vertical cuts first, then tilt the blade to make the angled cuts and complete the joint. Cut the back (I) to size and shape from ⅜-inch hardwood-faced plywood.

Lower Case Assembly

The first step is to place glue on dovetails on the inside desk top (H) and the drawer support frames (F,G). Then push them into the side slots from the back, until they are all seated properly in the sides (A). The inside desk top should be flush with the front edges of the sides. The front of the drawer frames should be flush with the back of the rabbet at the back inside edge. Place glue in the rabbet onto piece (B) and put it in place. Fasten it with glue and countersunk flathead wood screws. Place this assembly on its back on a smooth, flat surface and stand

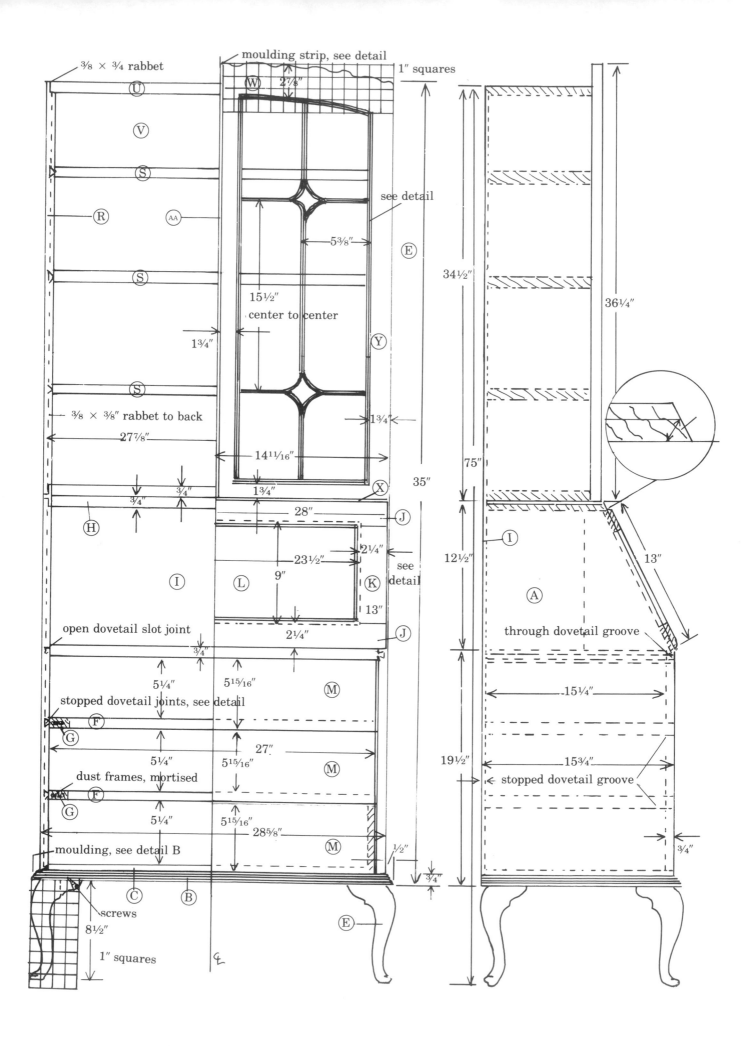

⅜ × ¾ rabbet

moulding strip, see detail

1" squares

2⅞"

Ⓤ

Ⓦ

Ⓥ

Ⓢ

Ⓡ

ⒶⒶ

see detail

Ⓔ

5⅜"

15½"
center to center

1¾"

Ⓢ

Ⓨ

⅜ × ⅜" rabbet to back

27⅞"

Ⓢ

1¾"

14¹¹⁄₁₆"

1¾"

Ⓧ

35"

34½"

36¼"

75"

¾"

¾"

28"

Ⓙ

Ⓗ

23½"

2¼"

see
detail

Ⓘ

9"

Ⓛ

Ⓚ

Ⓘ

12½"

13"

Ⓐ

open dovetail slot joint

Ⓙ

2¼"

13"

through dovetail groove

¾"

5¼"

5¹⁵⁄₁₆"

Ⓜ

15¼"

stopped dovetail joints, see detail

Ⓕ

Ⓖ

27"

Ⓜ

5¼"

5¹⁵⁄₁₆"

19½"

15¾"

dust frames, mortised

stopped dovetail groove

Ⓕ

Ⓖ

5¼"

5¹⁵⁄₁₆"

Ⓜ

28⅝"

¾"

moulding, see detail B

½"

¾"

Ⓒ

Ⓑ

screws

Ⓔ

8½"

1" squares

⌀

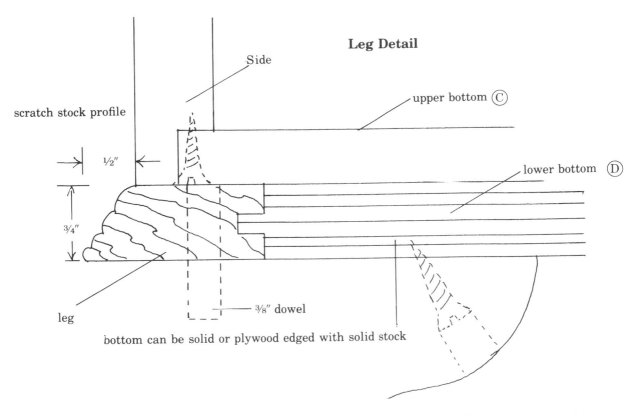

Leg Detail

Side

upper bottom Ⓒ

scratch stock profile

lower bottom Ⓓ

½"

¾"

leg

⅜" dowel

bottom can be solid or plywood edged with solid stock

Dovetail Joint

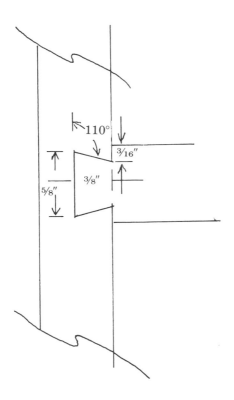

110°

3/16"

3/8"

5/8"

the upper bottom (C) against it, making sure the back edges of both the bottom and case sides are flush. Then fasten it in place to the sides with flathead wood screws, driven up into the sides. Do the same with the other bottom piece (D), fastening it to the upper bottom with screws.

While the case is still on its back, bore holes into the underside of the bottom for the leg dowels. Fasten the legs (E) in place with glue on the dowel and with countersunk wood screws through the wings.

Now carefully turn the piece upright, making sure that you don't put stress on the back legs as you turn it.

Inside Desk Construction

Construct the desk partition unit (BB) from ¼-inch solid stock using dado joints for the dividers (see detail drawing). Then construct the drawer of ¼-inch solid stock using the same materials and small dovetails for the joints. The bottom of the drawer is glued in place. Sand all pieces smooth before assembly and finish the unit before installing it in the desk. It simply slides in place from the back and can be installed just before you put on the back.

Desk Lid Construction

The desk lid (J-L) is frame-and-panel construction. The frames are assembled using standard, shaper-cut "cabinet joints." These are made by using special male and female cutters for a shaper (available from the Freud Company). The stiles (K) are cut to create the female shape, while the rails (J) are cut with the mating male shape.

Drawer Support Frame Detail

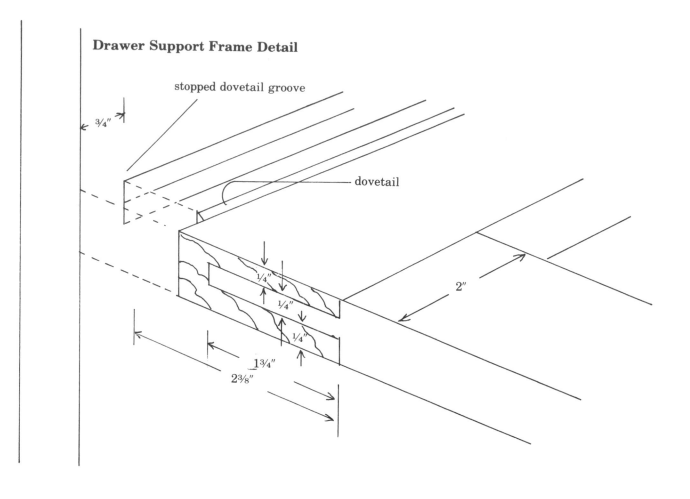

stopped dovetail groove

¾″

dovetail

¼″

¼″

¼″

2″

1¾″

2⅜″

Inside Desk Partition Unit

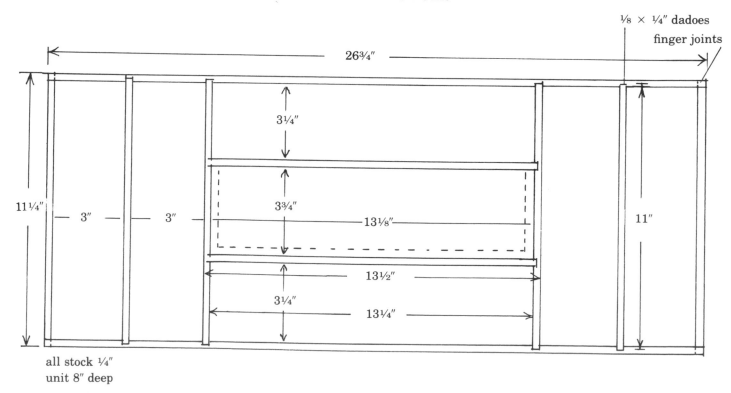

⅛ × ¼″ dadoes

finger joints

26¾″

3¼″

3¾″

13⅛″

11″

11¼″

3″

3″

13½″

3¼″

13¼″

all stock ¼″
unit 8″ deep

Desk Lid Detail

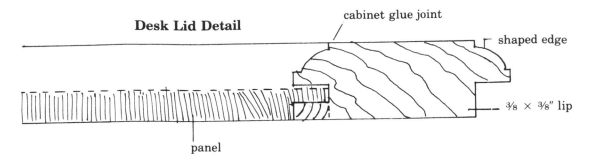

cabinet glue joint

shaped edge

⅜ × ⅜″ lip

panel

Lower Drawers

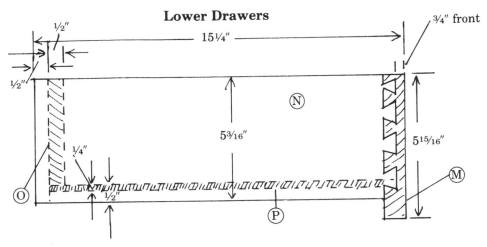

½″

15¼″

¾″ front

½″

Ⓝ

5³⁄₁₆″

5¹⁵⁄₁₆″

¼″

Ⓜ

Ⓞ

½″

Ⓟ

Ⓠ moulding carving for desk lid

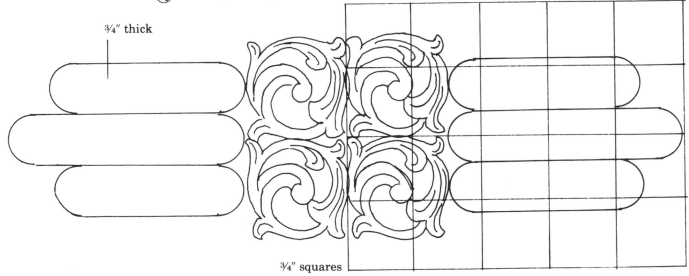

¾″ thick

¾″ squares

Bookcase Door Frame Detail

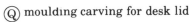

leaded glass panel

wood retaining strips

Bookcase Door Overlap

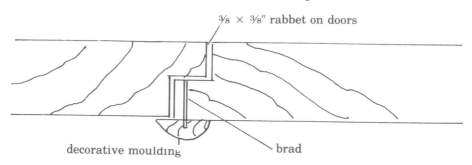

⅜ × ⅜″ rabbet on doors

decorative moulding   brad

After being cut to shape, the frame is glued and clamped together until the glue sets. Then shape or rout the bottom edge of the frame so that it will overlap the case slightly. This is done by using a shaper or with a radial arm or table saw to create the lip. Then the outside top edge of the frame is shaped on a shaper (with stock turned upside down) or with a router and router table. Cut the panel to size from solid stock (or plywood) and fasten it to the inside of the frame with glue.

Drawers

Make the drawers by dovetailing the sides (N) into the front (M) and using a dado joint for the back (O). The bottom (P) is held in dadoes in the front and sides, and extends past the back. It is held to the bottom of the back with small, countersunk flat-head wood screws. Note that the drawer front extends below the drawer sides ¾ of an inch to cover the drawer support frames (F,G).

After constructing the drawers, sand, stain, and finish all parts of the base, then slide the inside desk unit in place from the back. It is not anchored in place. Install the desk lid using drop-lid hinges mortised into the lid and the inside desk top piece (H). Install the lock by mortising it into the top of the lid. Then, finally, install the drop-lid supports on either side of the lid, making sure the drop lid is held properly in relation to the inside desk top when open. The panel of the drop lid is covered with leather, glued in place. You may want to use felt instead.

Enlarge the squared drawing and carve the applied plaque (Q) for the center of the desk lid. Glue it in the center of the desk lid.

The last step in bottom case construction is to fasten the back in place with flat-head wood screws, slightly countersunk through the back. Then install the hardware on the drawers and slide them in place.

Bookcase Construction

The bookcase is constructed in much the same way as the bottom case. First, cut the side pieces (R), then cut dovetail slots into the inside face of each for the shelves. Cut the dado joints on each end of the sides. Then cut the top (U), bottom (T), and shelves (S) (with end dovetails) to size.

Assemble the case by pushing the dovetails into their slots after putting glue on the dovetails. Then put the top and bottom in place in the end dadoes. Fasten with glue and countersunk brass wood screws. Install the back (V). Note that the sides and top have a ⅜ × ⅜-inch rabbet for the ⅜-inch-thick plywood back. The bottom, however, is cut ⅜ of an inch narrower than the rest of the cabinet, so the back can run full length. Anchor the back in place with wood screws countersunk through the back.

Constructing the Doors
The doors are constructed in the same manner as the bottom desk lid, using a "cabinet joint." Enlarge the squared drawing and make a pattern for the arched door rails (Z). Cut these to size and shape using a band saw or sabre saw. The top ends of stiles (W,Y) must be shaped as well. Then using the shaper, cut the cabinet joints on the rails and stiles. Glue and clamp together and allow to set. The front doors must also be cut to overlap at their joints. Then make the small, rounded decorative bead for the front of the right-hand door (AA). Fasten it in place with glue and small screws from the back of the door rabbet. Rout out the inside edge of the frame for the leaded-glass panel.

Sand, stain and finish all pieces to the top. Then hang the doors using mortised butt hinges. Install the hardware. Make the leaded-glass panels, or have them made, and then install them, using small wooden retainer strips, as shown.

Materials List
Case Bottom
A—Sides—¾ × 15¾ × 31", 2 req'd.
B—Top—¾ × 10½ × 28⅝", 1 req'd.
C—Upper bottom—¾ × 14⅝ × 27⅞", 1 req'd.
D—Bottom—¾ × 16¼ × 29⅝", 1 req'd.
E—Legs—4 × 4 × 8½", 4 req'd.
F—Drawer support frame, front and back—¾ × 2 × 27⅛", 4 req'd.
G—Drawer support frame, sides—¾ × 2⅜ × 14⅝", 4 req'd.
H—Inside desk top—¾ × 15¾ × 27⅞", 1 req'd.

I—Back—⅜" plywood × 27⅞ × 30½", 1 req'd.
J—Desk lid rails—¾ × 2¼ × 28", 2 req'd.
K—Desk lid stiles—¾ × 2¼ × 9", 2 req'd.
L—Desk lid panel—¼ × 9 × 23½", 1 req'd.
Drawers
M—Fronts—¾ × 5¹⁵⁄₁₆ × 27", 3 req'd.
N—Sides—½ × 5³⁄₁₆ × 15", 6 req'd.
O—Backs—½ × 4⁷⁄₁₆ × 26", 3 req'd.
P—Bottoms—¼ × 14½ × 26", 3 req'd.
Q—Plaque—¾ × 2½ × 7½", 1 req'd.
Top Bookcase
R—Sides—¾ × 9 × 34½", 2 req'd.
S—Shelves—¾ × 8⅝ × 27⅞", 3 req'd.
T—Bottom—¾ × 8⅝ × 27⅞", 1 req'd.
U—Top—¾ × 9 × 27⅞", 1 req'd.
V—Back—⅜" plywood × 27⅞ × 34⅛", 1 req'd.
W—Door stiles—¾ × 1¾ × 36¼", 2 req'd.
X—Door rails—¾ × 1¾ × 11¾", 2 req'd.
Y—Door stiles—¾ × 1¾ × 35", 2 req'd.
Z—Arched door rails—¾ × 1¾ × 11¾", 2 req'd.
AA—Moulding strip—⅜ × ½ × 36¼", 1 req'd.
BB—Inside desk partition unit
   Top & bottom—¼ × 8 × 26¾", 2 req'd.
   Ends—¼ × 8 × 11¼", 2 req'd.
   Upright dividers—¼ × 8 × 11", 4 req'd.
   Horizontal dividers—¼ × 8 × 13½", 2 req'd.
Drawer front—¼ × 3⅝ × 13⅛", 1 req'd.
Drawer sides—¼ × 3⅜ × 7¾", 2 req'd.
Drawer back—¼ × 3⅜ × 13⅛", 1 req'd.
Drawer bottom—¼ × 7¾ × 13⅛", 1 req'd.
Hardware
Drop-leaf hinges—1 pair req'd.
Drop-leaf supports—1 pair req'd.
Drawer pulls—6 req'd.
Keyed lid lock—1 req'd.
Keyed door lock—1 req'd.
Brass butt hinges—1½", 2 pair req'd.
Glass or leaded glass—11¾ × 32½", cut to fit, 2 req'd.

Pot Cupboard

Circa 1858

This unusual hutch design is called a pot cupboard. Since it doesn't have any plate grooves or rails for displaying dishes and glassware on the upper shelves, it probably was used only for storing pots and pans. The original shown here was made in England from "punkin pine," a large species of pine tree that was indigenous to England up until the middle of the 19th century.

Punkin pine was once a popular furniture wood in both England and New England. The wood has a beautiful mellow tone, and one of the reasons for its popularity was that it was available in wide boards for "easy" furniture construction.

This project could be constructed of sugar, white or even yellow pine to achieve the same look. But any knots in the yellow pine should be extremely solid and sound.

Construction

The original hutch was made by simply nailing wide pieces of pine stock together using square-cut forged nails. In fact, many of the nail heads are still evident. The same technique can be used today, using No. 8 finish nails with the heads set. Fill the holes with wood putty or wood dough. Or use countersunk wood screws and cover their tops with wooden plugs or wood putty.

Base

As with most projects of this type, work starts with the cabinet base unit. You will have to dowel and glue up narrower boards to make up the wide stock required for some parts. Or you can use sugar-pine-faced plywood, if you prefer.

The first step is to cut the bottom (A) to size and shape. This can be a single piece of plywood, or you can use two pieces of 1 × 12 cut to the correct width and dowelled and glued together. Or you can simply fasten them in place to the bottom support (B) with glue and finishing nails and corrugated fasteners on their edges. In any case, the bottom must be fastened securely to the bottom support blocks with glue and nails. Then dowel and glue up the sides (C) or cut them from plywood.

Position the bottom assembly on a smooth, flat surface. Put the side pieces (C) in place and nail them to the bottom support pieces, making sure the assembly is square.

Cut the back (E) and front (D) support pieces to size and fasten them in place with nails and glue to the top edges of the sides. Fasten the top side support pieces (F) in place in the same manner. Then cut the side cleats (G) and fasten to the sides of the unit. Note that the shelves (H) are also the support for the drawers; so the top edges must be flush with the top edges of the facers between the drawers.

Make the shelves (H) to size from plywood or glue up from solid stock. Make sure the entire case is square by checking with a carpenter's square; then fasten the shelves securely in place with nails and glue. Fasten drawer stop (AA) in place.

Cut the front facer pieces (I-N) slightly oversize, joint their edges down to the correct size, and install them. Start with the vertical facers (I) on the front sides, then the two vertical facers in the center part of the front, and finally the top horizontal facers (K,M) between the uprights. Cut the drawer divider (N) facers and install them between the two uprights. Fasten the front drawer facers securely to the shelves and to the vertical facers with nails and glue. Again, make sure the top edges of these facers are flush with the shelves. Then install the bottom (J) and bottom center (L) facer between the vertical facers and to the bottom.

Top

Create the wide top (O) by dowelling and gluing up the solid stock, cutting to shape and size, then routing or shaping the edge around the front and sides. Position on top of the base and fasten in place with wood screws driven through the front, back, and side support strips (D,E,F). Make sure the screws don't protrude up through the top.

Drawers

The drawers (W,X,Y) are flush fronts and are simply constructed with dovetail joints on both front and back. The bottom is ½-inch set up ½ inch from the bottom in a groove in the sides, back, and front edges. The bottom is also fitted with a ½-inch-thick wooden drawer guide to fit down over a ½ × ¾-inch single drawer slide (Z) fastened to the center top of each of the shelves (H).

The first step is to construct the drawers and create the guides. Cut the guide and temporarily place it in position on the shelf. Insert the drawer and position the slide accurately from the back of the cabinet, making sure the drawer front is square with

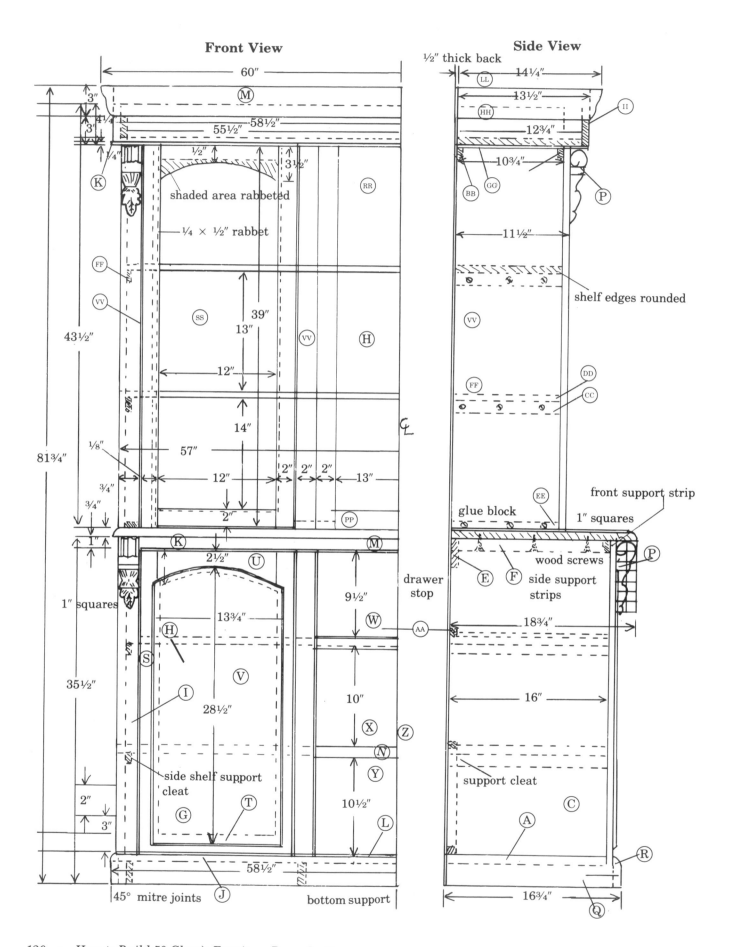

Front View

60"

M

3"

3"

4¼"

3"

¼"

K

58½"

55½"

½"

3½"

shaded area rabbeted

RR

¼ × ½" rabbet

FF

VV

SS

39"

13"

VV

H

12"

43½"

14"

⅛"

57"

81¾"

12"

2" 2" 2"

13"

¾"

2"

PP

¾"

1"

K

M

2½"

U

W

1" squares

H

S

13¾"

9½"

drawer
stop

W

AA

35½"

V

I

10"

28½"

X

Z

side shelf support
cleat

N

Y

2"

G

T

10½"

L

3"

58½"

45° mitre joints

J

bottom support

Side View

½" thick back

14¼"

LL

13½"

HH

II

12¾"

10¾"

GG

BB

11½"

shelf edges rounded

VV

FF

DD

CC

C̶L̶

EE

front support strip

glue block

1" squares

E

F

wood screws

side support
strips

P

18¾"

16"

support cleat

C

A

R

16¾"

Q

Drawer Detail

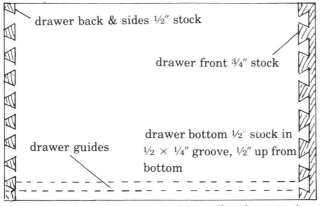

drawer back & sides ½" stock

drawer front ¾" stock

drawer guides

drawer bottom ½" stock in ½ × ¼" groove, ½" up from bottom

note: drawer fronts are ⅛" smaller than opening

Back Detail

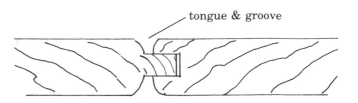

tongue & groove

the front of the cabinet and slides easily. Then anchor the slide in place, nailing from the back.

Bottom Moulding

Cut the bottom moulding (Q,R) to the correct size and create the rounded edge on a shaper, with a shaper head in a radial arm or table saw, etc. Then measure for the side pieces. Cut to length with a 45-degree mitre on their ends and fasten in place with glue and screws. Note that the top edge should be just flush with the top edge of the bottom (A). Then measure between the two side pieces to cut a snug-fitting front moulding piece. Nail and glue in place.

Bottom Doors

The bottom doors are of frame-and-panel construction with the panels (V) unusually set out rather than recessed. The frames are made using mortise-and-tenon joints. The top rail (U) pieces are cut first, using a band saw or a sabre saw, then the stiles (S) and bottom rails (T). Then the frame pieces (S,T,U) must be assembled. Make sure they fit into the cabinet opening properly and that they have been assembled squarely. Clamp securely and allow the glue to dry.

Cut the front panel pieces (V) from solid stock and use a shaper or router to rout the ¼ × ¼-inch rabbet on the back edge of the panel. Then use a shaper or router to lightly round the front edges. Fasten the panel in place over the door frame with glue and small screws driven from the back of the frame into the panel. Make sure the screws don't break through the thin edge of the panel.

Hang the doors using mortised 1½-inch brass butt hinges and install cabinet catches on the bottom inside of the cabinet to hold the doors shut.

Install hardware on the doors and drawers.

Cabinet Top Unit

The cabinet top is put together in a manner similar to the base. The side pieces (FF) are first cut to size and shape. Install the shelf support cleats (CC) and

the bottom support cleat (EE). The bottom support cleat is used to anchor the top unit to the base and is fastened in place with glue and screws.

Cut the shelves (DD) from ¾-inch stock, round their front edges, and run a plate groove along the back. Use a table or radial arm saw for this. Then glue and nail the shelves in place. Fasten the top back cleat (BB) in place.

Cut the top (GG) and nail it in place to the side pieces. Note that it protrudes out past the side pieces in the front to hold the extended front moulding.

Cut the top trim moulding pieces (HH-MM) to size and nail and glue them in place to the upper edges of the top side pieces and across the front top. Then cut the small ¼ × ¼-inch trim strips and fasten in place on the bottom with glue and small brads. Note that the corners of the strips are mitred. Cut the top moulding using a shaper and mitre the corners. Fasten it in place with glue and screws driven from the back of the case into the moulding.

With the basic top framework assembled, mount it in place on top of the base unit and fasten securely in place with screws down through the holding cleats (EE) into the top of the base unit. Make sure the top unit sits squarely and that the measurement between the two side pieces is exactly the same, top and bottom.

Then cut the side and center facer strips (UU) and fasten them in place. The center facer strips are held in place at the bottom with glue blocks. Make sure the bottom ends of center facers are the correct distance from the back of the cabinet.

Upper Door Construction

The upper doors (NN-TT), including the two swinging doors and the center fixed door, are constructed in basically the same way as the bottom doors. The frames are held together with mortise-and-tenon joints and glue. Then the inside edge is rabbeted with a ½ × ½-inch groove to accept the glass and small glass retaining strips. To avoid cutting the top edge of the glass in the rounded shape, you can rout out a flat square area on the back edge of the door frame as shown.

Anchor the center door in place with glue blocks and wood screws. Then hang the two side doors with mortised butt hinges and install the pulls and door catches at the bottom.

Carvings

The carvings (P) are fairly simple and add a great deal of flavor to the piece. They are constructed from 2-inch-thick stock. The first step is to enlarge the squared drawings for both sides and front and transfer them onto the carving blocks. Then use a band saw to rough out the carving block. Finally, finish-carve as per the pattern.

Back

The back (VV) on this piece is quite unusual in that it is ½ inch thick and made up of tongue-and-grooved planks nailed to the back edges of the assembly. Exposed edges were rounded as shown in the back detail drawing, and planks were not glued or secured together other than by the tongue-and-groove joints. You could, of course, substitute plywood.

Materials List

Cabinet Bottom

A—Bottom—¾ × 16 × 55½", 1 req'd.
B—Bottom supports—¾ × 2¼ × 16¾", 3 req'd.
C—Sides—¾ × 16 × 35½", 2 req'd.
D—Front support strip—¾ × 1 × 55½", 1 req'd.
E—Back support strip—¾ × 2½ × 55½", 1 req'd.
F—Side support strip—¾ × 1 × 14½", 2 req'd.
G—Side cleats—¾ × 1 × 16", 4 req'd.
H—Shelves—¾ × 16 × 55½", 2 req'd.
I—Vertical facers—¾ × 2 × 33¼", 4 req'd.
J—Bottom facers—¾ × ¾ × 16", 2 req'd.
K—Top facers—¾ × 1 × 16", 2 req'd.
L—Bottom center facer—¾ × ¾ × 17", 1 req'd.
M—Top center facer—¾ × 1 × 17", 1 req'd.
N—Drawer facers—¾ × 1 × 17", 2 req'd.
O—Cabinet top—¾ × 19 × 58½", 1 req'd.
P—Carvings—2 × 2 × 7¼", 4 req'd.
Q—Bottom side trim—¾ × 3 × 17½", 2 req'd.
R—Bottom front trim—¾ × 3 × 58½", 1 req'd.

Doors

S—Stiles—¾ × 2 × 31½", cut to fit, 4 req'd.
T—Bottom rails—¾ × 2 × 13¾", cut to fit, 2 req'd.
U—Top rails—¾ × 4 × 13¾", cut to fit, 2 req'd.
V—Panels—¾ × 13¾ × 28½", 2 req'd.
W—Drawer
  Front—¾ × 9⅜ × 16⅞", 1 req'd.
  Back—½ × 9⅛ × 16⅞", 1 req'd.
  Sides—½ × 9⅜ × 15¾", 2 req'd.
  Bottom—½ × 15¼ × 16⅜", 1 req'd.
X—Drawer
  Front—¾ × 9⅞ × 16⅞", 1 req'd.
  Back—½ × 9⅛ × 16⅞", 1 req'd.
  Sides—½ × 9⅞ × 15¾", 2 req'd.
  Bottom—½ × 15¼ × 16⅜", 1 req'd.
Y—Drawer
  Front—¾ × 10⅜ × 16⅞", 1 req'd.
  Back—½ × 10⅛ × 16⅞", 1 req'd.
  Sides—½ × 10⅜ × 15¾", 2 req'd.
  Bottom—½ × 15¼ × 16⅜", 1 req'd.
Z—Drawer slides—¾ × ½ × 15¼", 3 req'd.
AA—Drawer stops—¾ × 2 × 2", 3 req'd.

Cabinet Top

BB—Top back cleat—¾ × 2 × 55½", 1 req'd.
CC—Shelf support cleats—¾ × 1 × 10¾", 4 req'd.
DD—Shelves—¾ × 10¾ × 55½", 2 req'd.
EE—Bottom support cleats—¾ × 1 × 10¾", 2 req'd.
FF—Sides—¾ × 10¾ × 43½", 2 req'd.
GG—Top—¾ × 12¾ × 55½", 1 req'd.
HH—Top mouldings—¾ × 4¼ × 13½", 2 req'd.
II—Top trim strip—¾ × 4¼ × 58½", 1 req'd.
JJ—Trim strips—¼ × ¼ × 14", 2 req'd.
KK—Trim strip—¼ × ¼ × 60", 1 req'd.
LL—Top trim—¾ × 3 × 14¼", 2 req'd.
MM—Top trim strip—¾ × 3 × 60", 1 req'd.
NN—Stiles—¾ × 2 × 38¾", 6 req'd.
OO—Bottom rails—¾ × 2 × 14", 2 req'd.
PP—Bottom rail—¾ × 2 × 15", 1 req'd.
QQ—Top rails—¾ × 3½ × 14", 2 req'd.
RR—Top rail—¾ × 3½ × 15", 1 req'd.
SS—Glass—12½ × 35½", 2 req'd.
TT—Glass—13½ × 35½", 1 req'd.
UU—Upright facers—¾ × 2 × 39", 4 req'd.
VV—Back—½ × 57 × 81¾", 1 req'd.

Muffin Stand

Circa 1920

These folding pastry racks were originally made in England. But they soon became a favorite in America and the one shown here was made in this country. Muffin stands were used to hold pies, cakes, and muffins while they cooled.

The racks have recently become popular again and are used as decorative stands. They are perfect for china painters. The recessed center is just the right size to hold a painted 6-inch china tile.

Walnut was used on the rack shown. But almost any type of wood can be used, including oak, mahogany, cherry, or pine.

Construction

Although the construction is fairly simple, you will need a lathe with a faceplate to make the plate-turnings and the side pediments. The first step is to enlarge the squared drawing and cut the top (D), bottom support brace (C) and the feet (B) using a band saw or sabre saw. Then enlarge the squared drawing for the side pediments (E) and turn them. Be sure to make the small dowels on their ends. These fit into dowel holes in the tops of the side posts (A).

Turn the plate shelves (F) using a faceplate on your lathe. Note that the outside is rounded on the back and a decorative moulding is cut on the front. The center is recessed about 3/16 of an inch to allow a 1/4-inch tile to protrude above the wood surface and act as a hot pad.

The final step is to cut the side posts and the back shelf support piece (G). Sand and smooth all pieces.

Assembly

Start by fastening the back shelf support to each of the shelves (F) with a small brass hinge. Fasten the side posts (A) to the feet (B) with dowels and glue. Install the top piece (D) with dowels and glue as well; then fasten the bottom support bracket (C) in place with glue and screws.

The final step is to install the hinge shelf assembly. Use round head brass screws that extend through the side posts into the shelves. Holes in the side posts must be drilled slightly larger than the screw shanks. Glue the side pediments (E) to the post tops.

Sand, stain and finish.

Materials List

A—Sides—3/4 × 3/4 × 39½", 2 req'd.

B—Feet—3/4 × 3 × 18", 2 req'd.

C—Bottom support brace—3/4 × 4 × 11½", 1 req'd.

D—Top—3/4 × 5 × 11½", 1 req'd.

E—Side pediments—3/4 × 3/4 × 2½", 2 req'd.

F—Shelves—3/4 × 11 × 11", 3 req'd.

G—Back shelf support piece—3/4 × 1 × 33", 1 req'd.

Brass round head screws—1½", 10 req'd.

Brass hinges, 3 req'd.

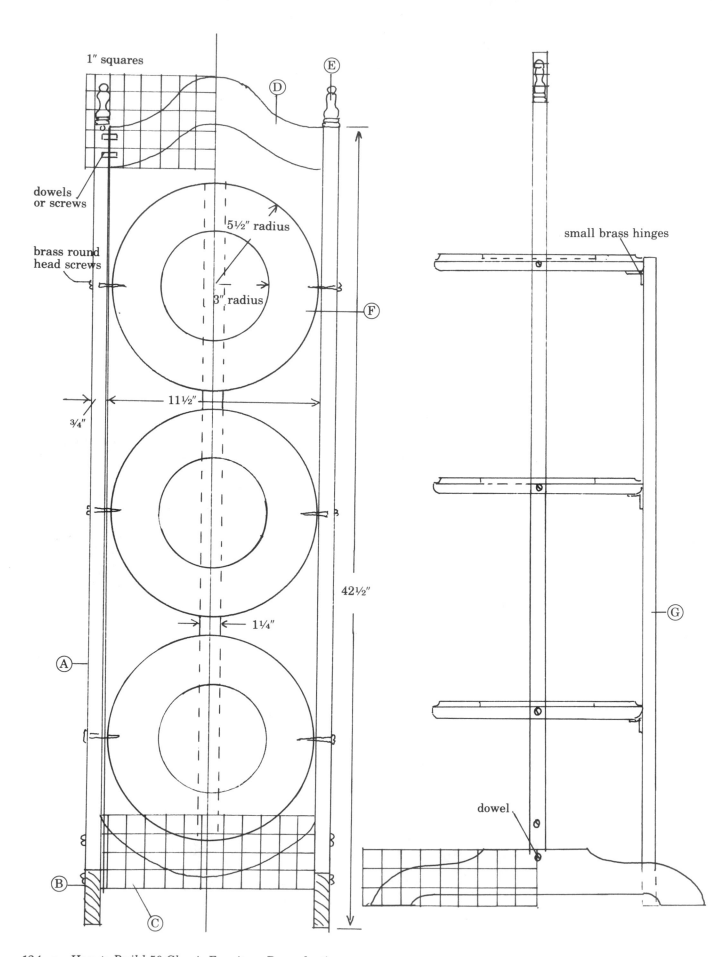

1" squares

dowels
or screws

brass round
head screws

5½" radius

3" radius

11½"

¾"

1¼"

42½"

A

B

C

D

E

F

G

small brass hinges

dowel

Quilt and Towel Rack

Circa 1850

Racks of this type were produced by 19th-century manufacturers and were usually made to go along with a specific bedroom suite. Consequently, there were many different styles, but they were generally used to hold towels alongside a commode or washstand. The rack shown was made in America from solid walnut. Most of the original racks were made from either walnut or mahogany.

Today these racks are popular decorative pieces that can be used for holding lightweight quilts and towels or as a drying rack in the kitchen. They can be made of walnut, ash, oak, mahogany, or even pine and make an excellent project, one that is both useful and easy to build. In fact, you might want to make up a "keeping pattern" for this project, because you'll be asked time and time again to make racks for friends and relatives.

Construction

The project is simple and doesn't take very long to complete. But it does require some straightforward lathe work, as well as some expertise in using a band saw to cut the long, shaped legs.

Legs

Construction starts with the legs (A). Enlarge the squared drawing and make up a pattern for the legs. Transfer it to the stock and cut to shape. Use a belt or drum sander to smooth the legs as much as possible. Then bore holes for the turned stretchers (B). Cut mortises for the top stretchers (C) as well as for the horizontal rack pieces (F).

Turned Stretchers

Enlarge the squared drawing and use a lathe to make stretchers (B) to size and shape, including round tenons on each end. Sand pieces smooth while they are still in the lathe.

Top Stretchers

Cut the top stretchers (C) to size and make tenons on their ends to fit into the mortise in the inside of the leg pieces. Cut the top center pieces (D) from ½-inch stock and finally use a band saw to cut the curved top pieces (E) patterned after the enlarged squared drawing.

Horizontal Rack Pieces

The last step is to cut the horizontal rack pieces (F). Use a shaper or router in a router table to round the

top edges of all rack pieces. Cut tenons on their ends to fit into the legs.

Assembly

Assembly starts with the ends. The first step is to place glue on tenons of the turned stretchers (B) and a top stretcher (C). Fit the tenons into mortise and dowel holes in the legs (A). Then clamp the parts of each end section together and allow the glue to dry thoroughly. Fasten the top center piece (D) to the underside of the top piece (E) with glue and screws. Now fasten this top assembly to the top stretcher on the end assembly, again with glue and screws.

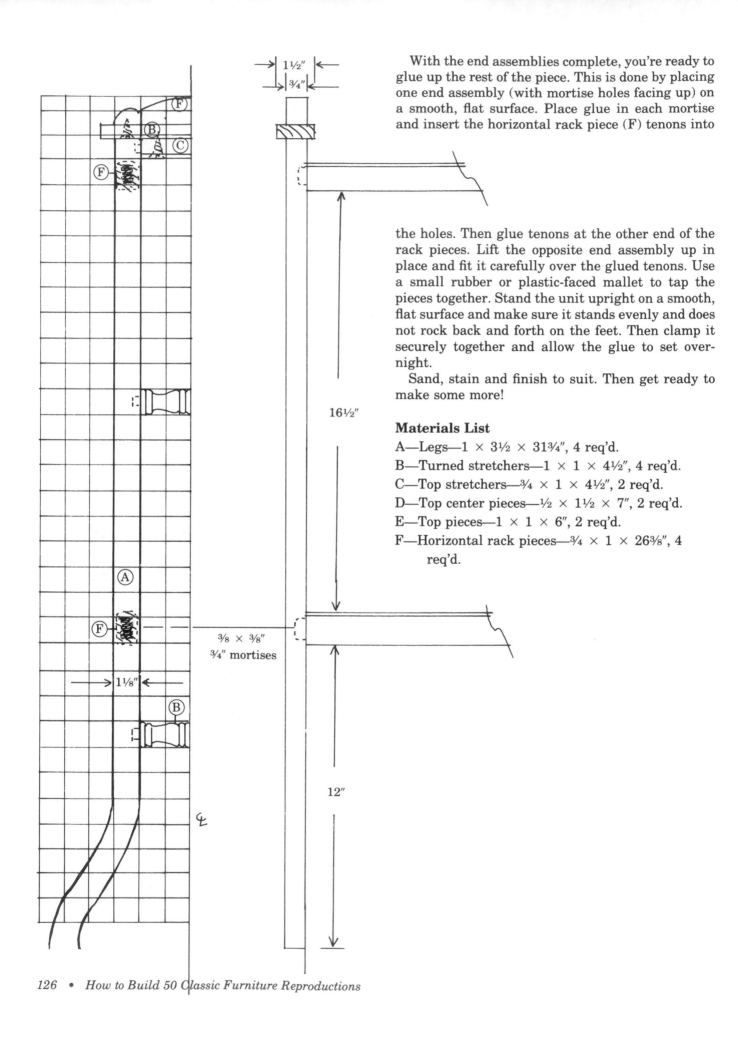

1½"

¾"

16½"

⅜ × ⅜"
¾" mortises

1⅛"

12"

₡

With the end assemblies complete, you're ready to glue up the rest of the piece. This is done by placing one end assembly (with mortise holes facing up) on a smooth, flat surface. Place glue in each mortise and insert the horizontal rack piece (F) tenons into the holes. Then glue tenons at the other end of the rack pieces. Lift the opposite end assembly up in place and fit it carefully over the glued tenons. Use a small rubber or plastic-faced mallet to tap the pieces together. Stand the unit upright on a smooth, flat surface and make sure it stands evenly and does not rock back and forth on the feet. Then clamp it securely together and allow the glue to set overnight.

Sand, stain and finish to suit. Then get ready to make some more!

Materials List

A—Legs—1 × 3½ × 31¾", 4 req'd.
B—Turned stretchers—1 × 1 × 4½", 4 req'd.
C—Top stretchers—¾ × 1 × 4½", 2 req'd.
D—Top center pieces—½ × 1½ × 7", 2 req'd.
E—Top pieces—1 × 1 × 6", 2 req'd.
F—Horizontal rack pieces—¾ × 1 × 26⅜", 4 req'd.

Clock Shelf

Circa 1920

Along with the popularity of manufactured furniture in the early 1900s came a vogue for matched sets of furniture. Included in these groupings were small pieces such as the oak clock shelf chosen for this project.

This clock shelf was manufactured in America and was designed to match the oak table, chairs and china cabinets that are also included in this book (projects 23, 24, 30, and 31, respectively). Though these shelves were usually made of oak, almost any hardwood will do.

Construction

Construction of this piece is very easy compared to other projects in this book, and it's a good project for anyone interested in getting started in furniture making.

The first step is to enlarge the squared drawing and cut the back (A) and two side pieces (B) to size and shape using a band saw. Do the same for the drawer (E) front. Then make the two stopped dadoes in the side support pieces.

Cut the drawer support piece (C) and make the tongues on its ends to fit into dadoes in the side pieces. Saw the top (D) to size and shape as well.

Assembly

Assemble the unit by placing glue on the ends of the tongues of the drawer support piece (C) and inserting the tongues into the side (B) dadoes. Fasten this section to the back (A) with glue and screws driven in from the back. Then fasten the top (D) in place with glue.

Drawer

Construct the drawer (E) by gluing the pieces together, including the ¼-inch-thick bottom. Then turn the drawer knob and fasten in place with a screw from the inside of the drawer front.

Sand, stain and finish to suit.

Materials List

A—Back—½ × 7 × 19¾″, 1 req'd.
B—Sides—½ × 5½ × 6¾″, 2 req'd.
C—Drawer support—½ × 4¾ × 14½″, 1 req'd.
D—Top—³⁄₁₆ × 6⅝ × 19¾″, 1 req'd.
E—Drawer
   Front—½ × 4 × 13⅞″, 1 req'd.
   Sides—½ × 2½ × 4¾″, 2 req'd.
   Back—½ × 2½ × 13⅞″, 1 req'd.
   Bottom—¼ × 4¾ × 13⅝″, 1 req'd.
F—Knob—¾ × 1 × 1″, 1 req'd.

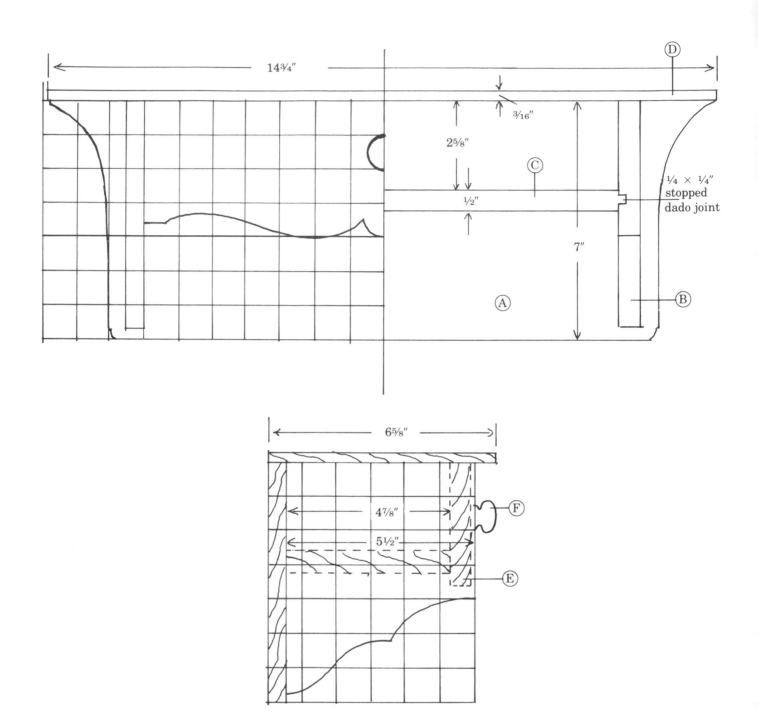

14¾"

³/₁₆"

2⅝"

C

½"

7"

A

D

¼ × ¼"
stopped
dado joint

B

6⅝"

4⅞"

5½"

F

E

Classic Nightstand
Circa 1900

Some types of furniture seem to be popular forever, and this little nightstand is a perfect example. Produced by the author, it was patterned after designs from a turn-of-the-century bedroom suite. But the finished piece can be used in the hallway or living room as well as in the bedroom.

The table has special value to our family, because it was constructed from home-cut and home-cured walnut. The stock was sawn from our own timber, using a chain saw and slabbing accessory and was stored in our barn loft for about 9 years.

You could use walnut or another hardwood, such as mahogany or cherry, oak, or pecan. Pecan would give the nightstand a more contemporary look.

Construction
Although the table is not particularly hard to build, it does require a fairly well-equipped shop and some expertise in turning, dowelling and shaper work.

Gluing Up Stock
The first step in construction is to dowel and glue together the stock needed. If you have 2-inch-thick (surface) stock, you can use it for the legs (J). If not, you will have to glue up these turning blocks from thinner stock. Make the blocks slightly oversize (for later surfacing). Select only good heartwood for the pieces. Sapwood is lighter in color, softer, and doesn't turn quite as sharply. Glue and clamp the pieces together securely, using several large C-clamps. Allow the glue to set overnight.

You will also have to dowel and glue together the wide top piece (A) from narrower strips to prevent it from warping. Or you could use veneered plywood for the top, if you prefer. When gluing up the top, alternate heartwood and sapwood sides on the pieces to help prevent warping. Allow the glue to set overnight.

Turning the Legs
After the glued-up turning blocks have been removed from the clamps, run the glued surfaces over a jointer, removing the glue runs, smoothing all four surfaces, and sizing them correctly.

Enlarge the squared drawings for the turned legs (J) and make a cardboard template. Then turn the legs to size and shape on a lathe. Once the first leg has been shaped, a lathe duplicator can save a great deal of time in turning the legs.

Cut away the turning waste on the lower ends of the legs, and finish-cut them so that they are of equal lengths. You can measure the legs and mark them accurately by placing a small square against the rip fence on your radial arm saw. Put the turned leg end against the square arm. Then mark all four legs on the opposite end to the correct length. Cut them to length on the radial arm saw.

Dowelling the Framework

The sides (D), back (B) and legs (J) are all held together with dowels. Cut the side and back pieces to size and joint their top and bottom edges. To start the assembly, place the two back legs in place on a smooth, flat surface. Then place the back between them. Mark dowel centerlines on the mating back and leg surfaces. Label one end of the back piece "A" and the corresponding leg surface "A." Then label the opposite end of the back piece "B," and that leg surface "B."

Now turn one leg two turns to the side and position the side piece (D) in place against it. Position a front leg on the opposite end of the side piece and mark dowel centerlines on this section. Label the mating dowelling surface "C" and then "D." Do the

opposite side in the same manner, continuing with "E" and "F."

Make sure during the marking process that you offset dowel holes on adjacent sides of the same leg. Otherwise, you will run into trouble while inserting the dowels.

Lower Moulding

The next step is to cut the lower moulding (E) that will be placed below the side pieces. A front moulding piece (C) is used to create the front drawer support. Make the moulding using a shaper cutter or a moulding head on a radial arm or table saw. Shape the edge on a wide piece of stock and then rip it to the correct width. Note that the front piece (C) is left wide as extra support for the drawer. Cut this front

Side View

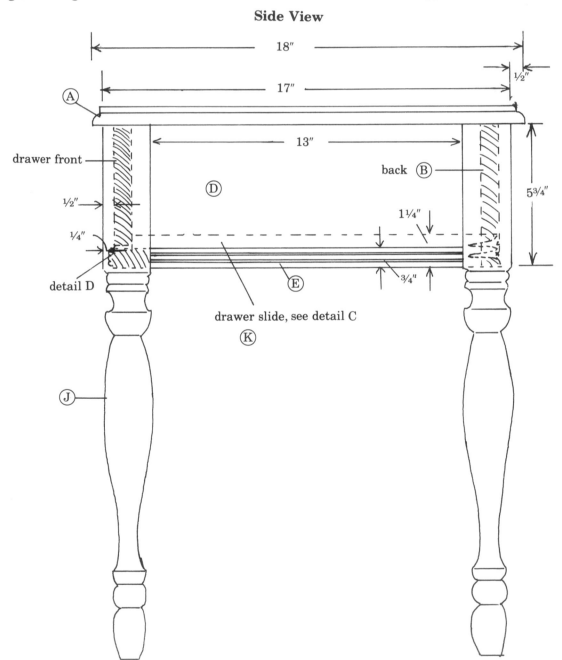

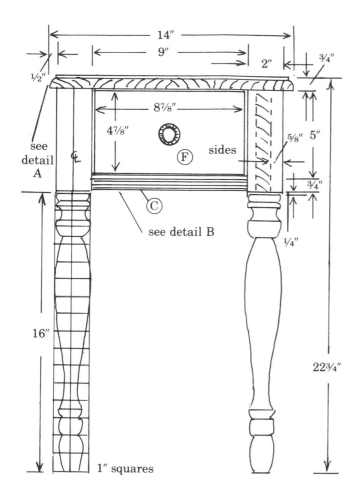

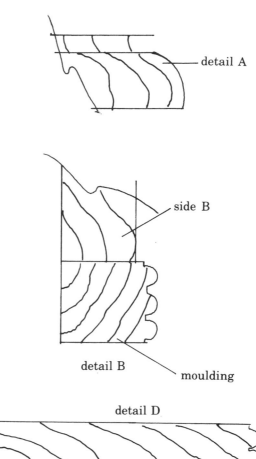

detail A

side B

detail B

moulding

detail D

1" squares

piece to size and then position it between the two front legs. Mark the dowel locations on it.

Using a dowelling jig, bore all the dowel holes needed. First set the jig to the centerline for the thinner apron stock and bore all those holes; then set the bit guide to the centerline of the wider leg stock and bore those holes as well.

With all holes bored, lay the pieces out on a flat surface and dry-fit each piece without glue to make sure they all fit together properly. Then run each piece lightly over a belt or disc sander to remove any burrs produced by the dowelling process.

Position all pieces on a smooth, flat surface and place some glue in the dowel holes. Run a thin bead on the ends of each joining piece as well. Then assemble the pieces starting with the sides (D) and legs (J). Once the side sections have been assembled, put the back (B) and the front moulding (C) between them.

When gluing in the front piece, use a temporary spacer block between the leg tops so they will not be skewed inward by the action of the clamps. Use a soft mallet or a wooden block and a hammer to tap the pieces solidly together.

Stand the leg and frame upright and make sure the legs all rest solidly on the surface. Rack the piece in any direction needed to make it square. Use a

square on the inside surfaces as well. Then use bar clamps to clamp the entire assembly tightly. Check again to make sure the assembly is square. Wipe away all excess glue with a warm, wet cloth and allow the glue to set overnight.

You can also glue up the pieces a section at a time if you don't have enough bar clamps. First glue up each side, then the back, and finally the front.

It's a good idea to completely sand each piece before final assembly. For one thing, it's almost impossible to get a sander into the lower areas of the sides between the legs. A finish polishing with medium grade steel wool will give them a professionally burnished look.

Shaping the Top

While the glue on the frame assembly is setting, you can shape the top. Using a belt sander, remove any glue lines that may have been formed. (A stop block placed on the table or workbench top will prevent the piece from sliding backwards as you work on it.) Then square off the ends using a table or radial arm saw. Make sure you use a fine-toothed finishing blade to prevent the finished edge from chipping.

The top edge of the top is shaped with either a router, a shaper, or a moulding head in a radial arm saw or table saw. Make the end-grain cuts first to

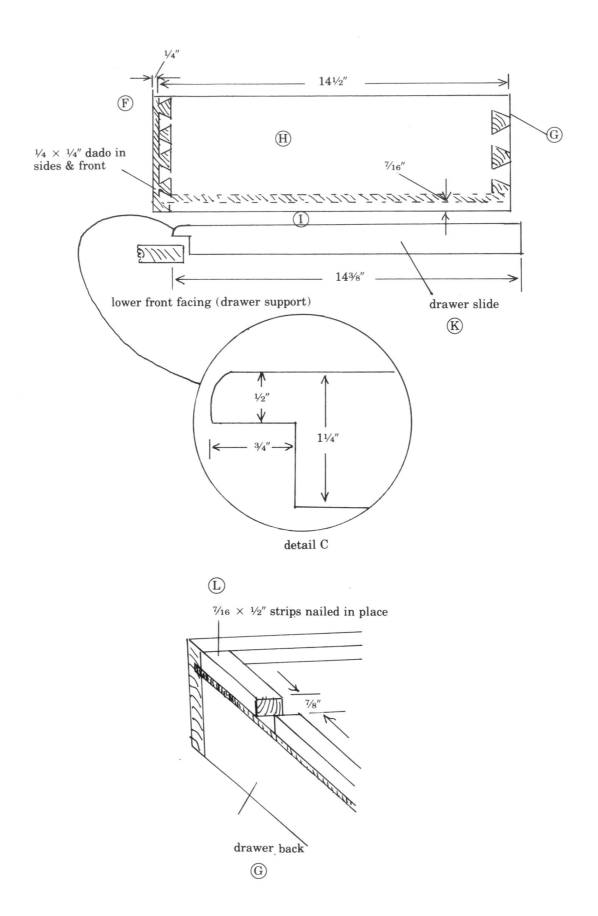

¼"

14½"

F

G

¼ × ¼" dado in
sides & front

H

7⁄16"

I

lower front facing (drawer support)

14⅜"

drawer slide

K

½"

¾"

1¼"

detail C

L

7⁄16 × ½" strips nailed in place

7⁄8"

drawer back

G

prevent the sides from splintering, then make the with-the-grain cuts. Finally, fine-sand the top and bottom surfaces.

Drawer Construction

After the glue on the frame assembly has set, remove the clamps and start construction of the drawer. Note that in the original the drawer front (F) and front support (C) were cut from the same piece of stock. The matching grains produced an attractive effect. In any case, cut the drawer front to size and joint and sand the edges smooth. Then cut the sides (H), back (G), and bottom (I) to size. Note that the sides and back are constructed of ½-inch drawer stock. This is available in pine, sycamore, and various other woods. These lightweight, strong woods make a solid but easy-sliding drawer.

The tops of the sides are "relieved," or shaped, up to within an inch of the drawer front. This is typical of most well-crafted furniture pieces and can be done with a router or shaper. The sides are dovetailed into the drawer front, using a router and dovetailing attachment. The back and sides can also be dovetailed together or they can be jointed with a dado joint.

The bottom is held in place with a dado joint in the sides and front. It extends out over the bottom edge of the back. Glue blocks will add additional support under the drawer edges if necessary.

Make sure the drawer is square before gluing and fastening the pieces together. Because the drawer front is flush construction, extra care must be taken to ensure that both the drawer and front opening in the table are perfectly square. The drawer front, however, is about ⅟₁₆ inch smaller on all four sides than the opening to allow for swelling.

Drawer and Top Installation

Cut the center drawer slide (K) to size and shape, as shown in the drawing. With the table standing upright, put the slide in place and fasten it on the front drawer support (C) with a countersunk wood screw. Now put the drawer into the frame and push it all the way back. Make sure the drawer front is square and properly positioned in the opening. Then mark the location of the back end of the drawer slide on the inside of the back (B) and remove the drawer. Fasten the slide in place to the back with wood screws. Make sure the drawer slides properly, then glue a couple of wooden drawer stops in the back of the unit.

Place the top upside down on a smooth, clean surface. Put the table frame assembly down on the top and fasten it in place with glue blocks and wood screws.

Wipe away excess glue and turn the assembly upright. Install the front hardware and apply the finish.

Materials List

A—Top—¾ × 14 × 18", 1 req'd.
B—Back—¾ × 5¾ × 9", 1 req'd.
C—Front moulding—¾ × 1¾ × 9", 1 req'd.
D—Sides—¾ × 5 × 13", 2 req'd.
E—Side bottom moulding—¾ × 1 × 13", 2 req'd.
F—Drawer front—¾ × 4⅞ × 8⅞", 1 req'd.
G—Drawer back—½ × 4⅜ × 7⅜", 1 req'd.
H—Drawer sides—½ × 4⅞ × 14½", 2 req'd.
I—Drawer bottom—¼" hardboard × 7⅞ × 14¼", 1 req'd.
J—Legs—2 × 2 × 22", 4 req'd.
K—Drawer slide—¾ × 1¼ × 14⅜", 1 req'd.

Enclosed Washstand

Circa 1880, American

Typical of early turn-of-the-century manufactured furniture in America, this classic oak washstand goes well with today's contemporary furniture styles. Its clean and simple design could also provide a nice contrast to much of the ornate and sophisticated furniture of other periods.

Washstands were made in many different sizes and styles and were used in both bedrooms and kitchens. A towel bar on the back was used for drying and holding towels.

The stands were made of several different woods, including pine, oak, and walnut. The stand shown is made of oak and is a very sturdy piece. It also looks quite good when done in antiqued pine, a favorite with furniture reproduction manufacturers.

Construction
The sides and back are frame-and-panel design with the legs acting as stiles for the panels, a construction technique typical of "assembly line" construction of the period. The front facers are mortised into the legs. All mortises are simple grooves routed in the legs.

Legs
The first step in construction is to cut the legs (A) to the correct size and length. Joint their edges for smoothness on all four sides. Rout the grooves for the side crosspieces (B,C) and panels (D) as well as for the back rails (X,Y) and panels (Z,AA) and for the front facers (E,F). Use a dado head on a table or radial arm saw or a router and router table. To make the piece a bit sturdier, you may wish to cut mortises for rails and facers a bit deeper with a mortising attachment on a drill press. But the original utilized only the ½-inch depth of the panels and a single groove running the full length of the legs.

Sides
Cut the bottom and top crosspieces (B,C) to size and rout a groove in their inside edges for the panel. Then, cut the tenons on their ends to fit in the grooves cut in the legs. Cut the panels from ¼-inch stock that is either solid wood or plywood. Cut the L-shaped drawer glide supports (S), the top support cleats (T), bottom support cleat (TT) and shelf supports (U). Cut tenons on their ends to fit into the grooves in the legs as well.

Side Assembly
Place glue on the ends of the side frame assembly, including the inside drawer glide supports (S) and cleats (T) and shelf supports (U). Put side assembly pieces together and fit all their tenons into grooves cut in the legs. Do not apply glue to the edges of the panels. Make sure the assemblies are square and true; then clamp and allow the glue to set overnight.

Back
The back is made of frame-and-panel as well, and the rails (X,Y) are cut to size from ¾-inch stock. Grooves must be cut in them for the panels (Z,AA). Then cut tenons on their ends to fit into the grooves in the back legs.

Incidentally, you could also use a solid ¼-inch back if you prefer, fitting it into the ¼ × ½-inch rabbets on the inside of the legs. This is a little easier to make than the traditional frame-and-panel arrangement.

Front Facers
Cut the front facers (F) and front bottom facer (E) to size and shape and make tenons on their ends to fit into grooves in the legs. Note that the bottom facer or foot board sits back from the front edge of the leg ¼ inch and a special mortise must be cut for it. Note also that in all cases the panels are not glued in the crosspieces or legs, although the crosspieces are glued to the legs.

Case Assembly
Place one of the side assemblies, with the groove facing up, on a smooth, flat surface. Put glue on the tenons of the back rails (X,Y) and insert them into the back leg of the side assembly. Insert the back panels between them as you do this, but without letting any glue touch the panel edges. Place glue on the ends of the front facer tenons (E,F) and fit them into the front leg of the side panel. Apply glue on all the exposed tenons on the opposite ends of both front and back pieces. Lift up the opposite side panel and carefully fit the tenons in place in the leg grooves. Use a soft mallet to tap the side panel assembly firmly together.

This type of assembly will probably take more than two hands, and a good helper would come in handy. After all pieces are in place, stand the entire assembly upright on a smooth, flat surface. Make sure it is square and doesn't rock on the legs; then clamp securely and allow the glue to set overnight.

After you remove the case from the clamps, you can strengthen the joints between crosspieces and legs with flat-head screws driven from inside.

Bottom
Construct the cabinet bottom (R) of solid wood. Cut it to fit and position it in place on the back rail (X) and the front facer (E). Fasten in place with glue and screws.

Shelf
Cut the shelf (V) to the proper size and drop it down

in place on the shelf support cleats (U). Fasten with screws if you wish.

Top
Cut the cabinet top (W) to the proper size. You will probably want to make up the top from several smaller widths of stock dowelled and glued together. Sand smooth both upper and lower surfaces, and finish the underside of the top before it is installed. This is especially important to prevent warping if you utilize a solid, one-piece top.

Cut the drawer tilt strip (SS) and fasten it in place to the top underside. The top is fastened in place with screws through the top support cleats (T) on

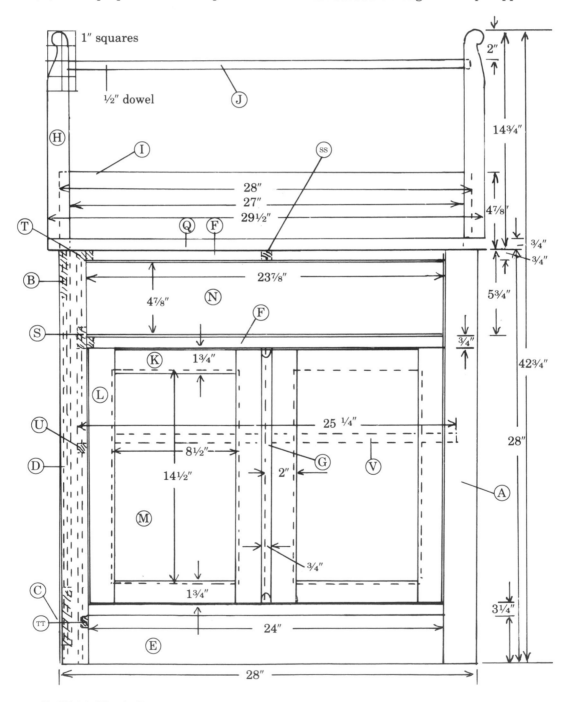

the side and from the underside of the top front facer (F).

Towel Rack

Cut the splash board (I) to shape and size and cut tenons on each end. Then cut the upper back uprights (H) to size and shape by following the square-drawing pattern shown at the top of the front view. Cut matching mortises in them for the splash board tenons. Bore the holes for the towel rack (J).

Assemble with glue and clamp solidly overnight. Fasten the towel rack to the back edge of the top with countersunk flat-head wood screws and no glue.

Doors

The doors are typical frame-and-panel with mortise-and-tenon joints. The first step is to cut the door stiles (L) to size and shape; then cut the groove on their inside edges for the door panel (M). Cut the mortises for the door rail (K) tenons. Then cut door crosspieces to size and rout the groove for the panel in them. Make the tenons to fit in the mortises of the uprights.

Cut the panels to shape and put together door assemblies with glue and screws. Fasten the doors in place with brass butt hinges.

Note that the doors overlap and have a decorative door trim strip (G). It is cut to shape on the edge of a piece of stock and ripped off with a circular saw. The upper and lower ends of it are flared using a band saw. Fasten this in place to the front closing overlap with small brass brads and glue. Note also that a wooden knob with a back wing is used to hold the doors shut, as shown in the door detail drawing.

Drawer

The drawer consists of a ¾-inch solid oak front (N) with ½-inch pine sides (O), and back (P), and a ¼-inch plywood bottom (Q). The sides, back and front are held together with dovetails, as shown, and the drawer bottom fits in a dado in the pieces.

The last step is to finish the piece and install the period hardware, including the porcelain casters in the bottoms of the legs.

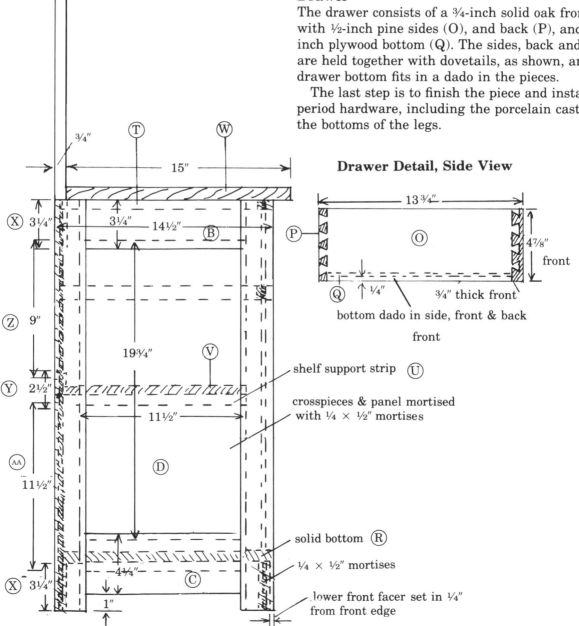

Drawer Detail, Side View

Materials List

A—Legs—2 × 2 × 28″, 4 req'd.
B—Top side crosspieces—3⁄4 × 31⁄4 × 111⁄2″, 2 req'd.
C—Bottom side crosspieces—3⁄4 × 41⁄4 × 111⁄2″, 2 req'd.
D—Side panels—3⁄4 × 111⁄2 × 193⁄4″, 2 req'd.
E—Front bottom facer—3⁄4 × 31⁄2 × 26″, 1 req'd.
F—Front facers—3⁄4 × 2 × 24″, 2 req'd.
G—Door trim—3⁄4 × 1⁄2 × 171⁄4″, 1 req'd.
H—Upper back uprights—3⁄4 × 11⁄2 × 143⁄4″, 2 req'd.
I—Splash board—3⁄4 × 47⁄8 × 28″, 1 req'd.
J—Towel rack—1⁄2″ dowel × 28″, 1 req'd.
K—Door rails—3⁄4 × 13⁄4 × 81⁄2″, 4 req'd
L—Door stiles—3⁄4 × 13⁄4 × 171⁄4″, 4 req'd.
M—Door panels—1⁄4 × 81⁄2 × 141⁄2″, 2 req'd.
N—Drawer front—3⁄4 × 47⁄8 × 237⁄8″, 1 req'd.
O—Drawer sides—1⁄2 × 47⁄8 × 131⁄2″, 2 req'd.
P—Drawer back—1⁄2 × 47⁄8 × 237⁄8″, 1 req'd.
Q—Drawer bottom—1⁄4 × 227⁄8 × 123⁄4″, 1 req'd.
R—Cabinet bottom—3⁄4 × 14 × 261⁄2″, 1 req'd.
S—Drawer glide supports—11⁄4 × 11⁄4 × 111⁄2″, 2 req'd.
SS—Drawer tilt strip—3⁄4 × 3⁄4 × 111⁄2″, 1 req'd.
T—Top support cleats—3⁄4 × 11⁄4 × 111⁄2″, 2 req'd.
TT—Bottom support cleats—3⁄4 × 11⁄4 × 111⁄2″, 2 req'd.
U—Shelf support cleats—3⁄4 × 3⁄4 × 111⁄2″, 2 req'd.
V—Shelf—3⁄4 × 113⁄4 × 251⁄4″, 1 req'd.
W—Cabinet top—3⁄4 × 15 × 291⁄2″, 1 req'd.
X—Back rails—3⁄4 × 31⁄4 × 25″, 2 req'd.
Y—Center back rail—3⁄4 × 21⁄2 × 25″, 1 req'd.
Z—Back panel—1⁄4 × 9 × 25″, 1 req'd.
AA—Back panel—1⁄4 × 111⁄2 × 25″, 1 req'd.

Door Detail

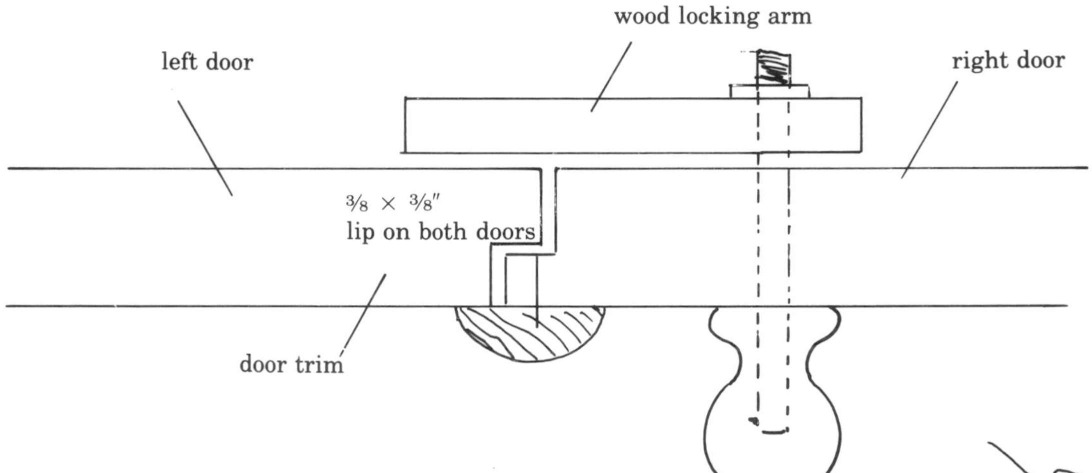
wood locking arm
left door
right door
3⁄8 × 3⁄8″
lip on both doors
door trim

Leg and Panel Detail

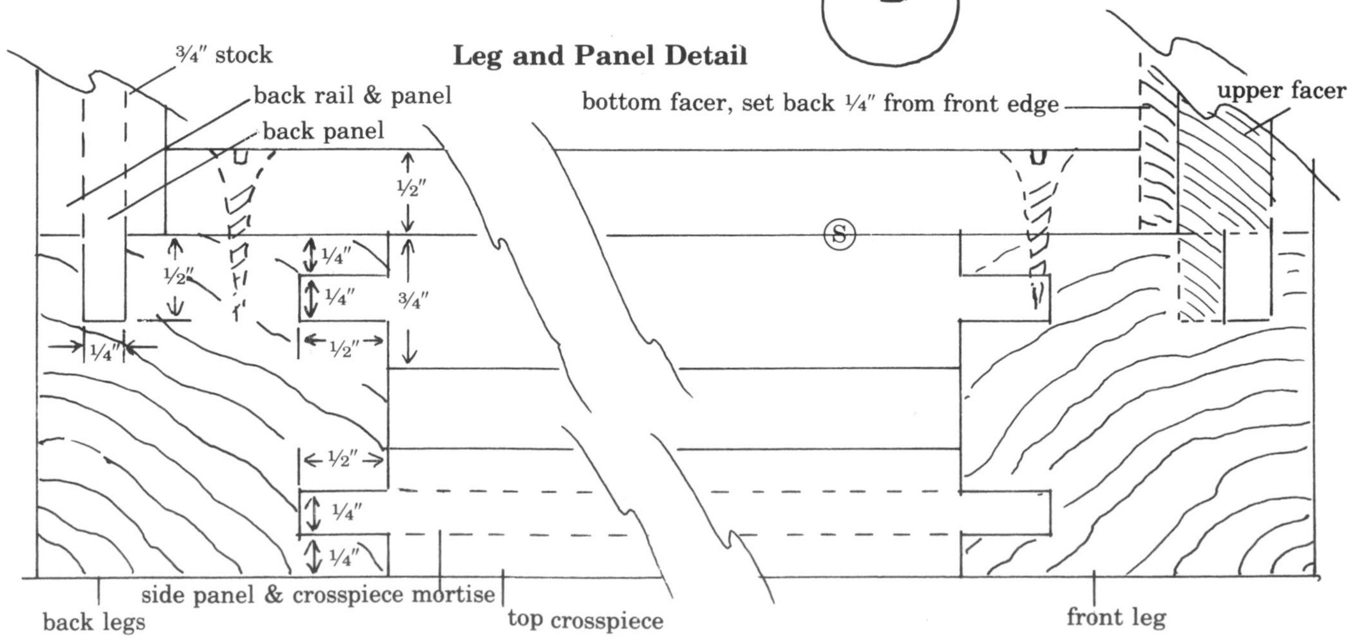
3⁄4″ stock
back rail & panel
back panel
bottom facer, set back 1⁄4″ from front edge
upper facer
1⁄2″
1⁄4″
1⁄4″
3⁄4″
1⁄2″
1⁄2″
1⁄4″
1⁄2″
1⁄4″
1⁄4″
S
back legs
side panel & crosspiece mortise
top crosspiece
front leg

Round Victorian Table

Circa Late 1800s

The round oak tables made by manufacturers, cabinetmakers and American craftsmen of the early Victorian period are very popular items with collectors and are also quite popular as reproduction furniture pieces. Several furniture-kit manufacturers offer these tables and they are also available unfinished for those who simply wish to add the finish of their choice.

There are a great number of different styles ranging from simple tables with square-cut legs and pedestals to the more heavily carved claw-foot tables with turned pedestal posts. Shown is a typical example of the latter. Although early pieces were made of walnut, mahogany, and oak, oak seems to be the choice with most collectors, and so it is the traditional wood to use.

Construction

Although at first glance the table appears to be quite complicated, it's not hard to build. However, it does require a good, heavy-duty lathe for turning the large hollow post and also requires a good band saw and precision in cutting and fitting the apron board pieces.

The top is made in two halves joined with dowel guide pins between them. Table extensions, fastened

to the underside of the top, enable the table to be extended out and additional leaves added. Two drop-down legs, anchored to the underside of the top halves with hinges, provide extra support when the table is extended full. The lower ends are stored up between the extensions when not in use.

Support Column
Construction starts with the support post segments (A). These are hollow wooden columns. They are made by cutting a number of wooden segments to the angles shown in the drawing. These are fitted with support post splines (B) in slots cut in their joining angled edges.

Once all pieces have been cut to size and shape, insert glue on the splines and join the segmented circle together. Use band clamps to clamp the column securely together and allow it to set overnight or until the glue is thoroughly dried. Remove from the clamps and cut 9-inch-diameter circles from ¾-inch plywood to fit over each end. Locate the exact center of the circles. Fasten these end caps in place with wood screws over the ends of the column, making sure they align properly. Then place the large, hollow column in your lathe and turn it to shape at a very slow speed. Turn and sand smooth while still in the lathe.

After the piece has been turned to the proper size and shape, remove from the lathe and, using a small square, divide the bottom plywood-holding circle into four equal parts. Mark this line down the sides of the hollow post. This will locate the exact position of each of the four legs around the outside of the circle. Then remove the plywood end caps from the hollow turned column.

Legs
The legs (C) are made by gluing up stock to make up the thickness needed. Then enlarge the squared drawing for the claw foot portion and carve to shape.

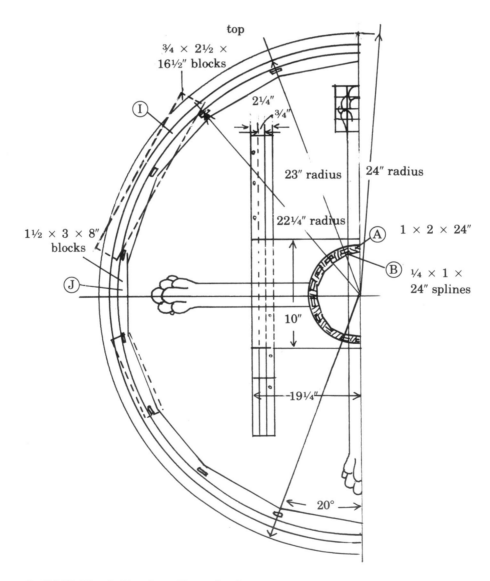

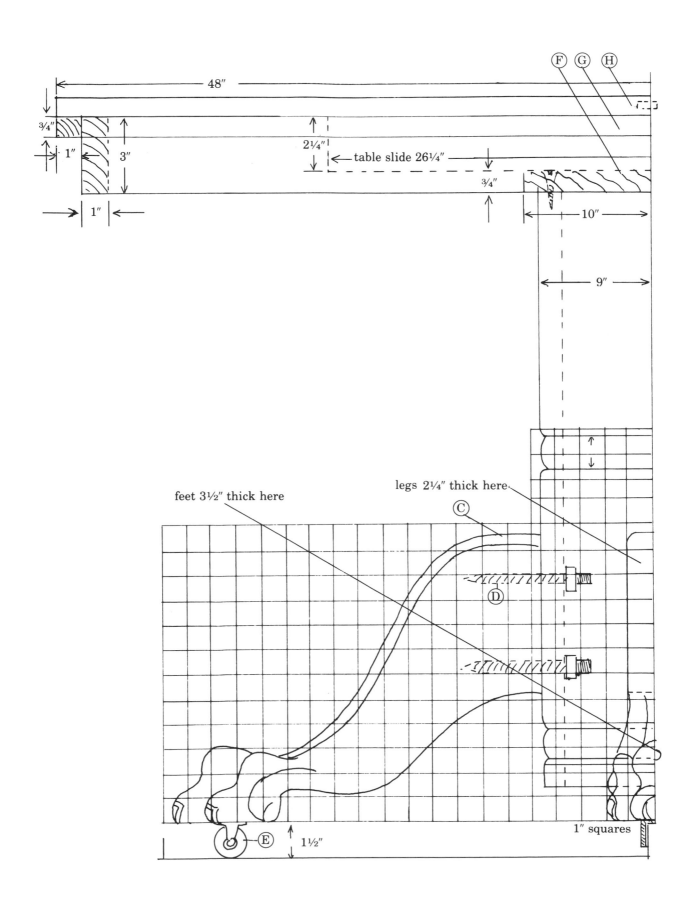

48″

¾″

1″ 3″

1″

2¼″

← table slide 26¼″ →

¾″

Ⓕ Ⓖ Ⓗ

10″

9″

feet 3½″ thick here

legs 2¼″ thick here

Ⓒ

Ⓓ

Ⓔ 1½″

1″ squares

With a duplicating carver you can easily duplicate the carving from one foot to another and cut down a great deal on the time and effort needed to build the table.

After carving all four legs to the correct size and shape, including the rounded inside end to fit up

against the turned column, locate the holes for the holding bolts and bore them. Then bore matching holes in the lower portion of the turned column.

The legs are held to the post with special lag bolts and washers (D). These have a screw thread cut on one end which is turned into the leg. The opposite end is threaded for a nut. After turning the bolts into the legs, insert the bolts into the mating holes in the turned column and install washers and nuts to fasten the feet solidly in place.

Table Slides

The table extension slides (G) are purchased; however, you can also make them up yourself, as shown in the detail, using slotted dovetails to create the slides. Cut the extension support block (F) to size and shape and install the slides on top of it with screws. Then fasten the slides and block assembly in place to the turned pedestal with screws down through the block into the top of the pedestal.

Tabletop

Construction of the top (H) of the table is fairly simple; however, construction of the apron is a bit more complicated. The top is two separate pieces made of solid stock glued up from smaller-width stock. Again this can be tongue-and-groove or can be made with dowel joints. Glue up to the rough size and then use a large shop-made compass or trammel point to create a cutting line for the circular top halves.

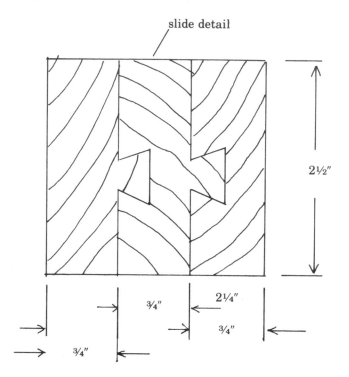

slide detail

2½"

¾"   2¼"

¾"

¾"

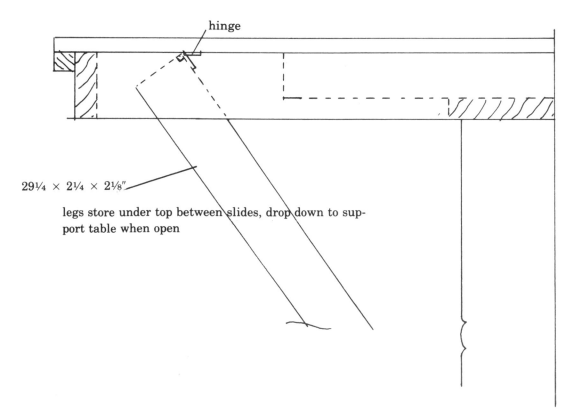

hinge

29¼ × 2¼ × 2⅛"

legs store under top between slides, drop down to support table when open

Saw the top pieces to the correct circumference using a band saw or sabre saw. You can make a band saw table extension and guide pin jig to assure the circle is cut perfectly round.

The edge of the tabletop is thickened with an additional piece of stock glued to the underside of the edge. This edge thickener (I) is made using the segment method as for the center column. Cut the segment pieces to the rough shape and size as shown in the drawing. Then make a pattern for the circumference, transfer this to the segment pieces, and cut them to shape on the band saw. Fasten these in place to the underside of the top with glue and screws. Make sure their meeting edges join smoothly and perfectly.

Apron

The apron is one of the hardest portions of the table to build. On the original it was cut from one solid piece steamed and bent to shape. However, you will probably need to make it of segmented pieces (J). You can make these of solid oak, leaving the joint lines showing, or you can cover the outside of the apron with oak veneer to cover the joint lines.

Again cut the segment pieces to the correct size and rough shape; you can even create an exact pattern for cutting each of the segments to shape. Cut the segment angles, then cut a slot for the apron splines (K) using a dado blade in a table or radial arm saw. Finally, cut the outside rounded edge of each segment using a band saw. You can also make up this large segmented circle with the blocks in the rough; temporarily fasten it to a piece of plywood with screws and then use a table extension and pin guide on your band saw to cut the circle. The latter will result in a truer, more finished appearance. Sand as smooth as possible and fasten to the underside of the tabletop as well as to the lower bottom tabletop lip with glue and screws countersunk in place. You might also wish to add glue blocks for extra strength.

Bore the pin guide holes for the table-leaf halves and smooth the two ends of a couple of dowels, then glue their opposite ends permanently in the holes in one side. They mate with holes bored in the opposite side of the table.

Assembly

Turn the top upside down on a smooth, flat surface and invert the pedestal assembly down in place over it. Fasten the extensions in place to the tabletop to secure the two assemblies together.

Drop Support Legs

Cut the drop support legs (L) to size, joint their edges, and sand smooth. Then install to the underside of the tabletop with butt hinges. Install the table-leaf catch. Make up as many leaves as needed; sand the entire project smooth, install the casters (E), and stain and finish to suit.

Materials List

A—Support post segments—1 × 2 × 24″, 18 req'd.

B—Support post splines—¼ × 1 × 24″, 18 req'd.

C—Legs—3½ × 12 × 15½″, glued up, 4 req'd.

D—Lag bolts & washers—⅜ × 4½″, 8 req'd.

E—Casters—1½″, 4 req'd.

F—Extension support block—¾ × 10 × 19¼″, 1 req'd.

G—Table extension slides—1 purchased set req'd.

H—Tabletop—¾ × 24 × 48″, 2 req'd.

I—Edge thickener—cut from—¾ × 2½ × 16½″, 9 req'd.

J—Apron blocks—1½ × 3 × 8″, 18 req'd.

K—Apron splines—½ × 1 × 3″, 18 req'd.

L—Drop support legs—2 × 2 × 30¼″, 2 req'd.

Butt hinges—1½″, 2 pair req'd.

Table-leaf catch hardware

Dowels—⅜″ as needed

Table leaves—¾ × 12 × 48″, as desired

Cane-Bottom Chair

Circa 1920

Although "younger" than many of the other furniture pieces, this "country" classic is popular with today's reproduction furniture builders. The chair goes well with the round Victorian table. Because of the bending needed to form the back and front legs as well as the arm supports and back splats, this chair is rather complicated. The chair shown is made of oak. It should be made using this material, although almost any hardwood could be used.

Legs
First turn the back (B) and front legs (A). Then bend them into the shape shown in the squared drawing using the methods on page 24.

Locate and bore the counterbored holes in the back legs for countersunk screws to hold the seatboard (H-J) to the legs.

Back Splats
Cut the top back splat (L) to the correct shape. Enlarge the squared drawing and carve the piece. Then bend it to shape.

Cut the lower back splat (K) to the proper size and shape and bend it as well.

Side Supports
Turn the side supports (G) to the proper size and shape on a lathe, then bend them to the shapes needed. It will take a great deal of work to get both of these in the exact shape needed to match them up correctly. However, this must be done or they can force the chair out of square during assembly.

Bore the holes for the back spindles (M) in the underside of the top piece and the upper side of the bottom splat.

Chair Rungs
Turn all the rungs (C-F) to the proper shape and size, including the tenons on each of the rungs.

Seatboard
Make the seatboard framework of ¾-inch-thick pieces (H-J) held together with dowels and glue. Then rout a recess in the top inside edge of the framework for the cane and spline. (*Note:* Installation of cane is discussed on pages 160 and 161.) Use a sabre saw or coping saw to round the corners of the seatboard and cut the back recesses for the back legs.

Then sand the edges round on both top and bottom of the seatboard. Bore the holes in the bottom of the seat.

Assembly
Assembly of a chair of this type is done all at one time, as opposed to the front and back construction done on some other chairs in this book.

Place a bit of glue on each tenon or dowel end before insertion, but not enough to run out or down onto the surrounding wood surface. Proper sizing of the tenons and dowel ends is very important for a properly constructed chair, one that will last without falling apart when the glue dries out. The tenons and dowels should be snug, but not a hard, "driven-on" fit, or there will be no room for the glue to hold them securely in place.

Assembly starts with the front legs. Drive their dowelled ends up into the holes bored in the seat bottom. Then place the front rungs between them and temporarily clamp together. Place this assembly aside for a few moments and assemble the lower back-leg assembly, placing both the lower back splat and the back lower rung between the legs and clamping this assembly together. Place the side rungs in place in the back-leg assembly, and position the front-leg assembly in place with the side rungs in their correct holes. Locate the position of the seatboard back edge and fasten it in place with a countersunk wood screw driven through the counterbored holes in the back legs.

Set the leg assembly on a smooth, flat surface and make sure it doesn't rock and has all four legs solidly planted. Clamp the entire assembly with band clamps. Install the side support pieces with screws into the seatboard and the back legs.

Upper Back Assembly
Assemble the upper back by inserting the back spindles (M) into the holes in the lower rail and then sliding the upper back piece down over their ends. Anchor the upper back to the back legs with countersunk, oval-head wood screws through the back legs into the chair-top back piece. Make sure none of the screws penetrates through the top piece.

Stain and finish to suit after a thorough sanding, then install cane. Ready-made cane and spline materials are widely available to finish this project.

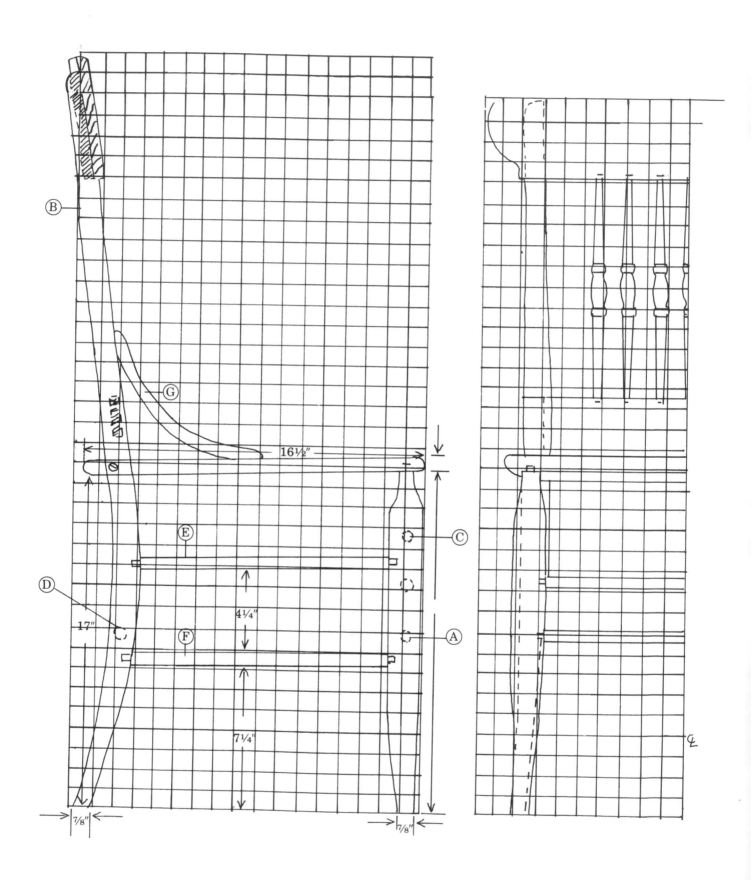

Materials List

A—Front legs—1¾ × 1¾ × 17½", 2 req'd.
B—Back legs—1¾ × 1¾ × 36", 2 req'd.
C—Front rungs—⅝ × ⅝ × 14½", 3 req'd.
D—Back rung—⅝ × ⅝ × 14½", 1 req'd.
E—Top side rungs—⅝ × ⅝ × 12¾", 2 req'd.
F—Bottom side rungs—⅝ × ⅝ × 13¼", 2 req'd.
G—Side supports—⅝ × ⅝ × 11½", 2 req'd.
H—Seatboard, front—¾ × 3½ × 18", 1 req'd.
I—Seatboard, back—¾ × 3 × 16", 1 req'd.
J—Seatboard, sides—¾ × 3½ × 9½", 2 req'd.
K—Lower back splat—¾ × 2¼ × 15", 1 req'd.
L—Top back splat—¾ × 5½ × 21½", 1 req'd.
M—Back spindles—¾ × ¾ × 11¼", 7 req'd.
Cane to fit

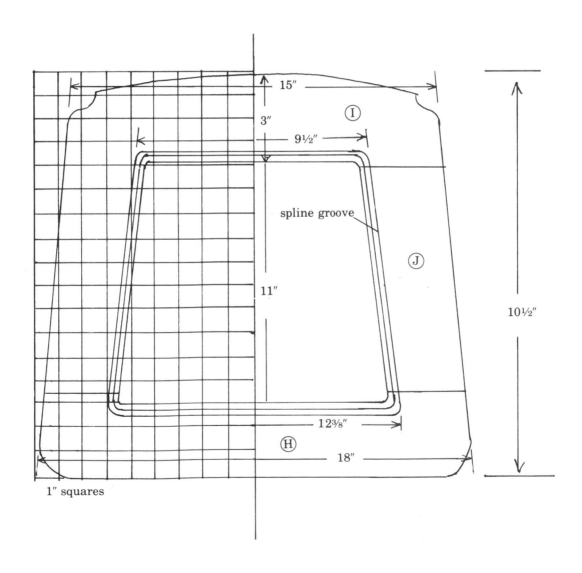

1" squares

Antique American Rocker

Circa Late 1800s

This oak rocker is typical of manufactured Early American country furniture. It features a stamped or embossed back piece and a pressed, embossed cardboard seat. The style of this rocker is classic, and any number of reproduction designs are still manufactured today, many of them for the unfinished furniture market. These rockers are usually made of oak. However, many of the modern-day replicas are made of pine that has been stained dark for a "country antique" flavor.

Construction
Most of the project consists of turnings; however, there is also some bending required on the back. If you want, you can cut the curved back pieces to shape on a band saw instead of bending them to shape. There is also some carving involved in recreating the embossed back piece design. But the carving isn't much of a problem because the relief is fairly shallow and the background is stippled. The biggest problem is in getting the correct compound angles so that all the pieces fit.

Turnings
The first step is to enlarge the squared drawings and create the turnings for the legs (A), stretcher (B,C), back posts (K) and the front arm posts (I). Turn the spindles (N) for the seat back and arm spindles (J). Make sure to turn tenons on the ends of each. After turning the back posts, cut mortises into their inside surfaces for the back pieces (L,M).

Seat
The seat is actually made up of four pieces; a seatboard front (E), back (F), and two sides (G). They are joined with dowels. The first step in assembly is to rough-cut the pieces to size, but do not use the band saw to shape them yet. Lay them out together and mark and drill the dowel holes to connect the pieces. Enlarge the squared drawing for the outline and for the center cutout and transfer it to the pieces. Use a band saw to cut the inside cutout shape on each piece, then glue and dowel and clamp the pieces together until the glue sets. Finally, cut the outside outline for the seatboard to shape using a band saw. Sand all edges thoroughly.

Arms
Enlarge the squared drawing and cut the arms (H) to shape. Lightly round their upper edges using a shaper or a router in a router table.

Back
Cut the back pieces (L,M) to the correct size and either cut or bend them into the shapes required. Cut tenons on their ends. Carve the upper back piece to the pattern shown on the squared drawing.

Rockers
Enlarge the squared drawing for the rockers (D) and cut to shape. Round their top outside edges slightly with sandpaper.

Boring the Holes
One of the single most important factors in building a chair of this type is getting all the holes for the pieces bored at the correct angles. Many of them are compound angles. Use a portable electric drill with a homemade jig, or use a tilting arm drill press to bore the holes at the precise angles needed. A bit with a square bottom, such as a Forstner bit, should be used. Since most of these are stopped holes, a depth gauge on the drill bit is also necessary to ensure that you don't bore completely through the stock.

Start with the holes in the bottom of the seat for the legs (A). Then bore holes in the top of the seat for the back posts (K) and arm posts (I). Once the seatboard holes have been made, drill holes in the rockers (D), legs (A) and stretchers (B,C). Bore holes in the underside of the arm (H) and countersunk screw holes in their back ends to fasten them to the back posts. Bore holes in the upper and lower back pieces (M,L).

Then finally cut mortises into the inside part of the back posts (K) to accept the back pieces (M,L). These are somewhat tricky to cut and a great deal of trial and error is needed to get a good, tight-fitting joint.

Assembly
Because of the number of odd angles of the piece, the chair is assembled all at once, rather than in sections. You will need a wide variety of clamps, including several band clamps, to clamp all the pieces properly.

Assembly starts by laying all the sanded and smoothed parts in order on a smooth, clean tabletop. Then dry-fit each piece in place before you do the

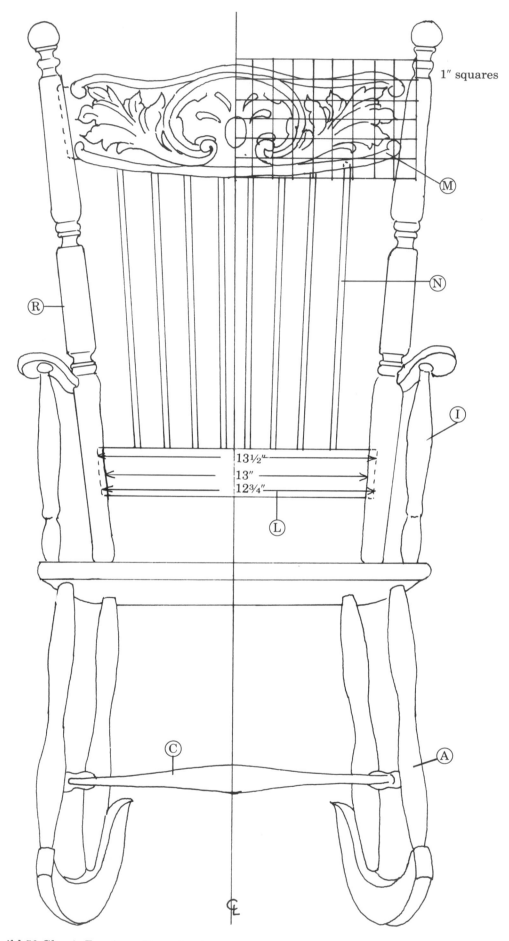

1" squares

M

N

R

I

13½"
13"
12¾"

L

C

A

C L

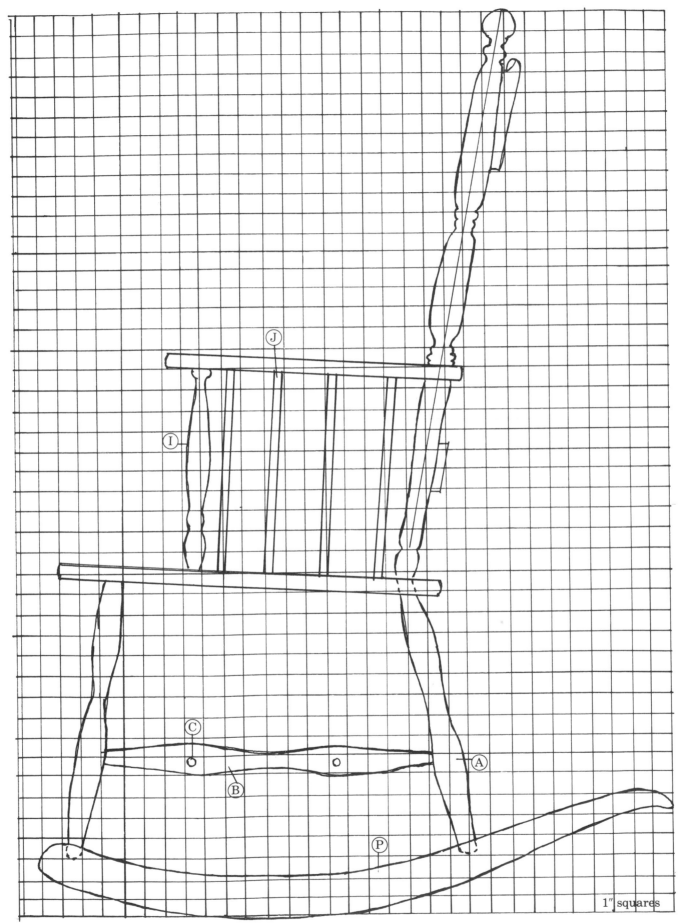

1″ squares

final assembly with glue. This doesn't mean you should hammer the pieces together, just check to see that all tenons fit snugly in their appropriate holes and that all the holes are bored at the correct angles. Once you get glue on the parts, refitting or remaking a piece becomes quite a problem.

After you're sure all pieces fit properly, place glue on the bottoms of the legs and the ends of the side leg stretchers (B). Fit the stretchers between the legs, then insert the legs into the rockers. With both side sections assembled in that manner, place the two center stretchers (C) between the side assemblies. Tap all pieces solidly in place, then put a single band clamp around the leg assembly (at the point of the leg stretchers). Slip the assembled seatboard over the ends of the leg tenons and tap it firmly in place with a soft rubber, plastic, or rawhide mallet.

Stand the seat-leg assembly on a smooth, flat surface, and make sure the chair is square by checking to see that it is not tilted to one side, that one leg is not pushed out farther than the others, etc. Since there is no reference that can be used in this case, it will have to be done by eye. If there is any problem, correct it at this time by loosening the clamps and tapping the pieces into place. Then retighten the clamps. You may also have to adjust the clamps themselves, because they can sometimes pull a piece out of shape.

The next step is to assemble the back section by placing spindles (N) into the proper holes in the back

pieces. Then fit the back pieces into the back post mortises (K). Again clamp with band clamps and set aside.

Insert the front arm posts (I) and spindles (J) into the holes in the seat, then place the arms (H) down over them and clamp with bar clamps. Finally, put the back assembly in place, fitting the post ends down into the seatboard holes. Fasten the arms to the back posts with countersunk brass, oval-head wood screws.

Leave the unit clamped overnight, then sand smooth, cut away any glue runs, and finally stain and finish. For authenticity, fasten the pressed cardboard seat (O) in place with the decorative tacks.

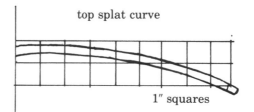

top splat curve

1″ squares

bottom splat curve

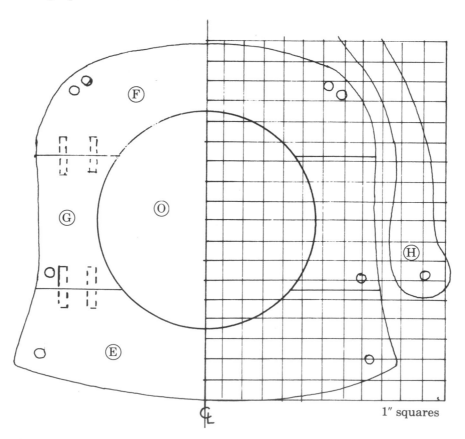

1″ squares

Materials List

A—Legs—1½ × 1½ × 14″, cut to length, 4 req'd.

B—Side stretchers—1½ × 1½ × 17″, cut to length, 2 req'd.

C—Center stretchers—1½ × 1½ × 17″, cut to length, 2 req'd.

D—Rockers—⅞ × 6 × 31½″, 2 req'd.

E—Seat board front—¾ × 5½ × 20″, 1 req'd.

F—Seat board back—¾ × 6 × 18″, 1 req'd.

G—Seat board sides—¾ × 5 × 7″, 2 req'd.

H—Arms—¾ × 6 × 15″, 2 req'd.

I—Front arm posts—1½ × 1½ × 11″, cut to fit, 2 req'd.

J—Arm spindles—⅜″ dowel × 11″, cut to fit, 6 req'd.

K—Back posts—1½ × 1½ × 29″, 2 req'd.

L—Lower back piece—¾ × 2½ × 15″, bent and cut to fit, 1 req'd.

M—Upper back piece—¾ × 6 × 19″, bent and cut to fit, 1 req'd.

N—Back spindles—⅜″ dowel × 15″, cut to fit, 8 req'd.

O—Pressed cardboard seat—12 × 12″, 1 req'd.

Decorative tacks

High Chair

Circa 1890

The owner of the chair shown here used it as a child in 1900, but was not certain how many years it had been in the family. But because he was the third child, it is very likely that the chair was purchased before 1900.

Although the original was made of red oak, you could use almost any solid hardwood, including walnut, cherry, or mahogany. Hickory would be the best choice for the bent parts. Oak would also serve well for the bent parts. The greener the wood is, the better when it comes to bending.

With some carving, wood turning and bending, the project does provide several challenges. Each taken step-by-step, however, makes the chair a less formidable project.

Make Patterns
The first step in construction of the high chair is to enlarge the squared drawings and make full-size patterns of those parts that will be turned, band-sawed, or bent to shape.

Seats
Cut the parts (K,L,M) for the seat to size and shape on a band saw. Note that the seat is made from four parts dowelled and glued together as shown in the detail drawing. After you assemble the seat portion, and without the center cut out, use a router with a pivot accessory guide to rout the circular groove that will hold the cane and spline. For this, use a 1/4-inch router bit and cut the groove 1/4 inch deep. Bore a starting hole in the seat center. Then, using a sabre saw or jig saw, cut out the seat bottom.

Mark the locations for the back supports (J,O) on the top of the seat and for the legs (A,B) on the bottom. To make the proper angles, bore these stopped holes with either a radial arm drill press or a portable electric drill with a wooden block jig.

You can make the block jigs. Each consists of a 2 × 4 with a hole the exact size of the one to be made in the bottom piece bored down the center of the block. Then cut the end of the jig on a compound angle that matches the angles of the legs—or back supports—as shown. The jig is clamped on the chair bottom to prevent it from sliding out of place. Use a depth collar or a piece of tape on the drill bit to mark the depth of the stopped holes.

Turnings
Note that the legs should be turned 2 inches longer on the bottom. They will then be cut off after the chair has been dry-assembled to ensure the chair stands straight. Turn the back spindles (O), side spindles (P), back uprights (J), and legs (A,B) to shape. Then turn the 5/8-inch dowel stretchers for the back (E,F), sides (C,D) and the 3/4-inch front (G). Note that these dowels are shouldered down to 1/2 inch on each end for fitting in the legs, etc.

Legs
Bore holes in the legs (A,B) for the stretchers. Clamp the leg to the drill press table to ensure that the holes are drilled straight. Note that the side stretcher holes are bored at an angle.

Cut the mortise in the upper part of the back upright using a mortising attachment in a drill press. You could also drill a series of 1/4-inch-deep × 1/4-inch-wide holes in a line. Then use a very sharp chisel to cut away the waste and make the mortise square-sided and smooth. Using a band saw, cut the footboard (H) to the proper size and shape.

Assembly
Lay out all the pieces in position on a smooth, flat worktable. Then sand and smooth until each piece fits properly. Fit each piece and finally assemble the entire chair without glue. Lay a steel square across the bottom edge of each leg and flat against the table surface and mark the angle to cut the bottom of each leg. Then cut this angle.

Reassemble the chair without glue and make sure it stands properly, doesn't rock, etc. If it does, adjust the leg cuts until the chair is square. Disassemble, place a bit of carpenter's glue in each hole and glue it together, starting with the side stretchers (C,D). Put in the back (E,F) and front (G) stretchers. Tap each piece soundly in place using a wooden or leather mallet. Then wipe away all glue runs using a cloth dampened with warm water. Clamp the chair securely together using band clamps, one at the locations of the upper stretchers, and one on the top of each leg. Tap the seatboard down solidly in place. Again, wipe away excess glue with a warm, damp rag.

Make sure that the seatboard sits squarely on the legs and is not tilted to one side or the other; then weight it down securely with heavy weights. Allow this assembly to dry overnight. Tap the foot board supports (I) in place. Fasten the foot board (H) to the supports using countersunk wood screws driven up from the support dowels into the front board.

The Upper Back

The upper back (N) can be cut from a thick block of wood (see detail drawing), or thin stock can be bent to shape after it has been cut with a band saw and carved. If you cut it to shape, make the first cut from the top to the bottom edge. Then cut the front profile. Make ¼ × ¼-inch tenons on its ends to fit in the

back upright mortises. Put the carving pattern in place with a piece of carbon paper under it. Transfer the carving pattern to the wood stock. Carve the reliefs with small gouges and chisels. First outline the carving with a grooving chisel, then follow with a gouge to cut away the background. The carving should not be very prominent (approximately ⅛ inch), just enough to suggest background.

Bore holes for the spindles (O) in the upper back, again clamping the pieces in place to drill the holes straight.

If the back is to be bent instead of cut, cut the front profile to shape with a band saw and carve as before.

Front View

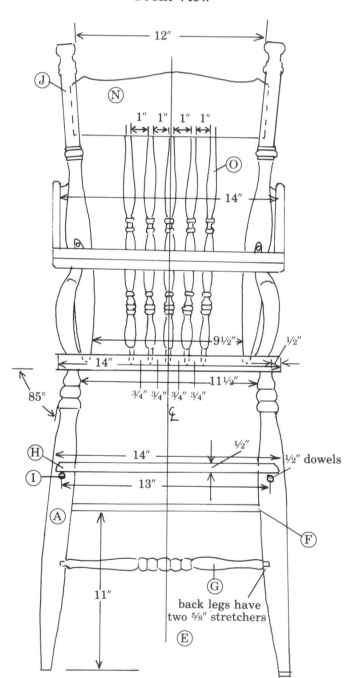

Side View

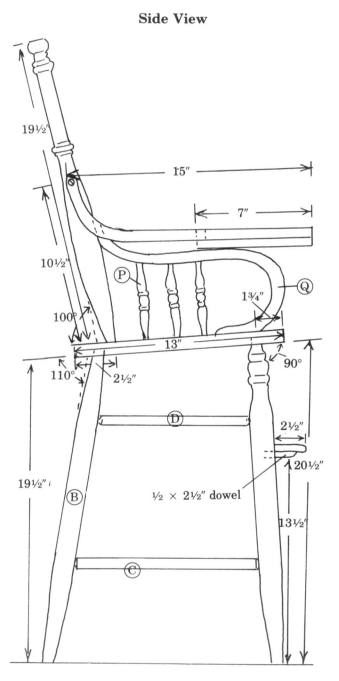

seat

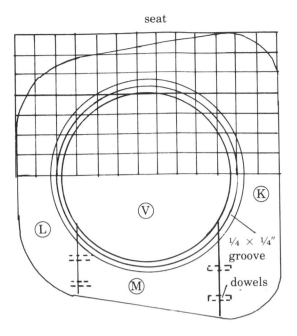

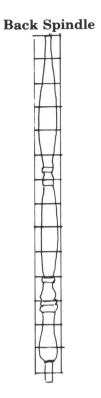

¼ × ¼"
groove

dowels

Back Leg **Back Upright** **Front Leg**

1" squares

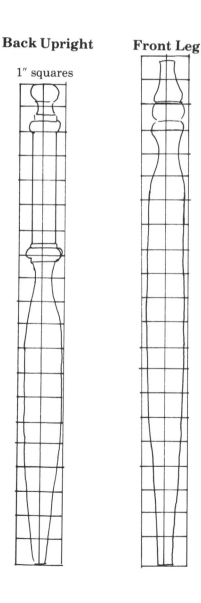

Front Stretcher

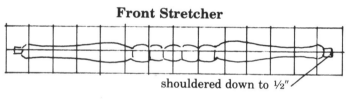

shouldered down to ½"

Bore the spindle holes in the bottom and cut the tenons. Then stream the wood or soak it for several hours in hot water. Bend it to shape using a wooden cawl (see detail) and allow it to dry overnight. Note that the curve of the cawl should be exaggerated because the wood will rebound somewhat.

Assemble the top back section of the chair. Again, you should first dry-fit all the parts to make sure they fit properly. When you are satisfied they fit, reassemble them using glue.

Place the upper back (N) tenons in the uprights (J) first and tap solidly in place using a wooden or rawhide mallet. Place the upper ends of the spindles (O) in the back piece. Fit the uprights and spindles into the chair seat holes. Tap solidly in place.

Use a single bar clamp running from the chair seat to the top of the upper back to pull the entire assembly down solidly to the chair seat. Then put a clamp across the front of the upper back piece and uprights. *Caution:* It is very easy, as you tighten the clamp, to accidentally twist and turn the uprights, causing tenons on the back piece to slip out of place. In fact, you may have to resort to a clamp on the back as well. Wipe away all glue runs with a warm, damp rag.

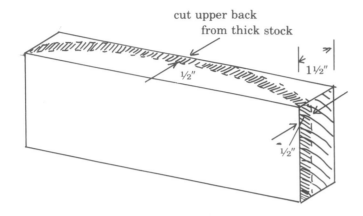

cut upper back
from thick stock

½"

1½"

½"

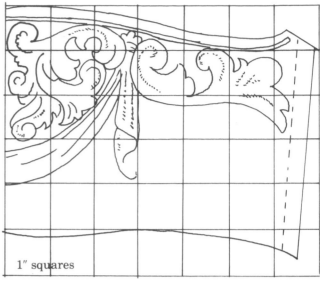

half pattern **Upper Back Carving Detail**

1″ squares

Bending the Arms

This step is the hardest. First the ends of the arms (Q) are cut to the shape shown in the squared drawing using a band saw. Round all edges smooth with sandpaper.

Steam or soak the stock for about 12 hours in hot tap water, constantly changing the water to keep it as hot as possible. Then bend the stock around a cawl as shown in the drawing. (Again, using unseasoned, "green" stock will help prevent the splitting

and splintering that may occur with kiln-dried stock.)

While the stock is still slightly damp, remove it from the cawl and fasten it in place with wood screws to the back uprights and the seat. Bore holes in the underside and fit the side spindles (P) in place at the same time. Then clamp down solidly from the arms to the seat bottom and leave the clamps on until the wood dries thoroughly.

The Tray

Cut the bottom part of the tray (R) from ½-inch stock using a band saw (see detail). Then cut the long strip of ½ × ⅝-inch stock (S) that will make up the outer edge of the top of the tray. This should be cut longer than needed; the excess will be cut off later. Soak and bend this strip to the outer shape of the tray, but before it has a chance to dry completely, fasten it in place with glue and clamps. Drive wood screws up from the bottom edge into the bent piece to hold it securely. Cut the back edge strip (T) and soak, bend, and install it in the same manner.

Then soak and bend the upper arm portion of the strip to the shape shown. Cut to length, round the ends and then bore holes for the holding screws. The spacers (U) are rounded on the inside to accept the shape of the uprights. Turn the outer spacer blocks; bore the screws holes in them. Fasten the tray to the chair using round head wood screws with washers between the spacers and the inside of the tray arms.

Finishing

Sand all parts of the chair as smooth as possible and apply finishing coats. Lacquer is a good choice because it can easily be sprayed onto curved surfaces. Give at least two coats of lacquer, then buff with steel wool.

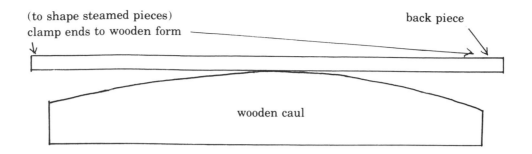

(to shape steamed pieces)
clamp ends to wooden form

back piece

wooden caul

Arm Detail

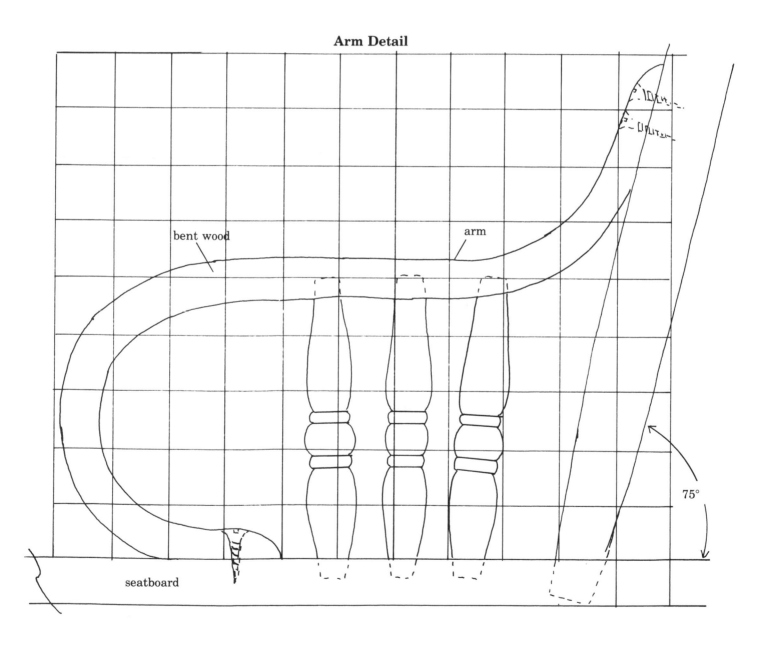

bent wood

arm

seatboard

75°

Tray 1″ squares

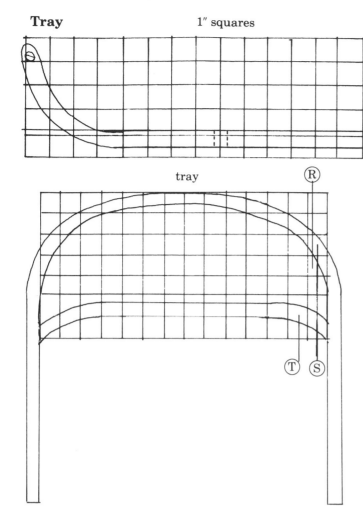

tray Ⓡ

Ⓣ Ⓢ

wooden spacer turned on lathe

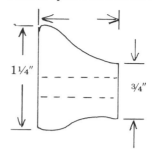

1¼″ ¾″

Caning

The cane for this project is pre-woven cane available in sheet form. The seat requires a single square foot of cane. Allow the cane and spline to soak for several hours in warm water before use.

Put the cane down over the grooved circle in the seat bottom. Start the end of the spline at the back for the seat, tapping it down over the cane, forcing the cane and spline down into the groove. Then, using a wooden block which has been cut down to the thickness of the spline, force the spline and cane in place. Do this by tapping lightly with a hammer on the edge of the wooden driver.

Don't try to seat the cane and spline in the bottom of the groove at this time; try to force it only about halfway down. Go entirely around the groove, tapping the spline into the groove until you get back to the starting point. Next, cut the excess portion of the spline away using a sharp chisel. Tap the end down to meet the starting end of the spline. Tap the spline and cane completely into the bottom of the groove using the wooden driver and hammer.

Then, using a sharp utility knife or razor, cut away the excess caning that is outside the edge of the spline. Run a slight bead of white glue around the outside edge, wipe smooth with a cloth, and allow to dry. Then give the chair several more coats of lacquer to finish it completely.

Materials List

A—Front legs—1¾ × 1¾ × 23″, 2 req'd.
B—Back legs—1¾ × 1¾ × 22″, 2 req'd.
C—Bottom side stretchers—⅝ round × 12″, 2 req'd.
D—Top side stretchers—⅝ round × 10″, 2 req'd.
E—Bottom rear stretcher—⅝ round × 13½″, 1 req'd.
F—Top rear stretcher—⅝ round × 13″, 1 req'd.
G—Bottom front stretcher—¾ round × 13½″, 1 req'd.
H—Foot board—½ × 2½ × 14″, 1 req'd.
I—Foot board supports—½″ dowel × 2½″, 2 req'd.
J—Back uprights—1¾ × 1¾ × 20″, 2 req'd.
K—Seatboard, front—¾ × 3 × 14″, 1 req'd.
L—Seatboard, back—¾ × 3 × 12″, 1 req'd.
M—Seatboard, sides—¾ × 5 × 7″, 2 req'd.
N—Upper back—½ × 6 × 15″, bent to shape, 1 req'd.
O—Back spindles—¾ × ¾ × 14½″, 5 req'd.
P—Side spindles—¾ × ¾ × 6″, 6 req'd.
Q—Arms—½ × 1½ × 26″, bent to shape and shaped, 2 req'd.
R—Tray bottom—½ × 6 × 14″, 1 req'd.
S—Tray outer rim—½ × ¾ × 54″, 1 req'd.
T—Tray inner rim—½ × ¾ × 16″, 1 req'd.
U—Spacers—¾ × ¾ × 1¼″, 2 req'd.
V—Cane for bottom—1 squared foot, spline as needed.

Drop-Leaf Desk and Bookcase

Circa 1920

Typical of the American manufactured furniture of the early 1900s, this oak desk and bookcase combination is very popular with nostalgic furniture buffs. It is so popular, several different styles and sizes have been offered through various kit furniture companies and through unfinished furniture outlets. The original pieces were usually made of oak, but they look good in walnut or even pine when it has a dark, antique-looking finish.

Construction

Construction of the piece is straightforward, and glued dado joints are used throughout. The dadoes are stopped back from the front edge on both sides and at the center divider section. The back is solid stock, although you may wish to substitute plywood. If so, you only need to use solid stock for the upper decorative part on the left side and the carved portion that holds the mirror on the right side.

Sides

Begin by enlarging the square drawing and making patterns to cut the two exterior sides (A,C) and the center side/divider (B) to shape. Note that the center side/divider is ¾-inch narrower front to back than the two sides. This is to compensate for the thickness of the back pieces. Cut ⅜-inch-deep by ¾-inch rabbets on the inside back edge of each side piece to accept the back. Use a router or radial arm or table saw.

Now make the stopped dadoes in the sides and the side/divider. Note that these are stopped ¾ inch from the front edge on each one except at the right-hand desk top (G), which is stopped 2½ inches back.

Shelves

Cut the left side shelves and top (D) to the correct length and width, making notches on the outside front corners for the stopped dadoes. Then shape the front of the top piece using a shaper or router. Cut the three shelves (D) to the correct size and shape.

Bottom

Then cut the left bottom piece (E) to the correct length. There are two bottom pieces, one for each side, and they both fit into dadoes in the center side/divider. Cut the opposite, right-hand bottom piece (F) to size and shape as well.

Drawer Support/Facers

Cut the drawer support/facers (I,J) to size and shape. The moulded front edge of the top one must be done with a shaper or router. Then make notches on their front corners to allow them to fit into the stopped dadoes.

Drop Lid

After cutting the drop lid (DD) to the proper size and shape, enlarge the squared drawing and carve the front to the pattern. Note that the carving is a simplified form of chip carving with the background cut down and stippled with a hand stamp. The end of a new nail set makes an excellent stipple maker for the background.

Note that the drop lid has a hardwood spline fitted in a dado in each end to strengthen it.

Backs

Cut the left back (K) to size and shape from glued-up solid stock. Or if you prefer, dowel a section of solid stock to the top of a piece of plywood to make up this portion. Cut the shaped edge on the back using a band or sabre saw.

Then make up the right back (L). As can be seen in the picture, the exposed portion consists of a solid stock frame to hold the mirror. It consists of uprights and crosspieces, held together with glue and a tongue-and-groove or dowelled joint. For the right back piece, the first step is to make up the joints. Then fit them together without glue and mark the outline of the opening for the mirror. Cut the mirror opening to size with a band saw or sabre saw. Then glue together the pieces to make up the frame.

Allow the glue to set overnight. Then remove from the clamps and cut the outside to the correct shape by following a pattern made from the squared drawing. Cut the decorative edging for the mirror opening using a router or shaper. Then rout out a groove on the back edge to hold the mirror. Transfer the carving pattern onto the piece and carve the decorative top portion to this design. Note that the background is also stippled.

Doors

Enlarge the squared drawing for the right-hand solid door (P) and cut it to shape on a band saw or with a sabre saw.

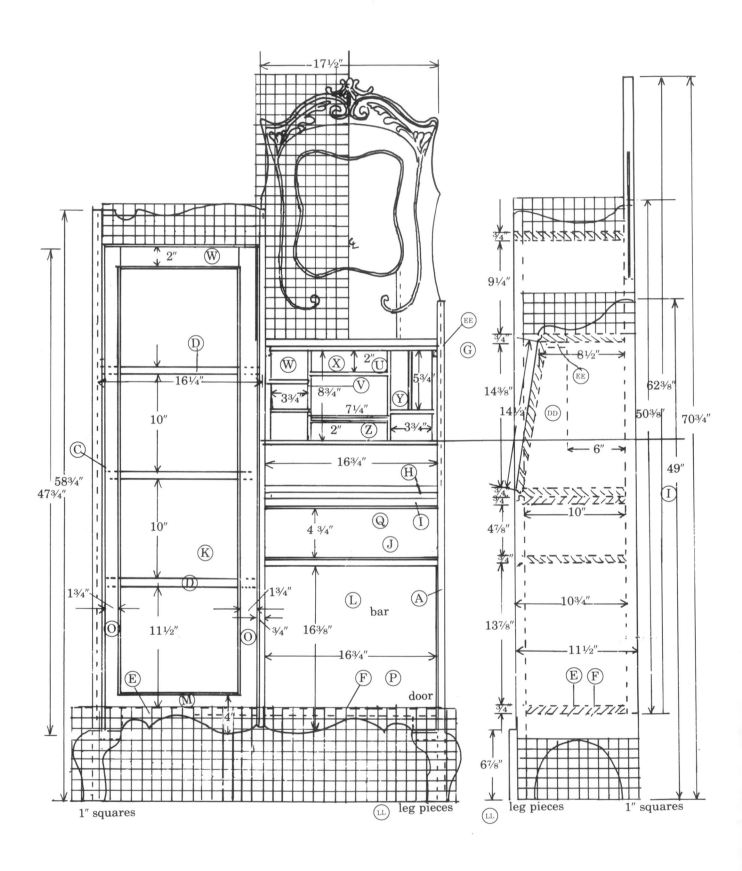

Drop Lid Carving (half pattern)

1″ squares

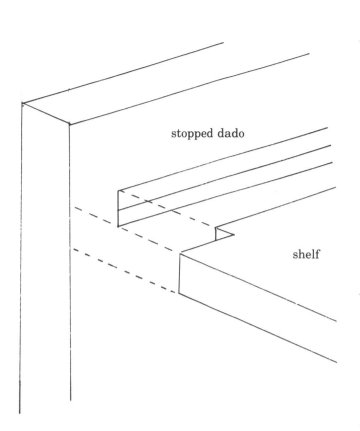

stopped dado

shelf

The left-hand door is a frame made of solid stock held together with a cabinet joint. Cut these joints on the ends of the stiles (O) and rails (M,N) using a shaper and a cabinet-joint cutter set. Then glue and clamp overnight. Make sure the door frame is square. It should not be twisted or buckled in any way and should be flat against the clamp bars as well.

After the glue has set, remove the door frame from the clamps, enlarge the squared drawing for the bottom rail, and cut it to shape on a band saw or with a sabre saw. Use a router to cut rabbets on the inside for the glass and glass-retainer strips.

Legs

Enlarge the square drawing for the leg pieces (LL) and cut them to shape and size on a band saw or with a sabre saw.

Mirror Installation

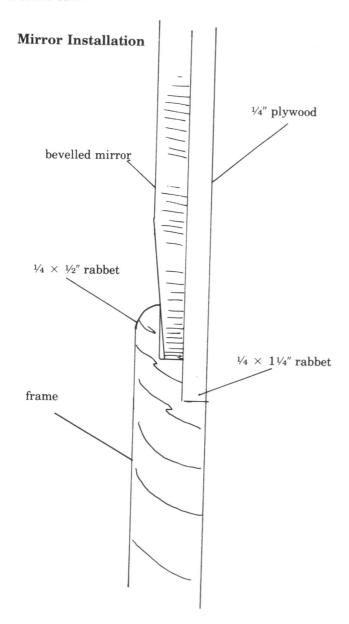

¼″ plywood

bevelled mirror

¼ × ½″ rabbet

¼ × 1¼″ rabbet

frame

Door Glass Retainer Detail

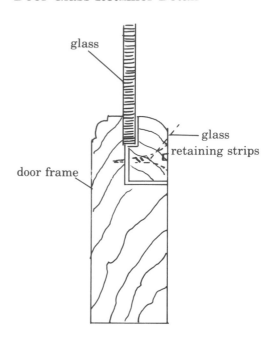

glass

glass
retaining strips

door frame

Assembly

Assembly is quite easy once you have all the parts on hand. The first step is to place glue on the edges of the left-hand shelves (D), the left-hand top piece (D) and the left-hand bottom piece (E). Then insert them into dadoes cut in the left-hand side.

Put the side/divider (B) in place over the opposite ends of the shelves, tops, and bottoms, fitting all pieces firmly into the dadoes.

Then fit the right-hand top (G), bottom (F), inside desk top (H) and the drawer support/facers (I,J) into dadoes in the side/divider. Install the right-hand side next.

Use a carpenter's square to ensure that the entire case is square, and clamp the front edge securely in place.

Place glue in the rabbets of the side/divider and top and position the left-hand back (K) in place. Install the right-hand back (L) in the same manner, then clamp the back of the case. Allow the entire assembly to remain in the clamps overnight. Then drive screws from the back into the sides and side/divider, as well as into the shelves, tops, and bottoms.

Drawer

Construct the drawer according to specifications. Note that it consists of a dovetailed front (Q) and side pieces (R) that overlap the back (S). The back fits into dadoes in the sides and the bottom is held in a dado in the front and sides.

Hang the right-hand lower door (P) with 1½-inch brass butt hinges mortised into the side and door. Install the wooden knob and a catch on the inside.

Fasten the front-leg pieces in place with wood

screws driven from the back of glue blocks and from the inside edges of the side legs.

Pigeonhole
Construct the pigeonhole (U-Y) and drawer unit (Z-CC). The pieces are held in dadoes with glue and the small drawer is simply glued up.

Finishing
Sand, stain and finish the pieces to suit, including the unhung left-hand door and the drop lid. Then install the bevelled mirror pieces.

Install the pigeonhole unit with screws through its top into the underside of the right-hand top piece (G).

Mount the drop lid (DD) in place using drop-lid hinges mortised to the front of the inside desk top (H) and the inside of the drop lid. Then install drop-lid supports, top lock, and knob. Note that there is a small holding stop block (EE) glued to each upper corner on the inside of the desk to stop the drop lid from going too far back into the desk. Its front surface should be just flush with the outside of the side piece.

Install knobs on the drawer and slide in place. Put the glass in the door for the left-hand side using small glass-retainer strips held in place with wood screws. Then hang the door and install the locking door catch.

Materials List
A—Right side—¾ × 11½ × 49", 1 req'd.
B—Center/side divider—¾ × 10¾ × 52", l req'd.
C—Left side—¾ × 11½ × 58¾", 1 req'd.
D—Left side shelves and top—¾ × 10¾ × 16¼", 4 req'd.
E—Left bottom—¾ × 10 × 16⅛", 1 req'd.
F—Right bottom—¾ × 10 × 16⅞", 1 req'd.
G—Right top—¾ × 8½ × 17½", 1 req'd.
H—Inside desk top—¾ × 10 × 17½", 1 req'd.
I—Top drawer facer—¾ × 10¾ × 17½", 1 req'd.
J—Bottom drawer support facer—¾ × 10¾ × 17½", 1 req'd.
K—Left back—¾ × 16¼ × 50⅜", 1 req'd.
L—Right back—¾ × 17½ × 62⅜", 1 req'd.
LL—Leg pieces—¾ × 6 × 7", 4 req'd.

Doors
M—Rail—¾ × 4 × 12½", cut to size, 1 req'd.
N—Rail—¾ × 2 × 12½", cut to size, 1 req'd.
O—Stiles—¾ × 1¾ × 47¾", 2 req'd.
P—Right door—¾ × 16⅜ × 16¾", 1 req'd.

Pigeonhole Drawer
Q—Front—¾ × 4¾ × 16⅝", 1 req'd.
R—Sides—½ × 4¾ × 10½", 2 req'd.
S—Back—½ × 4¼ × 16⅛", 1 req'd.
T—Bottom—¼ × 9¾ × 16⅛", 1 req'd.

Pigeonhole
U—Bottom and top—¼ × 6 × 16¾", 2 req'd.
V—Vertical dividers and ends—¼ × 6 × 9", 4 req'd.
W—Horizontals—¼ × 4 × 6", 3 req'd.
X—Center horizontals—¼ × 6 × 7½", 2 req'd.
Y—Right vertical divider—¼ × 6 × 6", 1 req'd.

Drawer
Z—Drawer front—¼ × 1⅞ × 7⅛", 1 req'd.
AA—Drawer back—¼ × 1⅝ × 7⅛", 1 req'd.
BB—Drawer sides—¼ × 1⅝ × 5½", 2 req'd.
CC—Drawer bottom—¼ × 5¼ × 7⅛", 1 req'd.

Drop Lid
DD—Lid—¾ × 14½ × 16⅝", 1 req'd.
EE—Drop lid stops—½ × ½ × 2", 2 req'd.

Hardware
Wooden knobs—4 req'd.
Drop-lid hinges—1 pair req'd.
Drop-lid support—1 pair req'd.
Brass butt hinges—1½", 5 req'd.
Drop-lid lock—1 req'd.
Door latch lock—1 req'd.
Bevelled mirror—13 × 13", cut to shape, 1 req'd.
Glass—12½ × 42½", 1 req'd.

Pie Safe

Circa 1920

Atypical example of manufactured furniture of the early 1900s, this pine pie safe was made in Boston. Pie safes are very popular reproduction furniture pieces and are offered through many mail order kit furniture companies.

The safe shown here features punched wood panels, applied mouldings, and etched glass for the front panels. The etched glass doors add a "Victorian" touch and help make this a fine example of manufactured furniture styling.

Although it is made of pine and finished with a light stain, it would also look good in a dark antique stain. Oak could also be used. I have seldom seen pie safes made of more expensive woods, such as walnut, although these woods could be used.

Construction
Construction is the frame-and-panel system that was popular with the period. It is fairly simple and results in a sturdy, durable piece of furniture.

Upright Posts
Construction starts with the upright posts. The back posts (B) are cut to size and a ⅜-inch rabbet is cut into their inside back edges for the ⅜-inch plywood back. You could also make the back of the frames and panels to match the sides, as was done with the original. Here the back fits in a groove towards the back of the inside face of the post. However, the plywood back is probably a more practical approach for many. In any case, cut the groove ¼ inch from the outside corner on the front face of the post. This is for the side panel stiles.

Now cut the front posts (A) to correct size. Round their front edges with a router or shaper. Cut the ¼ × ¼-inch grooves into the inside front faces and the back faces.

Side Panels
The side panel is made of four ¾-inch-thick rails (D-G), three ¼-inch plywood panels (H-J) and two stiles (C). Top and bottom edges of panels fit in grooves cut into edges of the rails; side edges of panels and tongues on rails fit in grooves in the stiles. These frame assemblies fit into the upright front and back posts (A,B).

The first step is to cut rails (D-G) to the correct size. Then use a dado head in a table or radial arm saw to cut grooves in their upper and lower edges.

Use a dado head to cut tongues on each end to fit into the posts. Note that upper and lower exposed edges of rails must be lightly rounded. Use a router or shaper.

Cut panels (H-J) to size. Upper panels (H,I) have holes bored in them to provide ventilation. Make up a pattern for the holes (see drawing) and trace it onto the panels. Then bore the holes using a ³⁄₁₆-inch bit.

Make the upright stiles (C) for the sides, and cut a tongue on their outside edges to fit into the grooves in the posts (A,B). Then make a groove on their inside edges to accept the rails and panels. Use a band saw or sabre saw to shape decorative lower ends of stiles as shown in the drawing.

Front Facers
Saw front facers (K,L) to size and make tongues on their ends to fit into the front posts (A). Cut a ⅜ × ¾-inch rabbet in the inside face of the bottom facer (L) to accept the bottom (N). Then rout a ¼-inch groove in the bottom edge of the bottom facer for the lower front bracket (BB) tongues to fit up into.

Interior Partitions
Make up the bottom (N) to the correct size. Unless you use plywood, you will have to glue this up from small pieces to get the needed width. Here, plywood is an acceptable choice because none of the edges are exposed. The bottom drawer support (R) and inside upper bottom (U) must all be notched to fit around the posts.

Cut the shelves (P,X), upper bottom (U) and the drawer support. They are all the same size and shape (and the drawer support is solid, one-piece). Cut the side support cleats (O-Q-S-V-Y) to size and shape. Install the drawer glides (T).

Back
Cut the back (M) to the correct size, or make it up from panels and rails, if preferred.

Assembly
Assembly of the unit starts with the side panels. Work from top to bottom and, for the moment, do not use any glue. Starting with top rail (D), insert the panel (H) in it, then position the next rail (E) over the lower edge of the panel. Now follow with a second panel (I), the next rail (F), the bottom panel (J), and the bottom rail (G). Next, place glue on tongues

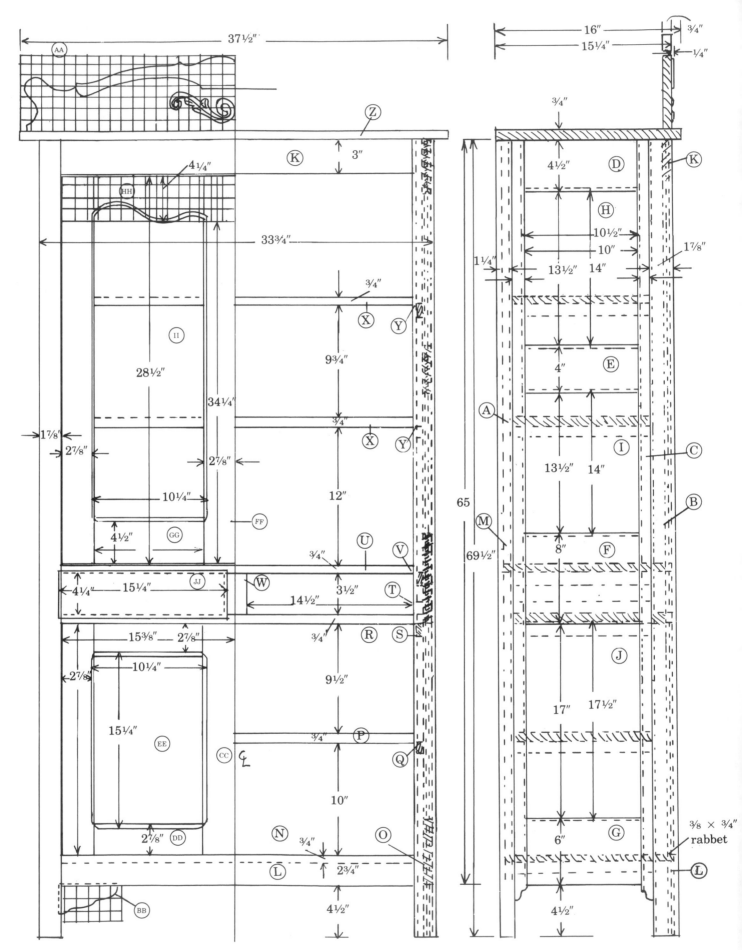

Ventilating Holes for Upper Panels

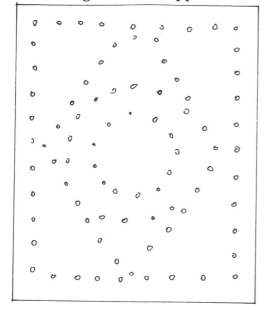

both assemblies, and allow the glue to set for several hours. When clamping make sure you don't damage the thin tongues on the stiles. Clamp lightly, and only until the glue sets. Then remove the clamps, glue the tongues of the stiles, fit them into grooves in front and back posts (A,B) and clamp securely overnight.

Remove sides from the clamps and mark the location of the shelf, bottom, and drawer support cleats (O,Q,S,Y). Fasten these to the inside face of the side stiles (C) with glue and screws. Mark the location of the bottom front facer (L) on both side assemblies, glue the ends of facer tenons, and fit them into grooves on the front posts. Then slide the top facer (K) into place in the same manner and clamp both lightly in place. Make sure the upper edge of the top facer is flush with the ends of the posts. Clamp top and bottom facers lightly in place.

(*Note:* If you choose to use a frame-and-panel back, it will have to be installed at the same time the facer pieces are installed.)

Make sure the unit is square, then place on the front under edge of the bottom (N) and position it in the rabbet in the lower front facer. Fasten the bottom in place with screws through its front edge into the lower facer and with screws driven down into the side support cleats.

Glue the lower front bracket tongues (BB) and insert into the bottom front facer and front posts.

of the rails. Do not glue any part of the panel edges, either in the rails or the stiles. Position the stiles (C) over tongues of the rails and the protruding edges of the panels. Make sure the assembly is square. The top ends of stiles should be flush with the upper edge of the top rail.

Do the other side panel in the same manner; clamp

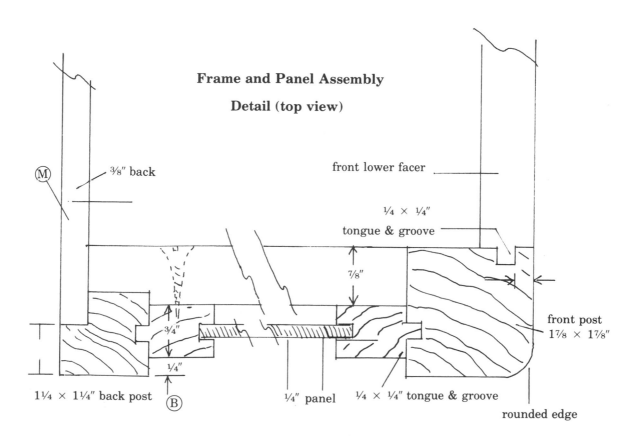

Frame and Panel Assembly

Detail (top view)

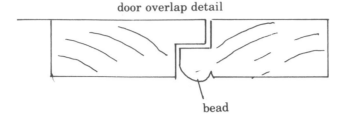

door overlap detail

bead

Fasten the bottom shelf (P) in place with screws driven up through the side cleats.

Install the drawer support (R) in the same manner, followed by the center facer (W) and inside upper bottom (U). Then saw the small center to size, and glue and screw it in place. Drive screws through from the underside of the drawer support and from the top of the inside upper bottom.

Install the upper shelves by fastening with screws through the side shelf supports.

Cut the top (Z) to the correct size and install it with screws driven down into the front top facer and upper side rails (D). Install the back (M) with glue and screws.

Bottom Doors

The doors are frame-and-panel joined with a simulated cabinet joint. This is done by simply cutting a groove in the end of each stile (CC) and tongues to fit on each rail (DD). Then glue the frames together. After they have been glued together, rout out an edge on the back for the ¼-inch panel and shape the outside edge on a shaper. Insert the wood panel (EE) and fasten in place with small brass butt hinges and install the lock and wood locking knob.

Both the upper and lower doors have overlapping adjoining edges with a small bead cut on the right-hand door. This is done by using a router and router table.

Upper Doors

Construct the upper doors in the same manner as the lower doors, cutting grooves in the stiles (FF) and matching tongues on the rails (GG,HH). Then enlarge the squared drawing and cut the upper rails (HH) to the correct shape.

Assemble with glue and clamps and allow the glue to set. Then rout out a recess on the back for the glass (II) and glass-holding wood strips. Shape the front edges on a shaper or with a router. Hang doors with brass butt hinges and install the knob and lock.

Drawers

Make the drawers using a ⅜-inch lip on the front piece (JJ) with overlapping joinery on front and back. The bottom (MM) is ¼-inch hardboard fitted in a ¼ × ¼-inch dado cut in the front and sides (KK), and extends past the bottom edge of the back (LL).

Top Board

Enlarge the squared drawing for the top board (AA) and cut it to shape using a band saw. Then cut the thin upper decorative scroll piece to shape on a band saw and fasten it to the edge with glue and screws driven from the back. Carve (or purchase) the applied moulding for the center and fasten it with glue and small screws from the back. Make sure you don't break or mar the carving with the screws. The top board is installed with small angle irons and screws, so it can be removed if necessary.

Install the glass and drawer hardware after staining and finishing.

Materials List

A—Front posts—1⅞ × 1⅞ × 69½", 2 req'd.
B—Back posts—1¼ × 1¼ × 69½", 2 req'd.
   Sides
C—Stiles—¾ × 1 × 66½", 4 req'd.
D—Rails—¾ × 4½ × 10½", 2 req'd.
E—Rails—¾ × 4 × 10½", 2 req'd.
F—Rails—¾ × 8 × 10½", 2 req'd.
G—Rails—¾ × 6 × 10½", 2 req'd.
H—Panels—¼ × 10½ × 14", 2 req'd.
I—Panels—¼ × 10½ × 14", 2 req'd.
J—Panels—¼ × 10½ × 17½", 2 req'd.
K—Front facer—¾ × 3 × 31¼", 1 req'd.
L—Bottom front facer—¾ × 3 × 31¼", 1 req'd.
M—Back—⅜ × 33¾ × 65", 1 req'd.
N—Bottom—¾ × 14⅜ × 31¾", 1 req'd.
O—Bottom side support cleats—⅞ × 1 × 14", cut to fit, 2 req'd.
P—Bottom shelf—¾ × 14⅜ × 31¾", 1 req'd.
Q—Bottom shelf side support cleats—⅞ × 1 × 14", cut to fit, 2 req'd.
R—Drawer support—¾ × 14⅜ × 31¾", 1 req'd.
S—Drawer side support cleats—⅞ × 1 × 14", cut to fit, 2 req'd.
T—Drawer glides—⅞ × 1 × 14", cut to fit, 2 req'd.
U—Upper bottom—¾ × 14⅜ × 31¾", 1 req'd.

Drawer Detail

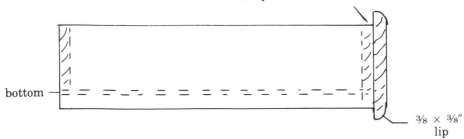

overlap sides and front

bottom —

⅜ × ⅜″
lip

V—Upper bottom side support cleats—⅞ × 1 × 14″, cut to fit, 2 req'd.

W—Center facer—¾ × 2 × 3½″, 1 req'd.

X—Shelves—¾ × 14⅜ × 31¾″, 2 req'd.

Y—Shelf side support cleats—⅞ × 1 × 14″, cut to fit, 4 req'd.

Z—Top—¾ × 16 × 37½″, 1 req'd.

AA—Top board—¾ × 6½ × 36″, 1 req'd.

BB—Lower front brackets—¾ × 3 × 6″, 2 req'd.

Lower Doors

CC—Stiles—¾ × 2⅞ × 20¼″, 4 req'd.

DD—Rails—¾ × 2⅞ × 10¼″, 4 req'd.

EE—Panels—¼ × 10¼ × 15¼″, 2 req'd.

Upper Doors

FF—Stiles—¾ × 2⅞ × 34¼″, 4 req'd.

GG—Bottom rails—¾ × 4½ × 10¼″, 2 req'd.

HH—Top rails—¾ × 4¼ × 10¼″, 2 req'd.

II—Glass—10¼ × 28″, 2 req'd.

Drawers

JJ—Front—¾ × 4¼ × 15¼″, 2 req'd.

KK—Sides—½ × 3⅜ × 13″, 4 req'd.

LL—Backs—½ × 3 × 13⅜″, 2 req'd.

MM—Bottoms—¼ × 13¼ × 13⅞″, 2 req'd.

Kitchen Cupboard

Circa 1900

This project is a two-piece kitchen cupboard, dough board, flour storage, and plate and glassware cabinet. It is both practical and simple in design and makes an attractive display piece. The fact that the cupboard shown here was made of walnut, rather than oak, makes this particular piece unusual. In fact, the top cutting and mixing surface is made of walnut, and there are many knife and "use" marks in the beautifully grained wood. The piece would also look quite good in oak or even antiqued pine, although when using pine you probably should make the cutting top of a hardwood such as maple.

Construction

As with any piece of this size, there are two sections: a base and an upper cabinet joined to it. Construction starts with the base.

Legs

The first step is to enlarge the squared drawing for the legs (A) and make a pattern for the turned, bottom portion of the legs. Cut the legs to the correct length and size. Note that you may have to glue up stock to make legs to the thickness needed. After cutting to rough size, run the legs over a jointer to smooth their surfaces. Mark the center on both ends of the stock, then slightly round all corners using a shaper or router. Once this has been done, turn the bottom portion on a lathe.

Aprons

Cut the back (C) and side aprons (B) and the front facers (D,E,F) to the correct size and shape. (Note that the front piece is constructed of several pieces joined as shown.) The front, back, and side pieces are fastened to the legs using pinned mortises. The first step is to cut tenons on these pieces; then cut mortises in the legs to fit.

Assembly

Smear glue on the ends of the tenons of one side piece and fit them into mortises in the legs. Position and clamp the pieces securely. Make sure the legs are square with the bottom edge of the side. Do the other side assembly in the same manner, and allow the glue to set overnight.

Front Assembly

Fasten the side facers (E) to the front facer (D) using glue and dowels. Install the center back support strip (N) with glue and screws. Make the breadboard slot by using a drill for starting holes at the ends and then a coping or sabre saw to complete the cut.

Construct the center facer (F) assembly as shown in the center facer detail and fasten it securely to the front facer. The support strips (N) are installed at this time. Note that the front of the divider strip is rounded. This is done with a moulding head on a table saw. Or you can use a shaper to round the edge of a piece of stock. The edge is then ripped off to the proper thickness. Backer strips that fit between the center facer and sides of the drawer openings are glued and screwed to the back of the rounded decorative divider strip. Then the entire unit is screwed and glued in place on the front facer.

Bottom Framework Assembly

Once the facer has been assembled and the glue has set, remove side and front pieces from the clamps and assemble the bottom framework on a smooth, flat surface. Place glue on the tenons of the back (C) and front assembly and insert into mortises in the legs. Tap together with a soft wooden mallet and clamp securely overnight. Make sure the entire assembly is square. It shouldn't rock or tilt on one leg, and legs should be square and flush with the tops of the back, side, and front pieces.

Pinning the Mortises and Tenons

After all the joints have set, use a sharp chisel to cut away any glue runs. Then bore dowel holes through the legs from the back so that they do not show and insert wooden dowels to pin the joints together.

Make wood glue blocks and fasten them to the inside top edges of the sides with glue and screws.

Drawer and Cutting Board Glides

Cut the drawer and cutting board glides (G-L) to the correct shape and size and fasten them in place to the front assembly using glue blocks. Fasten to the back of the unit in the same manner, or you can use flat-head screws driven in from the back, countersunk and covered with wood plugs.

You will note that the upper drawer glides that hold the cutting board in place also are a tilt strip for the drawers below, preventing them from tipping down when pulled out. The center support strip (N) behind the center facer (F) runs up to just under the cutting board to provide extra strength to this part

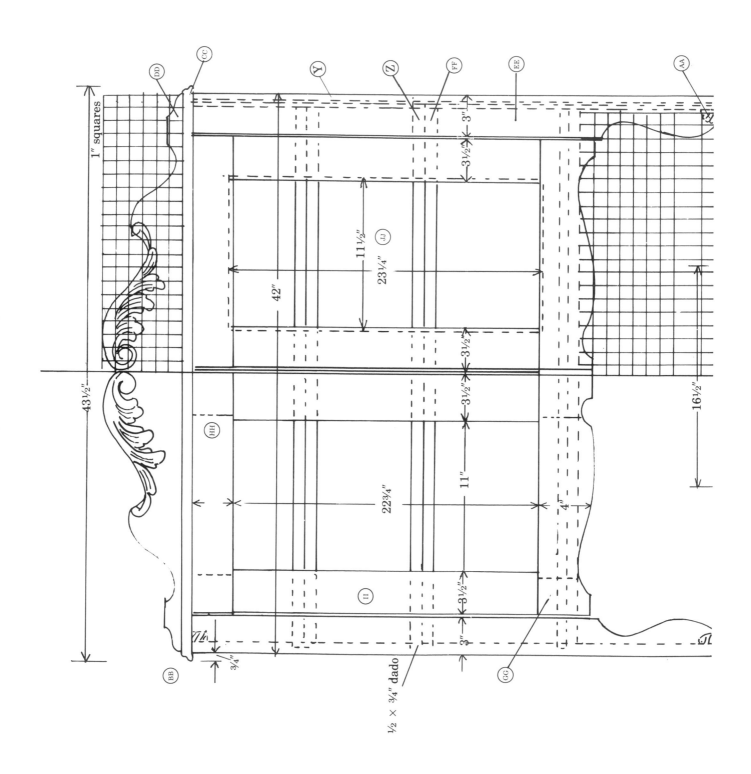

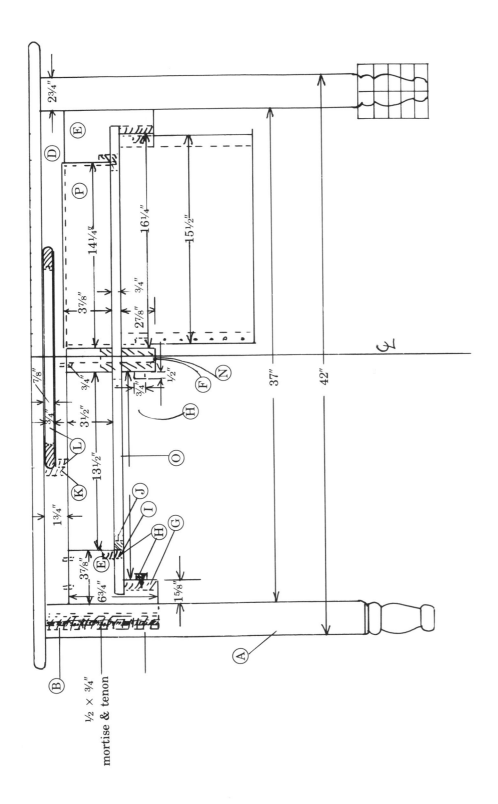

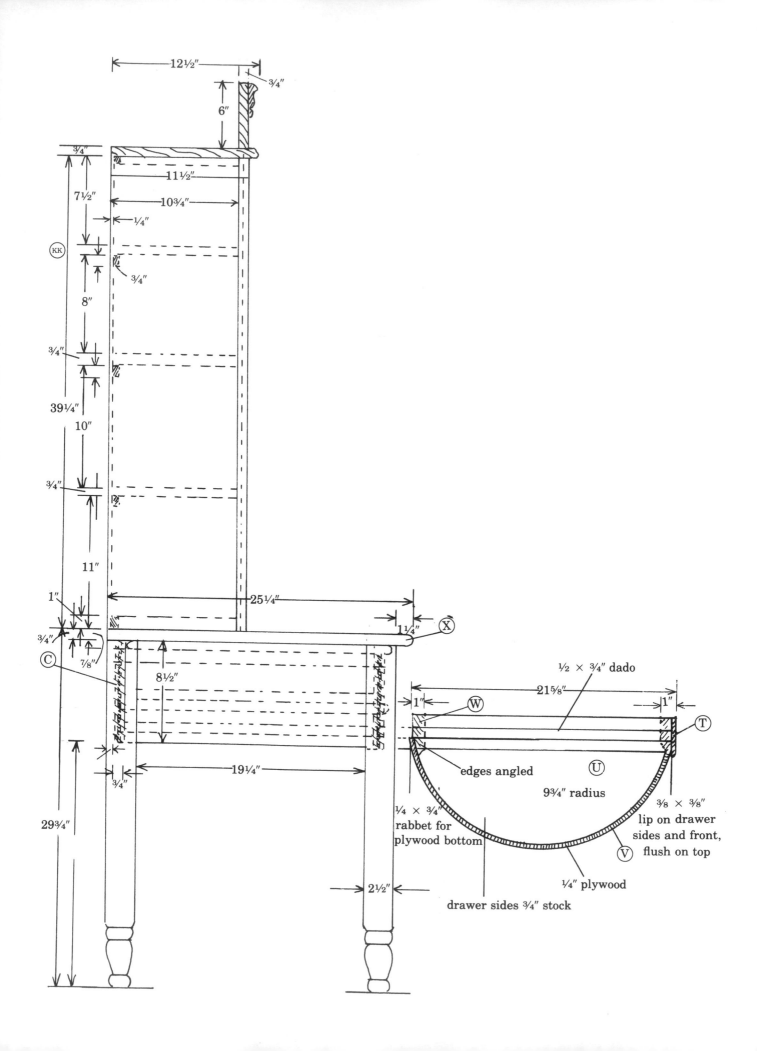

12½"

¾"

6"

¾"

7½"

10¾"

¼"

KK

¾"

8"

¾"

39¼"

10"

¾"

11"

1"

25¼"

1¼"

X

¾"

C

7⁄8"

8½"

½ × ¾" dado

21⁵⁄8"

1"

W

1"

T

edges angled

U

9¾" radius

19¼"

¾"

¼ × ¾"
rabbet for
plywood bottom

⅜ × ⅜"
lip on drawer
sides and front,
flush on top

V

29¾"

¼" plywood

2½"

drawer sides ¾" stock

Leg and Apron Mortise and Tenon

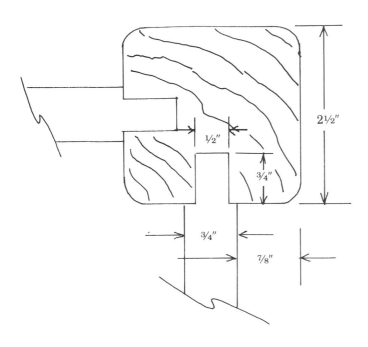

of the front facer. Make sure you get the back ends of the drawer slides properly positioned so that when drawers are inserted they will fit flush and won't tilt to one side or the other.

Top

As mentioned earlier, if you are using a softwood for this project, you may want to make up the top from maple to provide a hard cutting surface. In any case, dowel and glue up stock to make the wide top, sand the top and bottom smooth with a belt sander, follow with a finishing sander, and then lightly round all edges and corners. Position it on the bottom assembly so that the back edge of the top is flush with the back edges of the legs. Fasten it in place with screws driven up through glue blocks on the sides and through the cutting board holding strips (K). Make sure you don't allow the screws to protrude through the surface of the top.

Cutting Board

Assemble this part (M) as shown in the cutting board detail. First use waterproof glue to put together lengthwise pieces with tongue-and-groove joints. Allow these pieces to remain clamped overnight. Then cut tenons on the ends of the glued-up

Center Facer Detail (seen from back)

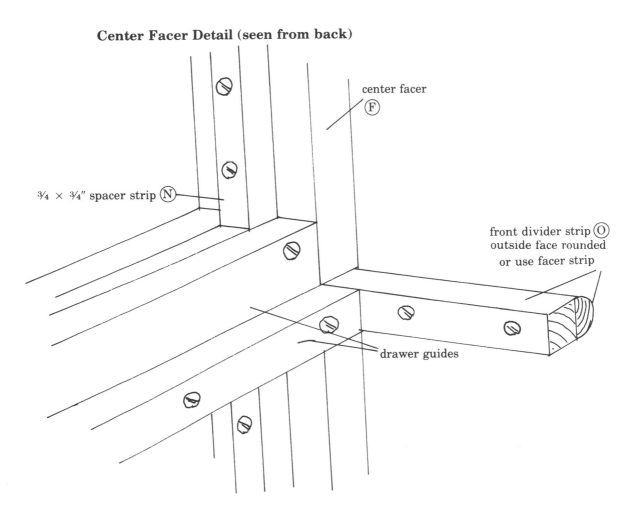

Cutting Board Detail

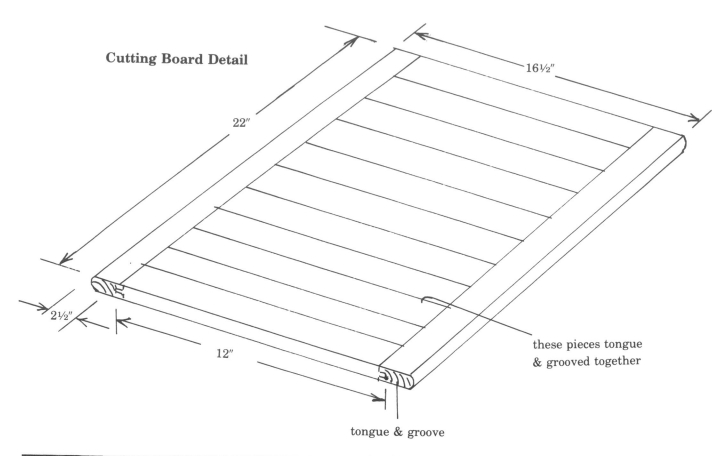

22"

16½"

2½"

12"

these pieces tongue
& grooved together

tongue & groove

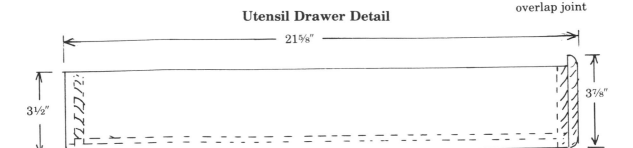

21⅝″

3½″   3⅞″

¼″ bottom ¼″ from bottom edge

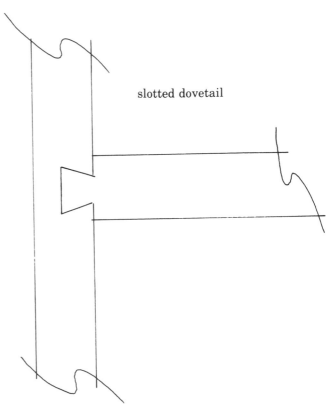

slotted dovetail

sections and a groove in a matching piece of stock to cap the ends. Glue and clamp these together, again using waterproof glue. After letting the glue set overnight, remove the clamps and sand all glue lines using a belt sander, followed by a finishing sander. Finally, round all edges using a shaper or router.

Utensil Drawers
The top silverware drawers are fairly standard in construction. They consist of ¾-inch front pieces with a ⅜-inch lip on top and both sides. The bottom is flush to fit against the ¾-inch rounded front divider strip (O). The sides (Q) are ½-inch material dovetailed to the drawer fronts. The bottom (S) fits in dadoes cut in the sides. Then the back (R) is installed. There is a typical silverware divider tray in each drawer.

Flour Bin Drawers
The bottom drawers are quite unusual and were used to hold flour, vegetables, etc. They are made by creating drawer fronts (T) similar to the utensil drawer fronts (P). These are joined to ¾-inch-thick sides (U). Make a pattern for the sides and cut them to shape on a band saw. Then cut the ¾-inch-wide × ½-inch-deep dadoes in the upper sides to fit the drawer slides, already fastened to the cabinet. The bottoms (V) are ⅛-inch plywood bent around the bottoms of the drawer sides and nailed in place. You could also utilize copper if you prefer. The ends fit in rabbets cut in the bottom of the drawer fronts and backs (W) as shown. The drawer sides, back, and front are held together with dovetails.

These unusual drawers can be used today as bread or vegetable bins. If they are to be used primarily for vegetables, you may want to bore a decorative pattern of holes in the sides to provide ventilation.

Construction of the Upper Cabinet
The top case construction is fairly simple. The first step is to cut the side pieces (Y), top (CC) and shelves (Z) to the correct size. The shelves are fitted with two plate grooves cut in them. The first is spaced 1¼ inches from the back, while the second is 3½ inches out from the back.

Note: The back (KK) on the original is frame-and-

panelled stock held in a dado in the back edge of the sides. But you may want to use ¼-inch hardwood-faced plywood to match the rest of the stock. In this case, you will need to cut a ¼ × ¼-inch rabbet, instead of the dado, on the inside back edge of both side pieces and the top.

The top and shelves are then installed in the mortised-in dadoes cut in the sides. (For a stronger joint you can utilize a slotted dovetail cut as shown on page 17.) *Note:* if you are using the back frames and panels, install them at this time.

Make sure that the case is clamped square and allow the glue to set. Then enlarge the squared drawings for the front facers (EE) and cut them to the correct size and shape using a band saw. Cut a groove into their back edges to accept the tongue cut on the front edge of the back side pieces. Then round their front outside edges on a shaper.

Cut the bottom glue blocks (AA) to proper size and shape and fasten to the bottom inside the pieces with

glue and screws. The screws can be covered over with wooden plugs if you wish. (*Note:* There are none on the original, but they will help hold the piece more securely in place.) Install top glue blocks (BB). Then fasten the front side facer in place by placing glue in the tongue-and-groove portion and on the bottom and top glue blocks. Wipe away all excess glue and allow to set overnight.

Top Carving

Enlarge the squared drawing for the top front piece (DD) and cut it to shape using a band saw. Sand thoroughly. Then enlarge the squared drawings for the carvings. Carve these on a separate block of wood to the shape shown, first roughing them out with a band saw. Then fasten them to the top front piece with glue and brads or with small screws through the back into the carving.

Fasten the top front piece in place with dowels and glue. Now put the upper cabinet on top of the base and fasten in place with brass round-head screws driven down through the glue blocks and into the top of the base. But make sure the upper cabinet is standing squarely in place first. You could also leave the top unattached for ease in moving.

Doors

The door frames are mortise-and-tenon assembly. Cut the pieces (GG-JJ) to the correct size, then cut the back rabbets on the inside edge of the doors and cut the glass-holding rabbets as well. Cut a bead on the outside edge of the right overlapping door using a shop-made scratch stock tool. Then cut the mortises and tenons. Glue and clamp the door pieces together.

Hang the doors using mortised butt hinges and put catches on the bottom shelf to hold them closed. Then put in the glass and secure it with small, glass-holding strips held in place with tiny screws or brads.

Install the hardware of your choice. The hardware on the original was unusual—a simple piece of wire bent as shown in the drawing and held in place with round head screws. You might prefer a more traditional hardware.

Stain and finish. A hand-rubbed oil finish will provide the best and most durable finish if you intend to put the cupboard to practical use.

Materials List
Base Cabinet

A—Legs—$2\frac{1}{2} \times 2\frac{1}{2} \times 29''$, 4 req'd.

B—Side aprons—$\frac{3}{4} \times 8\frac{1}{2} \times 20\frac{1}{2}''$, 2 req'd.

C—Back apron—$\frac{3}{4} \times 8\frac{1}{2} \times 38\frac{1}{2}''$, 1 req'd.

D—Front facer—$\frac{3}{4} \times 1\frac{3}{4} \times 38\frac{1}{2}''$, 1 req'd.

E—Side facers—$\frac{3}{4} \times 3\frac{7}{8} \times 6\frac{3}{4}''$, 2 req'd.

F—Center facer—$\frac{3}{4} \times 2\frac{1}{4} \times 6\frac{3}{4}''$, 1 req'd.

Drawer Glide Supports

G—$\frac{3}{4} \times 2\frac{1}{2} \times 17\frac{1}{4}''$, 4 req'd.

H—$\frac{3}{4} \times \frac{1}{2} \times 17\frac{1}{4}''$, 4 req'd.

Door Overlap

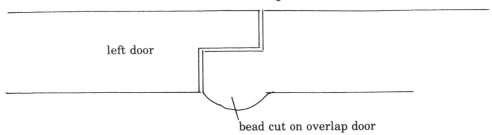

left door

bead cut on overlap door

Detail of Frame and Panel Construction for Back

Handmade Hardware

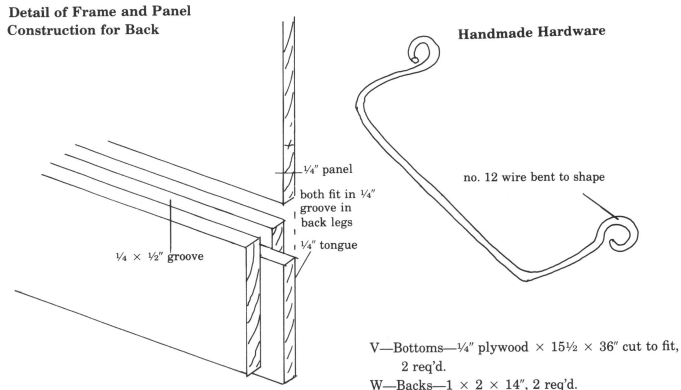

¼″ panel

both fit in ¼″ groove in back legs

¼″ tongue

¼ × ½″ groove

no. 12 wire bent to shape

I—¾ × 1½ × 17¼″, 2 req'd.

J—¾ × ½ × 17¼″, 4 req'd.

K—¾ × 1¾ × 17¼″, 2 req'd.

L—¾ × ⅞ × 17¼″, 2 req'd.

M—Cutting board, maple—glued up
    ¾ × 2 × 22″, 2 req'd.
    ¾ × 2 × 12″, 11 req'd.

N—Support strips, front & back—¾ × ¾ × 8½″, 2 req'd.

O—Front divider strip—¾ × 1¼ × 35″, 1 req'd.

Utensil Drawers

P—Fronts—¾ × 3⅞ × 14¼″, 2 req'd.

Q—Sides—½ × 3½ × 20″, 4 req'd.

R—Back—½ × 3 × 13½″, 2 req'd.

S—Bottom—½ × 13 × 19½″, 2 req'd.

Flour Bin Drawers

T—Fronts—¾ × 2⅞ × 16¼″, 2 req'd.

U—Sides—¾ × 9¾ × 21¼″, 4 req'd.

V—Bottoms—¼″ plywood × 15½ × 36″ cut to fit, 2 req'd.

W—Backs—1 × 2 × 14″, 2 req'd.

X—Top—¾ × 25¼ × 47½″, 1 req'd.

Top Cabinet

Y—Sides—¾ × 10¾ × 39¼″, 2 req'd.

Z—Shelves—¾ × 10½ × 41½″, 3 req'd.

AA—Bottom glue blocks—¾ × ¾ × 10½″, 2 req'd.

BB—Top glue blocks—¾ × 1½ × 10½″, 2 req'd.

CC—Top—¾ × 12½ × 43½″, 1 req'd.

DD—Top front piece—¾ × 6 × 42″, 1 req'd.

EE—Front side facers—¾ × 3 × 39¼″, 2 req'd.

Doors

GG—Bottom rails—¾ × 4 × 17½″, 2 req'd.

HH—Top rails—¾ × 3 × 17½″, 2 req'd.

II—Stiles—¾ × 3½ × 23¼″, 4 req'd.

JJ—Glass panels—11½ × 23¼″, 2 req'd.

KK—Back—¼″ plywood × 39½ × 41″, 1 req'd.

Curved-Glass China Cabinet

Circa 1900

This elegant curved-front china cabinet not only provides a touch of nostalgia, it also serves as an excellent display case for your favorite china or collectibles. The design of this project is typical of this type of cabinet that was popular during the early 1900s. The original cabinet was made in America from solid oak. The cabinet shown here, created by the author, is a simplified version without a lot of hand carving.

The curved glass side pieces are available by mail order from Hopcraft Glass Co. A price list and instructions for measuring and ordering the glass is available from them on request. The top back piece of the furniture features an "imitation" carved wood design using stamped-wood moulding. This is available from most wood supply mail-order houses.

The false bottom piece can be left unattached to make a secret hiding spot for valuables.

In some ways this is a rather challenging piece of woodwork. It is fairly complicated in the clamping and cutting procedures, but the cutting and shaping procedures are not especially difficult. So this would probably be a good piece of furniture for an intermediate woodworker to try.

The most important factor is proper clamping and gluing of the curved sections as they are being positioned on the top and bottom. If this is not done correctly, it will be extremely hard to mount the curved glass pieces. All joints are glued lap-and-mortise joints; so careful fitting of joints is extremely important. Also, the project requires the use of several power tools, including a shaper or router and a lathe.

Making Patterns

Enlarge the squared drawings for the top (A), bottom (B), the false top and bottom (O), inside support cleats (F) and the shelves (I). Then make full-size patterns for each. You will probably have to glue and dowel together stock to make it wide enough for the top and bottom pieces.

Cutting Pieces to Shape

Cut these pieces to shape and size using a band saw or sabre saw. Then sand all edges as smooth as possible using a disc sander. Note that shelves (I) are ⅜-inch-thick instead of ¾ of an inch. These must be run down to proper thickness using a planer. If you don't have a planer you can often get the building supply yard to do it for you. Cut a ¼ × ³⁄₁₆-inch-wide dado in the back top part of the shelves. This serves as a plate groove so the plates can be stood up against the back of the cabinet.

Then shape the bottom edge of the top piece (A), the top edge of the bottom piece (B) and both bottom and top edges of the shelves. Use a cove or ogee cutter in a shaper or router. Cut the false top and bottom pieces (O) ¼ inch narrower than the cabinet to allow for the ¼-inch plywood back.

Saw the ¾-inch-thick inside support cleats (F) to size and shape. Sand their edges smooth on a belt or disc sander and then glue and screw them in place on the top and bottom pieces using No. 8 × 1¼-inch flat-head wood screws countersunk in place. It's a good idea first to lay out the position of the pieces using a carpenter's square, to mark location of door opening, etc.

Curved Top and Bottom Apron

While the glue is drying on these pieces, cut the pieces for the curved sides (E). Make tenons on their ends to fit in the uprights (C,D). Then cut a ¼ × ½-inch rabbet on one of their inside edges (as shown in the drawing) to hold the glass. Next, make saw kerfs in the back of these pieces using a radial arm or table saw. These kerf cuts should come to within about ⅛ inch of the front of the piece and be ¼ inch apart. You will probably have to experiment a bit, and it may take several tries before you get them to bend without breaking on the saw kerfs.

Saw the front and back uprights (D,C) to width and joint their edges on a jointer. Then cut to length. For the front uprights, cut a dado directly in the center of the side edge of the piece. Then cut a ¼-inch rabbet into the inside back edge to accept the plywood back (P).

Shelf Holders

The shelves are made adjustable by using pin-type shelf holders. The pins are simply pushed into ¼ × ⅜-inch deep holes drilled in the back of the front uprights (D) and the inside of the back uprights (C). It is best to use a drill press for this and space them as shown. But you could use a portable electric drill as long as you have a stop gauge to prevent boring through the stock.

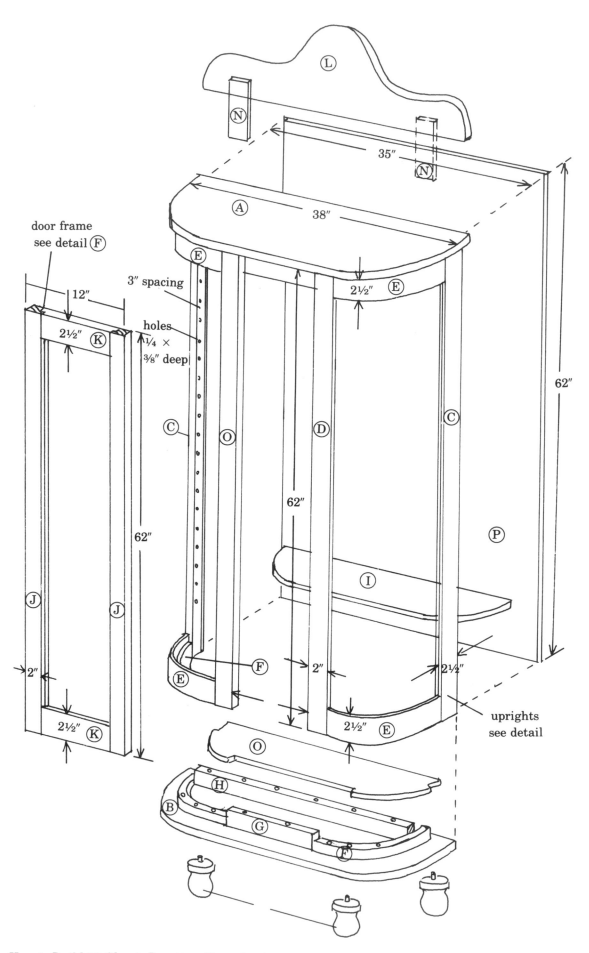

door frame
see detail (F)

3" spacing

holes
1/4 ×
3/8" deep

12"

2½" (K)

(C)

(J)   (J)

62"

2" →

2½" (K)

35"

(L)

(N)   (N)

(A)   38"

(E)

(E)   2½"

62"

(C)   (C)

(D)

(O)

62"

(P)

(I)

(F)   2"   2½"

(E)   2½" (E)

uprights
see detail

(O)

(H)

(B)

(G)

(F)

Case Assembly

After all these pieces have been cut to size, glue the curved inside support cleats (F) to the uprights (C,D). Clamp with bar clamps overnight. You will also have to use C-clamps to hold the wobbly kerfed pieces flat and prevent them from bending and breaking under pressure from the clamps. Use a carpenter's square to ensure that the unit is square.

Remove the assemblies from the clamps and make a dry run of positioning them in place on both top (A) and bottom (B) pieces to ensure they will fit properly. Note that these kerfed pieces can break quite easily, so handle them with care and go slowly.

If everything fits properly, smear glue on the bottom edges of the frames and run it into the kerfs. Then position the units. The back edge of the frame should align with the back edge of the top and bottom, and the front edge should hit the line where the

False Bottom & Top Detail

false bottom & top
¼″ plywood

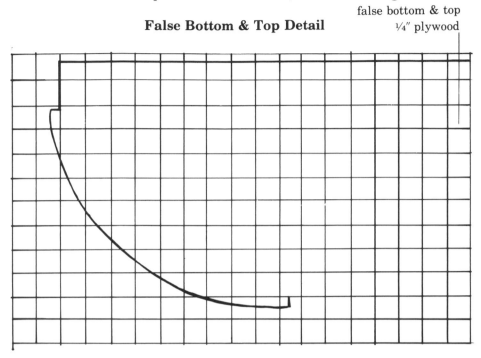

1″ squares

Top and Bottom Detail

top or bottom

uprights

back support cleat

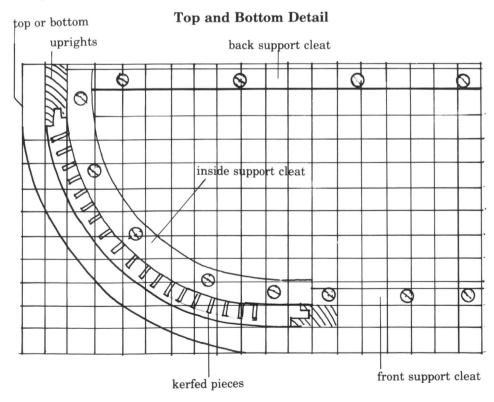

inside support cleat

kerfed pieces

front support cleat

door will be. Then clamp securely. You can do one assembly at a time, or both, depending on the number of clamps you have on hand.

Most woodworking glues react with oak, causing a dark blue stain. In addition, the joint between the curved pieces and the top (or bottom) is almost impossible to sand. So make sure you wipe away all excess glue. First use a warm, wet rag followed by a soft, dry cloth. It is especially important to clean all glue out of the kerfs in the area of the glass rabbets.

Make sure the front uprights are at right angles to the top and bottom and are not cocked in or out. The face of the back upright must be clamped so that it is at a 90-degree angle to the face of the front upright and it also shouldn't be cocked in or out. Then drive No. 8 × 1¼-inch flat-head wood screws through the top and bottom piece into the ends of the upright.

Turning Legs

Enlarge the pattern for the legs (M) and turn the legs on a lathe. You may have to glue up stock to make up the leg turnings. After turning and sand-ing the legs on the lathe, glue and dowel them in place. You may also want to add a couple of wood screws, driven down from inside the cabinet bottom.

Ordering and Fitting Glass

Very carefully measure the size of the glass side panels, make a pattern of their shape, and order glass to fit the side frames. While waiting for the glass to arrive, sand the entire case inside and out thoroughly.

Carefully fit the glass into the rabbets on the inside of the glass frames. The glass can be held in place with glazier points. Don't hammer these points or try to force the glass or you may crack it. You will probably have to cut away a bit of the rabbets here and there with a small sharp chisel to fit the glass correctly. Then cut ¼ × ¼-inch wood moulding strips. (First shape the edge using a quarter-round cutter in a shaper or router and then rip the strip away from the stock.) Glue these over the glass edges and use tape to hold them temporarily in place.

Shelf Detail

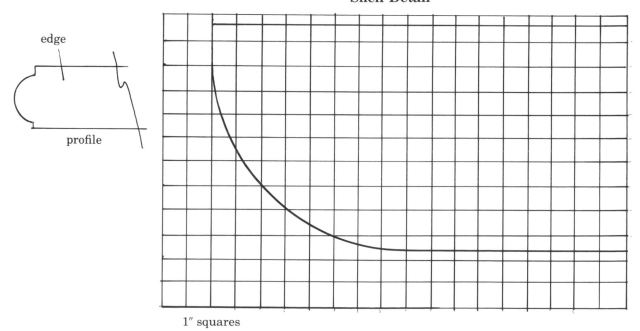

edge

profile

1″ squares

Uprights, Detail of Joint with Curved Piece

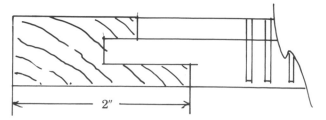

2″

kerfed piece

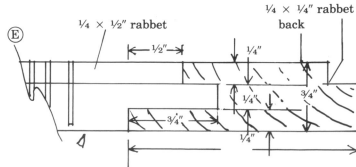

Ⓔ

¼ × ½″ rabbet

¼ × ¼″ rabbet
back

½″

¼″

¼″

¾″

¾″

¼″

Leg Detail

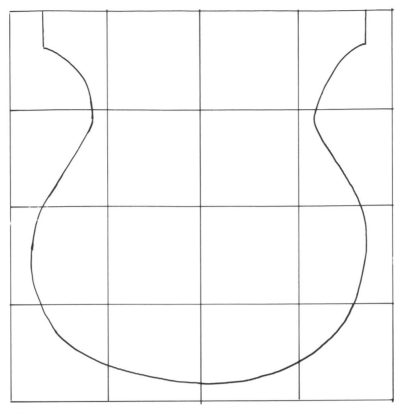

1″ squares

Decorative Top Detail

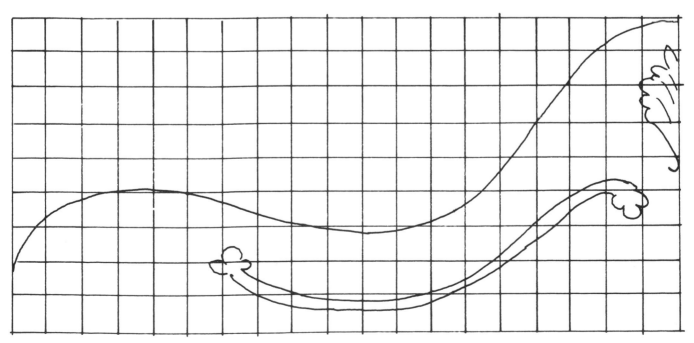

Cut the back (H) and front (G) support cleats for the false bottom and top. Glue and screw them in place, making sure the back pieces are set back flush with the inside edge of the rabbets in the back uprights (C). The front strips fit in behind the front uprights (D). Then glue and/or screw the false top in place. Glue and screw the bottom (O) in place.

Installing Purchased Carvings

Cut the decorative top piece (L) to size and shape following the squared drawing pattern. Then sand all edges using a drum sander and shape the top edge using an ogee cutter in a router or shaper. Glue the stamped wood carvings in place. Don't allow any glue to seep out under their edges, then sand thoroughly. Screw the decorative top supports (N) to the decorative top (L) and screw the bottom ends to the back uprights (C). Use No. 8 × 1¼-inch screws.

Door

Cut the door pieces (J,K) to size and shape and cut the rabbet and lap joints on their inside edges (see door frame detail). Assemble with glue, clamping solidly until the glue sets. Then sand thoroughly.

Final Steps

Cut the ¼-inch plywood back (P) to size, then sand it smooth. At this point, stain and finish all the pieces, including the case, shelves, door, and the decorative top piece. Because the glass has been installed, it will be best to use a brush-on finish instead of a sprayed one, unless you tape and cover all the glass. Even with a brush-on finish, you should run masking tape around the inside and outside edges of the glass to prevent getting stain and finish on it.

Next, install the hinges and pulls on the door. Put the glass in the door and then fasten the door to the cabinet and install a magnetic door catch.

Put in the shelves and fasten the ¼-inch plywood back in place using No. 8 × 1-inch flat-head wood screws. Drive them into the back uprights and false top and bottom support strips. Attach the top decorative piece using No. 8 × 1-inch flat-head wood screws.

Now all that's left is to move the cabinet in place and fill it with your collectibles.

Door Frame Joints (back view)

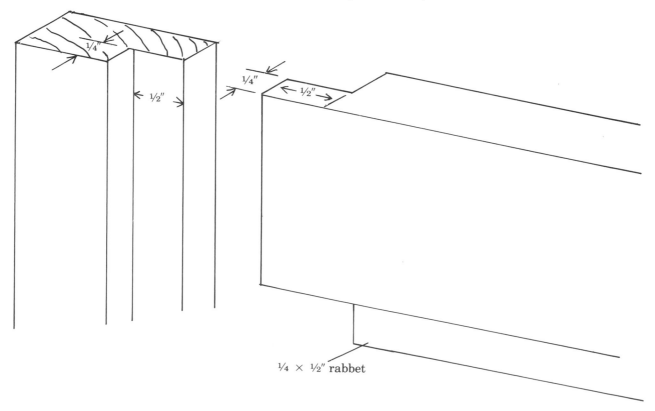

¼ × ½″ rabbet

Materials List

A—Top—¾ × 12 × 38″, 1 req'd.

B—Bottom—¾ × 12 × 38″, 1 req'd.

C—Back uprights—¾ × 2½ × 62″, 2 req'd.

D—Front uprights—¾ × 2 × 62″, 2 req'd.

E—Curved pieces—¾ × 2½ × 16″, 4 req'd.

F—Curved inside support cleats, top and bottom—cut from ¾ × 12 × 12″, 4 req'd.

G—Front top and bottom support cleats—¾ × 2 × 14″, 2 req'd.

H—Back top and bottom support cleats—¾ × 2 × 32″, 2 req'd.

I—Shelves—⅜ × 10 × 32″, 4 req'd.

J—Door rails—¾ × 2 × 62″, 2 req'd.

K—Door stiles—¾ × 2½ × 13″, 2 req'd.

L—Decorative top—¾ × 9 × 38″, 1 req'd.

M—Legs—4 × 4 × 4″, 4 req'd.

N—Decorative top supports—½ × 4 × 8″, 2 req'd.

O—False top and bottom—¼″ plywood × 10¼ × 36¼″, 2 req'd.

P—Back—¼″ plywood × 35 × 62″, 1 req'd.

Shelf support pins—16 req'd.

Glass to fit.

China Cabinet

Circa 1920

This is truly a classic of the manufactured oak furniture of the 1920s. There were many different styles made by manufacturers of the time and they ranged from the simple to such ornately carved cabinets as the one chosen for this project. Without a doubt, this unusual cabinet will prove both a challenging project and an impressive addition to your home.

Quarter-sawn oak was used in much of the casework for the grain pattern. Oak is the best choice for materials although walnut, or even pine, could be used. The curved glass panels are available from Hopcraft Glass Company.

Construction

Although this project is not particularly difficult, careful and accurate fitting of the side glass panels is extremely important. There is, of course, a lot of carving involved. But because it is all applied, it can be taken a step at a time. For authenticity, use quarter-sawn oak where possible. The door is latched with a lock only; no knob or catch is used.

Legs

The first step is to make up the back legs (B). These can be from solid blocks or you can glue up the stock to make the thickness. Then enlarge the squared drawing and cut the legs to size and shape. Bore a counterbored screw hole in each leg "wing" for anchoring to the bottom piece (A).

Enlarge the square drawing for the front legs (C), saw them to shape, and carve the feet. Bore angled, counterbored holes in their back undersides for anchoring to the bottom piece (A).

Case Bottom

Cut the bottom (A) to size from 1½-inch stock glued up to make the thickness. (Note that you could make the bottom outside edge a skirt board to make up the thickness. Simply join pieces of stock together in segments. Fasten with glue and wood screws through the bottom.)

Cut a ⅜ × ⅜-inch stopped rabbet in the upper back edge of the bottom. The back (F) will fit in this. Then cut mortises in the top face of the bottom for the front (H) and back (I) glass stiles. Finally, shape exposed outside edges of the bottom using a shaper or router.

Glass Stiles

Cut the back glass stiles (I) to size, including the tenons on their bottom ends to fit down into the bottom mortises. Cut the ⅜ × ⅜-inch rabbet in their back edge for the back and ¼ × ¼-inch dado in their front inside edge for the glass and rails.

Cut the front stiles (H) in the same manner. Then cut the tenons on their lower ends and the notches in their outside edges for the rabbets cut in the curved glass rails (D,E). Enlarge the squared drawing and carve the front stiles to the pattern.

Shelf Supports

The shelves (L) can be held on small wooden support blocks glued to the front and back stiles. But a better method is to use the metal shelf-support pins. Here you just drill a matching set of (stopped) holes in the stiles and insert the pin brackets to hold the shelves. The shelves can then be adjusted to suit your collection. Drill these holes in all stiles before assembly to make sure they all match up.

Glass Rails

Make the curved rail pieces (D,E). These can be done in several ways: they can be bent to shape, or kerfed and bent as shown in the Techniques Section. You can also cut them from a solid block of wood with a band saw. The latter is probably the best choice if you have stock thick enough to use.

After shaping the rails, cut tenons on their back ends to fit into the back stiles (I). Then cut the front ends with an overlap joint for the front stiles (H). Finally, round the top outside edge of the lower rail slightly and cut a glass rabbet in the outside edge of both top and bottom rails.

Top and Upper Fascia Board

Cut the top fascia board (M) to size and shape, then cut a notch in its bottom back two corners for the upper glass-holding rails. Cut the top (G) to size and shape, and shape the outer edge (as indicated in the drawing) using a shaper or router. Notch the front of the top to fit around the top fascia board (see top detail). Cut the back (F) to the correct size from ⅜-inch hardwood-faced plywood. Cut the shelves (L) to size; then shape the front underside of the shelves, as shown, with a shaper.

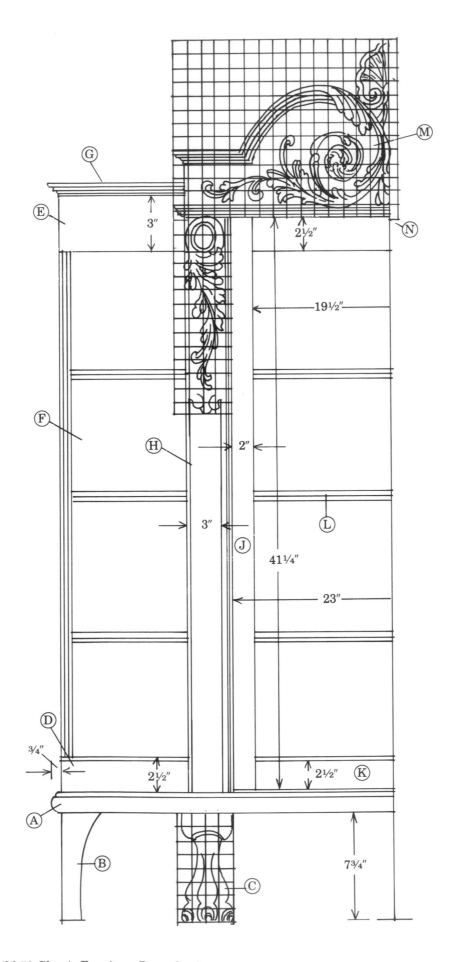

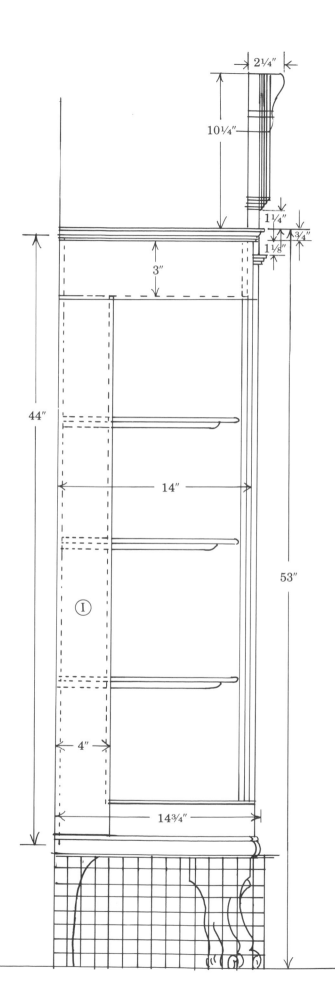

Case Assembly

The first step in assembly is to fasten the legs (B,C) to the bottom (A) with glue and screws driven up through the counterbored holes in the feet wings.

Fit rabbets of the glass rails (D,E) into notches cut in the front stiles (H) and fasten with glue and screws. Insert the back tenons of the glass rails into the grooves cut in the back stiles (I) and then fasten these assemblies to the bottom, placing the stile tenons into the bottom mortises. Fasten with glue and screws driven up through the bottom into the rails.

Temporarily put the back (F) and top (G) in place with countersunk wood screws to hold the assembly square until the glue sets. Temporarily fasten the top fascia board (M) in place as well, to assure proper spacing for it in the casework.

Door

The door (J,K) is constructed using basic cabinet joints cut with a shaper or router. The back of the frame must be rabbeted to hold the glass. After cutting the door pieces to size and shape, glue up using bar clamps to hold the assembly securely square until the glue sets. Then install on the case with three mortised butt hinges. Install the door lock.

Carvings

All carvings, including the upper moulding (N), are applied. First scroll-cut the stock and carve the pattern. Apply using glue. It will be easier to glue these in place by removing the fascia board (M) once the casework glue has set. Also remove the back (F) at this time as well.

After all the carvings have been installed, refit the top fascia board and sand, stain, and finish all pieces, including the back, shelves, etc. Insert shelves and reinstall the back with screws only.

Make up the glass-retaining strips for the curved side pieces as well as for the door and stain and finish them to suit. Then order the glass panels, after carefully measuring the spaces so that they will fit exactly. The last step is to fit the glass in place and install the glass-holding strips with tiny screws.

Materials List

A—Bottom—1½ × 14¾ × 49″, 1 req'd.
B—Back legs—3½ × 3½ × 7¾″, 2 req'd.
C—Front legs—3½ × 5 × 7¾″, 2 req'd.
D—Outside bottom glass rails—¾ × 2½ × 24″, bent or cut to shape, 2 req'd.
E—Outside top glass rails—¾ × 3 × 24″, bent or cut to shape, 2 req'd.
F—Back—⅜ × 44 × 46¼″, 1 req'd.
G—Top—¾ × 14¾ × 48½″, 1 req'd.
H—Front side stiles—¾ × 3 × 41⅜″, 2 req'd.
I—Back side stiles—¾ × 4 × 41⅜″, 2 req'd.

Bottom Detail

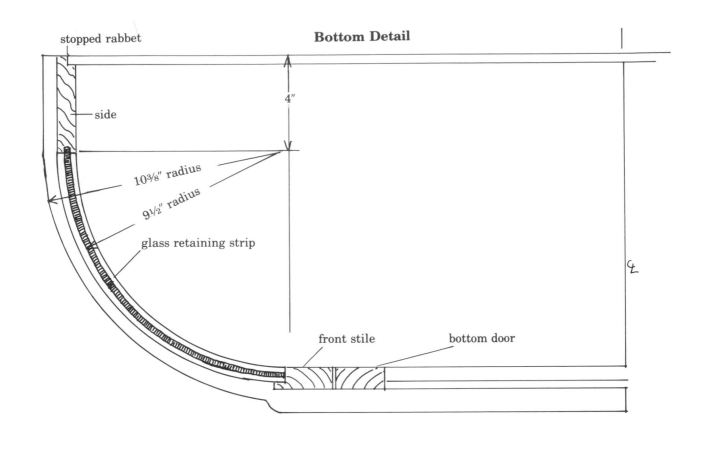

stopped rabbet

side

10⅜" radius

9½" radius

glass retaining strip

4"

front stile

bottom door

Top Detail

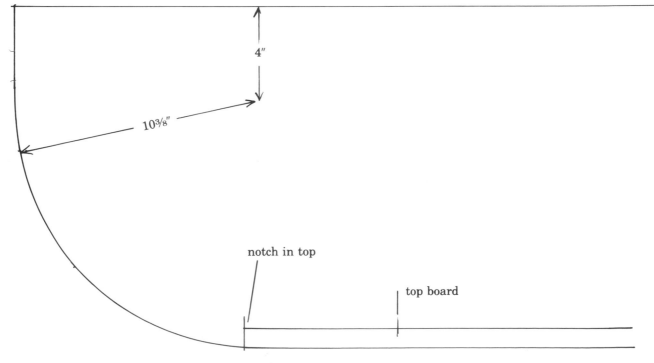

4"

10⅜"

notch in top

top board

J—Door stiles—¾ × 2 × 41¼″, 2 req'd.

K—Door rails—¾ × 2½ × 20″, 2 req'd.

L—Shelves—¾ × 12⅝ × 45″, 4 req'd.

M—Top fascia board—¾ × 12 × 30″, cut to size, 1 req'd.

N—Moulding—¾ × ¾ × 32″, cut to size, 1 req'd.

Curved glass pieces, measured after building, 2 req'd.

Door glass, measured after building, 1 req'd.

Brass hinges, 3 req'd.

Door lock, 1 req'd.

Detail of Glass-Holding Strips

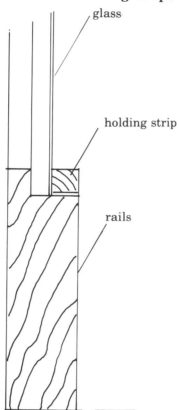

glass

holding strip

rails

Wishbone Victorian Bureau

Circa 1840

Though the original shown here was a manufactured item, it is a prime example of some of the finer American-made Victorian furniture pieces available. The craftsmanship is excellent and the walnut wood is beautifully grained.

There were many different styles and sizes of wishbone bureaus manufactured during the late 19th century.

While walnut is especially well-suited to this piece, mahogany was also sometimes used. Some bureaus of this type were even made of oak.

Construction

These manufactured items were usually fastened together without dovetails, dowels, or mortise-and-tenon joints. They used butt joints, glue and glue blocks, with the occasional nail to strengthen the casework. This particular piece, however, shows some concern for craftsmanship in the use of slotted dovetail construction on the upper handkerchief drawers.

In making plans for this project, I have used mortise-and-tenon construction for the facer section and standard web-frame construction to add strength to the carcass. The sides are typical frame and panel. The front side facers are cut at an angle and split turnings are simply applied to create the decorative effect.

Sides

Start by creating the side assemblies. Enlarge the squared drawings for the pattern for the shaped side pieces and rough-cut the front (A) and back (B) stiles (uprights) to shape as well as the top (D) and bottom (C) rails. Then cut grooves into the inside edges of the stiles to accept panel edges and rail tongues. Cut a ³⁄₈ × ³⁄₈-inch rabbet on the inside back edge of the back stiles to accept a ³⁄₈-inch plywood back (T). Cut the grooves in the inside edges of the rails for the panel and then cut the tongues on their ends to fit into the stiles. Finally, transfer the squared drawing to the pieces and use a band saw to cut them to size and shape.

Cut the side panels (E) to size from ¼-inch hardwood-faced plywood. Apply glue on the tenons of the rails, put top and bottom rails over the panel, and insert the rails and the panel into the stiles. Do not apply any glue to the panel edges. Make sure

these side assemblies are clamped square and are not warped; then allow the glue to set.

Front Facer Assembly

First, saw the front side facers (F) to size and length. Cut the shaped portion of their bottom ends. Then cut the outside edges at a 45-degree angle. Cut the front side facers (F) to size, including the shaped lower portion. Cut the drawer facer strips (H) and top facer (G) to size, leaving them long for the tenons on each end. These fit into the side facers. Finally, cut the upper bottom facer (I) as well as the lower bottom facer (J) to size and shape. Use the enlarged squared drawing pattern and a band saw to make the skirt board.

Lay the front facer assembly together and mark the locations of the mortise-and-tenon joints. Cut these to the proper shape, and try-fit each piece without glue to get a good fit. Once all the joints have been cut, glue up the entire front facer unit as one assembly. Make sure the unit is perfectly square. Check each drawer opening with a carpenter's square, otherwise the drawers won't fit properly. Then clamp together with bar clamps, and recheck to make sure parts are still square, and allow the glue to set.

Web-Frame Assemblies

The drawers are supported with web frames (O,Q,R). These can be made of softwood to the size shown in the drawing. Cut mortise-and-tenon joints as described on pages 13–14. Glue, assemble and then clamp.

Basic Assembly

Now it is time to form the basic carcass. The first step is to locate the position of the web dust frames on the inside of the side section. Then fasten these in place to the side units with glue and screws driven from the inside of the web frames into the side stiles and rails. With both sides fixed to the web frames, put the front facer assembly in place with glue and screws. Drive screws through the web frames into the front facers and use glue blocks down the sides between the front and side pieces.

Back

Cut the back (T) to size and temporarily anchor it in place in the rabbets in the back edges of the sides

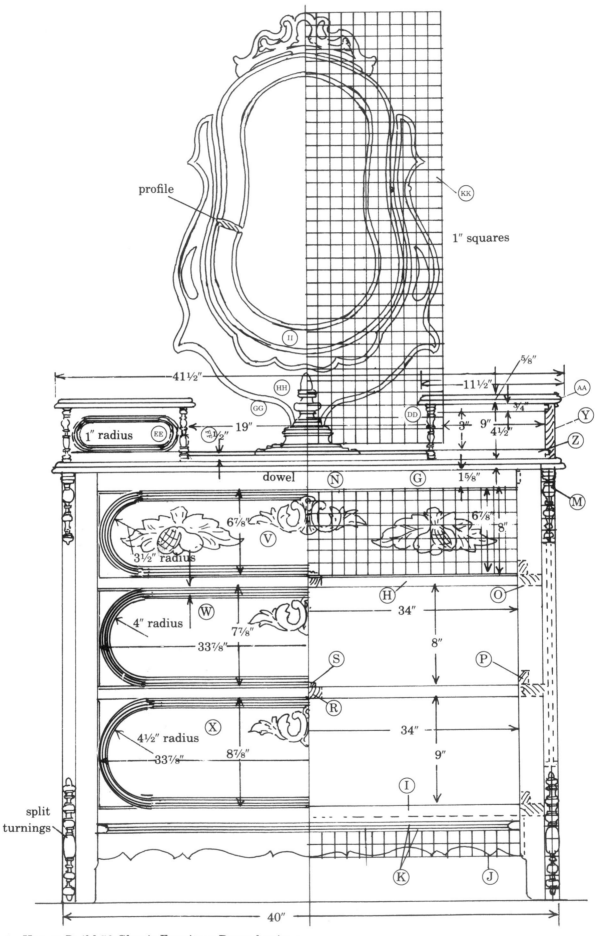

profile

1" squares

KK

II

41½"

HH

GG

19"

1" radius

EE

FF

1½"

dowel

N

G

DD

3"

9"

4½"

11½"

5⁄8"

3⁄4"

AA

Y

Z

1 5⁄8"

M

6 7⁄8"

3½" radius

V

6 7⁄8"

8"

H

O

4" radius

W

7 7⁄8"

34"

8"

P

33 7⁄8"

S

R

4½" radius

X

33 7⁄8"

8 7⁄8"

34"

9"

I

split
turnings

K

J

40"

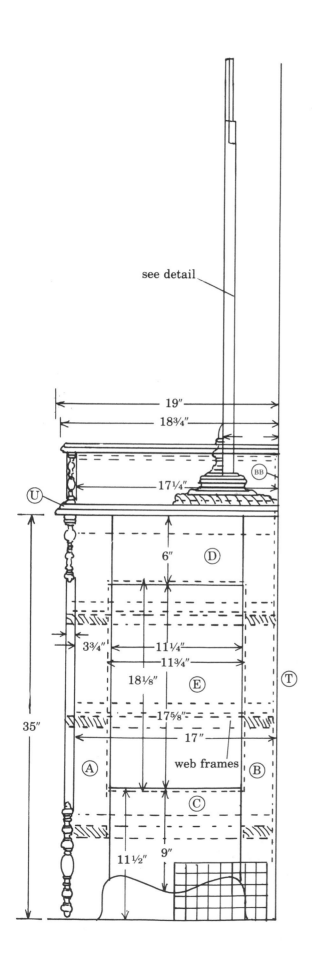

with screws. Then make sure the entire unit sits squarely on the floor. Clamp the assembly together until the glue sets.

Drawers

The drawers (V,W,X) are flush construction with dovetail joints front and back. The bottoms are made of ¼-inch hardboard that fits in dadoes in the sides, front, and back. Make the fronts from ¾-inch plywood; then cut the sides and back from ½-inch stock. Rout dadoes in the pieces for the bottom.

Assemble the drawers and cut a small slot in the back bottom edge of the back for the center drawer slides (S). Remove the plywood back of the unit and fasten the side drawer guides (P) in place to each web frame with glue and screws. Make sure they are exactly flush with the inside edge of the side pieces and perfectly parallel. Put each drawer in place; then fit the center drawer slide underneath, mark it and anchor it at the front center. Fasten it in place at the back of the case after again fitting the drawers in place to be sure the drawer front is square and flush with the front facers.

Once the drawers have been fitted, reinstall the plywood back with wood screws and glue.

Front Moulding

The drawers are fitted with applied moulding. Cut the long horizontal strips on the edge of a piece of stock. Then rip them off to the thickness needed. The half-circle mouldings are applied to the ends of each drawer to match up with the horizontal strips. These are cut on the face of a piece of stock with a router or shaper; then, using a band saw, cut the shaped mouldings from the stock. Use glue to apply the moulding to the drawer fronts. Note that there is also a small divider strip of moulding (K) applied to the bottom facer.

Split Turnings

Create the split turnings (L,M) for the side pieces by gluing up a couple of pieces of stock with a newspaper between them. Then turn the stock to size and shape and sand smooth while still in the lathe. Split the pieces apart using a sharp chisel or knife. Glue the turnings to the front of the facers.

Carved Mouldings

The drawer pulls and the escutcheons are carved from solid stock to the sizes and shapes shown in the squared drawing. Then they are anchored in place with glue. Drive screws inside the drawer fronts into the drawer pulls.

Top

Cut the top (U) to size and shape, rounding the front corners. Then rout the shaped edges on the front and sides. This edge is "stopped" back from the edge as shown in the side view drawing. Anchor the top in

place with screws and glue blocks, then add the center top drawer tilt strip (N) with glue and screws.

Handkerchief Boxes

The small boxes on top are made from solid stock and the top (AA) and bottom (Z) are fixed to the sides (Y) with a slotted dovetail joint. However, the front edges of the sides are first cut at an angle to match that of the lower case. The sides, bottom, and inner top pieces all have a $3/8 \times 3/8$-inch rabbet cut in their back edges for the $3/8$-inch plywood back pieces (BB).

Cut the outside top piece (CC) to size and shape and then fasten it to the inner top (AA), with glue and wood screws from the underside of the inner top. Then fasten the small cases together using glue in the slotted dovetail joints. After the small cases have set, remove them from the clamps and anchor them to the bureau top (U) with screws from the underside of the top. Construct the small drawers (EE) for the cases using the same joinery as on the larger drawers. Make the split turnings (DD) and attach to the case.

Mirror

Add the center mirror support plank (FF) between the two small cases, after first rounding its front edge. Glue and screw through the top into the support plank. Then locate the position of the swivelling mirror support (GG) and bore a hole through the top plank and carcass top for the mirror dowel.

Enlarge the squared drawing and create the mirror frame (II) from $3/4$-inch solid stock. Glue up the frame in segments, using dowels to join the segments. Then use a scroll saw to cut out the inside and a band saw for the outside. Sand all surfaces smooth with a drum sander. Use a shaper or router in a router table to shape the edges on the front, as well as to cut rabbets in the back for the mirror and a mirror holding piece of $1/8$-inch hardboard or plywood. Locate the position of the mirror support pins (KK), and bore holes for them. Then cut the top trim (JJ) from $1/4$-inch stock on a scroll saw. Fasten it in place to the mirror top by mortising and gluing it into the mirror frame.

The mirror support yoke (HH) is also made up of segments. Saw to shape on a band saw. Then use a router or shaper in the front edges to the shapes shown.

The mirror swivels on a turned support post (GG). Enlarge the squared drawing and turn the post to size and shape, including a dowel on its lower end. The dowel should fit smoothly but snugly into the dowel hole in the top of the carcass. Then saw away the top back part to make a notch for the mirror support yoke. Fasten this in place with screws and glue.

Sand the entire case as smooth as possible, stain, finish, and add the mirror. Then insert the swivelling mirror support piece in the dowel hole to complete the bureau assembly.

Materials List

A—Side stiles, front—$3/4 \times 3\frac{3}{4} \times 35''$, 2 req'd.

B—Side stiles, back—$3/4 \times 3 \times 35''$, 2 req'd.

C—Side rails, bottom—$3/4 \times 9 \times 11\frac{3}{4}''$, 2 req'd.

D—Side rails, top—$3/4 \times 6 \times 11\frac{3}{4}''$, 2 req'd.

E—Side panels—$1/4 \times 11\frac{3}{4} \times 18\frac{1}{8}''$, 2 req'd.

F—Front side facers—$3/4 \times 3 \times 35''$, 2 req'd.

G—Front top facers—$3/4 \times 1\frac{5}{8} \times 34\frac{3}{4}''$, 1 req'd.

H—Drawer facers—$7/8 \times 3/4 \times 34\frac{3}{4}''$, 2 req'd.

I—Upper bottom facer—$3/4 \times 1\frac{1}{2} \times 34\frac{3}{4}''$, 1 req'd.

J—Lower bottom facer—$3/4 \times 3 \times 34\frac{3}{4}''$, 1 req'd.

K—Lower moulding—$3/4 \times 3/4 \times 34''$, 1 req'd.

L—Lower split turning—$1\frac{1}{2} \times 1\frac{1}{2} \times 10\frac{1}{2}''$, split, 1 req'd.

M—Upper split turning—$1\frac{1}{2} \times 1\frac{1}{2} \times 6''$, split, 1 req'd.

N—Center top drawer tilt strip—$3/4 \times 1\frac{5}{8} \times 17''$, 1 req'd.

O—Web frame sides—$7/8 \times 2\frac{1}{4} \times 17''$, 6 req'd.

P—Drawer guides—$3/4 \times 1 \times 17''$, 6 req'd.

Q—Web frame front & back—$7/8 \times 2 \times 38\frac{1}{2}''$, 6 req'd.

R—Web frame centers—$7/8 \times 2 \times 14''$, 3 req'd.

S—Drawer slides—$1/4 \times 1 \times 17''$, 3 req'd.

T—Back—$3/8''$ plywood $\times 36 \times 39\frac{1}{4}''$, 1 req'd.

U—Top—$7/8 \times 19 \times 41\frac{1}{2}''$, 1 req'd.

V—Top drawer

    Front—$3/4 \times 6\frac{7}{8} \times 33\frac{7}{8}''$, 1 req'd.

    Sides—$1/2 \times 6\frac{7}{8} \times 17\frac{1}{2}''$, 2 req'd.

    Back—$1/2 \times 6\frac{7}{8} \times 33\frac{7}{8}''$, 1 req'd.

    Bottom—$1/4 \times 17\frac{1}{2} \times 33\frac{3}{8}''$, 1 req'd.

    Moulding curve blocks—$5/8 \times 4 \times 7''$, 2 req'd.

W—Middle drawer

    Front—$3/4 \times 7\frac{7}{8} \times 33\frac{7}{8}''$, 1 req'd.

    Sides—$1/2 \times 7\frac{7}{8} \times 17\frac{1}{2}''$, 2 req'd.

    Back—$1/2 \times 7\frac{7}{8} \times 33\frac{7}{8}''$, 1 req'd.

    Bottom—$1/4 \times 17\frac{1}{2} \times 33\frac{3}{8}''$, 1 req'd.

    Moulding curve blocks—$5/8 \times 4 \times 8''$, 2 req'd.

X—Bottom drawer

    Front—$3/4 \times 8\frac{7}{8} \times 33\frac{7}{8}''$, 1 req'd.

    Sides—$1/2 \times 8\frac{7}{8} \times 17\frac{1}{2}''$, 2 req'd.

    Back—$1/2 \times 8\frac{7}{8} \times 33\frac{7}{8}''$, 1 req'd.

    Bottom—$1/4 \times 17\frac{1}{2} \times 33\frac{3}{8}''$, 1 req'd.

    Moulding curve block—$5/8 \times 5 \times 9''$, 2 req'd.

    Drawer moulding—$5/8 \times 3/4 \times 96''$, cut to fit, 1 length req'd.

Drawer pulls—¾ × 3¼ × 8½", 6 req'd.

Drawer escutcheons—¾ × 3½ × 8", 3 req'd.

Top Handkerchief Boxes

Y—Sides—¾ × 4½ × 18", 4 req'd.

Z—Bottom—¾ × 9¾ × 18", 2 req'd.

AA—Inner top—¾ × 9¾ × 18", 2 req'd.

BB—Back—⅜ × 3¾ × 9¾", 2 req'd.

CC—Top—⅝ × 11½ × 18¾", 2 req'd.

DD—Split turnings—1 × 1 × 4½", split, 2 req'd.

EE—Drawer

    Fronts—¾ × 2⅞ × 8⅞", 2 req'd.

    Sides—½ × 2⅞ × 17½", 4 req'd.

    Backs—½ × 2⅞ × 8⅞", 2 req'd

    Bottoms—¼ × 8⅜ × 17½", 2 req'd.

    Moulding curve blocks—⅝ × 1½ × 3", 4 req'd.

Moulding—⅝ × ⅝ × 24", cut to lengths, 1 req'd.

Pulls—1 × 1", 2 req'd.

Mirror

FF—Center support plank—½ × 10½ × 19", 1 req'd.

GG—Mirror support post—7 × 8½ × 8½", 1 req'd.

HH—Mirror support yoke—¾ × 22 × 27½", glue up from segments, 1 req'd.

II—Mirror frame—¾ × 16 × 25", glue up from segments, 1 req'd.

JJ—Top trim—¼ × 5½ × 12", 1 req'd.

KK—Mirror support pins—2 req'd.

Mirror—12 × 21", cut to fit, 1 req'd.

Veneered Curved Chest

Circa 1920

This project is a classic example of an Early Victorian style of veneered chest. The chest is American-made and is an elegant, sturdy piece of furniture.

Veneer work is a major reason why the chest was included in this book, and the project will surely test your veneering skills. The chest is made of solid wood and is entirely veneered in flame-grained mahogany. The upper drawer, the edge of the bottom drawer, and around the top edge are veneered in a typical "waterfall" pattern (the grain runs vertically).

You can use almost any style of veneer, including curly maple, walnut, or rosewood, but the most commonly used veneer for this style furniture is fancy-grained mahogany.

Construction

Construction of the casework is fairly simple, but the veneering adds the challenge to this project. Although the original chest was made of solid wood and covered with veneer, you can substitute plywood, which is easier to work and less likely to warp. Standard web-frame construction is used to support the massive drawers.

Sides

The first step is to cut the sides (A) to size and shape from ¾-inch plywood or glued-up solid stock. Note that the back leg is an integral part of the sides. Enlarge the squared drawing and cut the back leg using a sabre saw or coping saw. (The size of the side

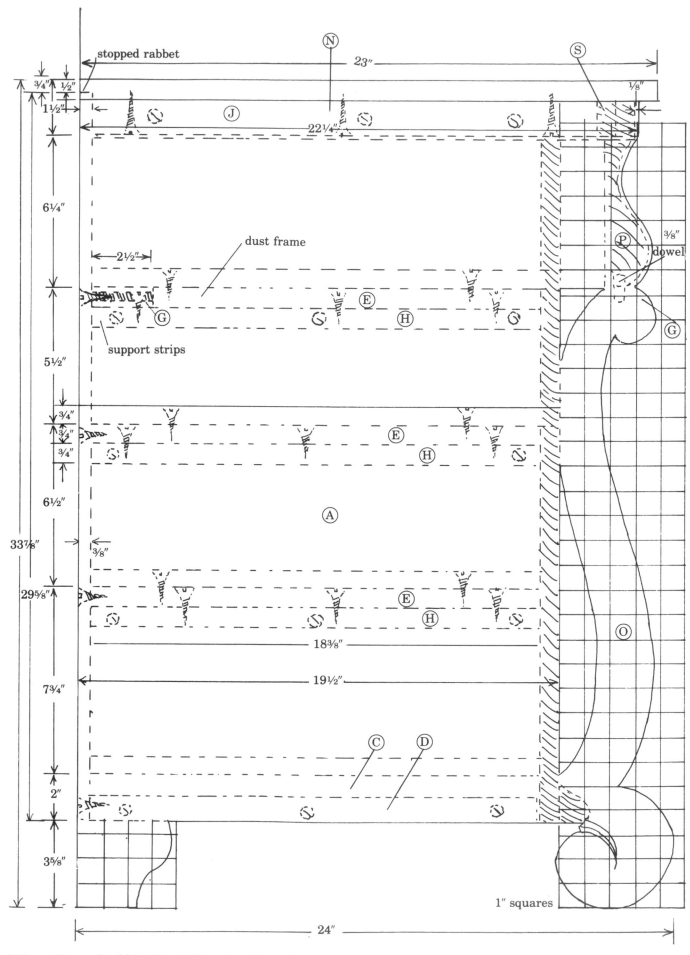

stopped rabbet

dust frame

support strips

dowel

1" squares

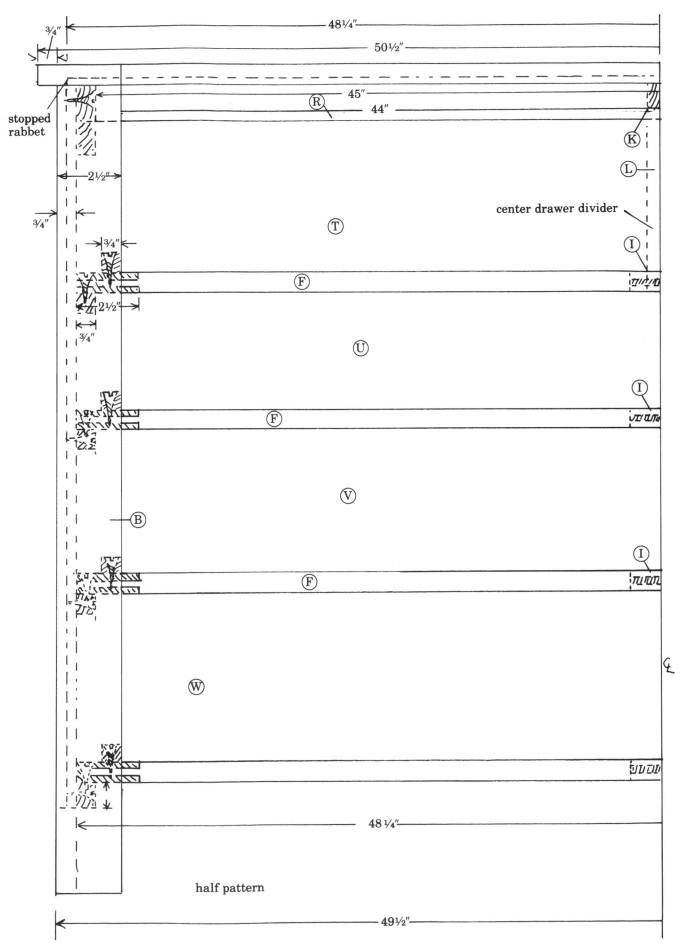

stopped rabbet

center drawer divider

half pattern

will make it to difficult to cut with a band saw.) Cut a ⅜ × ⅜-inch rabbet in the back edges of the sides for the back.

Cut the web frame side support cleats (H) as well as the bottom (D) and top (J) support cleats to size and shape. Fasten them in place to the sides. They should run to the rabbet on the back edge of the sides and be ¾ inch from the front edge. Make sure they are installed at a 90-degree angle to front and back of the side. Use a carpenter's square to lay out their position lines. Fasten with glue and screws.

Web Frames

Assemble the web frames (E,F,G,I) using mortise-and-tenon joints on their ends, as well as mortise-and-tenon joints for the center tilt strip (I). Make sure each frame is assembled perfectly square and is glued and clamped securely.

Cut the front inside facer pieces (B) to size and shape. Glue up bottom (C) from solid pieces or cut it to size and shape from plywood.

Case Assembly

Start by fastening the bottom (C) to the bottom support cleats (D) on the sides with glue and screws. Then install the web frames in the same manner, with the assembly lying on its back. Make sure it is fastened together squarely and securely.

Install the inside facer (B) to the sides, bottom, and frames with glue and screws. Cut the top facer strip (R) as well as the inside top facer (S) for it. Fasten them together with glue and screws and install in place with glue and screws.

Cut the back (M) to size and shape. Install it in the rabbets of the sides with glue and screws. It should be flush with the back edge of the bottom.

Cut the top drawer tilt strip (K) and fasten it between the back and the inside top facer (S) with glue and screws. A drawer guide (KK) is also fastened to the top of each side of the web frames and to the bottom, using glue and screws. Make sure they are perfectly flush with the inside edge on the back of the web frames. Install the top drawer divider (L) with glue and screws.

Veneering

The veneering starts at this point. Apply veneer to the front of the inside facers (B) up to the point where the top-scroll block (P) fits in place.

Front Scroll Pieces

Cut the top and bottom scroll pieces (O,P) to size and shape, including the lower carved section. Do this by enlarging the squared drawing, making a pattern and cutting the pieces to size and shape with a band saw. Bore holes for the dowel that joins them together.

Then veneer front and back surfaces of the bottom scroll pieces, running the veneer grain horizontally across the front faces. Do the same for the top scroll pieces. But veneer only the front and bottom surfaces.

Once these pieces have been veneered, place the top scroll piece in position and fasten it to the inside facer with glue and screws driven from the back of the facer. Place a dowel (Q) in the hole in the top of the lower scroll to join the two pieces together. Use just a tiny bit of glue here.

Make sure the lower outside face of the bottom scroll is flush with screws driven through the inside facer. Do not use glue because it might run down onto the exposed veneer between the two surfaces. It would be impossible to remove.

Veneering the Sides

Now you're ready to veneer the sides (A). Install the veneer sheet (with grain running vertically) and carefully cut around the scrolled front part of the chest. (Note that the veneer is cut away from the carved area on the front feet.) Veneer the insides of the front scroll pieces in the same manner (grain running vertically). Then lightly sand all veneered portions. Veneer the top facer (R) running the veneer grain vertically to create the "waterfall" effect.

Top

Cut the top (N) to size and shape and make the stopped rabbet in its back edge for the back. Then

Scroll Piece Detail

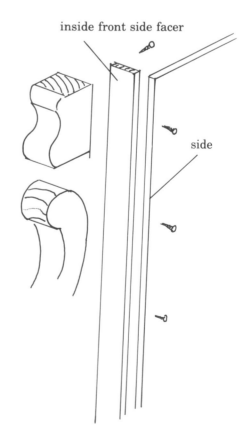

inside front side facer

side

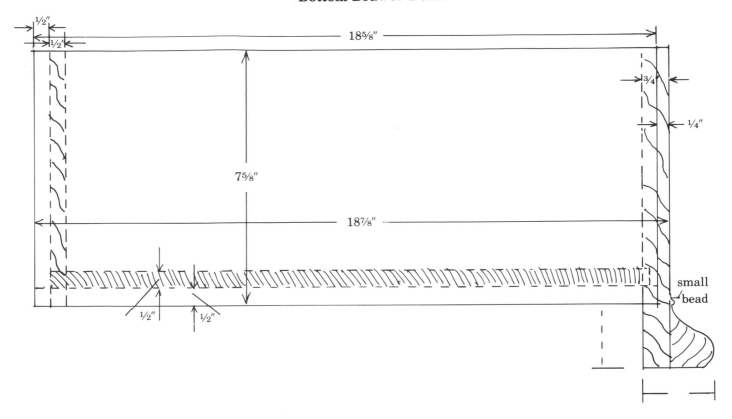

veneer the undersurface of the top. This can be a cheaper grade of veneer, or you can simply use pieces left over from veneering the sides.

Then veneer the top surface using a good-quality veneer. Finally, veneer its side and front edges using the waterfall grain pattern.

Install the top by positioning it and driving screws up from the top side supports (J) and top drawer tilt strip (K). Make sure the screws don't break through the top. Then anchor the upper back in the rabbet in the top.

Drawers

Now the fun starts. The two center drawers (U,V) are quite easy to build and veneer. They consist of ¾-inch solid stock or plywood fronts and ½-inch sides, back and bottoms. The joints are simple overlaps with the back in dadoes on the sides. The bottoms are fitted in dadoes in the front and sides, and extend back past the backs. Veneer the fronts and install drawer locks. Note that the inside sides are inset half the depth of the center drawer guide.

Bottom Drawer

The lower lip that appears to be a facer piece is actually part of the bottom drawer front. It drops down past the bottom (C) and bottom support cleat (D) and is flush with the bottom edge of the sides.

A small piece of moulding is used (as shown in the detail drawing) to help create this effect. It is glued and screwed to the bottom of the drawer front. Be-

fore installing it, however, you must cover it with veneer (see page 21 for information on veneering curved surfaces). Then veneer the drawer front and finally attach the veneered moulding strip.

Top Drawers

The two top drawers (T) have fronts cut to the shape shown. This is done by using a table saw set to cut a cove for the concave surface. Then make a series of angle cuts on the block to cut the convex surface to a rough shape. Final shaping is done with hand planes and sanders. The drawer fronts are then veneered in a waterfall effect, again using the techniques for veneering curved surfaces. Finally assemble the front with the drawer sides, back, and bottom and install the drawer locks. Construct the three lower drawers (U-W) and veneer their fronts as well.

Lightly sand the entire unit, stain and finish. Note that you should use a finish that is compatible with the glue used to install the veneer. Some lacquers will lift the veneer from some veneer cements.

Materials List

A—Sides—¾" plywood × 19½ × 33½", 2 req'd.

B—Inside facers—¾ × 2½ × 29¼", 2 req'd.

C—Bottom—¾ × 18⅜ × 48", 1 req'd.

D—Bottom support cleats—¾ × 1 × 18⅜", 2 req'd.

Top Drawer Front Detail

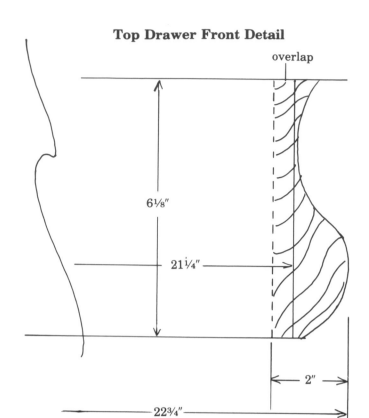

overlap

6⅛″

21¼″

2″

22¾″

Web Frames

E—Sides—¾ × 2½ × 18⅜″, 6 req'd.
F—Fronts—¾ × 2½ × 48″, 3 req'd.
G—Back—¾ × 2½ × 48″, 3 req'd.
H—Side support cleats—¾ × ⅜ × 18⅜″, 6 req'd.
I—Tilt strips—¾ × 2½ × 18⅜″, 3 req'd.
J—Top side supports—¾ × 1½ × 18⅜″, 2 req'd.
K—Top drawer tilt strip—¾ × 1½ × 18⅜″, 1 req'd.
KK—Drawer guides—¾ × 1 × 18⅜″, cut to fit, 8 req'd.
L—Top drawer divider—¾ × 1 × 6¼″, 1 req'd.
M—Back—⅜ × 29⅝ × 48¼″, 1 req'd.
N—Top—¾ × 23 × 50½″, 1 req'd.
O—Bottom scroll—2½ × 4½ × 25½″, 2 req'd.
P—Top scroll—2½ × 4 × 8¾″, 2 req'd.
Q—Dowel—½ × 1″, 2 req'd.
R—Top facer—¾ × 1½ × 44″, 1 req'd.
S—Inside top facer—¾ × 1½ × 45″, 1 req'd.

Drawers

T—Top
 Fronts—2 × 6⅛ × 21⅞″, 2 req'd.
 Sides—½ × 6⅛ × 21¼″, 4 req'd.
 Backs—½ × 5⅝ × 21⅞″, 2 req'd.
 Bottoms—¼ × 20⅞ × 21″, 2 req'd.
U—Second drawer
 Front—¾ × 5⅜ × 43⅞″, 1 req'd.
 Sides—½ × 5⅜ × 18⅞″, 2 req'd.
 Back—½ × 4⅞ × 43⅜″, 1 req'd.
 Bottom—¼ × 18⅝ × 43⅞″, 1 req'd.
V—Third drawer
 Front—¾ × 6⅜ × 43⅞″, 1 req'd.
 Sides—½ × 6⅜ × 18⅞″, 2 req'd.
 Back—½ × 5⅞ × 43⅜″, 1 req'd.
 Bottom—¼ × 18⅝ × 43⅞″, 1 req'd.
W—Bottom drawer
 Front—¾ × 9¾ × 43⅞″, 1 req'd.
 Sides—½ × 7⅝ × 18⅞″, 2 req'd.
 Back—½ × 7⅛ × 43⅜″, 1 req'd.
 Bottom—¼ × 18⅝ × 43⅞″, 1 req'd.
 Moulding strip—1¼ × 2½ × 43⅞″, 1 req'd.
Veneer to cover

Bureau with Mirror

Circa 1900

Although this is one of the "youngest" furniture pieces in the book, it is also a good representative of the manufactured furniture of the Late Victorian period.

The unusual figurine and other carving on the front of the mirror add some challenge to this project. But because all carvings are "applied," this part of the project is greatly simplified. The serpentine front also provides an interesting challenge to the woodworker.

While the oak used on this bureau produces a solid and impressive appearance, walnut or mahogany could also be used. Softwoods would not produce the crisp lines needed for the carved portion, nor would they look quite as appropriate.

Construction

Construction of the bureau is completed in two sections: the lower case, or bureau, and the upper mirror and mirror support frame. The case is standard web-frame carcass construction with panelled sides.

Legs

The first step in this project is to make the legs (A,B). The feet on the front legs (A) are shaped in a modified claw foot and must be cut with a band saw. For this reason, the best method is to first rip leg blocks to size for the upper part of the legs. Then glue pieces on the sides and front of the two to make up the extra thickness for the feet. Transfer the squared drawings and cut out the feet using a band saw. Round and carve the feet to suit.

The back legs (B) are simply square-cut blocks, except that the bottom foot portion is tapered on both the front and inside surfaces.

Once all four leg blanks have been shaped, then rout a ⅜ × ⅜-inch stopped rabbet into the back legs for the ⅜-inch plywood back (N). Make the ¼ × ¼-inch stopped dadoes in the front face of the back legs for the side panel (M) and rail pieces (K,L). Cut stopped mortises in the inside of the legs for the web frames. Then cut the notches or mortises for the bottom apron (C). Cut notches in the leg posts for the web frames (see top view detail).

Sides

The next step is to cut the side pieces and assemble the sides. Cut the rails (K,L) to length and make the tenons on their ends. Cut grooves into the proper edges for the side panel (M). Then cut the side panel to size.

Assemble the sides by placing glue on the tenons of the side rails and inserting the panel (without glue) between the two rails. Then fit this assembly between the two leg posts and clamp securely until the glue sets. Make sure each of the units is square by checking with a carpenter's square.

Web-Frame Construction

The fronts (D) of the frame drawer supports are made of solid stock to match the rest of the chest.

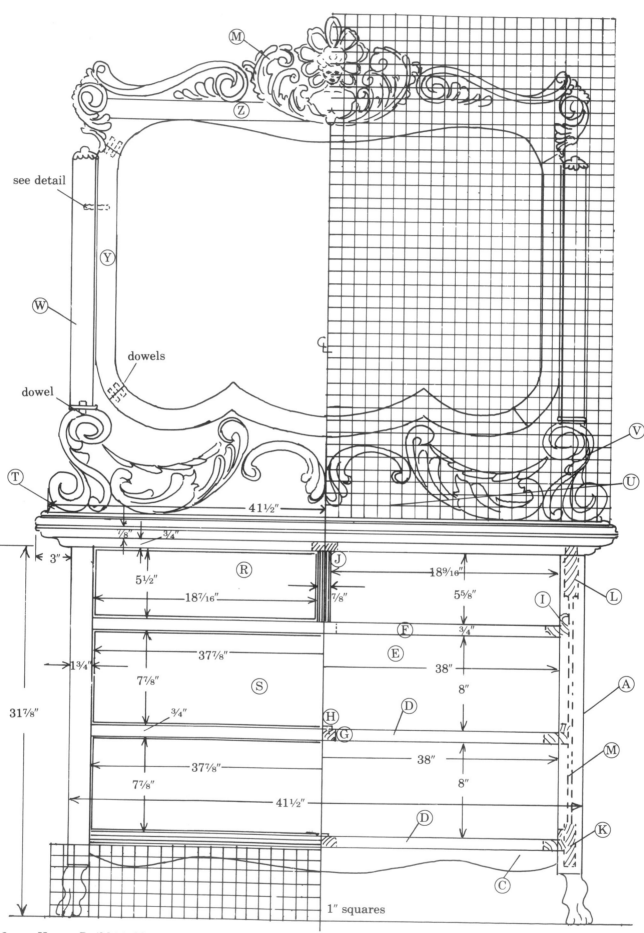

see detail

dowels

dowel

41½"

⅞" ¾"

3"

5½"

18⁷⁄₁₆"

18⁹⁄₁₆"

⅞"

5⅝"

¾"

37⅞"

38"

1¾"

7⅞"

8"

¾"

38"

31⅞"

37⅞"

8"

7⅞"

41½"

1" squares

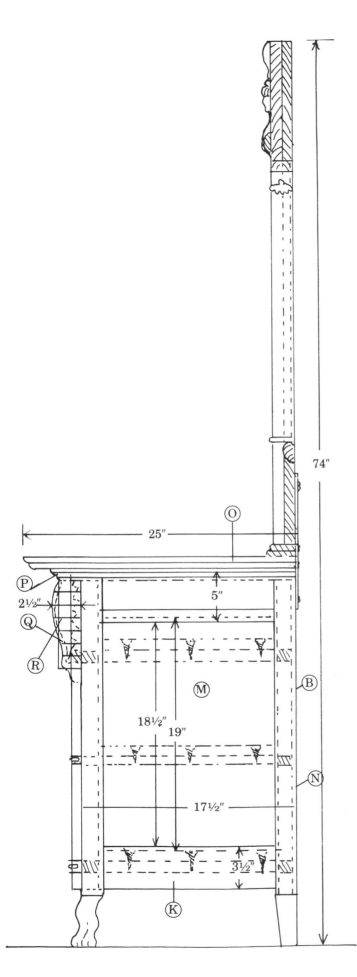

Other frame pieces are made of softwood such as pine.

The top web frame is a straight piece and is simply cut to width. Its front is then dressed on a shaper or router in a router table. The front frame piece also has a mortise in it for the web frame center (G). There is also a top web frame that fits between the sides but is flush only with the front squared portion as well as with the sides. A hardwood moulding covers its front edge after application.

The two lower web frames are serpentine shaped to match the drawers. Enlarge the squared drawing and cut to shape using a band saw. Then shape the frames' front edge to the moulding pattern (see top view detail). Cut the rest of the pieces (E,F,G) for the web frames and construct them using open mortise-and-tenon joints. Cut off part of the corners of the frames so that they fit into the notches made in the leg posts.

Bottom Apron

Enlarge the squared drawing for both surfaces (serpentine front, scroll-cut bottom) of the bottom apron (C) and cut it to size and shape. Then cut the tenons on each end to fit into the mortises cut in the leg posts.

Basic Carcass Assembly

Once the sides and web frames have been constructed, you're ready to assemble the casework. Work on a smooth, flat surface. Place glue on the ends of the bottom apron and insert its tenons into the front-leg mortises. Then put the web frames in place between the two side assemblies, gluing and clamping the chest together as you do. Make sure the entire chest is square and allow the glue to set before removing the clamps.

The center facer (J) is fitted in place down over the upper straight web-frame facer, mating into a mortise in the top of the straight web frame. Finally, fit the top straight web frame down over the center facer and fasten it in place in the notches in the top of the leg posts with glue. Fasten the drawer guides (I) in place on each side.

Front Side Pieces

Enlarge the squared drawing and cut the front side pieces (Q) to size and shape. Fasten them in place with glue and screws from the inside of the case, making sure they are flush with the outside edges of the leg posts.

Drawers

Drawer construction starts with the two upper drawers (R). The fronts on these are rounded, and the first step is to rough-cut the rounded shapes by using progressively sharper angles on a table saw. Then use a block plane to smooth up the surfaces. An alternative method is to turn the drawer fronts from a large block of wood, if you have a lathe large enough.

Cut the drawer fronts to the correct length and make the flats on their top and bottom edges. Finally cut the stopped dovetails into their side edges to mate with dovetails in the drawer sides. Cut the drawer sides and backs to size, and then cut the bottom dadoes in the sides, backs and fronts. Assemble the drawers and cut notches in their back bottom edges for the drawer slides (H).

The lower drawer (S) fronts must also be cut from heavy solid stock to create the serpentine front. Enlarge the squared drawing and use a band saw to cut the stock to the proper "wavy" shape. Then assemble these drawers with dovetail joints front and back. Put the drawers in place and, when you're sure they all fit flush on all sides, install the drawer slides (H) in place with glue and screws.

Top Moulding

Cut the top moulding (P) to shape and size and install it with 45-degree mitres at front corners.

Top

Note that the top on the original has a veneered surface. Cut the top (O) to the correct size and shape using a band saw or sabre saw. Then sand it smooth and use a router to shape the under edge. Finally, install the top in place with glue and screws driven up through the upper web frame.

Back

Cut the back (N) to the proper size and install it in place with screws.

Mirror Support Frame

The mirror support frame consists of three sections: a bottom scroll-cut section and two turned standards

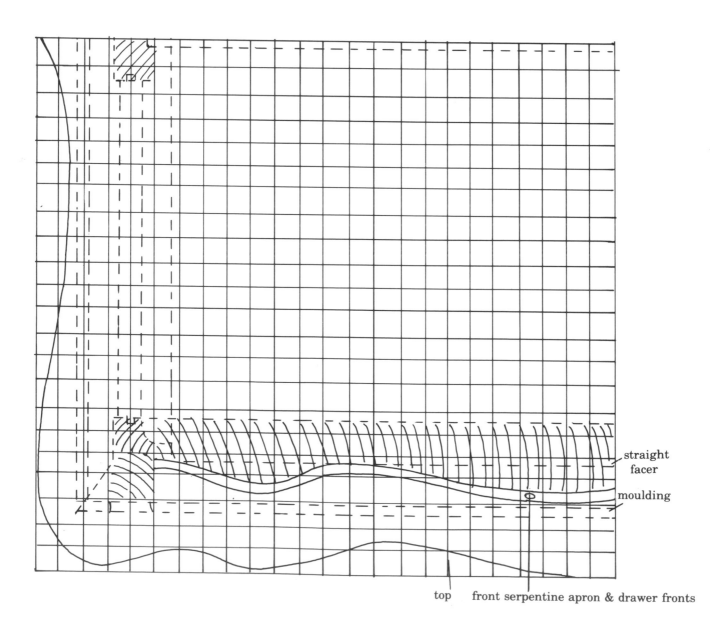

straight facer

moulding

top   front serpentine apron & drawer fronts

(posts). The first step is to enlarge the squared drawing and cut the support bottom (U) to size and shape. Sand it smooth. Then carve the applied carvings and glue them in place to the section. Turn the two mirror standards (W) and fasten them to the top of the support bottom with dowels. The backs of the posts must be flattened slightly so that a metal bracket can be mounted on them. These brackets hold the pins from the mirror frame and allow the mirror to tilt forward and back. Then, finally, cut the bottom support moulding (V) to size and shape and fasten it to the lower part of the support bottom with glue and screws. Turn the mirror standard pediments to shape, carve the pedestals, and glue the pediments to the post tops.

Mirror Frame

The mirror frame is made up of four pieces. Enlarge the squared drawing and cut the pieces (X,Y,Z) to the sizes indicated. Use a shaper to round the curved surfaces and to cut the mirror rabbet in the back of each piece. Join the pieces with dowels at each joint.

Carve the applied carving, as well as the figure-head at the top (AA), and glue to the front of the mirror frame. Then turn the upper "split turning" scroll piece (BB) on the lathe, split it down the middle, and glue it in place as well. Fasten the metal support straps to the mirror support frame and the back of the chest with round head screws. Install the mirror and mirror back; then mount the tilt pins on the back and install the mirror support moulding (T).

Sand, stain, and finish to suit.

Materials List

A—Front legs—$1\frac{3}{4} \times 1\frac{3}{4} \times 31\frac{7}{8}$", 2 req'd.
B—Back legs—$1\frac{3}{4} \times 1\frac{3}{4} \times 31\frac{7}{8}$", 2 req'd.
C—Bottom apron—$2 \times 3 \times 39$", 1 req'd.

Web-Frame Drawer Support

D—Web frame front—$\frac{3}{4} \times 3 \times 39$", 2 req'd.
E—Web frame back—$\frac{3}{4} \times 2 \times 40$", cut to fit, 2 req'd.
F—Web frame sides—$\frac{3}{4} \times 2 \times 17$", cut to fit, 4 req'd.
G—Web frame centers—$\frac{3}{4} \times 2 \times 17$", cut to fit, 4 req'd.

H—Drawer slides—$\frac{1}{4} \times 1 \times 17$", cut to fit, 3 req'd.
I—Drawer guides—$\frac{3}{4} \times \frac{3}{4} \times 14$", cut to fit, 7 req'd.

J—Center facer—$\frac{3}{4} \times 2 \times 6\frac{5}{8}$", cut to fit, 1 req'd.
K—Bottom side rails—$\frac{3}{4} \times 3\frac{1}{2} \times 14\frac{1}{2}$", 2 req'd.
L—Top side rails—$\frac{3}{4} \times 4 \times 14\frac{1}{2}$", 2 req'd.
M—Side panels—$\frac{1}{4}$" plywood $\times 14\frac{1}{2} \times 19$", 2 req'd.
N—Back—$\frac{3}{8}$" plywood $\times 26\frac{3}{4} \times 38\frac{3}{4}$", 1 req'd.
O—Top—$\frac{7}{8} \times 22 \times 47\frac{1}{2}$", 1 req'd.
P—Top moulding—$\frac{3}{4} \times \frac{3}{4} \times 90$", cut to fit, 1 length req'd.
Q—Front side pieces—$1\frac{3}{4} \times 2\frac{1}{2} \times 8\frac{1}{2}$", 2 req'd.
R—Top drawer
    Fronts—$2 \times 5\frac{1}{2} \times 18\frac{7}{16}$", 2 req'd.
    Sides—$\frac{1}{2} \times 5\frac{1}{2} \times 17$", 4 req'd.
    Backs—$\frac{1}{2} \times 5\frac{1}{2} \times 17\frac{7}{16}$", 2 req'd.
    Bottoms—$\frac{1}{4} \times 17\frac{15}{16} \times 18$", 2 req'd.
S—Lower drawer
    Fronts—$2 \times 7\frac{7}{8} \times 37\frac{7}{8}$", 2 req'd.
    Sides—$\frac{1}{2} \times 7\frac{7}{8} \times 17$", 4 req'd.
    Back—$\frac{1}{2} \times 7\frac{7}{8} \times 37\frac{7}{8}$", 2 req'd.
    Bottoms—$\frac{1}{4} \times 17 \times 37\frac{3}{8}$", 2 req'd.

Mirror

T—Mirror support moulding—$\frac{7}{8} \times 2\frac{3}{4} \times 47$", 1 req'd.
U—Mirror support bottom—$\frac{3}{4} \times 8 \times 47$", 1 req'd.
V—Mirror support moulding—$\frac{3}{4}$" thick
W—Mirror standards—$2 \times 2 \times 21$", 2 req'd.
X—Mirror frame bottom—$\frac{3}{4} \times 4\frac{1}{2} \times 36$", cut to fit, 1 req'd.
Y—Mirror frame sides—$\frac{3}{4} \times 3 \times 22$", cut to fit, 2 req'd.
Z—Mirror frame top—$\frac{3}{4} \times 11 \times 42$", cut to fit, 1 req'd.
AA—Carving—2" thick $\times 9 \times 15$", 1 req'd.
BB—Split turning—$1\frac{1}{2} \times 1\frac{1}{2} \times 17$", split, 1 req'd.

Canopy Button Bed

Circa 1850–1875

Spool-turned items were some of the first mass-produced, factory-built furniture pieces made in America. There are a number of variations, including motifs of spools and the more delicately turned "button" style used on the bed shown here. Beds were a popular spool-turned item and came in standard sizes and styles as well as in this high-post, canopy style. The bed shown is one of the better designs and it is one of the few originals left.

The posts on the original bed end just at the top of the top turning (marked AA on the drawing). Then decorative finial posts are added to complete the bed design. The bed can be used with either one of the two sizes of button tops, an acorn finial or, as shown in the photo, with a full post and canopy.

The wood most often used for these beds was walnut, although mahogany, walnut, and cherry are good alternatives.

Construction

This project is a wood turner's dream or nightmare, depending on how you look at it. The turning itself is quite simple, but there is so much of it that I ended up counting buttons in my sleep just from measuring them on the original bed to make the drawings. However, I can tell you that even though they were factory-made there was some discrepancy in the sizes and shapes of the buttons.

Naturally, you'll need a good lathe for this project, and if you have a lathe duplicator, you can save a great deal of the work of this project. The single most important step in the construction is to make sure you get all the buttons laid out and marked accurately on the turning stock. It's hard enough to turn evenly cut buttons, without the added problem of faint or irregular guide marks.

Posts

Start by making up full-size turning patterns for all the posts needed. Then turn the lower bedposts (A). (*Note:* These are 47 inches long, so they can be turned in a standard-size lathe.) Cut mortises in these posts for the lower part of the head and footboard piece (C). Then bore the holes for the tenon ends of the horizontal turned stretchers (D). Bore a hole in the top for the finial or top post joining dowel.

Headboard and Footboard

The headboard and footboard actually consist of horizontal turned button stretchers (D) with vertical spacers (E) between them. The headboard and footboard are exactly the same in size, placement, etc.

Turn the two horizontal pieces to size first. These pieces will require a long lathe bed, or you can turn them in two sections and join them with a dowel in the center if you wish. Turn the round tenons on each end of the horizontal stretchers. Bore holes in their sides for the vertical spacer tenons while the stock is still in the lathe, so that it can be held securely in place. Or you can use a V-block to hold the round stock in position for accurate boring with a drill press.

Turn the spacers (E) to size and shape. Note that they each have a double button on the top and bottom. Make tenons on their ends as well. Sand all pieces as smooth as possible while they are still in the lathe.

The bottom rail (C) of the footboard and headboard consists of a solid piece of 7/8-inch stock cut to the shape shown in the squared drawing. This rail also has tenons on each end to fit into the bedpost mortises. Large dowels could also be used for this joinery.

Assembly of Headboard and Footboard

With all parts shaped and sanded smooth, join the spacers (E) between the horizontal stretchers (D) with glue on their tenons, but make sure you use only a small amount. If excess glue runs down into grooves between the turned buttons it's almost impossible to remove. Temporarily clamp this assembly together; assemble the rest of one end section by placing a bit of glue in the mortises of two leg posts. Fit tenons of all pieces, including the bottom rail (C), in the leg mortises and holes. Make sure the entire unit is square, then clamp and allow the glue to set.

Bed Rails

The side bed rails (B) are also made of 7/8-inch-thick stock, cut to the length and shape shown in the drawing. They match the head and foot rails in design. Install the side rail support cleats (F) with glue and

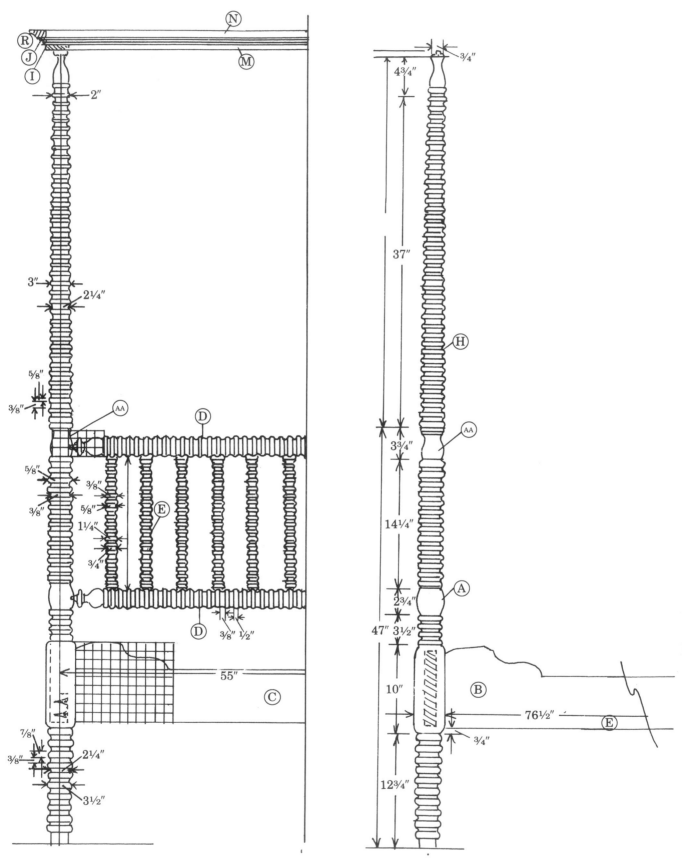

screws to the lower part of the inside face of the boards. Finally, obtain the bed bolt hardware, mortise it into the sides of the bedposts, and fasten it to the ends of the bed rails. Cut the slats (G) to the size needed. They are usually made from 1 × 3's.

Post

If you intend to use the short finials, turn them to the final shape as shown in the drawing. Include the turned tenons on their ends to fit down in the dowel hole in the top of the lower bedposts.

The upper bedposts (H) are turned in the same manner. Again, if you have a lathe bed that limits you to shorter turnings, just make up a couple of turnings for each post and join them with glue and a large wooden dowel. Note that the long posts are tapered and that the taper should be cut first. Then lay out the buttons on the taper and turn them to size and shape. The top of each post has a dowel turned on its end to fit up into the canopy support.

Canopy Support

The canopy bottom support (I,L) is made of 1 × 3's half lapped together at each corner. Bore holes through them at the corner so that the support frame will fit down on the bedpost dowels. Top moulding (J,K,M,N) is run on a shaper or with a router. Install it around the outside edge of the canopy frame with glue and small brads or with wood screws from the back.

Materials List

A—Lower bedposts—3½ × 3½ × 47″, 4 req'd.
B—Side bed rails—⅞ × 9 × 76½″, 2 req'd.

C—Head- and footboard rails—⅞ × 9 × 51½″, 2 req'd.
D—Head- and footboard horizontal turnings—2¼ × 2¼ × 52½″, 4 req'd.
E—Head- and footboard vertical turnings—1⅜ × 1⅜ × 15½″, 24 req'd.
F—Side rail support cleats—1 × 3 × 76½″, 2 req'd.
G—Slats—1 × 3 × 55″, cut to tight fit, 5 req'd.
H—Upper bedposts—2½ × 2½ × 42½″, 4 req'd.
   ### Canopy
I—Side bottom canopy—¾ × 3 × 82½″, 2 req'd.
J—Side canopy trim—¾ × 1 × 84″, 2 req'd.
K—Side canopy top trim—1 × 2 × 88″, 2 req'd.
L—End bottom canopy—¾ × 3 × 58½″, 2 req'd.
M—End canopy trim—¾ × 1 × 60″, 2 req'd.
N—End canopy top trim—1 × 2 × 64″, 2 req'd.
Bed fasteners

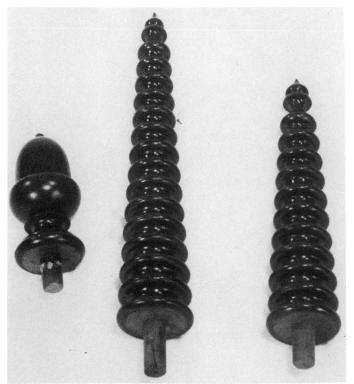

Button Bed Tops

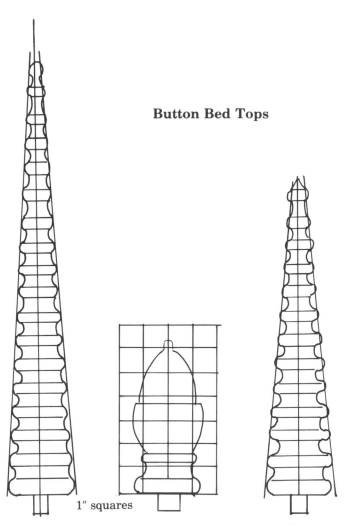

1″ squares

Corner Chair
Circa 1850, England

This corner chair design is from the beginning of the Victorian period of furniture building in England. It is, however, patterned after an earlier Chippendale corner chair made between 1750 and 1780.

The chair shown was made of English oak, though the earlier Chippendale versions were made of mahogany. The Queen Anne corner chair was also similar to this design. It had Queen Anne legs and feet. There was a front cabriole leg, while the sides and back had turned legs and Queen Anne-style feet.

Construction

Although ornate and complicated in appearance, the corner chair is relatively easy to build. Because of the location of the three turned legs, it is sturdier than some of the more delicate chair styles. Rails are held to the legs with mortise-and-tenon joints pegged with wood dowels.

Legs

The first step in construction is to enlarge the squared drawing and make a pattern for the front cabriole leg (A). Then shape and carve it to specifications. Note that the side wings of the leg are glued in place to the center post. After carving, cut the inside corners in the top of the front leg to allow the seatboard to be placed in position. Then round the tops of the outside edges. Cut mortises for aprons (C).

Enlarge the squared drawing for the back and side legs (B) and trace them off on a turning blank. Locate and cut mortises in them. Then turn the legs to shape, making sure to turn a dowel on the top end of each to fit up into the splats (E).

Arm

Enlarge the squared drawing for the arm and transfer this to two pieces of stock. Cut the 45-degree mitre joint where the two pieces join in the center and join with glue and dowels. Clamp overnight. Then cut the arm to shape on a band saw or with a sabre saw. Locate and bore the dowel holes on the bottom side of the arm for the leg dowels. Locate and cut mortises on the underside of the arm for the splat tenons (E). Note that you will have to place the squared drawing over the arm (make sure it is positioned correctly) to locate these mortises. A great deal of care is needed here for a good, accurate fit.

Cut the backrest (G) from a piece of stock, following the pattern from the square drawing. Sand and smooth it to shape and fasten it in place to the upper center of the arm with glue and dowels or countersunk screws. Allow it to dry overnight; then lightly round the edges on the top and bottom of the arm.

Splats

Enlarge the square drawing for the splats (E) and trace them off onto ½-inch solid stock. Bore starting holes in the proper places and use a scroll saw to cut away and create the fretwork. Note that there is a slight carved effect in the center of the pattern under the two sweeping arms. This is achieved by undercutting the bottom portion up to this point, as shown in the drawing. Sand the splats as smooth as possible and cut mortises on their upper and lower ends.

Seat Frame

Cut the two front seat aprons (C) to proper length and shape, including the rounded arch on the bottom. Then cut tenons on each end, cut rabbets into the inside top edges, and lightly round the outside top edge. Cut the back apron pieces (H) to shape. Use a table saw to cut the cove on the front edges and then a band saw to make the back sweep cuts. Use scratch moulding or a chisel to carve the tiny moulding shape at the top of the upsweep. Then cut the mortise in the top of the splat tenons.

Assembly

With all the pieces shaped, and well sanded, the next step is the assembly. Join with glue and work on a clean, smooth flat surface. The first step is to place some glue on the tenons of the front aprons (C) and fit them into the front leg (A). Then place tenons at the other end of the front apron into mortises in the side legs (B). Put the back aprons (H) in place with their tenons in mortises in the back of the side legs. Finally, put the back leg in place.

Position the chair upright on a smooth, flat surface. Make sure it is square and doesn't rock or tilt from leg to leg. Clamp the assembly securely. Without applying any glue, temporarily place the arms (F) down over the leg dowels. This will ensure that the legs are clamped squarely, and that their tops or bottoms have not tilted in or out. Leave the entire assembly overnight.

After the bottom assembly has been completed, cut and install the seatboard supports (I), or glue

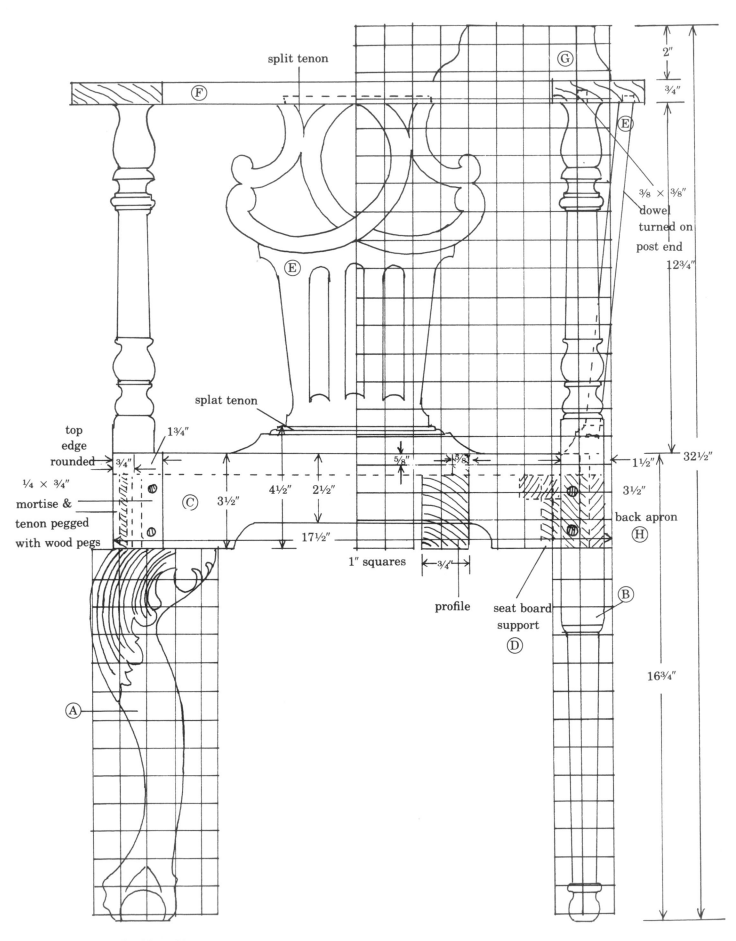

split tenon

top edge rounded

⅛ × ¾"
mortise & tenon pegged with wood pegs

split tenon

splat tenon

1¾"

¾"

⅜ × ⅜"
dowel turned on post end
12¾"

2"

¾"

32½"

1½"

3½"

back apron

Ⓗ

3½"

4½"

2½"

⅝"

⅝"

17½"

1" squares

¾"

profile

seat board support

Ⓓ

Ⓒ

Ⓕ

Ⓖ

Ⓔ

Ⓔ

Ⓐ

Ⓑ

16¾"

½"

¼'

85°

17½"

14½"

blocks and fasten them in place with glue and screws.

You could, of course, glue and clamp the entire chair together at this time, but it would take a large number of clamps. The easier method is to clamp seat frame, aprons, and legs together first. Once the glue has set, bore holes through the mortise-and-tenon joints and drive the wooden pegs in place with glue in the holes to secure the entire seat-frame assembly.

To assemble the top portion, apply some glue in the bottom mortises of the back seat frames and then put the splats (E) in place. Place a bit of glue on the top dowels of the chair legs and the tops of the splat tenons. Then carefully fit the chair arms (F) in place. This operation will take about fifteen hands, so you may need some help. Clamp the arm securely in place, or weight it down with heavy books. Clean away all excess glue and allow to sit overnight. Then stain and finish.

Assemble the seatboard (J) from ¾-inch stock and upholster it with an appropriate fabric over a foam

Arm, Half Pattern

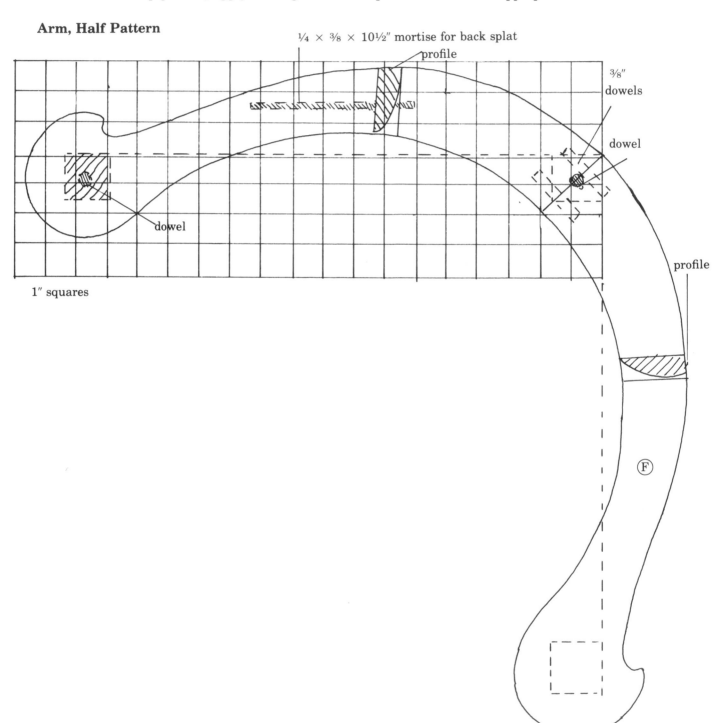

¼ × ⅜ × 10½" mortise for back splat

profile

⅜"
dowels

dowel

dowel

1" squares

profile

F

profile

pad. Fasten the fabric on the bottom underside edges. Then fasten the seatboard in place with screws through the seat supports from the bottom.

Materials List

A—Front leg—5 × 5 × 16¾″, 1 req'd.

B—Back and side legs—1½ × 1½ × 29½, 3 req'd.

C—Front seat aprons—¾ × 3½ × 15¼″, 2 req'd.

D—Seatboard supports, back—¾ × 2¼ × 14½, 2 req'd.

E—Splats—½ × 9 × 12½″, cut to shape, 2 req'd.

F—Arms—¾ × 6 × 19″, cut to shape, 2 req'd.

G—Backrest—2 × 10 × 15″, cut to shape, 1 req'd.

H—Back aprons—1½ × 4½ × 15½″, 2 req'd.

I—Seatboard supports, sides—¾ × 2 × 2, 4 req'd.

J—Seatboard—¾ × 15⅜ × 15⅜, 1 req'd.

Seat Frame

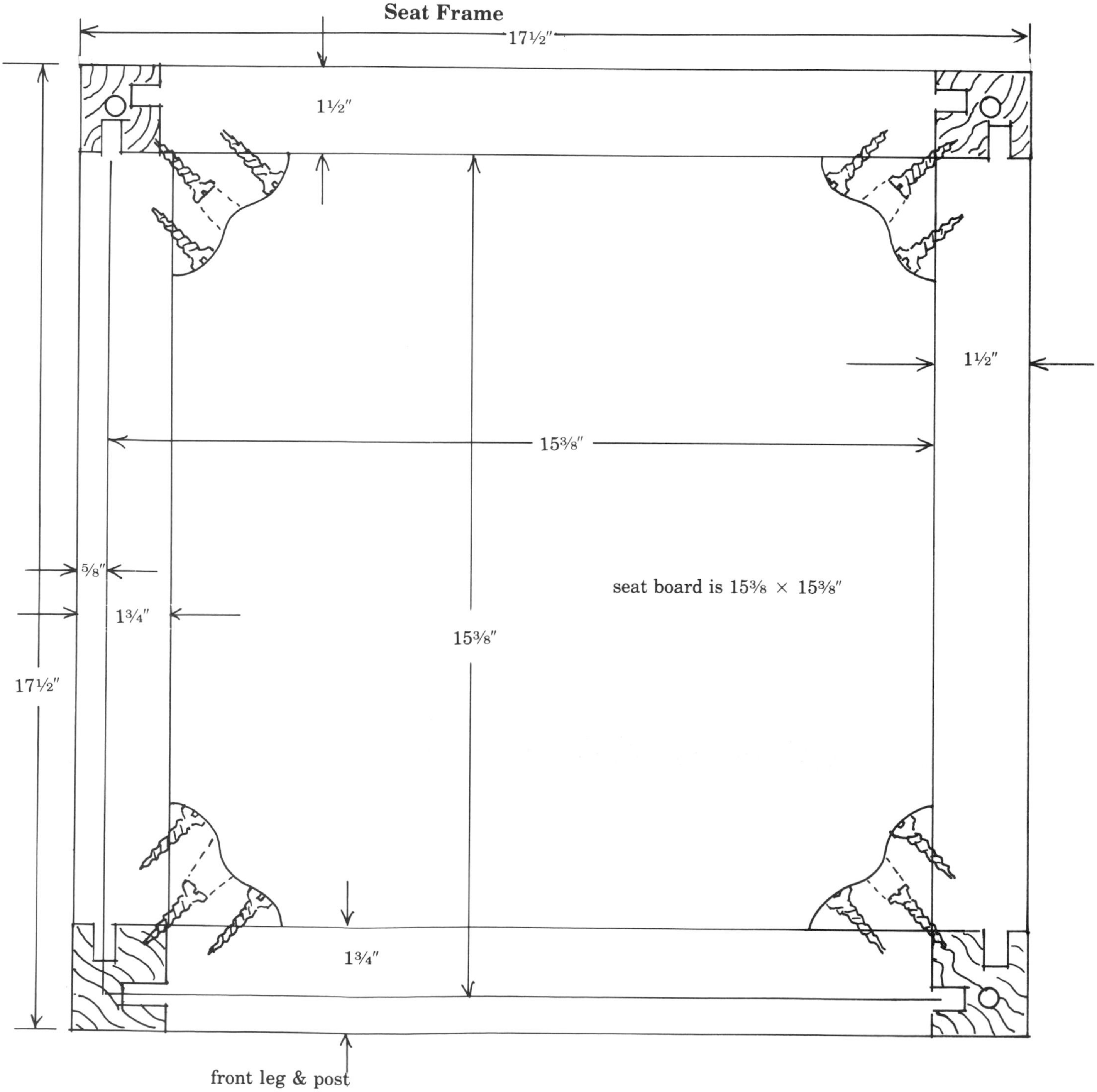
17½″
1½″
1½″
15⅜″
⅝″
1¾″
seat board is 15⅜ × 15⅜″
15⅜″
17½″
1¾″
front leg & post

Round Tilt-Top Table

Circa 1750
The Metropolitan Museum of Art, Rogers Fund, 1925

This walnut table is an excellent example of the Chippendale-style tripod, tip-and-turn tables that were manufactured in Philadelphia during the height of the period-furniture boom of 1850 to 1880. These tables were extremely popular and quite ingeniously designed.

The top was usually made of one solid piece of stock, and it was recessed to create a lip around the outer edge. In cheaper versions, the lip was applied or glued on, but it invariably separated. On better-quality tables, the lip was one with the top.

The edge was also sometimes left smooth and round, while other versions had various types of designs cut into them. At times, designs had the appearance of the "pinched" top of a piecrust, thereby giving rise to the name "piecrust tables." These tops can be routed quite easily with modern equipment. In fact, the Sears® Craftsman Edgecrafter, which is used with a router and router table, is designed primarily for this job.

One of the main features of these tables was that the top was hinged to tip down. Then the table could be stood in a corner and out of the way until needed. With the top tipped up it could be used as a tea table or for other purposes.

In addition, many of the better tables also had a bird-cage design at the top of the pedestal. This was fitted with a slotted tenon and peg. When the peg was removed, the table was free to revolve. Although the original table shown here is made of walnut—the most popular material of the time—either mahogany or cherry would be excellent alternative woods.

Construction
The simple, serpent-foot design and bulbous turning of the table shown makes it fairly easy to construct. Instructions for edging the top are given on page 11.

Post
Start by enlarging the squared drawing and turning the post (A) to size and shape, including the long dowel-like tenon on its upper end. Note that the bottom of the post has small indentations cut into it to form a decorative scalloped edge. This is done with a woodworking rasp or a medium-size gouge.

Turn the post upside down and divide the bottom face into thirds using a protractor. Mark locations for the dovetailed slots for the legs (B). With the stock in the lathe, make the slots using a dovetail cutter in a router. To cut slots while the stock is in the lathe, mount the router in a special fluting jig or remove the stock from the lathe and use a router and router table. Or you can use the Craftsman Routercrafter. These methods are covered on page 11.

Sand the entire post as smooth as possible while it is still in the lathe. Cut the mortise for the top locking pin (G) using a portable electric drill to make the preliminary hole, then smooth it up with chisels.

Feet
Enlarge the squared drawing for the legs (B). Before cutting them to shape from the stock, mark the locations of the dovetails on their ends. Cut them to size and shape using a table or radial arm saw. Set the saw blade at a bevel to make the initial cuts from the end; then saw down from the sides to complete the cut.

Make the dovetails fit snugly in post slots. This will take a bit of experimentation and will depend on how sharp your saw blade is, what kind it is, etc. It's a good idea to cut the post slots and then experiment with a piece of scrap stock until you get the right setting on your saw for the leg tenons. Cut the legs to rough shape on a band saw. Then use drum sanders and slap sanders in a portable electric drill to round the edges and create the serpentine feet. You could also use large wood rasps to do the rough shaping.

Bottom-Post Assembly
Once all the leg pieces have been properly cut, shaped and sanded, place glue in the dovetail slots of the post bottom and tap the legs into place. Stand the unit upright on a smooth, flat surface and make sure it doesn't wobble or tilt to one side. Use a large carpenter's square to determine if the post is perfectly vertical.

Bird Cage
Cut the bottom (C) of the bird cage assembly to size and shape and drill a hole through it for the top of the post (A) to slide through. The hole must be sized to fit the post dowel so that the tabletop turns easily. Cut the stopped dowel holes for tenons on the bird cage turnings (E).

Cut and shape the top (D) of the bird cage in the same manner. Then bore the hole through its end for the dowel pivot pin (H) that holds the tabletop. Enlarge the squared drawing and make the bird cage turnings, including their tenoned ends.

Assemble the bird cage by sliding the bottom piece down over the post dowel. Then slide the locking collar (F) down over it. Fasten this in place with a small brad or wooden dowel through it and the post dowel.

Then put the bird cage turnings in place, position the bird cage top piece in place and glue and clamp

until the glue sets. Make sure that you don't get any glue down in the joint between the post dowel and the bottom piece. If you do, the bird cage unit will not turn on the dowel. Cut and shape the locking pin (G) that slides through the mortise in the post dowel. This pin makes it possible to keep the tabletop from revolving.

Top

Although the original top (J) was made using a single solid piece of stock, the best bet is to glue up the stock. Use dowels or tongue-and-groove joints and

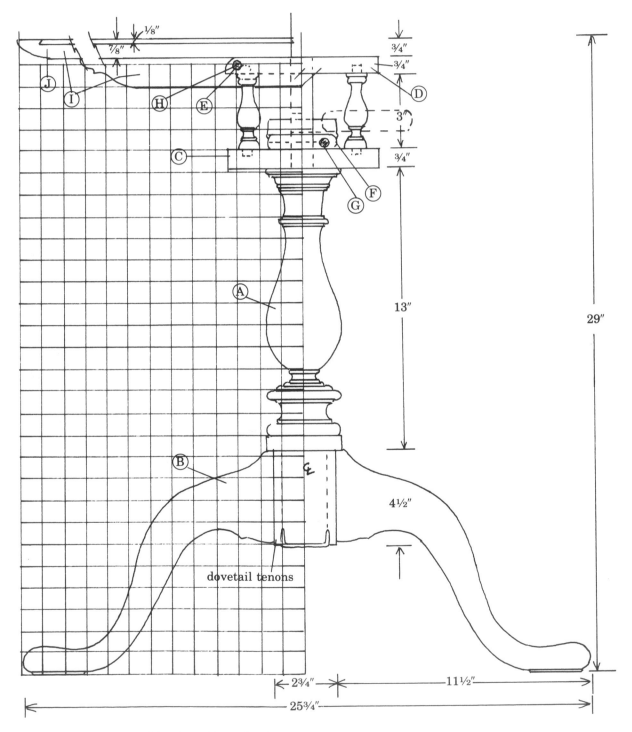

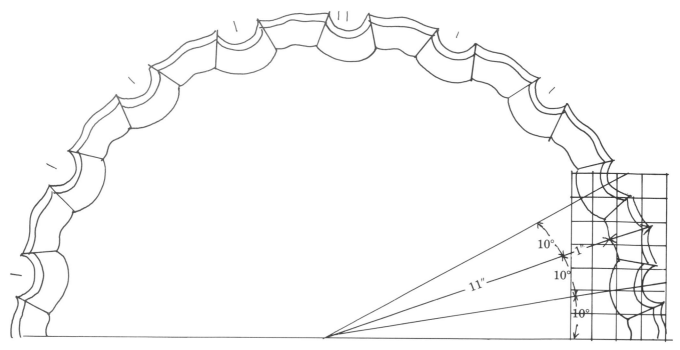

Piecrust Pattern

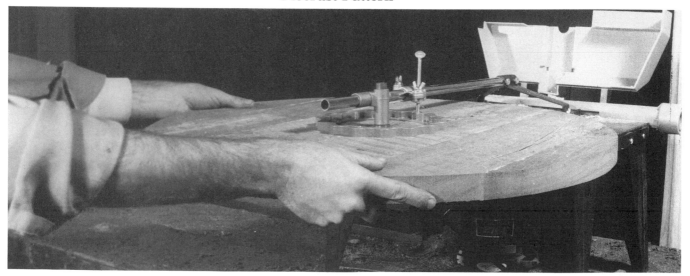

glue the stock into a stable, flat, smooth surface. Then cut away glue lines and sand the top smooth with progressively finer sanding machines and sandpaper.

Then saw the top to shape. You can make the lip on the smooth, round top using the faceplate on the out-feed end of your lathe, if your lathe is equipped with one. If you prefer, you can make the scalloped-shape top (see detail drawing) using the pin and guide method or the Edgecrafter, as shown on page 11. Sand and smooth the table surface completely. Cut the top cleats (I) to size and shape and fasten them to the underside of the tabletop with glue and screws.

The last step is to connect the top to the bird cage by inserting the holding dowel pin (H) through holes in the top cleats and the bird cage top. Then install

the small tilt-top table catch, available from period-furniture hardware supply companies.

Sand, stain, and finish.

Materials List

A—Post—$3\frac{1}{2} \times 3\frac{1}{2} \times 22''$, 1 req'd.

B—Legs—$1\frac{1}{2} \times 10\frac{3}{8} \times 12''$, 3 req'd.

C—Bird cage bottom—$\frac{3}{4} \times 7 \times 7''$, 1 req'd.

D—Bird cage top—$\frac{3}{4} \times 7 \times 7''$, 1 req'd.

E—Bird cage turnings—$1 \times 1 \times 4\frac{3}{8}''$, 4 req'd.

F—Locking collar—$\frac{1}{2} \times 3 \times 3''$, 1 req'd.

G—Locking pin—$\frac{1}{2} \times 1 \times 3''$, 1 req'd.

H—Holding dowel—$\frac{3}{8} \times 8\frac{1}{2}''$, 1 req'd.

I—Top cleat—$\frac{3}{4} \times 1\frac{1}{4} \times 20''$, 2 req'd.

J—Top—$\frac{7}{8} \times 28 \times 28''$, glued up, 1 req'd.

Chippendale-Style Chair

Circa 1850

With its traditional Chippendale styling, this graceful and elegantly designed chair goes well with almost any traditional decor. The original piece shown here was made in England following designs typical of Thomas Chippendale, one of the most famous 18th-century furniture makers. The flared back, carved apron, and delicately carved splat are all typical of Chippendale styling.

The chair this project is patterned after is a sturdy, well-built piece of furniture. With proper care in construction, your reproduction will be every bit as durable as the original.

In almost all cases, earlier Chippendale pieces were constructed of mahogany. The original shown here was made during a later period, and walnut was used. The chair could also be made of cherry or other fruitwood, but wouldn't be nearly as traditional in appearance.

Construction

Constructing a chair of this type is a challenge for even the most advanced woodworker. The decision to produce a set for a dining room should be considered very carefully unless you have a carving duplicator that can be used to duplicate the cabriole legs and other carvings. Note that there are no stretchers between the legs.

Front Legs

The first step is to enlarge the squared drawing and create patterns for the cabriole legs (A). Glue wing blocks to the sides of leg posts with dowel and glue, taking care to ensure that dowels are out of the cutting lines of the leg.

Then cut the leg to shape on a band saw. Carve the ball-and-claw foot on the bottom. Again, if you have or can get a carving duplicator, it will make this job quite easy.

Rough-cut the tops of the posts to the correct shape for the seatboard-frame insert, then cut mortises in the leg posts for apron (F,G,H,I) tenons.

Aprons

Cut the side aprons (H) to size and shape and round the top outside edge slightly. Cut the chair seat rabbet on the inside edge. Cut tenons on each end of the aprons.

The front apron (F) must be cut on a band saw and you will have to use a shaper, hand plane, or router to cut the shaped rabbet on the inside edge. Again, slightly round the outside top edge.

Cut the bottom carved decorative apron (G) for the front with a band saw and make tenons on each end. Carve the apron by following the squared drawing pattern. Cut the side decorative aprons (I) in the same manner, make tenons on their ends and carve them to shape as well.

Cut the back apron (E) to size and shape, including the tenons on each end. The procedure for cutting is to first cut the front cove shape for the inside top part using a table saw set for coving. A shaper can also be used. Next, cut side wings to shape with a band saw and rabbet plane or small chisels. Finally, cut the mortise in the top for the back splat.

Back Legs

Enlarge the squared drawing for the back legs (B) and saw them to shape on a band saw. Cut the small beading on the outside front edges, as shown in the drawing. Cut mortises in the front and sides for aprons, and make tenons on each end to fit into the back top pieces (C). (See profile in side-view drawing.)

Chair Back

Cut the chair back top piece (C) to size and shape, again on a band saw and following the pattern. Cut mortises into the underside of each end of the top piece for back leg (B) tenons. Then make mortises for the back splat (D). Carve the chair back top piece to shape with the small beading on the front. Round the back edge to match the chair leg tops. Try-fit this piece several times until you get a perfect match between the chair leg tops and the mating bottom ends of the chair back top piece.

Back Splat

Enlarge the squared drawing for the back splat (D) and cut it to shape using a scroll saw for the open parts. Cut tenons on each end to fit into the back apron (E) and chair back top piece (C). The back splat may need to be steamed to bend; then carve the splat to the correct shape, as shown in the drawing.

Assembly

Assembly of the chair starts with the back legs (B). It's a good idea with a project this complicated to make a dry run of assembling the pieces to ensure

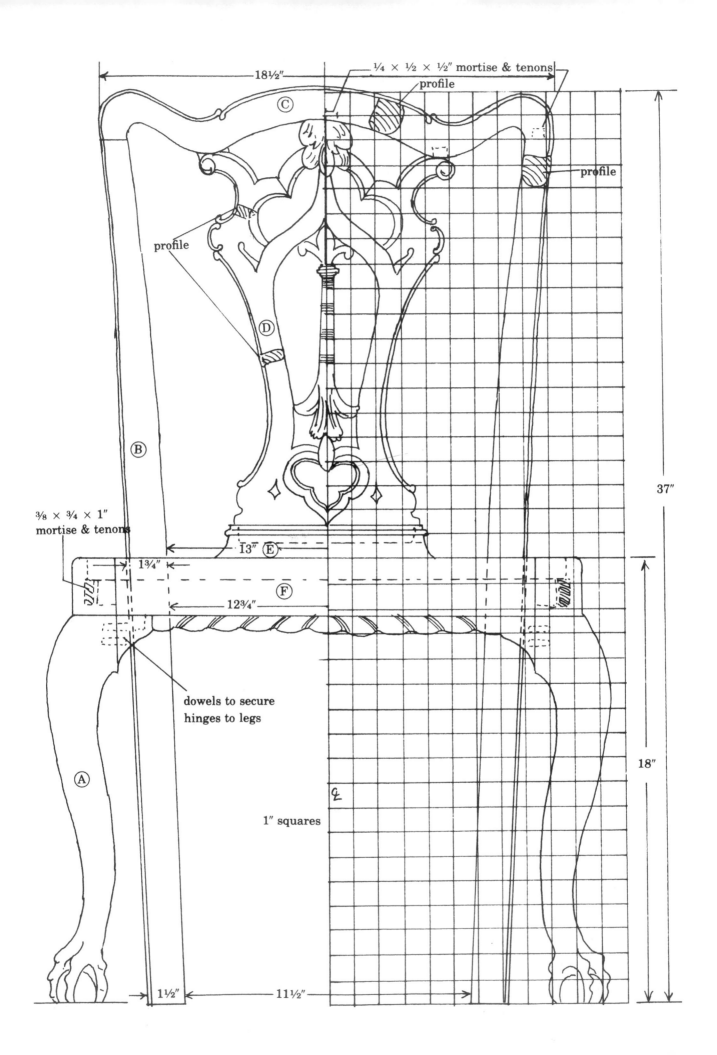

18½"

¼ × ½ × ½" mortise & tenons
profile

Ⓒ

profile

profile

Ⓓ

Ⓑ

37"

⅜ × ¾ × 1"
mortise & tenons

13" Ⓔ

1¾"

Ⓕ

12¾"

dowels to secure
hinges to legs

Ⓐ

18"

Ȼ

1" squares

1½"

11½"

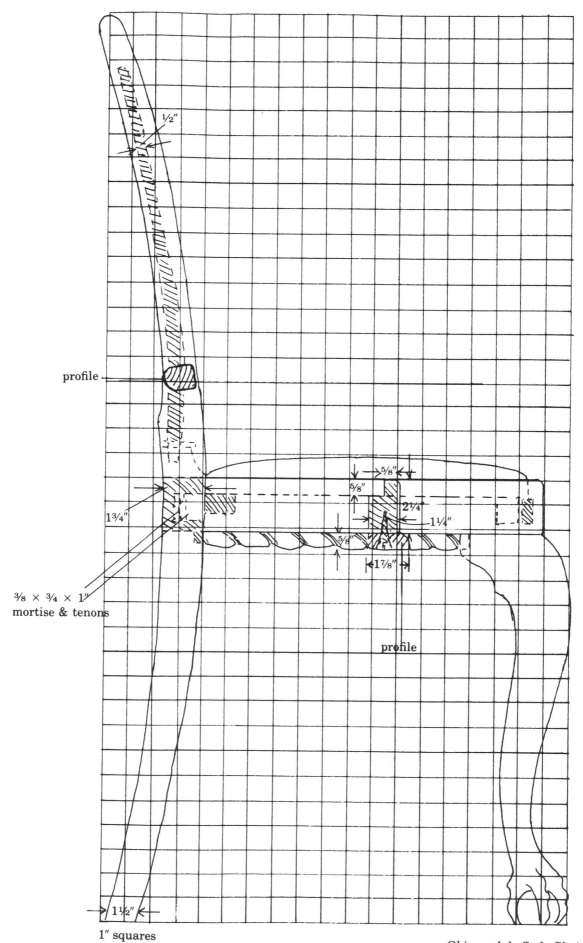

profile

½"

profile

1¾"

⅜ × ¾ × 1"
mortise & tenons

⅝"
⅝"
⅝"
2¼"
1¼"
1⅞"
1½"

1½"

1" squares

that all tenons fit properly in mortises and that pieces mate properly. Once you have glue in place, it's too late to stop and shave off a bit of material for a proper fit. Use a soft mallet to hammer and tap the pieces together without glue.

Once you have checked for a good fit, assemble the pieces as follows, placing glue on the ends of the tenons. The standard procedure is to put glue on the ends of back apron (E) tenons and fit them into the chair leg mortises first. Then place the back splat (D) tenon in the back apron. Finally, position the chair back top piece (C) in place down over the tenons on the back splat and legs. Make sure the assembly is square, checking each joint carefully.

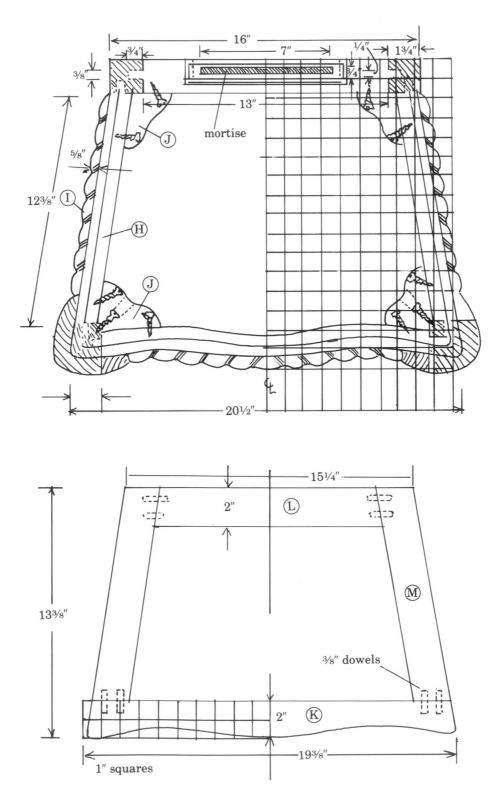

Joints should be solidly closed without cracks at any point. Then clamp securely with band clamps and allow the glue to set overnight.

Remove clamps from the back assembly. Fasten the bottom decorative aprons (G,I) to the undersides of the front (F) and side (H) aprons with countersunk wood screws. Then mate front apron tenons into mortises in the front legs. Repeat the step on the side aprons, placing tenons in the front-leg mortises first. Then position this entire assembly in place, mating back tenons of the side aprons into mortises in the back legs.

Now turn the assembly upright on a smooth, flat surface. Make sure it stands squarely with each foot solidly on the surface and does not rock from leg to leg. If it does, rack or twist it until it stands solidly. Then clamp parts firmly in place using bar and band clamps. Check again after tightening the clamps to assure the assembly is still square.

Allow the assembly to sit overnight and then install the seat cleats (J). Smooth up the rabbets on the inside for the seatboard. Cut away any dried glue runs with a sharp chisel and sand the entire piece glass smooth.

Construct the seatboard (K-M) as per the drawing (or cut from solid ⅝-inch plywood) and stain and finish the chair. Incidentally, if you plan to make up several chairs, it's a good idea to do it in an assembly-line procedure, making the same piece for all chairs at the same time.

Materials List

A—Front legs—4½ × 4½ × 18″, 2 req'd.

B—Back legs—1¾ × 4½ × 36″, 2 req'd.

C—Back top piece—1¼ × 3 × 18½″, 1 req'd.

D—Back splat—½ × 11 × 18″, 1 req'd.

E—Back apron—1¾ × 3⅝ × 14¾″, 1 req'd.

F—Front apron—1¼ × 2¼ × 20½″, 1 req'd.

G—Front decorative apron—⅝ × 1⅞ × 14″, 1 req'd.

H—Side aprons—1¼ × 2¼ × 13½″, 2 req'd.

I—Decorative side aprons—⅝ × 1⅞ × 11″, 2 req'd.

J—Front & back seat cleats—¾ × 3½ × 3½″, 4 req'd.

K—Seatboard, front—¾ × 2 × 19⅜″, 1 req'd.

L—Seatboard, back—¾ × 2 × 11⅜″, 1 req'd.

M—Seatboard, sides—¾ × 2 × 11½″, 2 req'd.

Chippendale Armchair

Circa 1760

If it weren't for the sheen and the smell of fresh wood, even an expert would have trouble distinguishing this reproduction from the original Chippendale. The armchair shown is a reproduction made by Mount Airy Furniture Company of Mount Airy, North Carolina, and it is a fine example of workmanship. The carving on the back splat is excellent and the general construction is quite true to the original.

The chair shown is made of walnut, though it would also look quite good made of mahogany. A lightweight wood, however, is not recommended for this project, because it would detract from the massive, yet elegant and graceful design of the chair.

Construction

As with any project of this nature, cutting and fitting the pieces properly is the hard part. Assembly, on the other hand, is fairly easy. There is quite a bit of delicate carving on the back splat. The cabriole legs, shaped and carved arms, and arm supports will also prove challenging for even the most skilled craftsmen.

Front Legs

Enlarge the squared drawing and cut the front cabriole legs (A) to size and shape. Then carve the legs to the pattern.

When this much carving is involved, and especially if you plan to build more than one chair, consider using a duplicating carving machine, such as the Dupli-Carver®. It can make this tedious chore fast and easy. All you do is carve one leg to the exact shape and then simply use the machine to duplicate carvings on any number of legs needed.

After carving, cut the top portion of the outside of the legs to size and shape, as shown in the top view of the chair. Then cut mortises in the sides of the leg posts for the front (C) and side (E) rails.

Rails

Cut the side rails (E) to size and shape, including the angled ends. Then cut the tenons that fit into the back legs and front legs. Incidentally, if you prefer to use dowels to join the legs and rails, it's a bit easier than trying to cut the angled mortise-and-tenon joints. But the dowelled joint is not quite as strong, an important consideration in a chair.

Cut the back rail (D) to size and shape, including its tenons, and then make the mortise in the top for the back splat (G). The front rail (C) is serpentine shaped on its front edge. First, cut the rail to length and make tenons on its ends to match the front-leg mortise. Then enlarge the squared drawing of the front edge and use it to create the serpentine shape. Sand the curves with a drum sander.

Back Legs

The back legs (B) are compound cut. Enlarge the squared drawing and cut them to size and shape. Cut the mortises in them for the side (E) and back (D) rails. Then cut the mortise notch for the arms (I).

Finally, make tenons on their top ends to fit into the top back piece (F) mortise. Then shape the moulded front and round the upper back part.

Back

The top back (F) and back splat (G) are cut using a band saw for the back and a scroll saw for the scrollwork on the back splat. Then make the relief carving of the pattern given on the drawing. Cut mortises in the top back piece. Make the tenons on the ends of the back splat to fit into the back rail and top back.

Arms

Enlarge the squared drawing and make the compound cuts to fashion the arms (I) to size and shape. Cut notched tenons in each to fit into the back-leg posts (see arm-joint detail). Then cut the mortises for the arm support posts. Carve the shallow relief carvings on the tops of the arms.

Enlarge the squared drawing and saw the arm supports (H) to size and shape. Shape their front edges (see arm-joint detail) and slightly round the rest of the edges. Then cut the tenons on their top ends to fit up into the arms.

Assembly

Before assembly, sand each piece as smooth as possible and fit all the pieces together without glue to make absolutely sure that all tenons fit into their mating mortises easily but snugly.

Assembly starts with the back assembly. Place glue on the bottom tenon of the back splat (G) and position splat and back rail (D) together. Then fit the back legs (B) over the tenons of the back rail. Finally, tap the top back piece (F) down over the

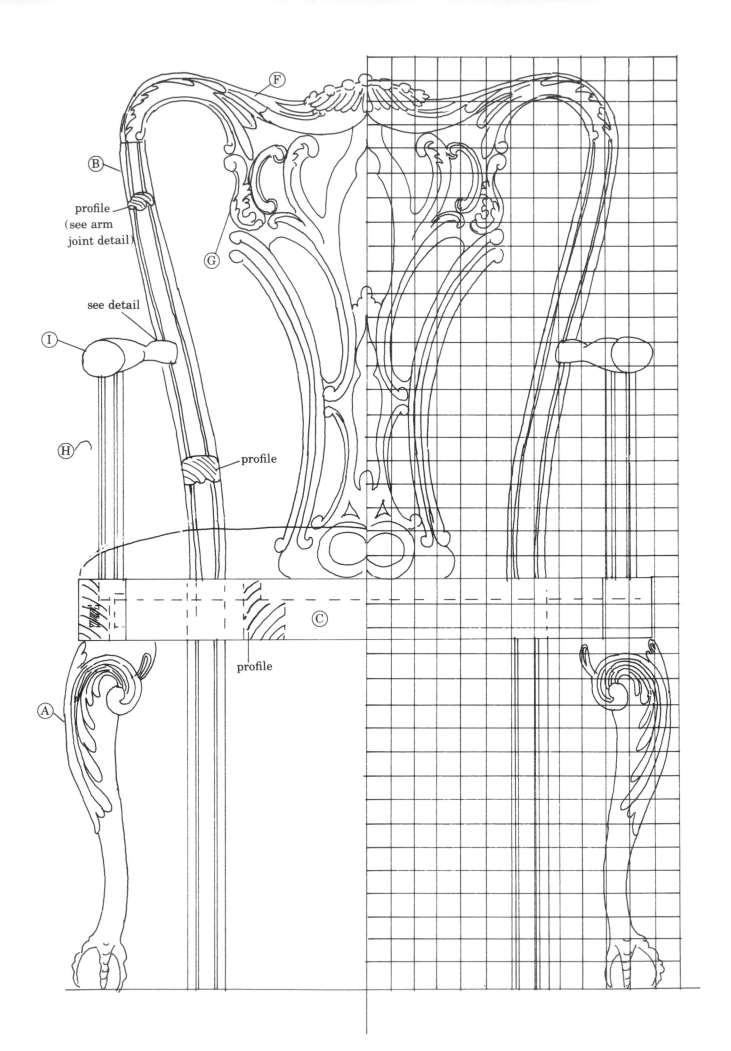

F

B

profile
(see arm
joint detail)

G

see detail

I

H

profile

profile

C

profile

A

back splat and leg posts. Temporarily clamp this together and assemble the front cabriole legs (A) and front rails (C). Then place the side rails (E) between the front and back sections. With the chair on a smooth, flat surface, make sure it stands absolutely square and clamp all pieces together. This will take quite a bit of clamping and some unusual clamps, including band clamps, to do a good job. Leave the assembly in clamps until the glue sets.

Remove the chair frame from the clamps and fasten the arms (I) and arm supports (H) together. Insert the arm tenons into the mortises of the back legs and fasten the arm posts to the chair side rails with glue and screws driven through the inside of the side rails.

Cut the corner braces (J) and fasten in place with glue and screws. In most instances for this type of chair a traditional seatboard arrangement is replaced by metal spring supports.

Sand, stain, and finish.

Materials List

A—Cabriole legs—4 × 4 × 17″, 2 req'd.
B—Back legs—5 × 5 × 39″, 2 req'd.
C—Front rail—2 × 2½ × 21½″, 1 req'd.
D—Back rail—1½ × 2½ × 12″, 1 req'd.
E—Side rails—1½ × 2½ × 17½″, 2 req'd.
F—Top back—1 × 3 × 22″, 1 req'd.
G—Back splat—1 × 6 × 20½″, 1 req'd.
H—Arm supports—1 × 3½ × 12″, 2 req'd.
I—Arms—2 × 4 × 17″, 2 req'd.
J—Seat corner braces—¾ × 2 × 2″, 4 req'd.

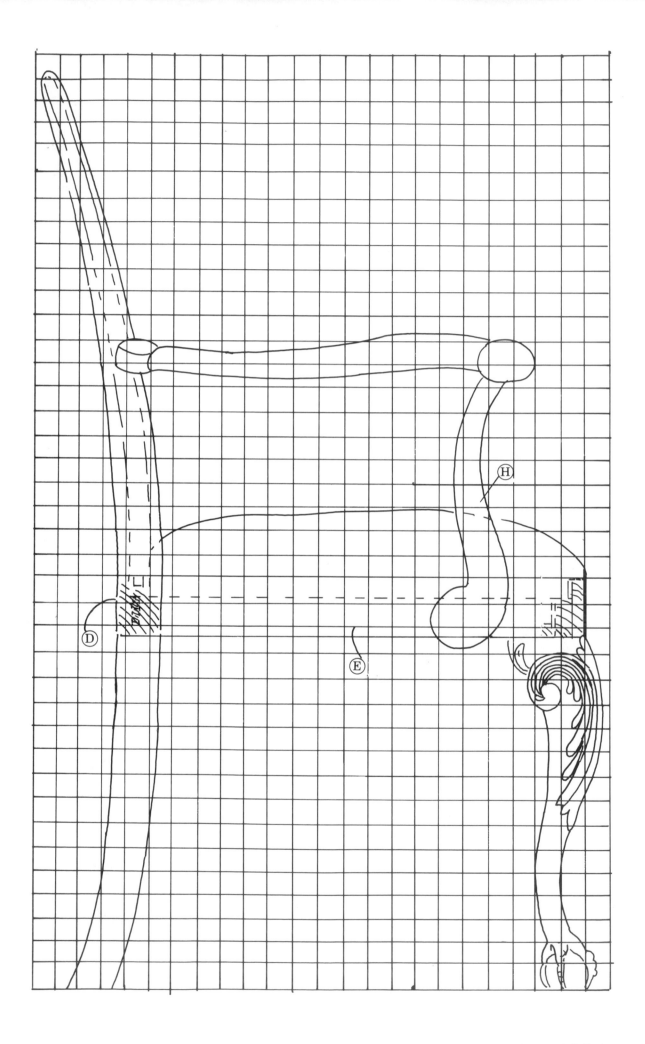

Top View

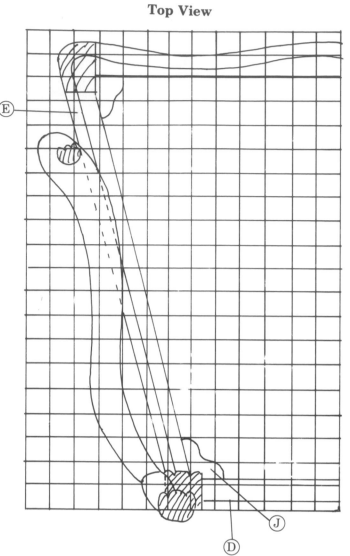

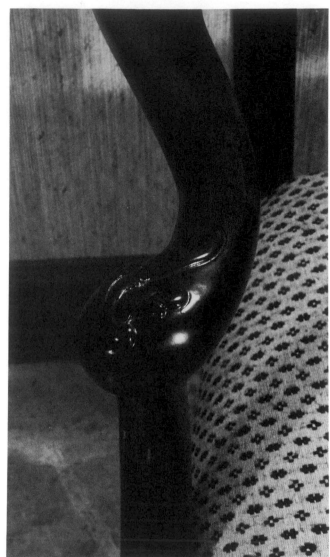

Arm Joint Detail

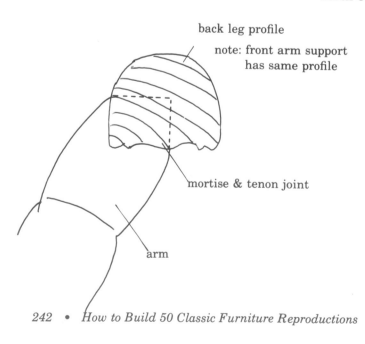

back leg profile

note: front arm support
has same profile

mortise & tenon joint

arm

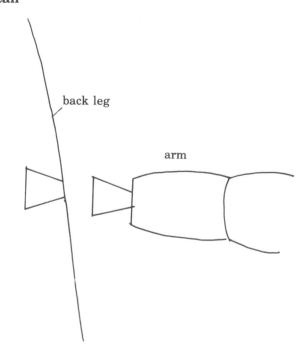

back leg

arm

Victorian Sofa Table

Marble-topped tables were quite popular around the turn of the century, and this little sofa table is a popular reproduction. Normally these were made of mahogany, but they would also look good constructed of pecan or walnut. These days, synthetic marble is also available if you're unable to obtain real marble of the size and shape needed.

Construction

Construction is fairly straightforward and a good project for the intermediate woodworker. Although small in size, the table is surprisingly challenging and a number of woodworking skills and tools are needed.

Top

The bulk of the construction of the table involves turning for the top (A) and the lower pedestal (B). The 1½-inch-thick top can be made of one solid piece, which produces the best appearance, but a block that size is fairly expensive, and you may prefer to glue it up by gluing ¾-inch-thick blocks to the underside of a ¾-inch-thick solid top piece. Regardless of which method is used, the top (A) is fastened to a faceplate and turned on a lathe. You will probably wish to cut the top block to square, then draw diagonal lines across the corners to first locate the center. Then use a compass to draw a circle the correct radius and rough-cut the top block to shape on a band saw. Fasten the faceplate in place with wood screws from the underside of the block, locating it directly over the previously drawn diagonal lines. Turn to the correct size and cut the small groove on the outside edge.

Pedestal

The pedestal (B) is turned from a single block of wood. One of the hardest problems is locating the dowels to hold the feet in place. It's a good idea to mark diagonally across corners on both the top and bottom of the block. Turn it to rough shape, and finish the lower leg-holding portion except for the bottom rounded tip. Then use the lines on both top and bottom of the rough-cut block to locate the position of the legs. Finish turning and sanding the pedestal, but leave in the lathe until you complete the next step.

Legs

Next, enlarge the squared drawing and make a pattern for the legs (C), then transfer this to the solid wood stock to be used for them. Cut on a band saw or

using a sabre saw, and sand the edges smooth using a drum sander.

Assembly

Mark locations on the edges of the legs (C) that join the pedestal, and bore ⅜-inch dowel holes into the ends of the legs. Place dowel points in these holes and position them in place on the pedestal (B) (still

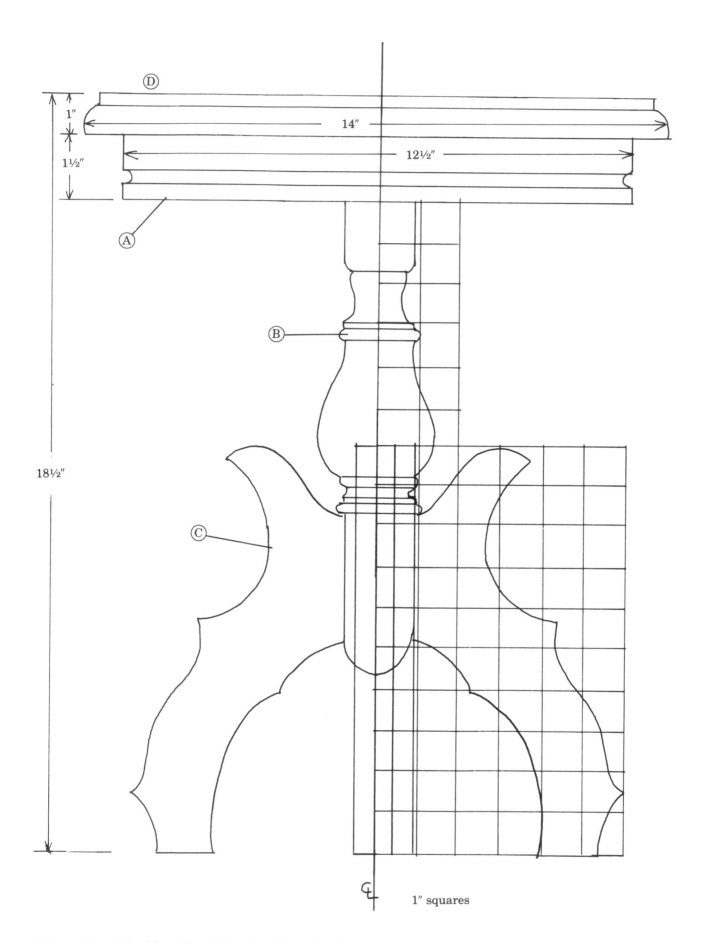

D

1"

1½"

14"

12½"

A

18½"

B

C

⌀

1" squares

in the lathe) and tap them firmly to locate the position of the dowel holes for each of the legs in the pedestal. Bore these using a ⅜-inch bit. Remove the pedestal from the lathe, and glue and dowel the legs in place to the pedestal. Set the table on a flat, smooth surface as you do this, and make sure it sits squarely on all four legs and is level. Clamp, using band clamps, and allow to dry overnight.

Anchor the wooden tabletop (A) to the top of the pedestal (B) with screws down through the top into the pedestal.

Sand thoroughly and finish to suit.

Note: The marble top can be anchored from the underside of the wooden top with screws in masonry anchors, but a better tactic these days is simply to glue it in place with epoxy glue.

Materials List

A—Tabletop—1½ × 12½ × 12½", 1 req'd.
B—Pedestal—2½ × 2½ × 11½", 1 req'd.
C—Legs—1 × 6 × 10", 4 req'd.
D—Marble top—1 × 14" diameter, 1 req'd.

Hepplewhite Serpentine Bureau

Circa 1790

The Nelson-Atkins Museum of Art, Kansas City, Missouri

This veneered mahogany bureau is a fine example of the Hepplewhite style of furniture. It is covered with crotch mahogany veneer. The graceful lines of the serpentine front, top, and moulding have helped make the bureau another classic of earlier times that is still copied by many manufacturers today. The matching Hepplewhite toilet mirror, which was often used on the bureau, is also included in this book.

Almost any good-quality hardwood veneer can be used (walnut, mahogany, cherry, etc.). However, grain patterns for the drawer fronts should be matched.

Construction

Construction is fairly simple: The bureau consists of solid wood sides and top; web-frame drawer supports are mounted in stopped dadoes in the sides. Originally there were small tenons on each dust frame that fit into mortises in the sides. But a stopped dado is easy to cut with today's power tools and makes a more stable and stronger case.

The top and sides may be solid stock, or you can use hardwood-faced plywood for the sides and back and solid stock for the top. Solid softwood stock is used for the curved drawer fronts, which are covered with veneer.

To start this project, you must figure the amount of material needed, including the flame-patterned crotch veneer on the drawers. Order and make sure you have all veneer on hand before beginning actual construction.

Sides

Construction starts with the sides (A). Again these can be glued-up solid stock, hardwood-faced plywood or softwood plywood covered with veneer. In any case cut them to the correct size and cut their front edges to the angle shown in the drawing. Cut stopped dadoes into the inside of the sides for the drawer dust frames. Use a dado head in a table or radial arm saw or router and guide strips. Make sure you stop these cuts back from the front edge. Then cut the rabbet into the inside back edges for the back.

Bottom

Enlarge the squared drawing for the front of the bottom (see bottom section detail) and cut the bottom (B) to shape. Make the serpentine front edge on a band saw. Cut the rabbet in the top back edge for the back piece.

Web-Frame Drawer Supports

Make up the web-frame drawer supports (E-G) from pieces of solid softwood stock, such as pine. Join them using mortise-and-tenon joints for all parts, including the center tilt strip pieces (G). The front pieces (D) of these frames must be cut on the same pattern as the front edge of the bottom. Make up a pattern from a piece of stiff paper or hardboard and use it for all the pieces including the web frame fronts and bottom.

Back

The back (S) on the original was made of solid ¾-inch stock, but you can substitute ⅜-inch plywood quite easily. The back fits in a rabbet cut in the back of the sides and bottom and in a stopped rabbet in the underside of the top.

Top

Glue up the top (C) from pieces of solid stock and sand both the bottom and top surfaces thoroughly. Round the corners using a coping or sabre saw and finally shape the top edge using a shaper or router (See top detail.)

Bottom Moulding

Enlarge the squared drawing (bottom section detail) and cut the front bottom moulding piece (L) to shape using a shaper or router on a wide piece of stock. Then use the front of the bottom as a pattern to cut the inside edges of the moulding piece. Cut it to shape (and away from the wide stock) using a band saw. Then shape the side moulding pieces (M) as well.

Feet

Enlarge the squared drawing for the feet (H-K) and cut to shape on a band saw. Note that the front feet (H) are compound cut. You will need a band saw with a throat height of 7 inches, or you can make the feet up of several blocks. First cut them to the shape shown in the drawing. Then glue them to together and cut the opposite curve of the compound curve, as shown in the detail drawing. Cut the recess in the

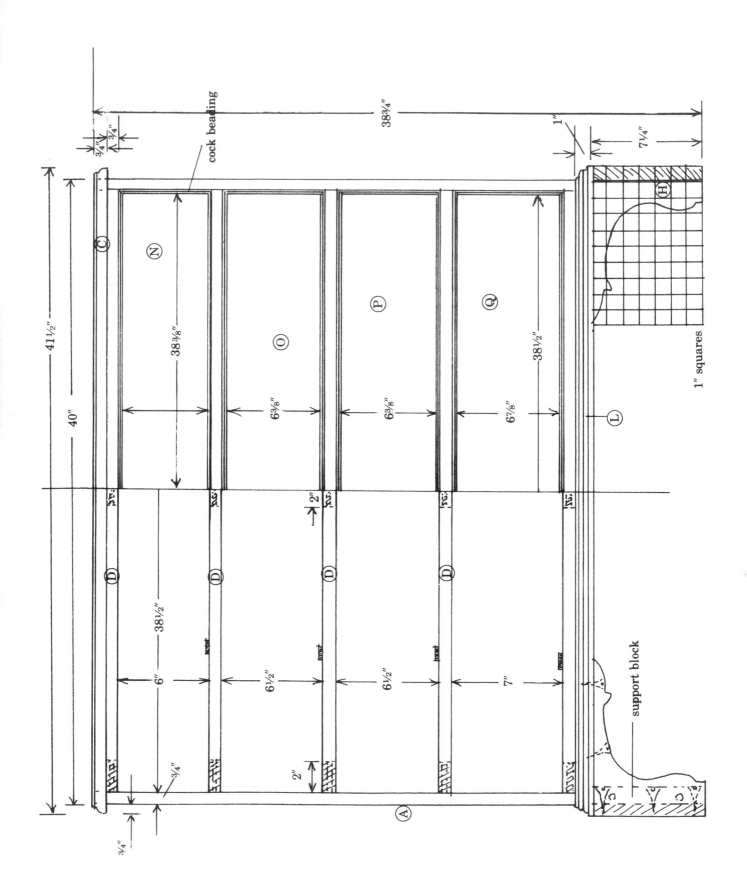

leg tops for the anchoring top piece. Fasten together with glue, screws, and a center support block, as shown in the detail.

Assembly
Start by anchoring the bottom board (B) to the sides (A) with glue and screws. Then slide the web frames (D-G) in place and anchor them to the sides with screws driven from the inside of the web frames. Make sure the screws don't break through the sides.

Anchor the feet (H-K) to the bottom in their proper positions.

Drawers
Cut the drawer front blocks (N-Q) to size from thick stock, as shown in the drawing. Then enlarge the squared drawing that shows the serpentine fronts. Transfer this to the stock and cut the fronts to shape using a band saw. Sand as smooth as possible.

Cut the backs and sides to shape and size. Note that the sides are anchored to the backs and fronts with dovetails. The bottom is set in a dado in the sides, front, and back. A notch in the back fits over a thin drawer guide (R) that is fastened to the web frames.

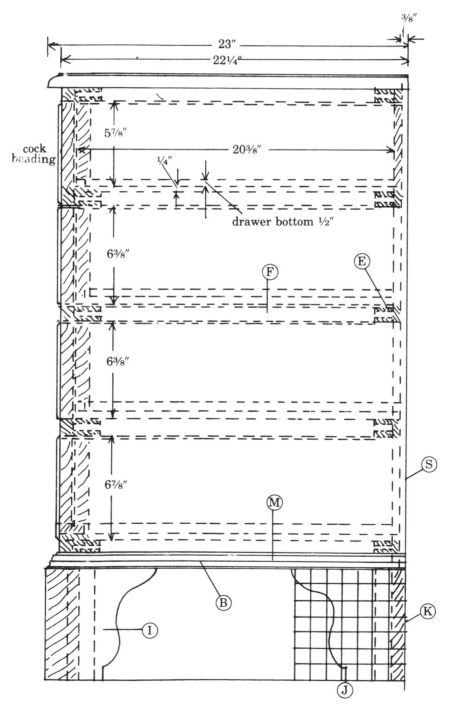

Angle of Front Edges of Sides

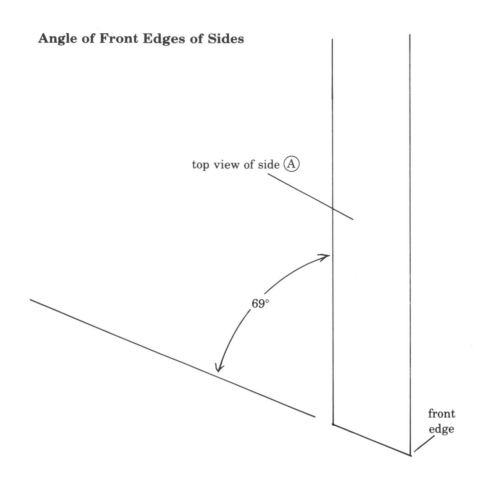

top view of side (A)

69°

front
edge

Sides: Stopped Dado

Top Detail

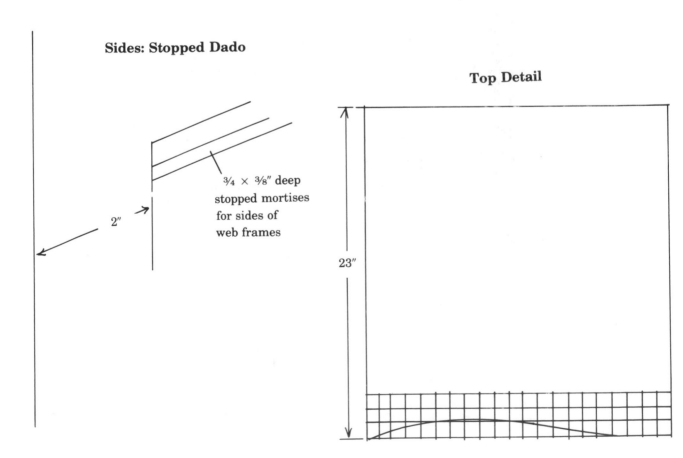

2″

¾ × ⅜″ deep
stopped mortises
for sides of
web frames

23″

Bottom Section Detail

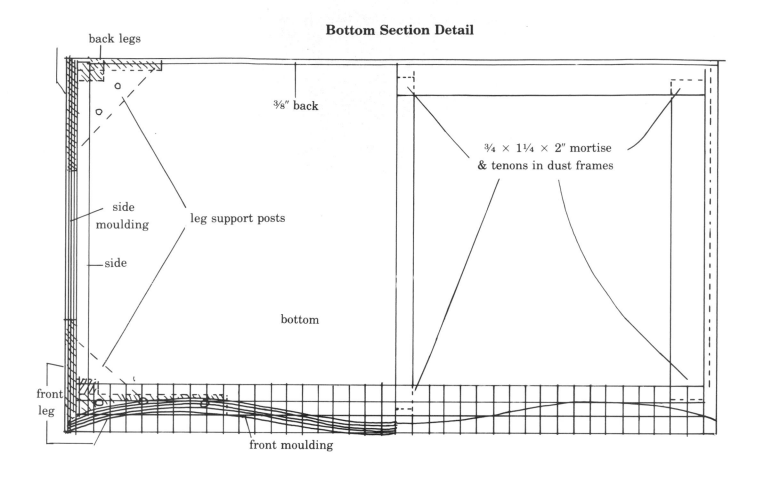

back legs

⅜″ back

side moulding

leg support posts

side

¾ × 1¼ × 2″ mortise & tenons in dust frames

bottom

front leg

front moulding

Drawer Front Detail

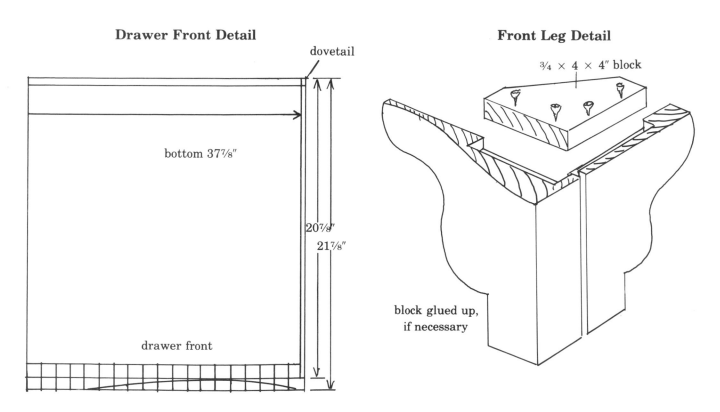

dovetail

bottom 37⅞″

20⅞″
21⅞″

drawer front

Front Leg Detail

¾ × 4 × 4″ block

block glued up, if necessary

Assemble the drawers with glue and clamp thoroughly. Put in the drawers and install the drawer guides when each drawer has been adjusted to fit perfectly in place. Then install the top (C), anchoring it with glue and screws driven up through the top web frame. Make sure the screws don't break through the top. Finally, install the back (S) in place.

Veneering

Veneering starts with the sides, followed by the front. Veneer the edges of the sides and then the fronts of the web frames, running the veneer on these in the "waterfall" pattern (where the grain runs vertically). Then veneer the feet and install the moulding on the front and sides. Mitre it carefully to fit the front corners. Fasten with glue. Veneer the drawer fronts, stain, and finish the piece. Then install the drawer locks and hardware. Apply cock beading to drawers as shown on page 23.

Materials List

A—Sides—$\frac{3}{4} \times 22\frac{1}{4} \times 31''$, 2 req'd.

B—Bottom—$\frac{3}{4} \times 21\frac{5}{8} \times 38\frac{1}{2}''$, 1 req'd.

C—Top—$\frac{3}{4} \times 23 \times 41\frac{1}{2}''$, 1 req'd.

D—Front facers—$\frac{3}{4} \times 2\frac{1}{2} \times 38\frac{1}{2}''$, 5 req'd.

Web Frames

E—Back—$\frac{3}{4} \times 2 \times 39\frac{1}{4}''$, 5 req'd.

F—Sides—$\frac{3}{4} \times 2 \times 20''$, 10 req'd.

G—Center tilt strip pieces—$\frac{3}{4} \times 2 \times 20''$, 5 req'd.

H—Front feet—$2\frac{1}{4} \times 7\frac{1}{4} \times 10''$, 2 req'd.

I—Side front feet—$\frac{3}{4} \times 5 \times 7\frac{1}{4}''$, 2 req'd.

J—Side back feet—$\frac{3}{4} \times 6\frac{1}{2} \times 7\frac{1}{4}''$, 2 req'd.

K—Back feet—$\frac{3}{4} \times 7\frac{1}{4} \times 10''$, 2 req'd.

L—Front bottom moulding—$1 \times 3 \times 41\frac{1}{2}''$, cut to fit, 1 req'd.

M—Side moulding—$\frac{3}{4} \times 1 \times 23''$, cut to fit, 2 req'd.

N—Drawer

Front—$2 \times 5\frac{7}{8} \times 38\frac{3}{8}''$, 1 req'd.

Sides—$\frac{1}{2} \times 5\frac{7}{8} \times 20\frac{7}{8}''$, 2 req'd.

Back—$\frac{1}{2} \times 5\frac{7}{8} \times 38\frac{3}{8}''$, 1 req'd.

Bottom—$\frac{1}{2} \times 20\frac{7}{8} \times 37\frac{7}{8}''$, 1 req'd.

O—Drawer

Front—$2 \times 6\frac{3}{8} \times 38\frac{3}{8}''$, 1 req'd.

Sides—$\frac{1}{2} \times 6\frac{3}{8} \times 20\frac{7}{8}''$, 2 req'd.

Back—$\frac{1}{2} \times 6\frac{3}{8} \times 38\frac{3}{8}''$, 1 req'd.

Bottom—$\frac{1}{2} \times 20\frac{7}{8} \times 37\frac{7}{8}''$, 1 req'd.

P—Drawer

Front—$2 \times 6\frac{3}{8} \times 38\frac{3}{8}''$, 1 req'd.

Sides—$\frac{1}{2} \times 6\frac{3}{8} \times 20\frac{7}{8}''$, 2 req'd.

Back—$\frac{1}{2} \times 6\frac{3}{8} \times 38\frac{3}{8}''$, 1 req'd.

Bottom—$\frac{1}{2} \times 20\frac{7}{8} \times 37\frac{7}{8}''$, 1 req'd.

Q—Drawer

Front—$2 \times 6\frac{7}{8} \times 38\frac{3}{8}''$, 1 req'd.

Sides—$\frac{1}{2} \times 6\frac{7}{8} \times 20\frac{7}{8}''$, 2 req'd.

Back—$\frac{1}{2} \times 6\frac{7}{8} \times 38\frac{3}{8}''$, 1 req'd.

Bottom—$\frac{1}{2} \times 20\frac{7}{8} \times 37\frac{7}{8}''$, 1 req'd.

R—Drawer guides—$\frac{3}{8} \times 1\frac{1}{2} \times 20''$, 10 req'd.

S—Back—$\frac{3}{8}''$ plywood $\times 30\frac{1}{4} \times 39\frac{1}{2}''$, 1 req'd.

Drawer pulls—8 req'd.

Drawer locks—4 req'd.

Veneer to cover

Hepplewhite Toilet Mirror

Circa 1780
The Nelson-Atkins Museum of Art, Kansas City, Missouri

Toilet mirrors were popular 18th-century bedroom pieces, and the mirror shown was made in America and constructed from mahogany. It goes with another project in this book, the Hepplewhite serpentine chest of drawers.

These small dressing mirrors were made of various types of wood and in various styles, but all were moulded on the same basic pattern. In addition, most were veneered with fine woods. The one shown here features mahogany veneer and ivory handles.

In some cases, the mirror standard was tilted back, and in others it was straight up. But the bottoms of the mirror standards were always cut with an angled forward shape to fasten them securely to the top. The mirror is held in place with decorative twist fasteners that can be tightened to hold it in any position. It hangs just a bit below center so it will stay in the vertical position, except when the tighteners are used.

Decorative touches sometimes included a satinwood inlay to outline the edge of the drawers or around the base front, sides and top edges. Cock beading was also sometimes used to protect the veneered edge. Scratch beading is used around the outside edge of the mirror standards, and the small, rounded embellishments on the front of the standards are scratch-cut into a piece and then applied to the standards.

This project could be made using almost any solid hardwood (walnut, mahogany, etc.), but the wood used should match an existing piece of bedroom furniture.

Construction
Construction is fairly straightforward in this project. Not only does the mirror complement the bureau, it also provides several woodworking challenges.

Case Construction
Start by enlarging the squared drawing and making the patterns for the top (A) and bottom (B). Then cut the top, bottom, sides (C), back (E) and center dividers (D) to the correct size. Use a band saw to cut the top and bottom pieces. Cut the half-lap rabbets on the ends of the top and bottom for the sides, and cut the dadoes in the top and bottom for the center di-

viders. Cut the mortises in the back of the top for the mirror standards (G).

Case Assembly
Assemble the top, bottom, back, sides, and center divider sections with glue and small finishing nails, setting them below the wood surfaces and filling over with wood putty. Sand the entire case as smooth as possible.

Veneer the case in the veneer chosen, starting

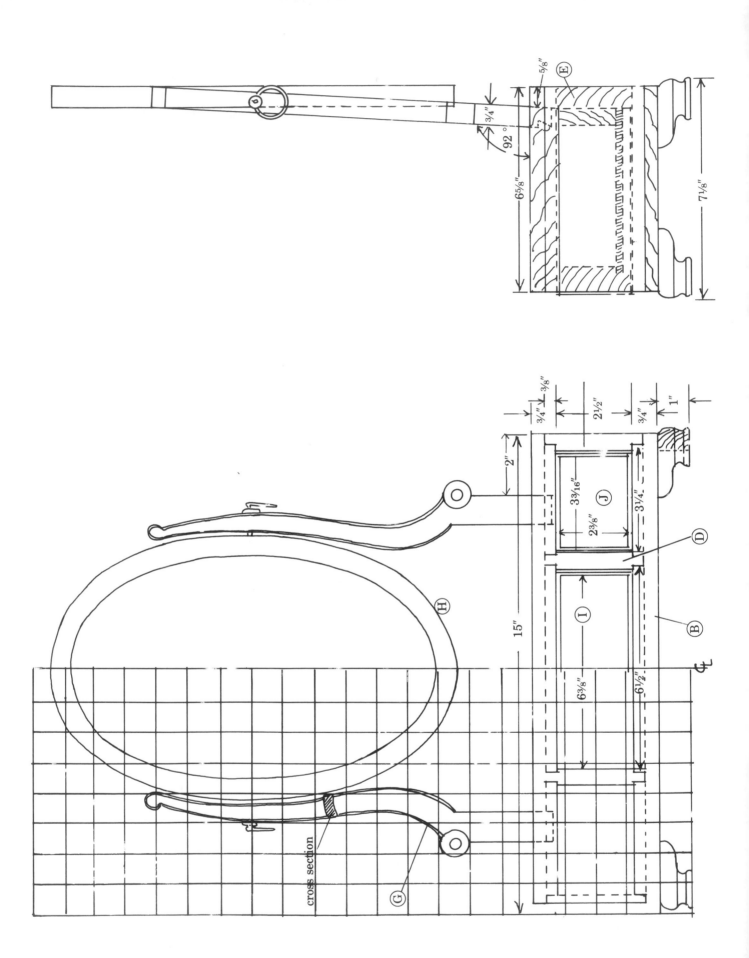

Top Pattern and Drawer Front

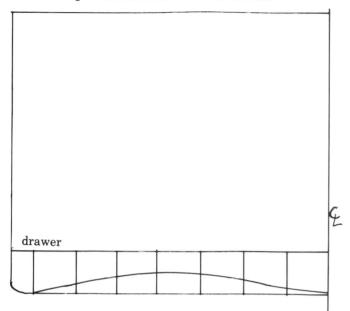

drawer

with the bottom, followed by the sides and then the top. Don't apply the back veneer at this time. Veneer the front in a "waterfall" pattern (the grain running vertically instead of horizontally). You can apply this in one piece and then use a sharp knife to cut out for the drawer openings. Or you can apply it in pieces to each section of the front.

Feet

The feet (F) are made in two pieces. First, cut the outside shape with a shaper or router on a wide piece of stock. Then rip to the correct width and cut a 45-degree mitre on the end of the stock pieces for each front and back piece of the foot. Saw a spline slot in the inside facers and cut a spline to fit. Bore holes in the bottom of the foot piece for a counterbored wood screw. Next transfer the squared drawing for the inside part of the foot and cut the small mitred sections of stock to size and shape using a band saw.

Sand each piece thoroughly and fasten the mitred corners together with glue and the splines. Anchor these pieces to the bottom of the case using screws driven up through the counterbored holes.

Mirror Standards

Enlarge the squared drawings and make the patterns for the mirror standards (G). Then cut them to shape from solid stock using a band saw. (Note the specially shaped tenons.) Cut the small bead in their front edge using a small chisel or scratch stock. Then carve the front decorative button to shape and glue in place. Bore holes for the mirror-standard knobs, and then sand completely. Fasten in place to the top by placing glue on the shaped tenons and pushing them into the mortises, tilting them in from the front.

Mirror Frame

The mirror frame (H) is cut from several segments of wood. These segments are made by first cutting the inside edge of the frame to shape from larger pieces of stock. Then cut the back rabbets on the inside back edge of the segments for the mirror and mirror-holding stock. Lightly round and shape the inside edge of the segments. Dowel and glue the segments together to form the inside oval. Then cut the outside outline to make the finished thin frame and install the mirror (K).

Drawers

Cut the thick front drawer (I,J) blocks to size and shape, then enlarge the squared drawing for the curve of the drawer fronts (same as curve for top). Cut these to shape on a band saw. The front, sides and back are held together with dovetails. The bottom rests in a dado cut in the front, back and sides. Cut all these pieces to size and shape, and then glue the drawers together. Veneer the fronts and add the cock beading strips. Then mount the drawer lock.

Finally, stain, finish and install the mirror with the support hardware.

Materials List

A—Top—¾ × 6⅝ × 15″, 1 req'd.
B—Bottom—¾ × 6⅝ × 15″, 1 req'd.
C—Sides—¾ × 3¼ × 6⅝″, 2 req'd.
D—Center dividers—¾ × 3¼ × 6⅛″, 2 req'd.
E—Back—¾ × 3¼ × 14¼″, 1 req'd.
F—Feet blocks—¾ × 1 × 2¼″, 8 req'd.
G—Mirror standards—¾ × 2½ × 13¼″, 2 req'd.
H—Mirror frame—¾ × 9 × 13¼″, or built up, 1 req'd.

Drawers

I—Center
    Front—1 × 2⅜ × 6⅜″, 1 req'd.
    Sides—½ × 2⅜ × 5⅜″, 2 req'd.
    Back—½ × 2⅜ × 5⅞″, 1 req'd.
    Bottom—¼ × 5⅜ × 6⅜″, 1 req'd.
J—Side
    Fronts—1 × 2⅜ × 3¼″, 2 req'd.
    Sides—½ × 2⅜ × 5⅜″, 4 req'd.
    Backs—½ × 2⅜ × 2¾″, 2 req'd.
    Bottoms—¼ × 2⅜ × 2¾″, 2 req'd.
K—Mirror—7½ × 12¼″, 1 req'd.
Mirror standard knobs—1 pair req'd.
Small drawer knobs—3 req'd.
Veneer to cover

Victorian Corner Cabinet

Circa 1850

The corner cabinet is one of the more unusual projects in this book. It is an elegant and beautifully constructed piece of furniture, but the ornately scrolled and carved top is a bit heavy in appearance. You might want to redesign it or build only the bottom section, leaving off the top. On the whole, however, this is an excellent piece to show off joinery, carving, and shaper work.

The front of the chest is supported on graceful Queen Anne–style legs joined with a curved stretcher. The stretcher extends to the back of the angled sides, as well. Frame-and-panel doors and an unusual carved drawer front complete the design. Probably the most interesting part of the upper section is the use of the carved split turnings.

Construction

Although this project is complicated, the piece itself is not particularly hard to construct. What is most important for this project is the ability to make clean cuts and tight joints. Because of the angles involved, a lot of trial and error fitting will be necessary, and you may waste quite a bit of stock before getting the joints cut to fit perfectly. Skill in shaper use is necessary for the panelled doors and for the top cutouts for the bevelled mirrors.

Bottom Case

Construction starts with the bottom case. The first step is to cut the side pieces (A) to size. Make the correct angle on their front edges. Cut the ⅜ × ¾-inch rabbet on their back edges for the back pieces (J,K). Then saw the ¾-inch-thick solid back pieces to shape. For the lower part of the back pieces, follow the squared drawing for the back "legs." The leg is cut on the inside back corner of each back piece. Cut rabbets into the back edges to create the overlap joint where the two back pieces meet (in the back corner).

Make the bottom (B) to size and shape, along with the bottom shelf (C) and the inside top (H) piece. These can be cut from plywood if you prefer. Edge the front of exposed pieces with solid stock for the sake of appearances. Shape the edge of the bottom shelf.

The drawer supports (E) as well as drawer tilt frame (G) and upper and lower facer strips are combined in the form of dust panels, as shown in the drawing. Or you can simply make them of solid

stock, if you prefer. This will make the job easier and probably result in a more accurate fit. You can use solid stock or plywood, edging the front of these pieces with wood to match the rest of the cabinet. But if you use solid wood on these pieces, you will have to use cleats on the inside of the sides and back to fasten them in place.

The next step is to fasten the bottom shelf supports (D) to the sides with glue and screws driven from the inside into the sides. Fasten the two side pieces (A) to the bottom (B), overlapping the sides down over the bottom. The angled edges of the sides must fit flush with the front of the bottom pieces. Fasten with glue and screws from the outside of the sides into the bottom. These will later be covered with moulding strips. Anchor the shelf to the cleats with glue and screws.

Assemble the dust frame and install in place with glue and screws through the dust frame into the sides of the cabinet. Cut a 7/16-inch-thick drawer slide (EE) and install it in place on the drawer support (E). Install the drawer support cleats (F). Finally, install the solid stock inside top (H) piece with glue and screws from the outside of the cabinet sides into the inner piece. Again, these screws will be covered with moulding.

Cut the top (I) to the correct size, and shape the edge on a shaper or with a router. Then cut the stopped rabbet in its lower back edge for the back pieces (J,K). Install it in place with glue and screws driven up from the inside top. Finally, attach the two back pieces, anchoring them in place with glue and screws to the sides, back, bottom, dust frame, shelves, and to each other. Attach a glue block to the inside corner of the back leg for reinforcement.

Leg Frames

Enlarge the squared drawing for the cabriole legs (L) and the aprons (M,N). Cut the legs to size and shape, and cut mortises in them for the aprons. Then rough in the top rounded portion of the aprons by bevel-cutting on a table saw. Trace the bottom shape onto the stock and cut the bottom part with a band saw. Then cut tenons on each end for the legs. Join the legs to the aprons with glue in the mortise-and-tenon joints and clamp securely. It will take a bit of work to get the entire frame section securely clamped.

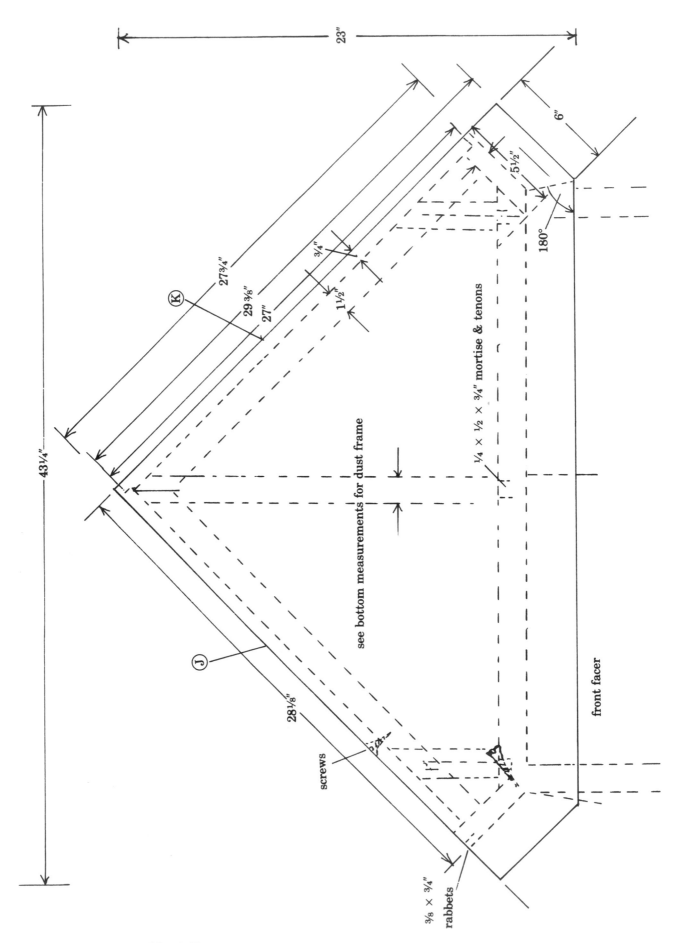

23"

6"

$5\frac{1}{2}$"

180°

$\frac{3}{4}$"

$1\frac{1}{2}$"

$27\frac{3}{4}$"

$29\frac{3}{8}$"

27"

Ⓚ

$43\frac{1}{4}$"

$28\frac{1}{8}$"

Ⓙ

screws

$\frac{3}{8} \times \frac{3}{4}$" rabbets

see bottom measurements for dust frame

$\frac{1}{4} \times \frac{1}{2} \times \frac{3}{4}$" mortise & tenons

front facer

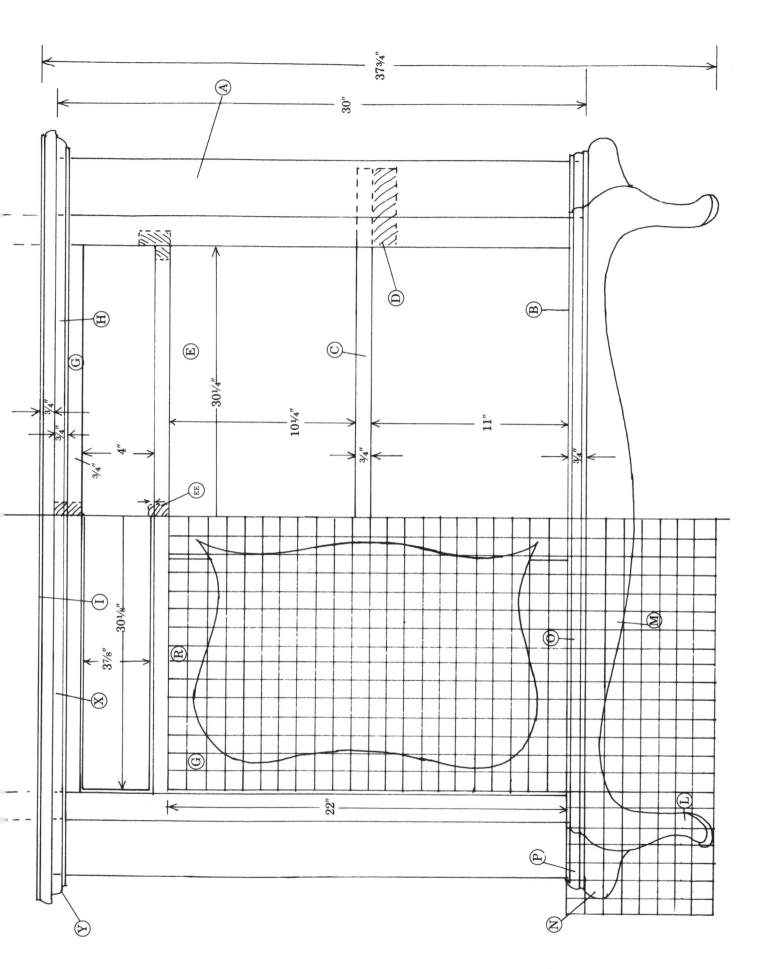

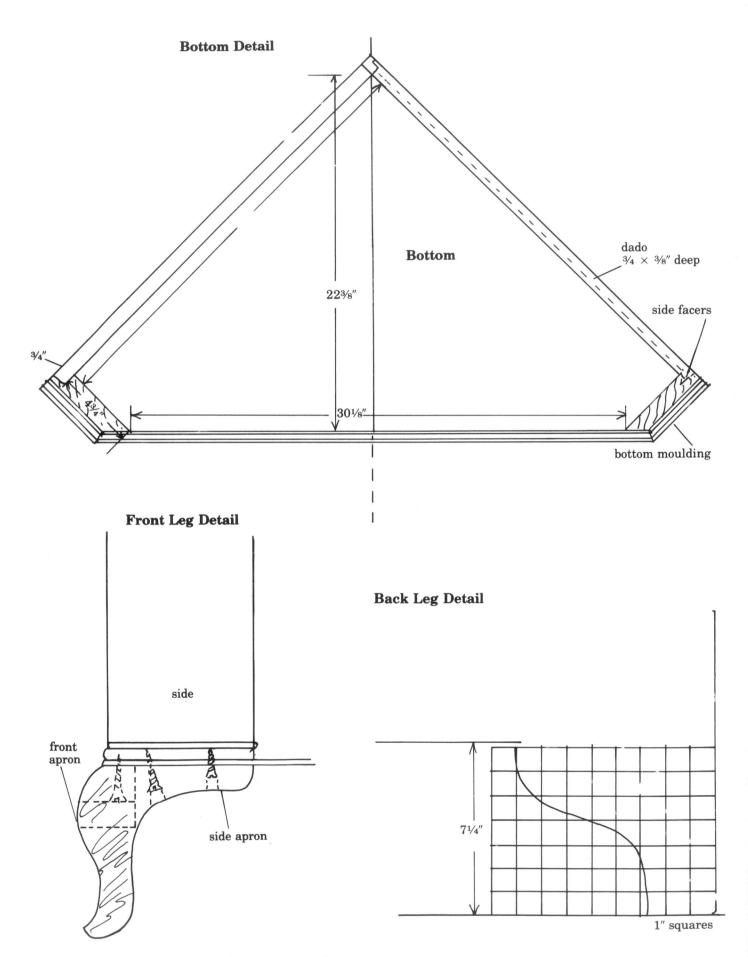

Bottom Detail

Bottom

dado
¾ × ⅜″ deep

side facers

22⅜″

¾″

4¾″

30⅛″

bottom moulding

Front Leg Detail

side

front
apron

side apron

Back Leg Detail

7¼″

1″ squares

Drawer Detail

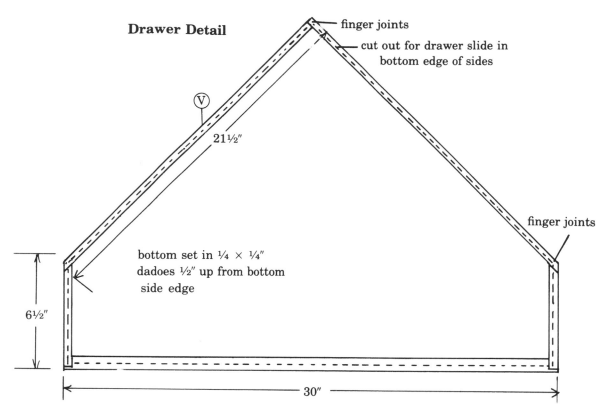

finger joints

cut out for drawer slide in
bottom edge of sides

Ⓥ

21½"

finger joints

bottom set in ¼ × ¼"
dadoes ½" up from bottom
side edge

6½"

30"

Allow the glue to set overnight; then finish rounding the aprons to match the front curvature of the cabriole legs. Anchor the legs and frames in place to the underside of the cabinet with glue and large, countersunk flat-head wood screws. Cut the front apron moulding (O) to fit, and install. Cut the top center (X) and side (Y) mouldings and join them with mitred joints and glue to the underside of the top and to the top front facing and sides.

Drawer

Cut the drawer front to shape and size. Transfer the carving pattern onto it and carve it to match. The small round scoops can easily be cut using a drill in a drill press, after vein-carving the straight lines.

Cut ¼ × ¼-inch dadoes in the front (T), sides (U), and back (V) pieces for the ¼-inch bottom; then fit the back and side pieces together with finger joints. Slide in the bottom (W) and anchor this assembly to the front with an overlapping joint. Notch out the back piece, up to the underside of the bottom, to allow for the drawer slide on the drawer support frame (E).

Doors

The doors are frame and panel, and a bit of exacting cabinet work is required here. The first step is to cut the rails (R) and stiles (Q) to length and width. Then cut tongue-and-groove joints to join them together. Put them together without glue, enlarge the squared drawing, and transfer the pattern of the frame onto the pieces. Disassemble and cut the parts of the frame to shape on a band saw. Carefully round and

sand all inside curves, making sure all jointing lines still meet properly. Then cut the groove on the inside of the rails and stiles with a shaper or router in a router table. Finally, round the outside edge lightly (see door frame detail).

Enlarge the squared drawing for the panels (S) and cut to shape with a band saw. Then shape the outer edges (which will be facing out) using a shaper or router in a router table. Finally, rout out the in-

Drawer Front Pattern

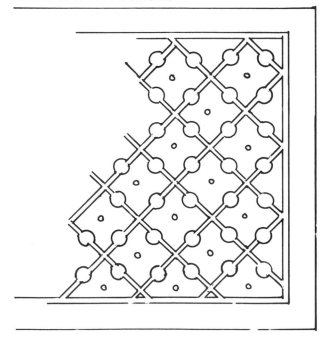

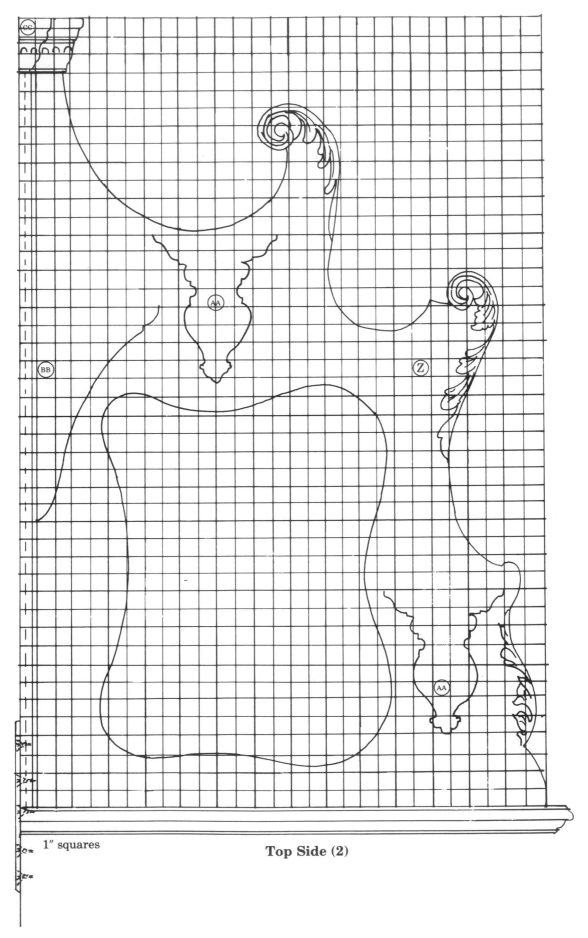

CC

AA

BB

Z

AA

1″ squares

Top Side (2)

Door and Mirror Frame Detail

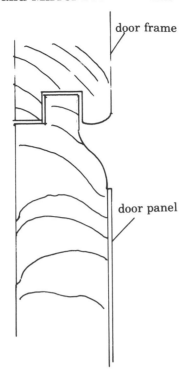

door frame

door panel

Corner Self Quarter Turning

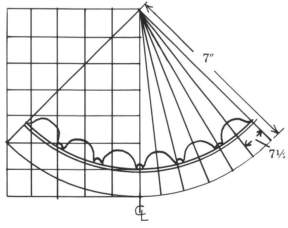

7"

7½

C̶L

side edge to create a ¼-inch-thick tongue all around the panel. This fits into the groove in the frame pieces (see door frame detail). Assemble the doors using glue in the frame tongue-and-groove joints, but do not get glue on any part of the panels. Cut the overlapping door joint edges and hang in place with mortised butt hinges. Sand, stain, and finish the base to suit; then add the hardware to doors and drawer.

Cabinet Top Unit

The top is not particularly complicated, despite its appearance. It is made of four pieces of solid stock (Z), joined to leave an open area for the bevelled mirrors. Cut the pieces and assemble them without

glue. Then lay out the opening for the mirror as well as the outside contour, using the squared drawing.

Disassemble the parts and cut out the opening with a band saw. Make the outside contours on the pieces and sand all parts thoroughly. Then join them with glue, clamp together, and leave overnight.

Remove from the clamps and rout a small bead on the inside front edge of the mirror opening (see door-and mirror-frame detail). Turn the back pieces over and rout out the area for the mirror, as well as for a ¼-inch holding piece for the back of the mirror.

Turned Shelves

The shelves are created by making split turnings with a piece of newspaper glued between them. The

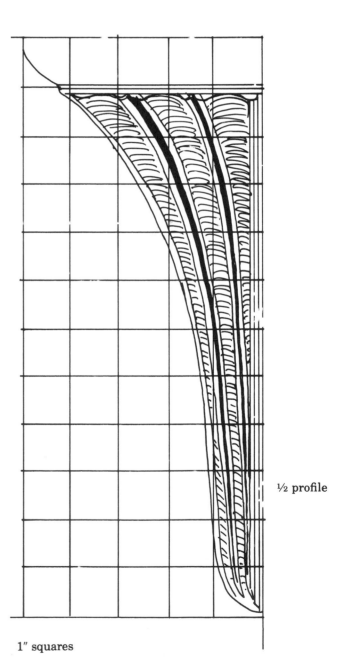

½ profile

1″ squares

two small shelves (AA) are half-shelves, while the center shelf (BB) is a quarter-turning.

Enlarge the squared drawing, turn to the correct shape, and split the turning apart. Then carve the surfaces to match the drawings. Fasten in place to the back pieces with glue and screws driven through the back.

Carvings
The carvings are applied. Enlarge the squared drawings, cut to shape with a scroll saw, then carve and mount them to the back pieces with glue.

Top Moulding
The top moulding (CC) is mitred in place as shown in the detail, anchoring it with glue and screws.

Half Turning

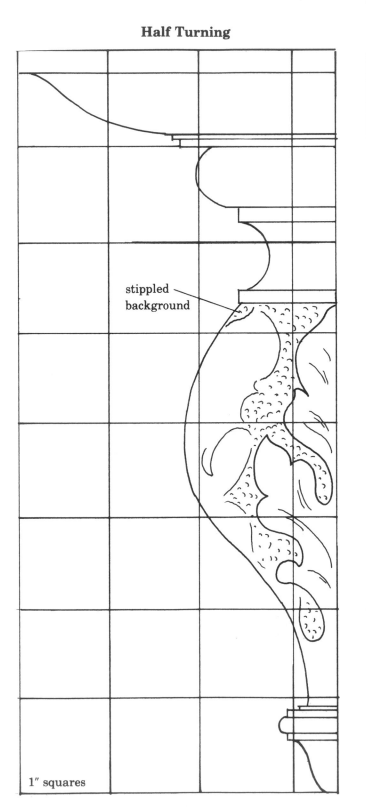

stippled background

1″ squares

Half Turning

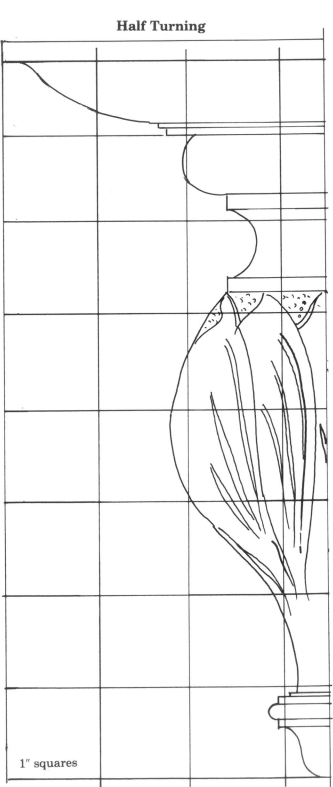

1″ squares

Mirror Installation

Stain and finish the entire top section; then install the mirror (DD) in place. Anchor the top to the bottom with metal straps and screws into the top and lower back pieces.

Materials List

Bottom Case

A—Sides—$1 \times 5\frac{1}{2} \times 29\frac{1}{2}''$, 2 req'd.

B—Bottom—$\frac{3}{4} \times 21\frac{3}{4} \times 37''$, cut to fit, 1 req'd.

C—Bottom shelf—$\frac{3}{4} \times 21\frac{3}{4} \times 37''$, cut to fit, 1 req'd.

Top and Bottom Edge Detail

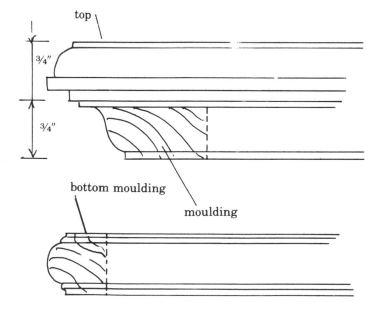

Mirror Detail

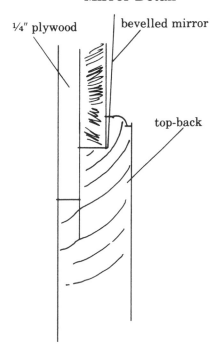

D—Bottom shelf supports—$\frac{3}{4} \times 1\frac{1}{2} \times 4\frac{3}{4}''$, 2 req'd.

E—Drawer supports—$\frac{3}{4} \times 21\frac{3}{4} \times 37''$, cut to fit, 2 req'd. (Or make up dust frames as shown.)

EE—Drawer slide—$\frac{7}{16} \times 1 \times 20\frac{1}{2}''$, 1 req'd.

F—Drawer support cleats—$\frac{3}{4} \times 1\frac{1}{2} \times 4\frac{3}{4}''$, 2 req'd.

G—Drawer tilt assembly/facer—$\frac{3}{4} \times 21\frac{3}{4} \times 37''$, cut to fit, 1 req'd. (Or make up dust frames as shown.)

H—Inside top—$\frac{3}{4} \times 21\frac{3}{4} \times 37''$, cut to fit, 1 req'd. (Or make up dust frames as shown.)

I—Top—$\frac{3}{4} \times 21\frac{3}{4} \times 43\frac{1}{4}''$, cut to fit, 1 req'd.

J—Left back—$\frac{3}{4} \times 28\frac{1}{8} \times 37\frac{3}{8}''$, 1 req'd.

K—Right back—$\frac{3}{4} \times 27\frac{3}{4} \times 37\frac{3}{8}''$, 1 req'd.

L—Legs—$3\frac{1}{2} \times 3\frac{1}{2} \times 7''$, 2 req'd.

M—Front apron—$2\frac{1}{2} \times 3\frac{1}{2} \times 30''$, 1 req'd.

N—Side aprons—$2\frac{1}{2} \times 3\frac{1}{2} \times 8''$, cut to fit, 2 req'd.

O—Front apron moulding—$\frac{3}{4} \times \frac{3}{4} \times 36''$, cut to fit, 1 req'd.

P—Side apron moulding—$\frac{3}{4} \times \frac{3}{4} \times 6''$, cut to fit, 2 req'd.

Doors

Q—Stiles—$\frac{3}{4} \times 2\frac{1}{2} \times 21\frac{3}{4}''$, 4 req'd.

R—Rails—$\frac{3}{4} \times 2\frac{3}{4} \times 12''$, 4 req'd.

S—Panels—$\frac{3}{4} \times 13 \times 19\frac{1}{2}''$, cut to size, 2 req'd.

Drawer

T—Front—$\frac{3}{4} \times 3\frac{7}{8} \times 30''$, 1 req'd.

U—Sides—$\frac{1}{2} \times 3\frac{7}{8} \times 7\frac{3}{4}''$, 2 req'd.

V—Backs—$\frac{1}{2} \times 3\frac{7}{8} \times 21\frac{1}{2}''$, 2 req'd.

W—Bottom—$\frac{1}{4} \times 20\frac{3}{4} \times 29\frac{5}{8}''$, 1 req'd.

X—Top center moulding—$\frac{3}{4} \times 2\frac{1}{2} \times 34\frac{1}{2}''$, cut to fit, 1 req'd.

Y—Top side moulding—$\frac{3}{4} \times 2\frac{1}{2} \times 6''$, cut to fit, 2 req'd.

Cabinet Top

Z—Sides—$\frac{3}{4} \times 29 \times 44''$, glued up from solid stock, 2 req'd.

AA—$\frac{1}{2}$ split turnings—$3\frac{1}{2} \times 7 \times 8''$, 4 req'd.

BB—$\frac{1}{4}$ split turnings—$7''$ radius $\times 12''$, 1 req'd.

CC—Top moulding—$2\frac{1}{2} \times 3 \times 12''$, cut to fit, 1 req'd.

DD—Mirror—$16 \times 22''$, 2 req'd.

Metal strips—$4''$, 4 req'd.

Hepplewhite Corner Washstand

Circa 1780

These small stands were designed to hold washing and shaving materials and, in addition to serving a practical purpose, they were a popular furniture item during the latter part of the 18th century. The washstand this project was patterned after was made in Boston and reflects the understated elegance and craftsmanship that is a mark of Hepplewhite furniture. It is graceful in design and has such interesting decorative details as inlays and fluted and shaped legs.

There are a number of variations on the basic design, but the washstands were almost always made of mahogany and mahogany veneer, with satinwood inlays in the front, rounded apron.

Construction

The washstand is not a particularly complicated piece to build, but because of the daintiness of design, careful fitting of all joints is especially important in this project.

Legs

Construction starts by enlarging the squared drawing and cutting the legs (A,B) to shape using a band saw. Then use a router or a router table, scratch stock, or a hand-held edge-shaping plane to create the fluting on the two front legs. Note that the back leg (B) is simply a straight-cut, undecorated leg.

After shaping the legs, notch the front and outside of both front legs for the aprons (G). Then notch the two back surfaces of the back leg for the back pieces (H,I). Cut the notches in the lower parts of the legs for the bottom shelf (C). Since these are exposed joints, very careful mortising and fitting is important.

Top

The top is actually three layers of wood. Cut the upper top (D) to size and shape, including the cutout in the center for the pitcher holder (see top detail drawing). Cut the center top piece (E) to shape as well. (*Note:* E and F are ¼ inch smaller in radius than D.) It also has a rounded front face for the front apron (G) and a hole in it for the pitcher holder. Notch it to go around the tops of the legs. Then cut the lower top (F) in the same manner. This piece, does not have a pitcher hole.

Make the front and side aprons from thin stock. Then cut the top back pieces (H,I) to the radius

shown. Note that they overlap, so one must be cut longer than the other by the thickness of the boards.

Upper Shelves

Cut the upper shelf pieces (J). This is best done by turning them full circle on a lathe and then turning the beads on their outer edges. Remove the circle from the lathe and cut it into quarters to create both shelves. Then remount a quarter-turning back in your lathe (on a faceplate) and cut the scoop depression in the center.

Assembly

First, place glue on the corners of the bottom shelf (C) and fit them carefully into mortises cut into the inside of each leg (A,B). Then put the lower top piece (F) in place and fasten it to the legs with glue and screws. Install the center top piece (E) by fastening it to the lower top with glue and screws. Then finally, fit the top (D) down over the center top and the ends of the leg tops. Fasten with glue and screws driven up through the bottom into the top. Be very careful not to go through the thin top piece.

Clamp the bottom section securely in place with band clamps. Place the unit on a smooth, flat surface, and make sure it is square and doesn't rock. Now put in the top back pieces (H,I), driving screws through the back into the legs and center and lower top pieces. Install the upper shelves (J) with screws driven through the top wing pieces.

Front Apron

Steam or soak the thin apron piece (G) and then install it in place with glue and screws driven into the tops of the legs and top pieces. Make sure all screws are sunk below the wood surface and that holes are filled over with wood putty. Then veneer the front apron and add the satinwood inlays and border pieces.

Stain and finish to suit.

Materials List

A—Front legs—⅞ × 3 × 30", 2 req'd.
B—Back legs—⅞ × 1⅛ × 30", 1 req'd.
C—Bottom shelf—¼ × 19 × 19", 1 req'd.
D—Top—¼ × 18¾ × 19", 1 req'd.
E—Center top—¼ × 18¾ × 18¾", 1 req'd.
F—Lower top—¾ × 18¾ × 18¾", 1 req'd.

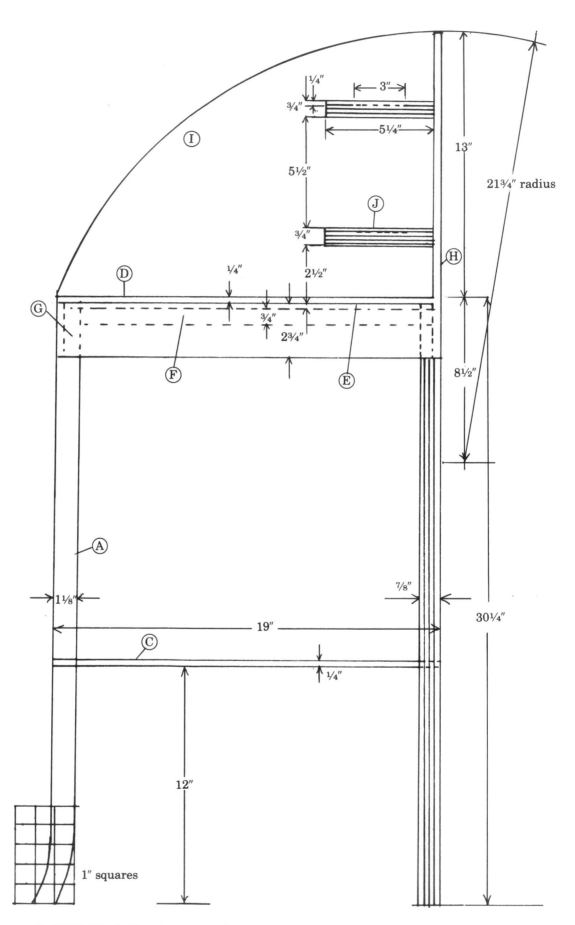

I

¼"

3"

¾"

5¼"

13"

5½"

J

21¾" radius

¾"

H

D

¼"

2½"

G

¾"

2¾"

F

E

8½"

A

7⁄8"

1⅛"

19"

30¼"

C

¼"

12"

1" squares

back view

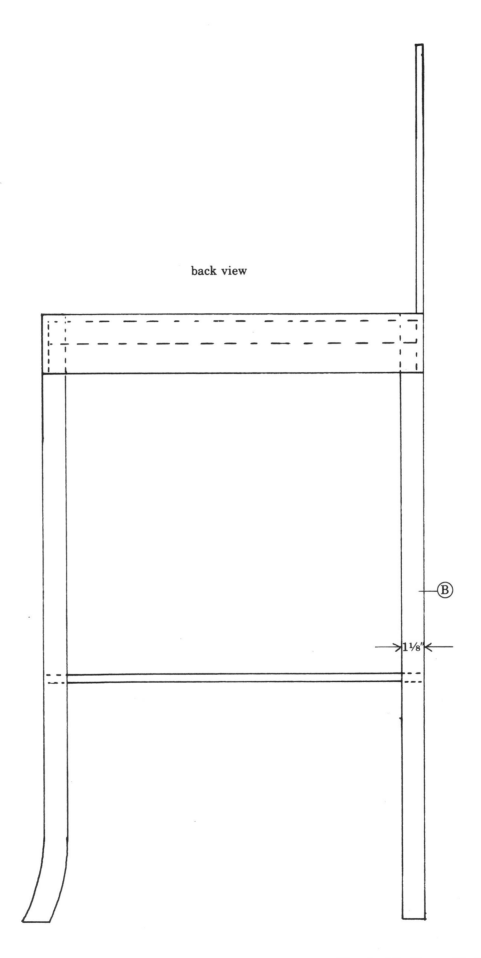

1⅛″

Ⓑ

G—Front apron—¼ × 2¾ × 34″, cut to length, 1 req'd.

H—Right-hand back piece—¼ × 15¾ × 19″, 1 req'd.

I—Left-hand back piece—¼ × 15¾ × 18¾″, 1 req'd.

J—Upper shelves—⅞ × 10½″, turning block, 1 req'd.

Veneer and inlays, as required

Top Detail

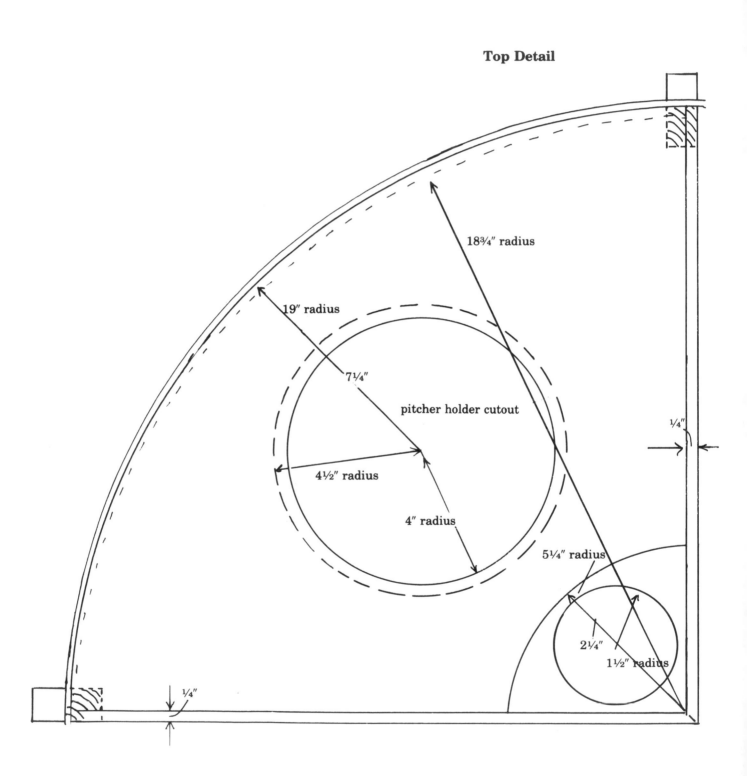

18¾″ radius

19″ radius

7¼″

pitcher holder cutout

4½″ radius

4″ radius

5¼″ radius

2¼″

1½″ radius

¼″

¼″

Shelf Joint Detail

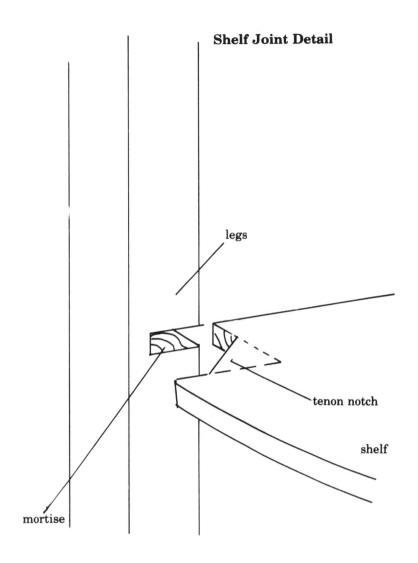

legs

tenon notch

shelf

mortise

Veneer Inlay

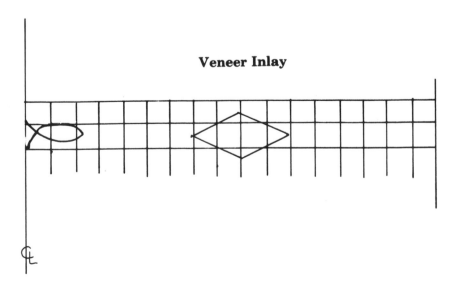

English Court Cupboard (Jacobean)

Circa 1850

This is one of the more "unusual" pieces in the book, and I selected it primarily because of the carvings and its massive appearance. It should go well with any "country"-style decor. The carving is mostly chip carving, plus a simplified style of relief carving that is typical of early English period oak furniture. Because the carving is fairly easy, even the first-time wood carver will have a chance to make a good-looking piece of furniture with this project. About the only real problem is the "applied gargoyle" in the center of the door.

Although the cupboard was built during the Victorian period, it is reminiscent of earlier periods. The carving suggests the early Oak period in England, which was from 1500 to around the middle 1600s. There is also a look of Jacobean styling in the piece as well. The cupboard is, of course, made of English oak and looks best when made of that wood. Although carving oak is somewhat more difficult than carving softwoods, the simplicity and shallowness of the cuts helps. A modified version could also be done using pine in the manner of the "primitive" carved furniture, so popular now in expensive reproduction pieces.

Construction

The piece is constructed of straightforward frame-and-panel assemblies. This includes the upper back, which consists of stiles on both sides and rails to hold the center carved panel and mirror frame.

Leg Posts

The first step is to cut leg posts (A,B) to size and shape, including the grooves in the back posts for the side panels (D). To make the piece easier to build, the lower back can be made using 3/8-inch plywood. The plywood panel is then set in rabbets cut in the back of the back posts (B), the bottom (E) and the top (Q).

Cut the grooves in the back of the front leg posts (A) for the side (panel and rail) tongues. Then cut the mortises for the upper facer (G), web-frame drawer facer front (J), and drawer support facer (N). Cut mortises as well for the bottom facer (H) and the bottom front "wing" (O).

Sides

The side panels (D) are made of solid stock glued to make up the width, or you can substitute hardwood-faced oak plywood, if you prefer. Cut dadoes on their inside faces for the drawer dust frame, lower shelves (M,W) and the bottom (E). Cut the vertical center divider (P) to size and make dadoes in it for the web-frame drawer support (J-L) and the shelves. Make a tenon on its end to fit in a dado to be cut in the bottom. Saw the side rails (C) to size and rout the grooves in their edges for the panels. Make tongues on each end and the rabbet on the inside top edge of each bottom rail. (See back-leg detail.)

Bottom

Saw the bottom (E) to size and cut the dado in its back edge for the back (F) and the dado across it for the center divider (P), as shown in the detail drawings. Cut the dado on its front bottom edge for the bottom facer (H).

Back

Cut the back to the proper size from 3/8-inch plywood or make it up from solid stock if you prefer.

Front Facers

Cut the top facer (G) to size and cut the tenons to fit into the top mortises in the top of the front-leg posts. Cut the web frame facer (J) and the rest of the web frame and assemble with glue (see detail drawing). Make the carved drawer support facer (N).

Cut the bottom facer strip (H) to size and cut tenons on each end. Then make the center vertical facer (I) and cut tenons on its upper and lower ends, as well as mortises in the side for the drawer support pieces. Cut a shallow dado in its back for the inside center divider piece (P).

Cut the bottom front wings (O) to size and shape.

Carving the Facers

The three front vertical facers and the bottom horizontal facer are carved using simple chip carving techniques. The first step is to lay out the vertical lines on the stock with a sharp pencil. Then mark locations of chisel-cut scoops. From this point on, the carving is simple. Use a gouge that is the proper size

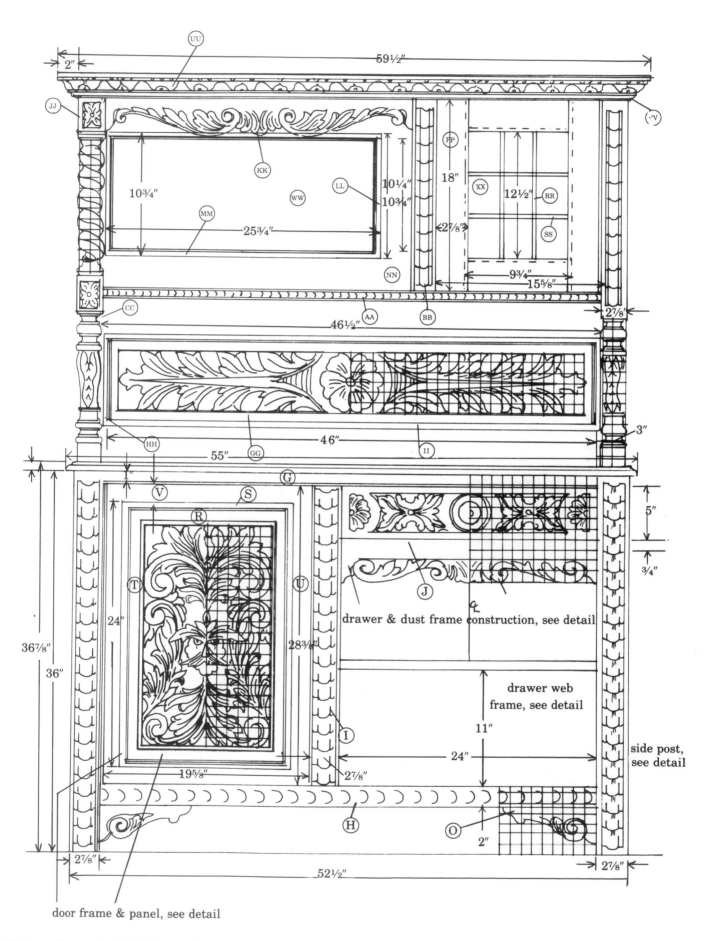

drawer & dust frame construction, see detail

drawer web
frame, see detail

side post,
see detail

door frame & panel, see detail

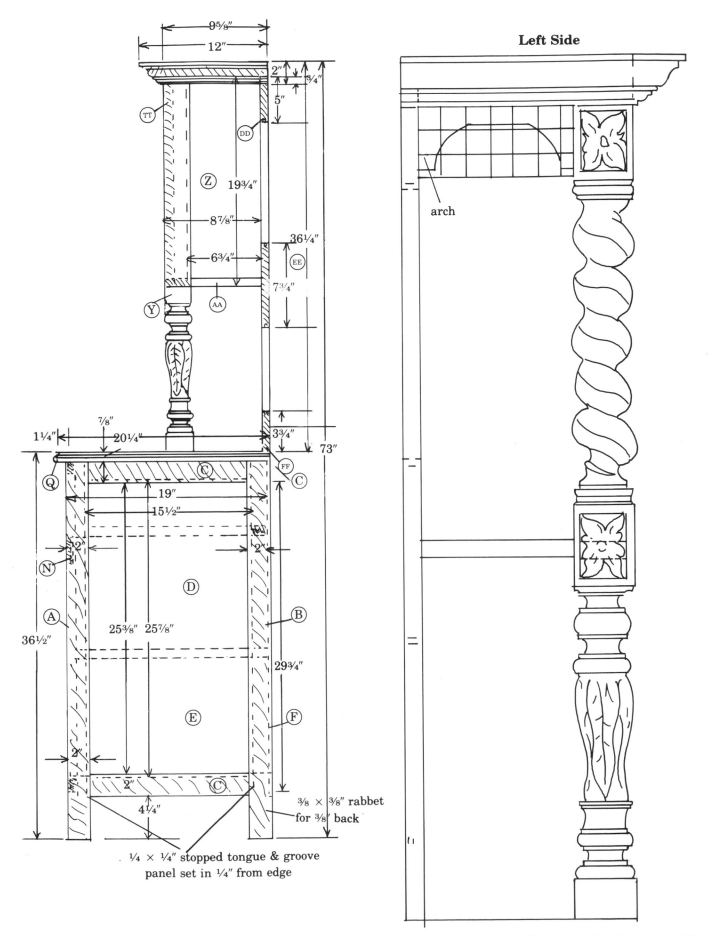

Left Side

arch

9⁵⁄₈″
12″
2″
³⁄₄″
5″

TT
DD
Z 19³⁄₄″
8⁷⁄₈″
36¹⁄₄″
EE
6³⁄₄″
7³⁄₄″
Y AA
73″
3³⁄₄″
7⁄₈″
1¹⁄₄″ 20¹⁄₄″
Q C C
FF
19″
15¹⁄₂″
2″ 2″
N
D
A B
36¹⁄₂″ 25³⁄₈″ 25⁷⁄₈″
29³⁄₄″
E F
2″
C
2″
4¹⁄₄″
³⁄₈ × ³⁄₈″ rabbet
for ³⁄₈″ back
¹⁄₄ × ¹⁄₄″ stopped tongue & groove
panel set in ¹⁄₄″ from edge

English Court Cupboard (Jacobean) • 275

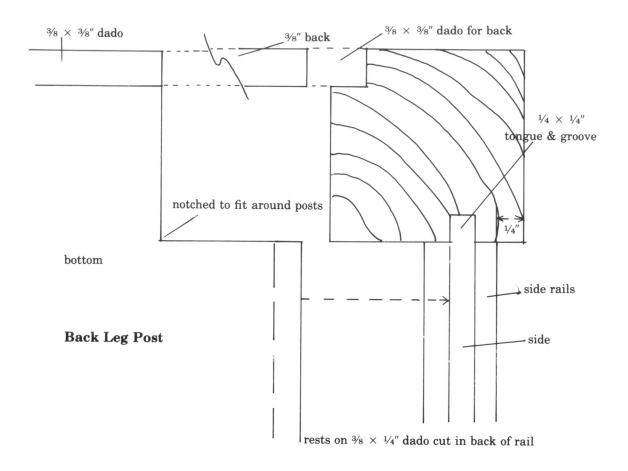

⅜ × ⅜″ dado

⅜″ back

⅜ × ⅜″ dado for back

¼ × ¼″ tongue & groove

¼″

notched to fit around posts

bottom

side rails

side

Back Leg Post

rests on ⅜ × ¼″ dado cut in back of rail

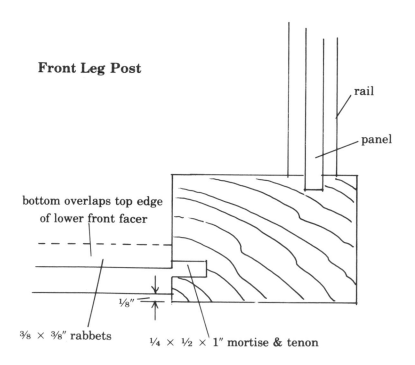

Front Leg Post

rail

panel

bottom overlaps top edge of lower front facer

⅛″

⅜ × ⅜″ rabbets

¼ × ½ × 1″ mortise & tenon

Front Leg and Center Divider Detail

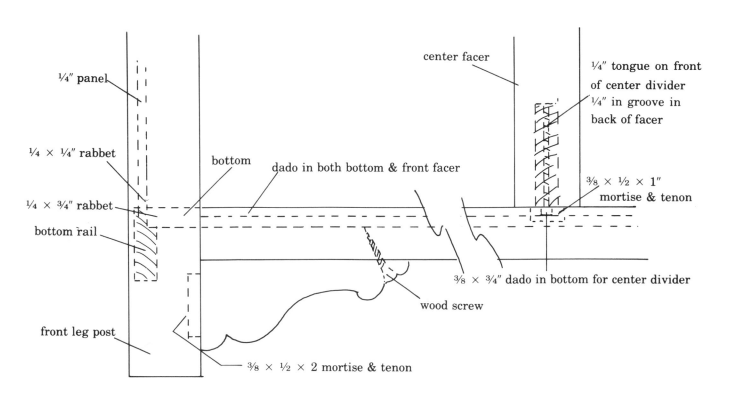

¼" panel

¼ × ¼" rabbet

¼ × ¾" rabbet

bottom rail

front leg post

bottom

dado in both bottom & front facer

⅜ × ½ × 2 mortise & tenon

wood screw

⅜ × ¾" dado in bottom for center divider

center facer

¼" tongue on front of center divider
¼" in groove in back of facer

⅜ × ½ × 1" mortise & tenon

Bottom Case Back Detail

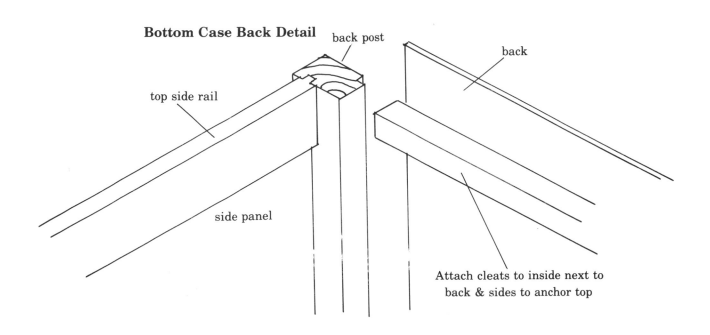

back post

top side rail

side panel

back

Attach cleats to inside next to back & sides to anchor top

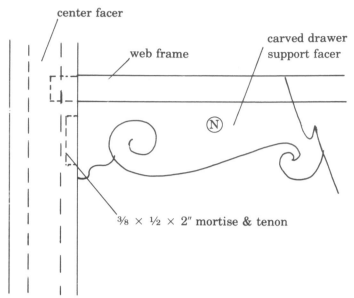

center facer

web frame

carved drawer support facer

Ⓝ

$3/8 \times 1/2 \times 2''$ mortise & tenon

of the "scoop" of the pattern. Hold the gouge upright for the rounded, or "stopped," part of the large center scoop. Strike the end with a hammer to make the cut straight down into the wood. Do this for all the scoops in the center section. Then do the smaller, side scoop cuts in the same manner. It will be easier to drive the smaller gouge deeper into the wood; so go carefully until you get the hang of it. You want to make all cuts to the same depth.

Once these "stopped" cuts have been made, drive the gouge in on an angle, scooping from the back of one stopped cut to the front of the next. This removes a curved chip from each stopped cut.

Smooth up any rough areas and use a tiny chisel to mark the fine veining lines in the center of each scoop. This type of carving is quite effective, is easy enough for even a first-timer, and is just plain fun to do. When doing the carving, however, make sure you have the stock held firmly in place on a sturdy table or workbench. Otherwise this job can be extremely frustrating.

The drawer support facer (N) and front wing pieces (O) are carved using standard relief-carving methods. The first step is to enlarge the square drawing, make up patterns and transfer them to the stock. Then use a fine veiner chisel to outline the pattern. Use larger chisels and gouges to remove the stock from the background and slightly round and relieve the surfaces of the stock. Last, fine-veining chisels are used to make the small cuts in leaves and flower petals.

Top
Glue and dowel up the top (Q) from solid stock. Shape the edge on a shaper or with a router.

Bottom Case Assembly
As with most other frame-and-panel assemblies, the first step is to assemble the sides. Put the side panels (D) in the side rails (C); then place the tongues of the side pieces into the front- and back-leg posts (A,B). Clamp these assemblies and allow the glue to set.

Now assemble the web-frame drawer support (J-L). Make sure this is square, and clamp it securely until the glue sets. Putting the side assemblies together with the rest of the casework will again take several hands to do correctly, so you may need some help. Place the bottom (E) over the rails of the two side assemblies and at the same time insert the glued tongues of the bottom facer strip (H) between the two front-leg posts. Before clamping in position, put in the vertical center divider (P), along with parts that fit into it—the web-frame drawer support (J-L), lower shelves (M,W) and carved drawer support facer (N). Next put the center vertical facer (I) in place with its tenon in the bottom facer (H). Note that the tenons on the web-frame

Drawer Web Frame Detail

side of web frame in ¼″ dado in center divider

back

mortise & tenon joints in web frame

note: solid shelf cut & fit in same manner

drawer guide ³⁄₁₆ × 1 × 17″

(YY)

cut web frames & mortises into notches cut in posts & center vertical facer

drawer support and the carved drawer support fit into it (see drawer web frame detail). Then finish the front installation by placing the top facer strip (G) down over the tenon on the front vertical facer. Insert top facer tenons in the mortises in the front-leg posts. Clamp the front assembly together, making sure all joints are square and tight.

Install the back (F) in the rabbets cut for it. Fasten with glue and wood screws driven in from the back into the sides, center divider, shelf, bottom, drawer web frame, etc. Add top support cleats to the inside of the back and sides. Cut them to fit and fasten with glue and screws.

Drawer

Cut the drawer front to the correct size and carve it according to the pattern. Then construct the drawer (X) using dovetail joints front and back. Cut a drawer guide slot in the bottom of the back and place a drawer guide (YY) in the center of the web frame to guide it in place. Install the drawer.

Door

The door is frame and panel also. It is made by first sawing the center panel (R) to size and shape, using a table saw and shaper or safety planer to cut the bevelled border around the carving. Then enlarge the squared drawing and make the relief carving. Note that the center carved gargoyle head is applied to the front of the panel. Carve the head to shape, making sure the grain runs the same way as the rest of the door panel, and apply with glue and small brads from the back of the panel. Then make up the decorative moulding (S,T) with a shaper or router (see door frame and panel detail). Glue and brad it

to the outside of the center raised panels and use 45-degree mitre joints at the corners.

Finally, construct the stiles and rails (U,V) using tongue-and-groove joints. Glue them together, inserting the center panel between the glued-up frame pieces. But do not glue the center panel in place. Note that the outside edge of the door has a small bead cut in it the same thickness as the butt hinge. This provides an unusual and nice touch and hides the mortised hinge. Hang the door and then install the door and drawer locks.

Fasten the bottom front wings (O) in place with glue on the tenons and a countersunk flat-head wood screw in the front end driven up into the bottom of the lower facer.

Install the top (Q) with glue and screws driven up through the bottom of the front facer and side and back cleats.

Upper Case

The upper case is also frame and panel. The first step is to create the front posts (Y). These are made by cutting the turning blocks to size and shape and then turning them on a lathe. You must carve the

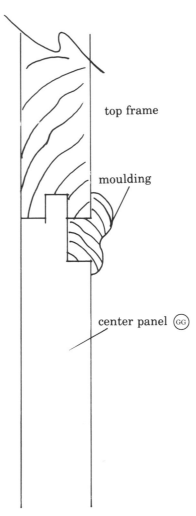

top frame

moulding

center panel (GG)

spiral on the upper left-hand side. This can be done while the stock is still in the lathe. A much easier method is to use a router crafter to cut the spiral. Then cut mortises into the inside face of each for the bottom piece (AA) and the groove in the right-hand post for side panel (Z). Finally, carve them to the patterns shown.

Casework

Cut the bottom (AA) to the correct size and carve the small chip-carved edges. Cut a shallow dado across it for the center divider and for the outside side piece. Then saw the center divider and side (Z) to size and shape. Cut a tongue on the front edge of the center divider to fit into the groove cut in the back of the front center divider (BB). Cut a tongue on both the front and back of the right-hand side piece (Z) to fit grooves in the posts (Y) and back piece. Cut dadoes in the inside face of the center divider for the shelf.

Make up the back frame and panel of solid stock, making the center carved panel and mirror panel (see mirror frame detail) separately and fitting them in rabbets cut in the front of the back panel. Use glue and screws from the back to anchor these in the back panel. Cut the top (TT) to the proper size and shape. Saw the upper scroll piece (KK) to shape and carve it following the pattern. Cut tenons on its ends. Make the left-hand side arch and cut tenons on its ends.

Top Case Assembly

Begin by positioning the center divider (P) and the right-hand side (Z) in the bottom (AA) dadoes. Then slip the posts (Y) over the corners of the bottom. Position the front center divider strip (BB) and fit the carved scroll piece (KK) between it and the outer posts.

Put the carved left side arch (JJ) in place and then move the panelled back assembly into position. Fasten the panelled back (CC-FF,NN) with glue and screws driven through the back into the appropriate pieces. Carve and install the panel (GG), then the moulding (HH,II) around it. Install the mirror with moulding (LL,MM).

Install the top (TT) with glue and screws driven

down through the top into the appropriate pieces. Then make the top moulding (UU) by first shaping it with a shaper or router and then carving the upper portion. Fasten it with glue and screws. Then make and add the lower moulding (VV) in the same manner. Install the shelf (OO).

Door

The door (PP-SS) is a frame and panel with cross-lap glass dividers mortised into the frame edges (see detail). The frames are joined with tongue-and-groove joints. Although the door shown utilizes stained glass (XX), the original probably had leaded glass. The door is hung using butt hinges (again cut a small bead to conceal the mortising of the hinges). Install the door lock.

Fasten the upper case to the back of the bottom case with metal strap supports screwed to the back panels and screws from the underside of the top (Q) into the posts (Y).

Stain and finish to suit.

Materials List

Bottom Case

A—Front-leg posts—2 × 2⅞ × 35¾″, 2 req'd.
B—Back-leg posts—2 × 2 × 35¾″, 2 req'd.
C—Side rails—¾ × 2 × 15½″, 4 req'd.
D—Side panels—¼ × 15½ × 25⅞″, 2 req'd.
E—Bottom—¾ × 18⅛ × 51″, 1 req'd.
F—Back—⅜″ plywood × 30 × 49¼″, 1 req'd.

Facers

G—Top—¾ × 1 × 47¾″, 1 req'd.
H—Bottom—¾ × 2 × 47¾″, 1 req'd.
I—Center vertical—¾ × 2⅞ × 23⅜″, 1 req'd.

Mirror Frame Detail

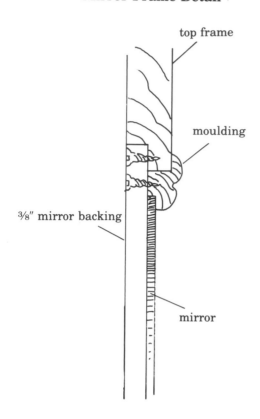

top frame

moulding

3/8" mirror backing

mirror

Web-Frame Drawer Supports

J—Front—1 × 3 × 27", cut to fit, 1 req'd.
K—Back—1 × 3 × 27", cut to fit, 1 req'd.
L—Sides—¾ × 3 × 18", cut to fit, 1 req'd.
YY—Guide—3/16 × 1 × 17", cut to fit, 1 req'd.
M—Shelf—¾ × 18 × 27", cut to fit, 1 req'd.
N—Drawer support facer—¾ × 3¼ × 24", 1
    req'd.
O—Bottom front wings—¾ × 4 × 9", 2 req'd.
P—Center divider—¾ × 18¼ × 30", cut to fit, 1
    req'd.
Q—Top—⅞ × 20¼ × 55", 1 req'd.
Door
R—Panel—¾ × 15½ × 24", cut to fit, 1 req'd.
S—Moulding—¾ × 1 × 16½", cut to fit, 2 req'd.
T—Moulding—¾ × 1 × 26", cut to fit, 2 req'd.
U—Stiles—¾ × 2 × 28¼", 2 req'd.
V—Rails—¾ × 2 × 16¼", 2 req'd.
W—Inside shelf—¾ × 16½ × 22", cut to fit, 1
    req'd.

Door Glass Dividers

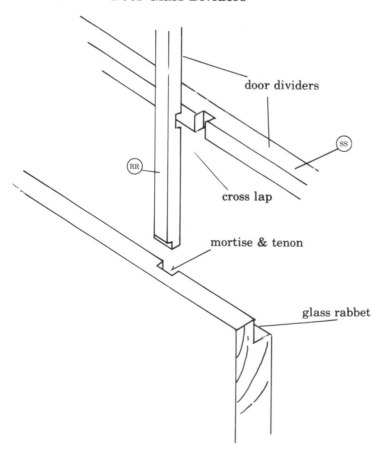

door dividers

SS

RR

cross lap

mortise & tenon

glass rabbet

Door Frame and Panel Detail

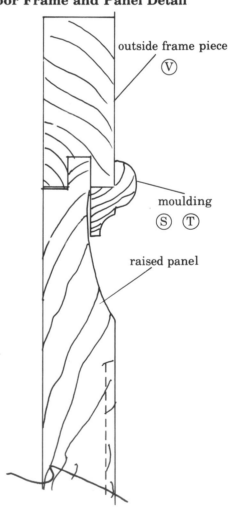

outside frame piece

V

moulding

S T

raised panel

X—Drawer

    Front—¾ × 4⅞ × 23⅞", 1 req'd.

    Sides—½ × 4⅞ × 18", 2 req'd.

    Bottom—¼ × 18 × 23⅜", 1 req'd.

Upper Case

Y—Posts—2⅞ × 2⅞ × 35¼", 2 req'd.

Z—Sides—¾ × 6¾ × 19¼", 2 req'd.

AA—Bottom—¾ × 8⅞ × 51¾", 1 req'd.

BB—Front center divider—2 × 2⅞ × 19", 1 req'd.

CC—Stiles—¾ × 3 × 35¼", 2 req'd.

DD—Rails—¾ × 5 × 46", 1 req'd.

EE—Rail—¾ × 7¾ × 46", 1 req'd.

FF—Rail—¾ × 3¾ × 46", 1 req'd.

GG—Panel—¾ × 7¾ × 46", cut to fit, 1 req'd.

HH—Moulding ¾ × 1 × 9", cut to fit, 2 req'd.

II—Moulding—¾ × 1 × 48", cut to fit, 2 req'd.

JJ—Left side arch—¾ × 3 × 6¾", 1 req'd.

KK—Upper carving—¾ × 4 × 30", 1 req'd.

LL—Mirror moulding—¾ × 1 × 12", cut to fit, 2 req'd.

MM—Mirror moulding—¾ × 1 × 27", cut to fit, 2 req'd.

NN—Back panel—¾ × 11¾ × 23", cut to fit, 1 req'd.

OO—Inside shelf—½ × 8 × 18", cut to fit, 1 req'd.

Door

PP—Stiles—¾ × 2⅞ × 18", 2 req'd.

QQ—Rails—¾ × 2⅞ × 9¾", 2 req'd.

RR—Vertical door dividers—¼ × ⅜ × 12½", 2 req'd.

SS—Horizontal door dividers—¼ × ⅜ × 9¾", 2 req'd.

TT—Top—¾ × 9½ × 52½", 1 req'd.

UU—Top moulding—1¾ × 2 × 95", cut to fit, 1 req'd.

VV—Top moulding—¾ × 1 × 95", cut to fit, 1 req'd.

WW—Mirror—11 × 23½", 1 req'd.

XX—Door glass—9¾ × 12½", 1 req'd.

Hardware

Door locks—2 req'd.

Drawer lock—1 req'd.

Drawer pull—1 req'd.

Brass butt hinges—1½", 2 req'd.

Chippendale-Style Secretary

Circa 1780

Secretaries were a very popular type of furniture during the boom in American furniture making in the late 18th century. There were numerous styles and types constructed by famous cabinetmakers of that time. But those patterned after original designs by Thomas Chippendale have had a lasting appeal and are still among the most popular types of furniture.

This secretary was made of mahogany, as were most of them in that period; however, both walnut and cherry were sometimes used. The secretary chosen for this project was made in America, based on Chippendale's designs. It is somewhat unusual in that most secretaries of that period had drawers rather than doors on the bottom portion. Nevertheless, the design of this piece is elegant and classic and the craftsmanship is superb.

Construction

The cabinet shown was constructed of solid, one-piece stock for the wide pieces. You, however, will probably have to glue up the stock if you intend to use solid stock. You could substitute plywood in many parts of the project. As is often the case with furniture pieces of this size, the secretary shown is constructed in two sections, a lower and upper case.

Lower Case

The first step is to make the sides (A) to size and shape, including the angled and shaped front top edges for the desk section. (Note the bottom profile of the sides, shown in the side view drawing.)

Cut stopped dadoes in the sides for the shelf (C), inner desk top (E) and the pull-out support facer (D). Cut rabbets into the inside top and bottom edge of the sides as well.

Cut the bottom (B) and top (F) pieces to size and cut a ⅜ × ½-inch rabbet on their back inside edges to accommodate the back piece (G). Note that the top also has half-lap rabbets on each end to fit down over the ends of the side pieces. In addition, the front edges have a double angle to match the slanted shape of the sides.

Cut the shelf (C) to size; then make up the pull-out support frame (D) as shown in the detail to the size and shape. Be sure to include the notches in its front end to create the stopped dadoes. Make up the inner desk top (E) from solid stock and cut it to the same shape, with notches in its front ends to allow it to fit in the stopped dadoes of the sides.

Enlarge the squared drawing and saw the side (I) and bottom aprons (J) to shape. These should be cut a bit long (lengthwise) and then mitred to fit the case after the rest of the bottom portion has been assembled. Run the moulding shape on their top edges with a shaper or router.

Lower Case Assembly

Place glue on the ends of the bottom, shelf, pull-out support frame, inner desk top, and top piece; and assemble. Make sure they are square; then clamp and allow the glue to set.

After this is done, measure for the back (G) and cut it to fit, but don't install it at this time. The back goes in after the pigeonhole assembly has been fastened in place.

With the basic case constructed, fasten the bottom aprons (I,J) in place using 45-degree mitre joints at their corners. The best method is to install the two side pieces first; then cut the front apron to fit between them, measuring carefully to achieve a good, tight joint. Use glue and screws from the inside to fasten the side apron pieces to the sides.

Doors

The doors are frame and panel. The pieces are joined with a cabinet joint, and the panels are inset in the rabbets created by the joint. The rails (L,M) and stiles (K) must be cut to length and their edges dressed to the proper shapes. For this job, use a shaper and the special cabinet-joint cutters, shown on page 20.

Pull-out

The pull-out (PP) is made of frame-and-panel construction as well. It has a thinner recessed center panel made to accommodate a felt or leather cover. The front edge of the pull-out has cock beading applied to it. Or you can recess the front by carving, if you prefer. After the pull-out is stained and finished, it is installed in the lower case. Put stop blocks on its back underside to prevent it from being pulled completely out of the cabinet. Install moulding (OO), mitring at the corners.

Desk Lid

The next step is to make the desk lid (H) to the

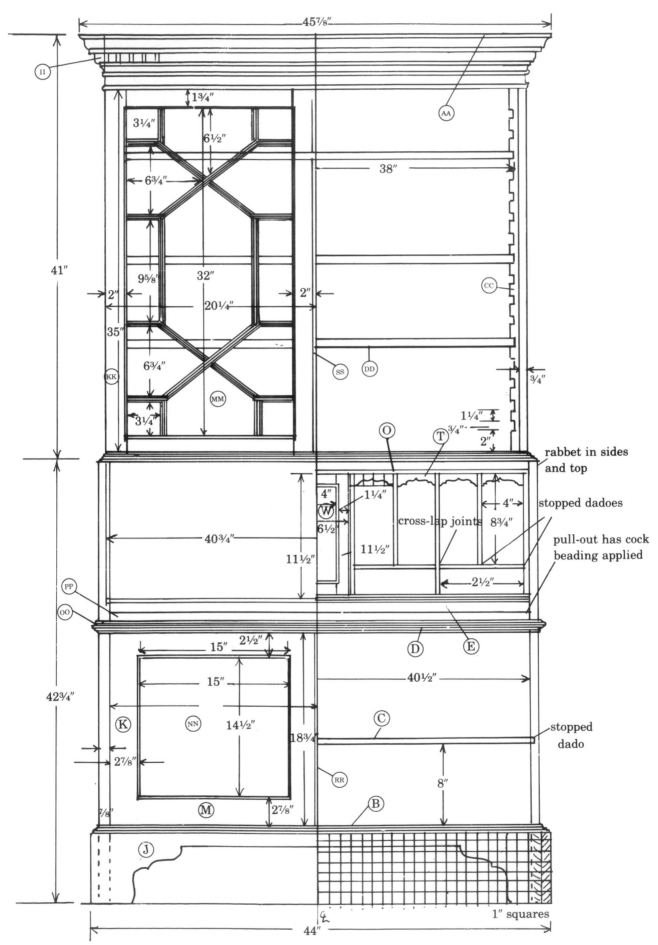

45⁷⁄₈"

II

1³⁄₄"
3¼"
6½"
6¾"

38"

AA

41"

9⅝"
2"
32"
2"
20¼"
35"

20¼"

CC

KK
6¾"

SS
DD

MM
3¼"

¾"

O
T
1¼"
¾"
2"

rabbet in sides
and top

W
4"
1¼"
6½"

11½"
cross-lap joints
8¾"

4"

stopped dadoes

40¾"
11½"

pull-out has cock
beading applied

PP

2½"

OO
D
E

15"
2½"

15"
40½"

K
NN
14½"
C

42¾"
18¾"

2⅞"

RR

8"

7⁄8"
J
M
2⅞"

B

1" squares

44"

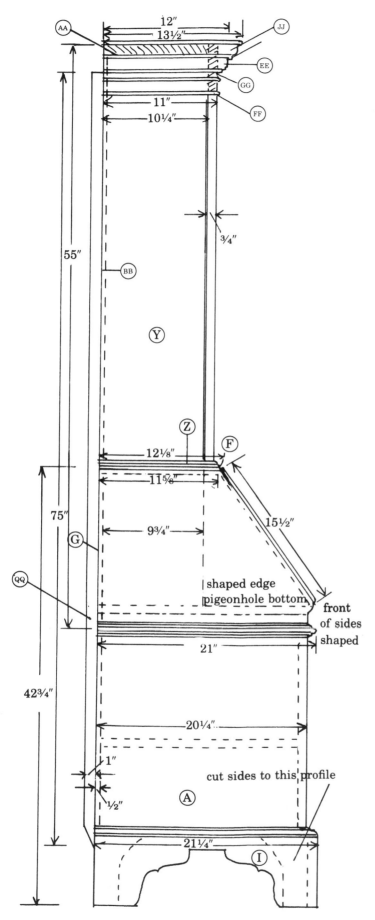

proper size. Then rout the ⅜ × ⅜-inch lip all around the inside edge along the top and two sides. Round all outside upper edges on a router and router table or shaper, mortise the drop-lid hinges, and install in place.

Pigeonhole Assembly

The pigeonhole is a highlight of the project and is a fine example of the craftsmanship and design of the period. It is constructed of ¼-inch stock using half-lap, slotted joints and glue. Upright pieces (P,Q,R) are held in stopped dadoes in the bottom (N) and top (O) pieces. The front edge of the bottom piece extends out past the front to the pigeonhole sections and has a shaped edge on it. The horizontal pieces (S) are fastened to the side pieces with stopped dadoes as well.

Tiny shaped arch pieces (T) are glued in place between the vertical dividers. The drawers are made of ⅛-inch stock glued together with half-lap joints. The tiny door is frame and panel. The panel (W) is inset in a moulding placed around it and in the rabbets of the door rails (V) and stiles (U) as shown in the detail. The door is hinged in place with tiny brass hinges and fitted with a key-operated door lock.

Stain and finish the lower case, including the pigeonhole unit. Then install the pigeonhole. Finally, put in the back, fastening it with glue and screws through the back.

Upper Case

The upper case is constructed as a simple box; then decorative embellishments, such as moulding, are added. The first step is to make the sides (Y) to size and shape. Then cut a ¼ × ⅞-inch rabbet into their bottom inside edges for the bottom (Z) and a ¼ × ¾-inch dado in the top inside edges for the top (AA). Cut the rabbets on their back inside edges for the back piece (BB).

Then cut the inside shelf supports (CC). This ingenious device for adjustable shelves is nothing more than a piece of solid hardwood stock cut with spaced dadoes. Cut these two pieces and the dadoes in them, making sure you get them all spaced properly; then fasten them to the sides with glue and counterbored screws, covered over with wooden plugs.

Fasten the bottom and top in place with glue and screws. Cut the back from a piece of ⅜-inch hardwood-faced plywood (the same wood as the rest of the case) and install it in place with glue and screws. Cut the top facer piece (EE) and fasten it with glue and screws through the top edge, which will be concealed by moulding, and into the front edge of the top piece.

Moulding

Cut the tiny bead moulding (FF) on the edge of a

piece of solid stock with a router or shaper; then rip from the edge of the stock and glue in place to the upper side and front facer pieces.

Make the other moulding pieces (GG-JJ), noting that the moulding is three separate sections. The center moulding has small decorative blocks (II) glued onto its outside face. Shape the stock, then cut moulding pieces for the sides to length, and fasten with glue and screws from the back of the sides. Now cut the front moulding pieces to fit between the mitred ends of the side pieces. Fasten them with glue and screws from the back of the front facer pieces (EE).

Doors
Cut the door rails (LL) and stiles (KK) to size and shape. Make the shaped inside edges on the front and the rabbets for the glass on the back. Cut the moulding pieces (MM) for the glass to shape and then join. As in the original secretaries, joining pieces here have very carefully cut butt joints. The outside pieces have small tenons and are mortised into the door frames. Then the glass pieces are cut to fit and glazed in place. After this step, the whole door, including the glazing, must be stained and finished.

Hang the doors with mortised butt hinges and install the door closure strip (SS) on the right-hand door, as well as the door lock.

Cut the shelves (DD) to the correct size and shape. Stain and finish the entire unit in the same manner as the lower case.

Final Assembly
To assemble the two units, cut the back brace (QQ) strips from 1¼-inch-thick stock and fasten the two pieces together with glue and screws. Screws driven from the underside of the desk top will also help anchor the pieces together.

Pull-Out Detail

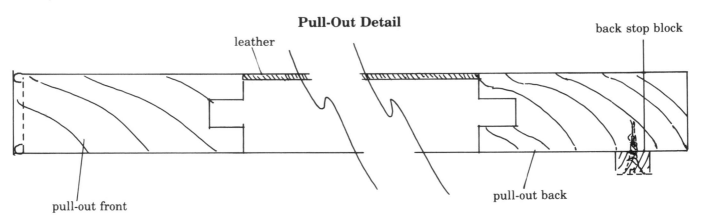

leather

back stop block

pull-out front

pull-out back

Pull-Out Frame Detail

Top Piece Detail

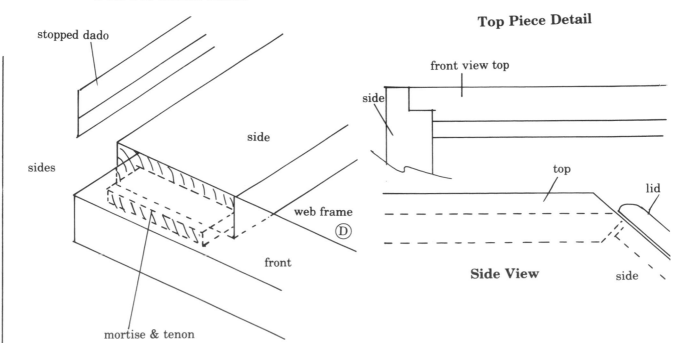

stopped dado

sides

side

web frame
Ⓓ

front

mortise & tenon

front view top

side

top

lid

Side View

side

Materials List

Lower Case

A—Sides—⅞ × 20¼ × 42⅝″, 2 req'd.

B—Bottom—¾ × 20¼ × 40¾″, 1 req'd.

C—Shelf—¾ × 18¾ × 40¾″, 1 req'd.

D—Pull-out support—¾ × 19¾ × 40¾″, 1 req'd.

E—Inner desk top—¾ × 19¾ × 40¾″, 1 req'd.

F—Top—¾ × 12 × 42″, 1 req'd.

G—Back—½ × 34¾ × 40¾″, 1 req'd.

H—Desk lid—¾ × 15½ × 40″, 1 req'd.

I—Side bottom apron—¾ × 7¾ × 22″, cut to length, 2 req'd.

J—Front bottom apron—¾ × 7¾ × 45″, cut to length, 1 req'd.

Doors

K—Stiles—¾ × 2⅞ × 18¾″, cut to length, 4 req'd.

L—Upper rails—¾ × 2½ × 15″, cut to length, 2 req'd.

M—Bottom rails—¾ × 2⅞ × 15″, cut to length, 2 req'd.

NN—Door panels—¼ × 14½ × 15″, 2 req'd.

RR—Door closure strip—½ × ¾ × 18¾″, 1 req'd.

OO—Moulding—¾ × 1¼ × 96″, cut to length, 1 req'd.

PP—Pull-out

Front—¾ × 2 × 40″, 1 req'd.

Back—¾ × 2 × 40″, 1 req'd.

Sides—¾ × 2 × 19″, 2 req'd.

Panel—⅝ × 16¼ × 36½″, 1 req'd.

Pigeonhole

N—Bottom—¾ × 10½ × 40″, 1 req'd.

O—Top—½ × 9¾ × 40″, 1 req'd.

P—Sides—½ × 9¾ × 11¾″, 2 req'd.

Q—Major verticals—½ × 9¾ × 11¾″, 4 req'd.

R—Minor verticals—½ × 9¾ × 9¼″, 4 req'd.

S—Center horizontals—½ × 9¾ × 17″, 2 req'd.

T—Arches—¼ × 1 × 3¾″, 8 req'd.

Pigeonhole Door

U—Stiles—¾ × 1¼ × 11½″, 2 req'd.

V—Rails—¾ × 1 × 4½″, 2 req'd.

W—Panel—½ × 4½ × 9½″, 1 req'd.

X—Pigeonhole Drawers

Fronts—½ × 2⅜ × 7⅝″, 4 req'd.

Sides—⅛ × 2⅜ × 9¼″, 8 req'd.

Backs—⅛ × 2¼ × 7⅛″, 4 req'd.

Bottoms—⅛ × 7⅜ × 8¾″, 4 req'd.

Upper Case

Y—Sides—¾ × 10¼ × 39¼″, 2 req'd.

Z—Bottom—⅞ × 11¾ × 39½″, 1 req'd.

AA—Top—¾ × 10¼ × 39½″, 1 req'd.

BB—Back—⅜ × 39½ × 55″, 1 req'd.

CC—Inside shelf supports—¾ × 9½ × 38½″, 2 req'd.

DD—Shelves—¾ × 9½ × 37¼″, 3 req'd.

EE—Top facer, front—¾ × 5 × 40½″, 1 req'd.

Moulding

FF—Bead moulding—¼ × ¼ × 144″, cut to lengths, 1 req'd.

GG—Moulding—½ × 1 × 144″, cut to lengths, 1 req'd.

HH—Moulding, ¼ × 1 × 160″, cut to lengths, 1 req'd.

II—Moulding blocks—¼ × ¾ × ¾″, 60 req'd.

JJ—Top moulding—1 × 1½ × 160″, cut to lengths, 1 req'd.

Upper Case Doors

KK—Stiles—¾ × 2¼ × 35″, 4 req'd.

LL—Rails—¾ × 1¾ × 16¼″, 4 req'd.

MM—Moulding—¾ × ¾ × 240″, cut to lengths, 1 req'd.

SS—Door closure strip—½ × ¾ × 35″, 1 req'd.

QQ—Back brace—1 × 1⅛ × 75″, 2 req'd.

Chippendale Breakfront

Circa 1800

The Chippendale breakfront is a classic furniture piece. The model for this project is actually an excellent reproduction of an original Chippendale made in the late 18th century. This reproduction is in a private collection and was crafted by the Mount Airy Furniture Company of Mount Airy, North Carolina. It shows what excellent craftsmen can do when reproducing a classic furniture piece. The choice of wood and craftsmanship are superb and greatly enhance the elegant design, created by one of the greatest cabinetmakers.

The reproduction is made of solid mahogany and has mahogany-veneered doors and drawer fronts. Even the glass-panelled door fronts are covered with veneer, which runs in a mitred, cross-banded pattern. Drawers and doors are also decorated with tiny boxwood cock beading. The center section of the two lower doors has burl figure in the veneer that adds to the beauty of the piece.

In addition to mahogany, original breakfronts were also often made of walnut. You could substitute hardwood-faced plywood for the sides. In fact, 3/8- or 1/2-inch hardwood-faced plywood is used for the back of all sections on the reproduction shown.

Construction

Because of the size of the project, it actually consists of six separate sections. There is a lower center section, an upper center section, and two upper and lower side sections. They are fastened together with countersunk flat-head wood screws through the sides and horizontal dividers. Construction of each section is done separately, although you will do some of the work, such as creating moulding, etc., for the whole project all at once.

Bottom Center Case

Start construction of the bottom center case by cutting the two sides (A) to size and shape. Use either hardwood-faced plywood or glued and dowelled solid stock. Cut dadoes in the inside surfaces of the sides for the bottom (B,C), the inside shelf (D), or shelves as desired. Cut rabbets in the back edges of the sides for the back. Then make the bottoms and shelves. You can use plywood with solid-stock edging, or make them up from solid stock for a more authentic reproduction.

Assembly

To assemble the bottom case, cut dadoes and rabbets in the sides for the bottom and inside shelves and back. Place glue in the dadoes and rabbets and insert the shelves. Cut and fit the 3/8-inch plywood back (H) in place, fastening it with glue and countersunk flat-head wood screws. Make sure the entire case is square, use a carpenter's square to check before driving the screws and allowing the glue to set overnight.

Moulding

Cut the bottom moulding (apron pieces with moulded tops) to size and carve it to the pattern shown. Note that there is also purchased moulding available that is a near match to the moulding shown. It is available from various woodworking supply houses.

Cut the two side moulding pieces (E) with a 45-degree mitre joint on each end. Fasten them in place with glue and wood screws from the inside of the sides.

Cut the front piece (F) to fit between the two, fastening with glue blocks and wood screws to the two side moulding strips and the front of the bottom piece. Note that at this point you may wish to add a bottom back piece and a bottom support strip. This will completely close off the bottom and add additional support in the center of the breakfront.

Doors

Now make up the doors (G) using solid stock or plywood. In either case the fronts of the doors are covered first with veneer, as shown on page 21. Cock beading is then applied to the front door surfaces as well. Note that the doors extend up past the sides of the bottom center case to mate with the drawer of the top center section.

Once the doors have been constructed and veneered, they are installed with brass butt hinges mortised in place. They meet flush in the center and magnetic catches are used to hold them securely in place.

Top Center Section

The first step is to cut the sides (I) to size, then cut the dadoes in them for the lower drawer support (J) and upper bottom (K). Cut dadoes for the lower top

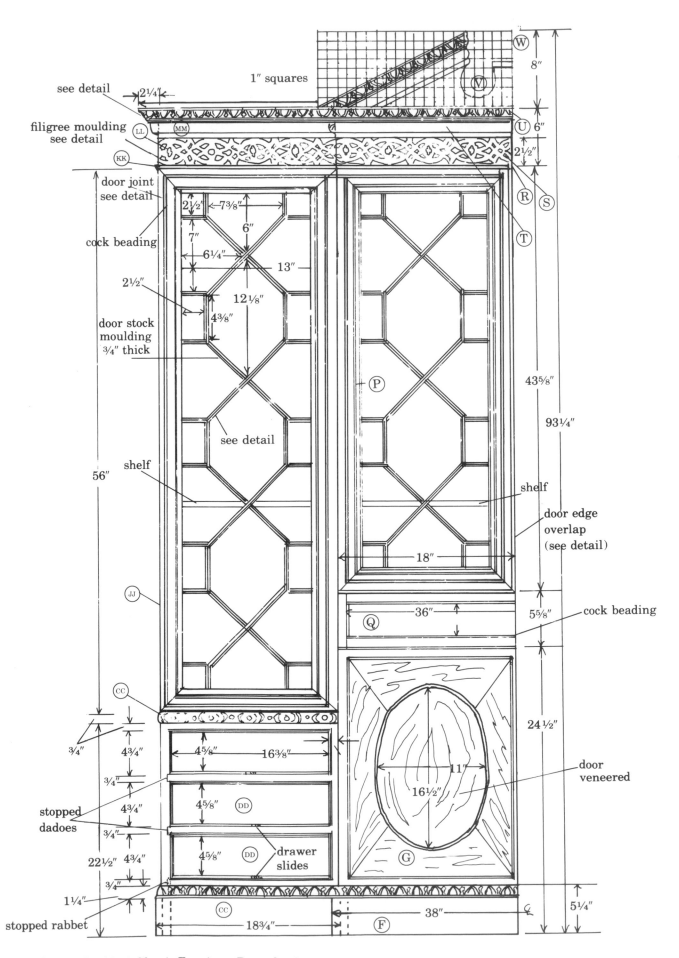

see detail

2¼"

filigree moulding
see detail

1" squares

door joint
see detail

cock beading

2½" ⟵ 7⅜"

6"

7"

6¼"

13"

2½"

12⅛"

door stock
moulding
¾" thick

4⅜"

see detail

shelf

56"

JJ

CC

¾"

4¾"

¾"

stopped
dadoes

4¾"

¾"

22½" 4¾"

¾"

1¼"

stopped rabbet

4⅝" ⟵ 16⅜"

4⅝" DD

4⅝" DD

drawer
slides

CC

18¾"

F

W

8"

V

U 6"

2½"

R
S

T

43⅝"

93¼"

P

shelf

door edge
overlap
(see detail)

Q 36"

5⅝"

cock beading

24½"

11"

16½"

door
veneered

G

38"

5¼"

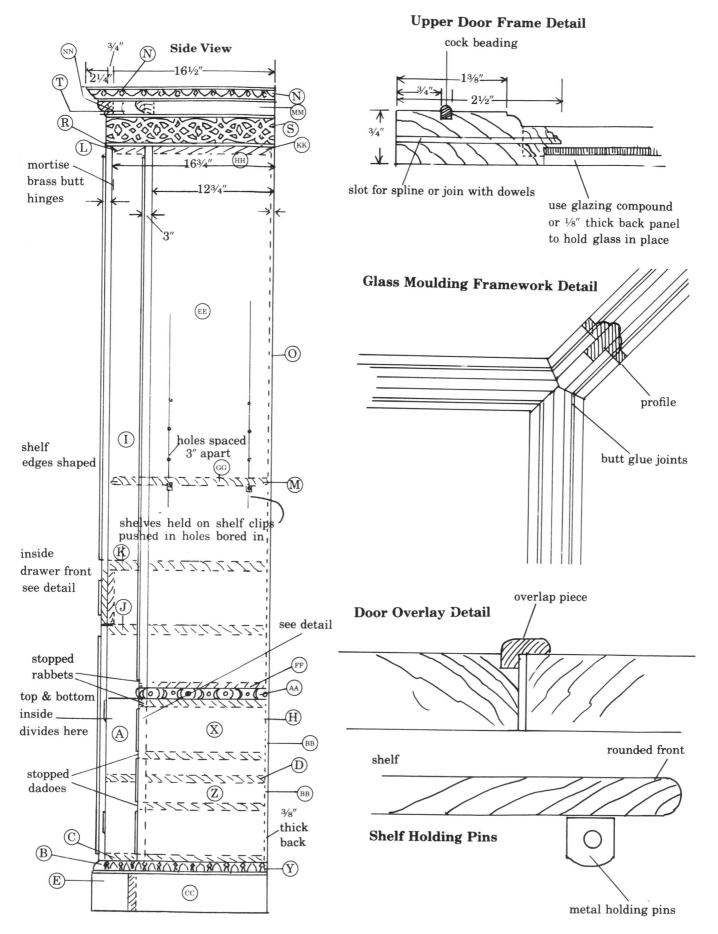

Side View

¾"
2¼"
16½"
16¾"
12¾"
3"

mortise
brass butt
hinges

shelf
edges shaped

holes spaced
3" apart

shelves held on shelf clips
pushed in holes bored in

inside
drawer front
see detail

stopped
rabbets

top & bottom
inside
divides here

see detail

stopped
dadoes

3/8"
thick
back

Upper Door Frame Detail

cock beading

1⅜"
¾"
2½"
¾"

slot for spline or join with dowels

use glazing compound
or ⅛" thick back panel
to hold glass in place

Glass Moulding Framework Detail

profile

butt glue joints

Door Overlay Detail

overlap piece

shelf

rounded front

Shelf Holding Pins

metal holding pins

piece (L) and then cut rabbets in the top ends of the sides for the top piece (N). Cut the rabbets in the back edges of the sides for the back piece (O).

Shelves

Shelves (M) are held in place with metal shelf-holding clips. These have a small metal pin that is slipped into stopped holes bored in the sides of the casework. The holes are spaced 3 inches apart from top to bottom of the case so that the shelves can be adjusted by simply moving the holding pins. Shelves are made of solid stock. Their front edges are shaped as shown in the drawing.

Assembly

Assembly of the top case starts by placing glue on horizontal pieces except for the top, and inserting them into dadoes cut in the sides. Make sure the unit is square, then cut the back piece from ⅜-inch hardwood-faced plywood and anchor it in place with glue and screws. Use countersunk flat-head wood screws. Clamp the entire unit until the glue sets.

Then fasten the upper top front facer (NN) in place with glue and glue blocks from the inside. It can also be anchored with screws into the inner top (L) as they will later be covered by the moulding.

Moulding

The top consists of a facer board covered with several different pieces of moulding to make up the configuration. The first is a small cock-beading-style moulding (R). This can be cut on the edge of thin stock and ripped off. Fasten it in place with glue, mitring it at the corners. Cut a 45-degree mitre at the back ends so that it will mate with the same moulding on the side units. To hold the cock beading firmly in place, you could cut grooves in the side and front facers and seat the moulding into it.

The next moulding is a filigree moulding (S) as shown in the detailed drawing. This is made by cutting stock down to ⅛-inch thickness. Then use a scroll saw to cut the filigree pattern. The moulding is then sanded, mitred and glued to the sanded facer board. Make sure that it meets properly at each corner. Above this is an ogee upper moulding (T). It is made on a shaper, then fastened in place with glue and screws, again being mitred at the corners. Then use the same carving design as the bottom section to make this moulding. Put the pediment moulding (U) in place over the ogee moulding, fastening it with glue and screws.

Top Pediment

The top pediment consists of a thin, scroll-cut piece (V), its bottom edge fit into a dado in a wider piece (UU). The top of the center of the pediment has a small wooden block (W) glued to it. The top outside slanted edges have moulding applied to three sides. Meeting corners of the moulding join at a 45-degree angle. The pediment is anchored to the top with glue and screws after it has been assembled. Fasten it so that the outside corners of the carved pediment moulding are flush with the outside edge of the carved pediment moulding (U) on the unit.

Upper Moulding Detail

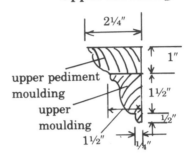

Center Drawer Detail

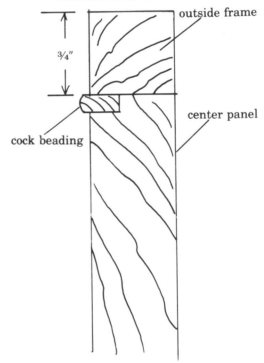

Lower Side Unit Moulding

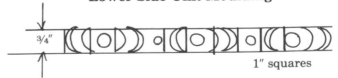

Doors

The doors (P) are made of solid stock and then their surfaces are veneered. The first step is to saw the stock to size. Then cut the shaped edges on their inside edges, as shown in the upper door frame detail drawing. Cut the cock bead holding groove with a router in a router table.

Next, the moulding framework that holds the glass in place is cut to size and shape. Use a shaper or router in a router table to create the moulding. There are two methods that can be used to hold the glass in place. The old-fashioned method was to cut individual glass pieces to fit into the sections. They were fastened in place with glazing points and compound. An alternative, and the one used in the reproduction, is to make up the front framework as shown in the detail and use one solid piece of glass. Then a second, very thin back frame that has been scroll cut and fits in place over the back of the glass is used to hold it in place.

In any case, before going any further with the doors, the glass-holding framework must be assembled (see glass-holding-framework detail). Cut tenons on the ends that fit into the inside edges of the door frame. Cut tiny mortises at these points in the door frame. Assemble with glue. The doors are assembled with splined mitre joints or dowels. The glass-holding frame goes in place at the same time.

After assembling the doors, install the veneer. Run it in crossband fashion over the entire door frame, joining it with 45-degree mitre cuts at the corners. Then use a sharp knife to cut it away from the cock-beading groove. Cut and install the beading, gluing it in place and joining it at the corners with mitred joints.

Hang the doors using brass butt hinges mortised into the sides and doors. Then install the front overlap piece and the door locks and hardware. Install the glass in the manner chosen.

Drawer

Construct the linen drawer (Q) starting with the drawer front. This is an overlap front and is fastened to an interior front with glue and screws. It is made of solid stock covered with veneer in the pattern shown and with cock beading applied in the same manner as on the lower and upper doors. Cut grooves for the cock beading with a router, then apply the veneer and the beading. Make up the drawer. Front, back, and sides are dovetailed together and the bottom is set in dadoes along the inside face of the front, back, and sides. Notch the bottom edge of the back for a drawer slide that is to be fastened to the inside of the bottom drawer support (J) with glue.

After assembly of the drawer, fasten the false front to the inner front with glue and screws driven in from the inside of the inner front, making sure

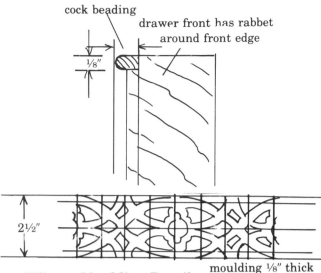

Side Drawer Cock Beading

cock beading

drawer front has rabbet around front edge

1/8"

2 1/2"

moulding 1/8" thick

Filigree Moulding Detail

screws don't break through the surface of the false front.

Side Units

Construction of the side units, particularly the upper sections, is much the same as the center section. The lower side units, however, consist of flush drawers, and it takes a bit of precise cabinetmaking to construct and fit them properly in place.

Lower Side Units

Make parts for both units as you go along. Again, the first step is to cut the side pieces (X) to size. Then cut stopped dadoes for the bottom pieces (Y) and center drawer divider supports (Z). Cut a stopped rabbet on the top ends for the top piece (AA). Cut rabbets in the back for the back piece (BB). Then make up the bottom, center divider and top piece by gluing a piece of solid stock as a facer to the front edge of a piece of plywood. Notch it so that the pieces will fit in the stopped dadoes and rabbets. Then assemble the unit, making sure it is square. Clamp it solidly together until the glue sets.

Make up the drawers (DD) using dovetail joints. The bottom of each fits in dadoes cut in the inside facers of the front, sides and back. The drawer front is covered with veneer and then cock beading is applied to the outside edges, as shown in the detail. Cut drawer slide slots in the backs of drawers, then make up the slides. Put the drawers in place in the unit. When they all fit properly, install the slides with glue. Then cut and install the plywood back (BB) in the rabbets of the sides, top and bottom. Cut, mitre, and install moulding (CC) on the bottom of the unit. Start with the outside piece and anchor it to the sides. Then fasten the front piece to the inner bottom piece. Mitre the end that joins to the center case moulding on a 45-degree mitre as well.

Create the top piece (AA) by gluing hardwood moulding to a plywood center piece. Anchor it to the top of the unit with glue and screws.

Upper Side Units
Construct these (EE-MM) in the same manners as the top center case.

Finishing
Sand, stain and finish all the units. Be sure to finish the inside cut edges that will join with other units.

Final Assembly
Start by placing all the pieces on a smooth, flat surface. Put the three bottom units together and anchor with screws through their sides. Put the top center case in place. Position the two upper side units against it. Anchor the lower side units to the upper side units. Then anchor upper side units to the top center case with screws through the sides.

Materials List
Center Case, Bottom
A—Sides—$3/4 \times 16\frac{3}{4} \times 22\frac{1}{4}''$, 2 req'd.

B—Inner bottom—$3/4 \times 16\frac{3}{8} \times 36''$, 1 req'd.

C—Upper bottom—$3/4 \times 16\frac{3}{4} \times 36''$, 1 req'd.

D—Shelf—$3/4 \times 16\frac{3}{8} \times 36''$, 1 req'd.

E—Side moulding—$3/4 \times 5\frac{1}{4} \times 6''$, 2 req'd.

F—Front moulding—$3/4 \times 5\frac{1}{4} \times 38''$, 1 req'd.

G—Doors—$3/4''$ plywood (or solid stock) $\times$ 18 $\times$ $24\frac{5}{8}''$, 2 req'd.

H—Back—$3/8''$ plywood $\times 17\frac{1}{2} \times 35\frac{1}{4}''$, 1 req'd.

Center Case, Top
I—Sides—$3/4 \times 16\frac{3}{4} \times 62\frac{1}{2}''$, 2 req'd.

J—Drawer support—$3/4 \times 16\frac{3}{8} \times 34\frac{1}{2}''$, 1 req'd.

K—Upper bottom—$3/4 \times 16\frac{3}{8} \times 34\frac{1}{2}''$, 1 req'd.

L—Inner top—$3/4 \times 16\frac{3}{8} \times 34\frac{1}{2}''$, 1 req'd.

M—Shelves—$3/4 \times 16 \times 34\frac{1}{4}''$, 4 req'd., or as desired

N—Top—$3/4 \times 17\frac{1}{4} \times 36''$, 1 req'd.

NN—Upper top front facer—$3/4 \times 6 \times 36''$, 1 req'd.

O—Back—$3/8''$ plywood $\times 35\frac{1}{4} \times 63\frac{1}{4}''$, 1 req'd.

P—Doors

Stiles—$3/4 \times 2\frac{5}{8} \times 43\frac{5}{8}''$, 4 req'd.

Rails—$3/4 \times 2\frac{5}{8} \times 18''$, 4 req'd.

Glass moulding—$3/4 \times 1 \times 24''$, cut to fit, 1 req'd.

Q—Drawer

Front—$3/4 \times 5\frac{5}{8} \times 36''$, 1 req'd.

Inside front—$3/4 \times 5\frac{5}{8} \times 34\frac{1}{2}''$, 1 req'd.

Sides—$1/2 \times 5\frac{5}{8} \times 16''$, 2 req'd.

Back—$1/2 \times 5\frac{5}{8} \times 34\frac{1}{2}''$, 1 req'd.

Bottom—$1/4 \times 15\frac{3}{4} \times 33\frac{1}{2}''$, 1 req'd.

Slide—$3/16 \times 3/4 \times 15\frac{3}{4}''$, 1 req'd.

R—Top moulding—$1/4 \times 1/4 \times 72''$, cut to fit, 1 req'd.

S—Filigree moulding—$1/8 \times 2\frac{1}{2} \times 72''$, cut to fit, 1 req'd.

T—Upper moulding—$2\frac{1}{4} \times 3 \times 80''$, cut to fit, 1 req'd.

U—Pediment moulding—$2\frac{1}{4} \times 3\frac{1}{4} \times 72''$, cut to fit, 1 req'd.

UU—Pediment-holding block—$3/4 \times 2 \times 32''$, 1 req'd.

V—Pediment center—$1/4 \times 4\frac{1}{4} \times 28''$, 1 req'd.

W—Pediment top—$1/2 \times 1 \times 4\frac{1}{2}''$, 1 req'd.

Lower Side Units
X—Sides—$3/4 \times 13\frac{1}{2} \times 22\frac{1}{4}''$, 4 req'd.

Y—Inner bottoms—$3/4 \times 13\frac{1}{2} \times 17\frac{3}{8}''$, 2 req'd.

Z—Drawer divider supports—$3/4 \times 13\frac{1}{8} \times 17\frac{3}{8}''$, 8 req'd.

AA—Top—$1 \times 13\frac{3}{4} \times 18\frac{1}{2}''$, 2 req'd.

BB—Back—$3/8''$ plywood $\times 17\frac{1}{4} \times 17\frac{3}{4}''$, 2 req'd.

CC—Lower moulding (front & sides)—$3/4 \times 5\frac{1}{4} \times 72''$, cut to fit, 1 req'd.

DD—Drawers

Fronts—$3/4 \times 4\frac{5}{8} \times 16\frac{3}{8}''$, 6 req'd.

Sides—$1/2 \times 4\frac{5}{8} \times 12\frac{1}{2}''$, 12 req'd.

Backs—$1/2 \times 4\frac{5}{8} \times 16\frac{3}{8}''$, 6 req'd.

Bottoms—$1/4 \times 12\frac{1}{2} \times 15\frac{7}{8}''$, 6 req'd.

Slides—$3/16 \times 3/4 \times 11\frac{3}{4}''$, 6 req'd.

Upper Side Units
EE—Sides—$3/4 \times 12\frac{3}{4} \times 61\frac{1}{2}''$, 4 req'd.

FF—Outer bottoms—$3/4 \times 12\frac{1}{4} \times 16\frac{1}{2}''$, 2 req'd.

GG—Shelves—$3/4 \times 12 \times 16\frac{1}{4}''$, 6 to 8 req'd., or as desired

HH—Outer tops—$3/4 \times 12\frac{1}{4} \times 16\frac{1}{2}''$, 2 req'd.

II—Tops—$3/4 \times 13\frac{3}{8} \times 18''$, 2 req'd.

JJ—Doors

Stiles—$3/4 \times 2\frac{5}{8} \times 56''$, 4 req'd.

Rails—$3/4 \times 2\frac{5}{8} \times 18''$, 4 req'd.

Glass moulding—$3/4 \times 1 \times 30''$, cut to fit, 1 req'd.

KK—Top moulding—$1/4 \times 1/4 \times 72''$, cut to fit, 1 req'd.

LL—Filigree moulding—$1/8 \times 2\frac{1}{2} \times 72''$, cut to fit, 1 req'd.

MM—Upper moulding—$2\frac{1}{2} \times 3\frac{1}{4} \times 80''$, cut to fit, 1 req'd.

OO—Upper top side facers—$3/4 \times 6 \times 18''$, 2 req'd.

Chippendale Lowboy

Circa 1770

The Nelson-Atkins Museum of Art, Kansas City, Missouri

The Chippendale-style lowboys made in Philadelphia during the latter part of the 18th century are some of the finest pieces ever made by American cabinetmakers. Most of these "originals" were made using drawings and plans from Thomas Chippendale's book, *The Gentleman and Cabinet-Maker's Director*.

Chippendale was one of the most influential furniture designers and his lowboys with their graceful cabriole legs, ball-and-claw feet, and elegant carvings provide an excellent woodworking challenge.

The lowboy shown, reproduced by the author, looks as elegant and beautiful today as it did in centuries past. It is truly a classic piece of furniture.

So many cabinetmakers were producing these lowboys during the late 18th century that they can be found in a great variety of sizes, surface embellishments, and modifications of design. On many, the outside columns are decorated with flutes. This is a quarter-turning set in a column recess on most of them. But on the lowboy shown here, the column itself is shaped and fluted.

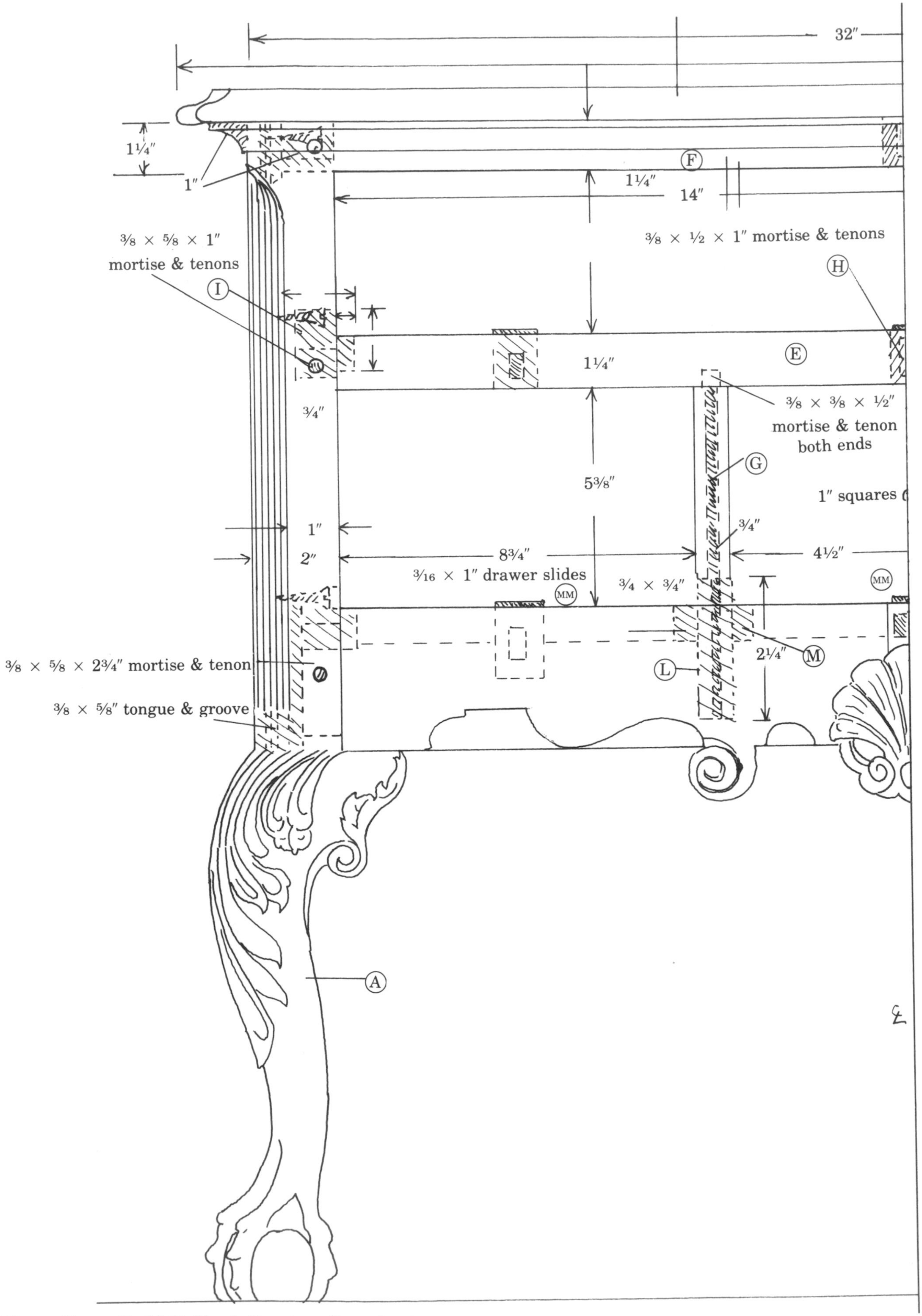
32″
1¼″
1″
Ⓕ
1¼″
14″
⅜ × ⅝ × 1″
mortise & tenons
⅜ × ½ × 1″ mortise & tenons
Ⓗ
Ⓘ
1¼″
Ⓔ
¾″
⅜ × ⅜ × ½″
mortise & tenon
both ends
Ⓖ
5⅜″
1″ squares
1″
¾″
2″
8¾″
4½″
3⁄16 × 1″ drawer slides
¾ × ¾″
MM
MM
⅜ × ⅝ × 2¾″ mortise & tenon
2¼″
Ⓜ
Ⓛ
⅜ × ⅝″ tongue & groove
Ⓐ

35½"

9⅜"

9"

Ⓝ

Ⓞ

Ⓟ

¾"

¾"

⅜"

4⅜"

14½"

5¾"

29½"

1"

13½"

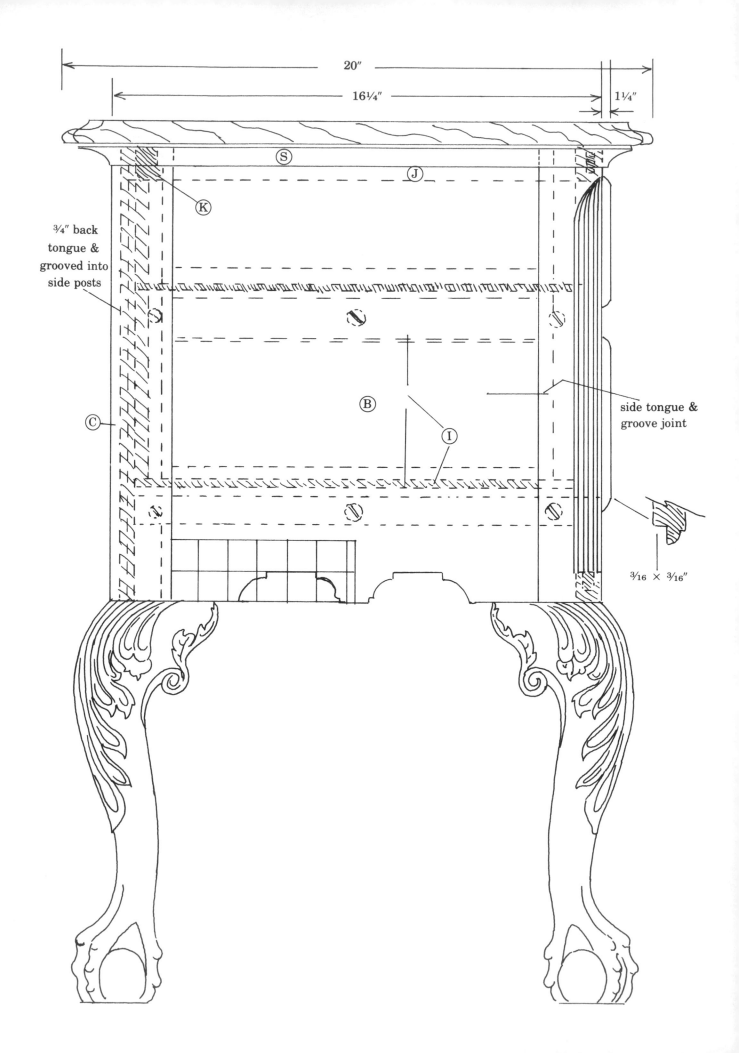

20"

16¼"

1¼"

Ⓢ

Ⓙ

Ⓚ

¾" back
tongue &
grooved into
side posts

Ⓒ

Ⓑ

Ⓘ

side tongue &
groove joint

3/16 × 3/16"

The lowboys tend to vary quite a lot in the quality of workmanship. The piece chosen for this project is one of the better designed and crafted lowboys. Note the pegged front mortise-and-tenon joints. The carvings on the skirt and drawer are not overdone, and the piece has excellent proportions.

Lowboys were made of several different kinds of wood. Walnut was used for the chest shown, but many were constructed of mahogany and cherry. Some were even made from maple.

Construction

Construction of a piece of furniture such as this requires a fairly skilled cabinetmaker, as well as a full collection of tools. Naturally, the original was made using hand tools alone. But power tools, such as a lathe, shaper, router, and a carving duplicator, can be used to ensure that parts fit accurately and to relieve the tedium of many of the chores.

In drawing up plans for this project, I have used the old furniture-building techniques that have made these pieces so long-lasting. But I did add side support strips to the inner top. This is a better way to anchor the top. The original used drawer tilt strips positioned away from the ends, which over time caused the top to loosen from the ends. This modification will not detract from the value of your reproduction; instead, it will make for an even longer-lasting "heritage" piece for your family.

Legs

The leg and upper post is all one piece. Unless you have a supply of large pieces of stock for the leg posts (A), they will have to be glued up from smaller pieces. One method of doing this is to cut a piece of stock to the correct diameter for the top part of the leg post and to the length of the whole leg. A wood block will later be glued to it to make up the extra width of the lower leg.

Cut the angled chamfer in it and then rout the flutes in the chamfer. This can be done by using a small hand-held router, with the leg post held in shop-made V-block jigs. Or you can mount the leg post between the centers of a lathe and use a special router guide to cut the reed flutes. In any case, the upper curved part will have to be finished by hand. The back-leg posts do not have the chamfer.

Cut grooves for the sides (B) and the back (C) into the leg posts. Make mortises for the front facers (D-G) into the inside edges of the front-leg posts. Then cut the extra-width blocks for the outside curve of the lower leg surfaces and glue them to the leg posts. Do each step on all the leg posts at the same time. For instance, cut all the full-length pieces, flute all of them, and mortise all of them.

Enlarge the squared drawing for the cabriole legs and transfer to the stock. Then cut the legs to size and shape using a band saw, as shown on page 27.

Smooth up all surfaces, then transfer the carving pattern to the stock and carve the legs. Allow the carving on the upper part of the leg to protrude about ⅛ to ¼ inch.

If you have a carving duplicator, this step is simply a matter of hand-carving the first leg and using the machine to make the remaining legs. In fact, you can probably duplicate the other three legs complete with carvings in less than one day, if the stock is glued up and ready to use.

Sides and Back

The sides (B) and back (C) can be made of glued-up solid stock, or plywood. For solid stock, glue pieces to the proper size and cut the shape on the bottom edges of the sides and back. Then cut the tongues on the ends of both sides and back to fit in the leg-post grooves. Cut mortises in the back for the bottom center drawer support (L) and tilt strips (H). Use extra care here. These pieces must be accurately marked, located, and cut, or the drawers will not fit properly. Regardless of how good a job you do on the rest of the cabinet, poorly fitted drawers will make the whole project look sloppy.

Front Facers

Construction of the front facer section starts with the lower facer (D). The carved lower apron can be done in two ways. The easiest is to use an applied carving for the shell. Just carve it to shape from a separate piece and glue it to the front of the apron; then carve the rest of the apron to the pattern. Orig-

Back Detail

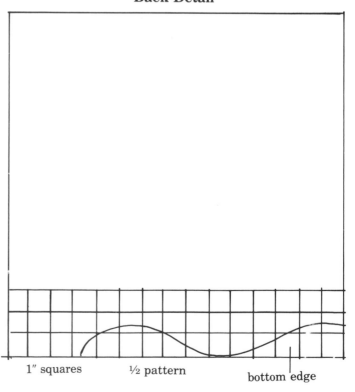

1" squares   ½ pattern   bottom edge

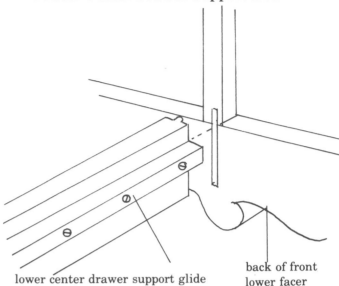

lower center drawer support glide

back of front
lower facer

inal lowboys had both applied and solid-stock carving, and the type used was usually determined by the amount of carving.

You can also cut the carving into the front of a single piece of stock. Use a router to cut down the stock around the carving and to cut the rest of the apron to the correct thickness. Then smooth up with scrapers and hand planes.

Regardless of the method used, the first step is to enlarge the squared drawing. Cut the bottom edge to the shape on a band saw. Then sand all the curves with a drum sander. Cut tenons on each end to fit into the front-leg posts (A). Cut mortises into the back face for the lower drawer supports (L) and in the top edge for the center drawer facer strips (G).

Center Drawer Facer

Saw the center drawer facer (E) that fits between the drawers to size and make tenons on each end to fit into the leg posts. Cut mortises in it for the center vertical facer (G) tenons, as well as for the center drawer tilt strips (H) and drawer slides (MM).

Upper Facer

Cut the top horizontal facer (F) to size and shape. Make tenons on each end to fit into the leg posts. Then cut the mortise in its center for the drawer tilt strip (H). Bore counterbored screw holes in the underside for anchoring the top (Q) in place.

Side Cleats

Cut the top side cleats (J) to size and shape. Bore holes for countersunk wood screws into both the underneath and inside surfaces of each.

Side Drawer Supports and Glides

Cut each of these (I) from a single piece of stock to the L-shape shown (see detail drawing). Each of

these must be notched on one end to fit around the leg posts and to go up against the back of the front facers. The other end goes against the back support piece. These can be made of pine or other less expensive softwood. This was done on the original.

Bottom Drawer Support Assemblies

Cut the bottom center drawer supports (L) from solid softwood stock and make tenons on each end. Then cut the center drawer glides (M) to size and shape and fasten them in place to the sides of the center drawer support with glue and screws.

Top Back Cleats

These cleats are ¾ × ¾-inch strips cut to fit between the leg post and the tilt strip (H). Rough-cut them now; then cut to fit during final assembly. They are used to anchor the top (Q) down in place on the back (C).

Top

Although the top (Q) on the original was made of one piece, it's best to make it up of several pieces joined with glue and dowels, or glue and tongue-and-groove joints. In either case, make sure that each piece is reversed to create a heartwood/sapwood alternating pattern. This eliminates warping problems. Sand both the bottom and top surfaces. Cut the corners as shown in the detail; then shape the edge using a shaper or router.

Top Moulding

Run the undertop moulding (R,S) to the proper shape on the edge of a wide piece of stock, using a shaper or router. Then rip the moulded edge from the stock.

Case Assembly

Assembly of the case starts with the back (C). Glue

the tongues of the back and place them in the grooves of the back-leg posts (A). Make sure the assembly is square and clamped securely. Allow the glue to set overnight.

Side Drawer Support Detail

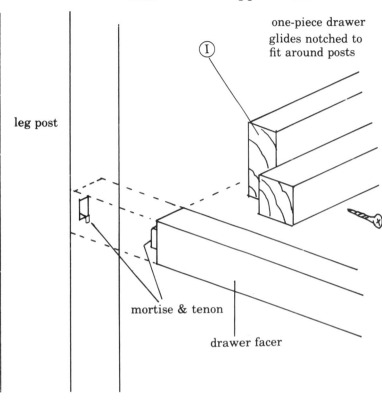

leg post

I

one-piece drawer glides notched to fit around posts

mortise & tenon

drawer facer

Full-Size Pattern for Top Corner

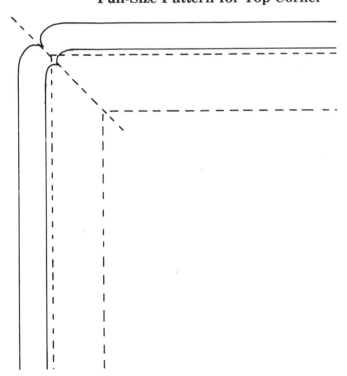

Bore holes into the mortise-and-tenon joints to "peg" the joints with wooden dowels. Insert the holding dowels. These can be hand-cut hardwood dowels, or you can use purchased dowel stock (covering the dowel ends with hardwood plugs, cut to fit the holes).

At the same time, you can start the front-apron assembly. This is done by first placing the center vertical facers (G) between the lower (D) and center facer (E) pieces. Glue and clamp them together. Use a small square to ensure that the facer assembly is perfectly square and then allow the glue to set overnight.

Remove this section from the clamps and place glue on the tenons on its ends. Put this assembly between the front-leg posts. At the same time, insert the top facer strips (F). Make sure the unit is clamped squarely and allow the glue to set. Again, insert dowels into the mortise-and-tenon joints to strengthen them further.

Now place the back assembly on its back on a smooth, flat surface. Put the side tenons in the back-post mortises. Fit back tenons of the drawer tilt strips (H) and lower drawer support assembles (L,M) into mortises in the back piece. Then carefully place the front assembly down over the tenons, fitting mortises over tenons of the tilt strips and support pieces.

Tap the construction together with a soft mallet and then carefully turn the assembly up onto a smooth, flat surface. Make sure it stands evenly on all four legs and that the assembly is not twisted or crooked; then clamp securely together. Again bore holes in mortise-and-tenon joints and insert holding dowels. Allow the glue to set.

An alternative method is to glue up the entire assembly at one time. The advantage of this method is it allows you to shift pieces slightly to correct for any misalignment. But it takes many clamps as well as several hands to assemble and hold all the pieces for clamping.

After the glue has set, put in the side drawer glides (I) with glue and screws. Attach the top (J) and back (K) cleats with glue and screws. Add top moulding (R,S).

Drawers

One of the major differences between handmade and factory-produced furniture pieces is that the drawers on handmade items are usually put together after assembly of the case. That way each drawer can be carefully fit in place.

I have made the entire drawer fronts on all drawers (N-P) lipped with an overhang, even though there is no lip on the bottom edge of the original piece. The lipped bottom edge covers any discrepancies in the drawer construction and hides any problems of warping and twisting that may occur later.

If you decide to leave the bottom lip off the drawer for a more authentic appearance, you will have to compensate and reduce the facers by the amount of the drawer lip.

The first step is to cut the drawer fronts to size and joint or sand all their edges. The center bottom drawer front (P) is a bit thicker to compensate for the extra thickness of the front carving. You could do the outside leaf portion of the carving as applied carving; however, it will look better carved into the drawer front to match the recessed carving of the interior shell.

Cut the rabbets 3/16 × 3/16-inch on the inside of all edges to create the lip fronts. Then cut the outside moulded shape on all four edges using a router or shaper. The outside shape for the center carved drawer will have to be lowered 1/4 inch to compensate for the surface being lowered around the carving.

Carving the Drawer Front

Next, carve the bottom center drawer (P) front. First outline the exterior convex relief carving of the leaves and vines. After the pattern has been marked on the drawer, use a sharp chisel to lower the surface around the carved portion. Then use a router to rout the rest of the top down to the correct thickness around the carving. A jig can be used to hold the carving block in place on your workbench and guide the depth for the router cut. Once this portion has been roughed in, then you can finish the carving with tiny chisels and hand-held rifflers. To carve the recess, first rough out the scoop shape. Then re-mark the pattern on the recess and carve the shell to the finished shape.

Drawer Assembly

The drawers are assembled in the same way, with dovetailed front and back. The bottom is held in with dadoes that are cut in the drawer front and sides, and it extends under the bottom of the back piece. This is a fairly standard drawer construction. There are, however, a couple of extra touches on these drawers that add a mark of craftsmanship. The first is to round the top edges of the drawer sides and backs. Thin guide blocks attached to the bottom of the back of each drawer fit down over the drawer slides (MM) and guide the drawers easily in and out of the case.

After completing each drawer, anchor its guide strip to the front of the facer assembly and then put the drawer in place. Once it fits perfectly, mark the location of the center guide strip and support cleat. Fasten them to the back with glue and screws.

Installing the Top

Remove the drawers, place the top (Q) upside down on a smooth, flat surface and then put the case assembly down on it. Fasten the case to the top with glue and screws driven through the side and front and back top aprons and support cleats into the top.

Set the unit upright and stain, finish, and add hardware. The hardware is available from a number of reproduction hardware companies.

Materials List

A—Leg posts—5 × 5 × 28¾", 4 req'd.

B—Sides—¾ × 13¼ × 15¼", 2 req'd.

C—Back—¾ × 15¼ × 29½", 1 req'd.

D—Lower front facer—¾ × 5 × 29½", 1 req'd.

E—Center horizontal facer—1 × 1¼ × 29½", 1 req'd.

F—Top horizontal facer—1 × 1¼ × 29½", 1 req'd.

G—Center vertical facers—¾ × 1 × 6⅜", 2 req'd.

H—Drawer tilt strips—¾ × 1¼ × 15½", cut to fit, 2 req'd.

I—Side drawer glides—2¼ × 2¼ × 12¼", 4 req'd.

J—Top side cleats—¾ × ¾ × 12¼", 2 req'd.

K—Back top support cleats—¾ × ¾ × 13½", 2 req'd.

L—Bottom center drawer supports—¾ × 3¼ × 15½", 2 req'd.

M—Center drawer guides—¾ × ¾ × 14½", 4 req'd.

MM—Drawer slides—¾ × 1⁷⁄₁₆ × 15½", cut to fit, 5 req'd.

Drawers

N—Top drawer

Front—¾ × 4⅜ × 28¾", 1 req'd.

Sides—½ × 3⅞ × 13", 2 req'd.

Back—½ × 3⅞ × 27⅞", 1 req'd.

Bottom—¼ × 12¾ × 26⅜", 1 req'd.

O—Outside lower drawers

Fronts—¾ × 5¾ × 9", 2 req'd.

Sides—½ × 5¼ × 13", 4 req'd.

Backs—½ × 5¼ × 8⅝", 2 req'd.

Bottoms—¼ × 7⅛ × 12¾", 2 req'd.

P—Center drawer

Front—1 × 5¾ × 9⅜", 1 req'd.

Sides—½ × 5¼ × 13", 2 req'd.

Back—½ × 5¼ × 8⅞", 1 req'd.

Bottom—¼ × 8⅜ × 12¾", 1 req'd.

Q—Top—¾ × 16¼ × 32", 1 req'd.

R—Front & back moulding—¾ × 1 × 34", cut to fit, 2 req'd.

S—Side moulding—¾ × 1 × 18", cut to fit, 2 req'd.

Chippendale Mirror

Elegant mirrors that matched lowboys or dressing tables were quite popular during the middle of the 18th century. The mirror shown here is from a design by the author, and it combines features of several different classic mirrors. It is designed to go with the Chippendale lowboy (another of the projects in this book). In fact, the mirror carving repeats the center shell pattern of the lowboy.

There was a great deal of variation in the shapes and carvings of the upper and lower parts of these 18th-century mirrors. The simplest mirrors were merely scroll-cut solid stock, while the more complicated pieces consisted of highly figured and carved frames. The wood used should match that of the lowboy the mirror will complement. It can be almost any good solid hardwood, although walnut or mahogany are traditional. In many instances, parts of the mirror were also covered with gold gilt.

Construction

One of the most interesting features of the mirror shown is that it has the same "broken" corner shape used on the top of the lowboy. This is made by cutting the top (C) and side (A) frame pieces to shape on a band saw. Cut the bottom frame piece (B) as well. Then use a shaper or router held in a router table to shape the ogee mouldings. This can be somewhat tricky—make sure you take all precautions during the operation. Once the moulding has been made, the rest is easy.

Transfer the squared drawing of the top panel (D) to a piece of stock. Note that it will probably have to be glued up to create the wide stock necessary. The grain must run vertically.

Saw the top scroll piece to size and shape on a scroll saw. Sand all edges as smooth as possible. Then carve the relief carving in the top. This can be applied or carved from the stock. These pieces were usually carved from the stock.

Assemble the mirror frame and cut the dado in its back top edge for the top panel. Assemble the frame with glue and mitred spline joints in the corners, as shown in the drawing. Glue the top section in place last. Allow the glue to set thoroughly. Then remove from the clamps and cut the groove for the mirror and the backing piece. Stain and finish the mirror frame to match the lowboy. Install the mirror (E) and the back piece (F), fastening the latter in place with small screws through the outside edge.

Materials List

A—Side frame moulding—1 × 1⅜ × 27″, cut to length, 2 req'd.

B—Bottom frame moulding—1 × 1⅜ × 17½″, cut to length, 1 req'd.

C—Top frame moulding—1 × 1⅜ × 16½″, cut to length, 1 req'd.

D—Top panel—¾ × 11 × 18″, 1 req'd.

E—Mirror—14½ × 28⅝″, 1 req'd.

F—Mirror back holding panel—⅜ × 14½ × 28⅝″, 1 req'd.

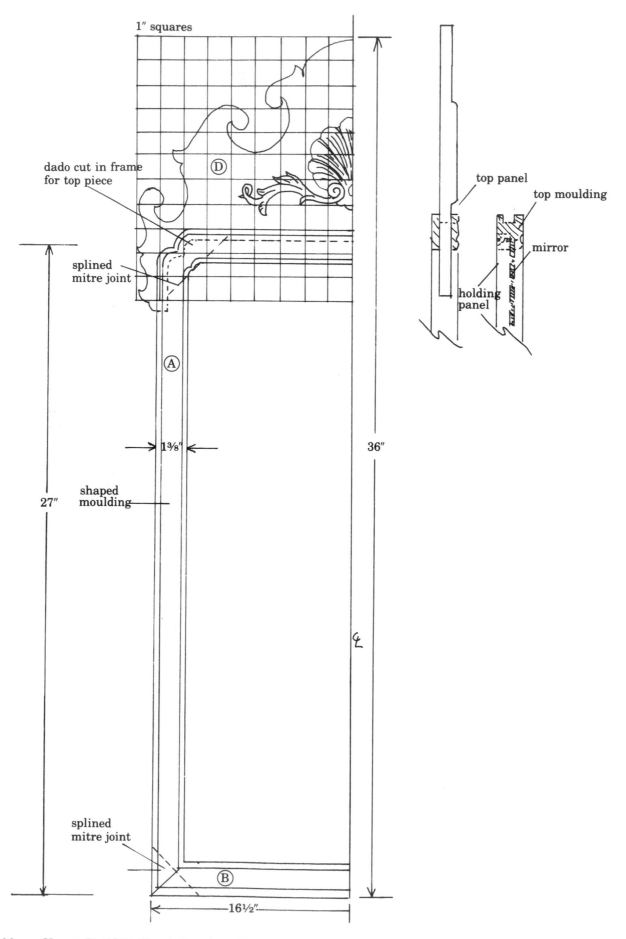

1" squares

dado cut in frame
for top piece

splined
mitre joint

Ⓓ

Ⓐ

1⅜"

shaped
moulding

27"

36"

splined
mitre joint

Ⓑ

—16½"—

top panel

top moulding

mirror

holding
panel

Philadelphia Highboy

Circa 18th Century
The Nelson-Atkins Museum of Art, Kansas City, Missouri

The Philadelphia cabinetmakers of the 18th century produced some of the finest examples of American furniture. Many of these pieces have become classics, and the Philadelphia highboy is just such a piece.

The highboy-style chest of drawers originated in Europe in the 17th century. The first designs were really imitations of ornate frames made for Oriental lacquered cabinets, then popular with English nobility. But the high chest became popular in its own right, and Oriental decorative touches were dropped. In later years the highboy became a prized centerpiece in many homes.

Although the Philadelphia craftsmen copied many of their designs from the European furniture builders, they nevertheless imparted a distinctly American flavor to them. The highboy chosen for this project is by an unknown cabinetmaker, but it is from the Philadelphia period. It is truly an elegant and masterful piece of work.

The original highboy is made of mahogany. But you could make it from walnut or cherry. Cherry is a popular wood with today's reproduction-highboy manufacturers.

Construction

This project isn't for the amateur. But those seasoned craftsmen who take this project one step at a time will be surprised at the "ease" with which this complicated piece can be built. Take the legs, for example. Carving four legs to the pattern shown is mind-boggling for most of today's time-conscious craftsmen. But with a carving duplicator you only have to carve one leg. The machine will do the other three legs.

Basic case construction is used on the highboy. All mortise-and-tenon joints are strengthened with dowel pins. The holes are slightly offset from each other to wedge the parts together.

Base Unit

The highboy is constructed in two separate parts: a base and a top unit. Make the base first.

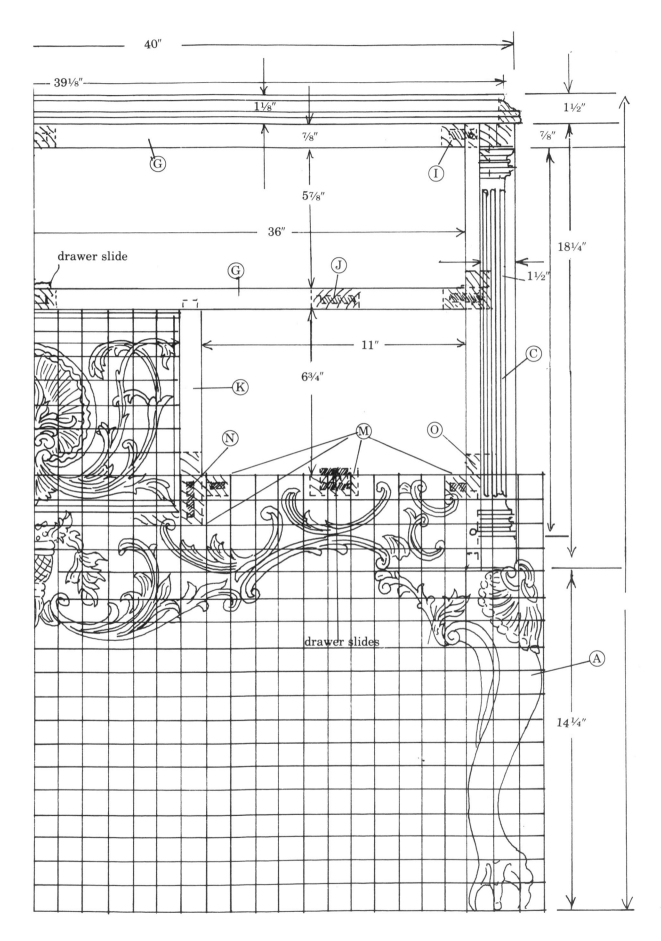

40"

39⅛"

1⅛"

7/8"

1½"

7/8"

G

I

5⅞"

36"

drawer slide

G

J

1½"

18¼"

11"

C

6¾"

K

N

M

O

A

drawer slides

14¼"

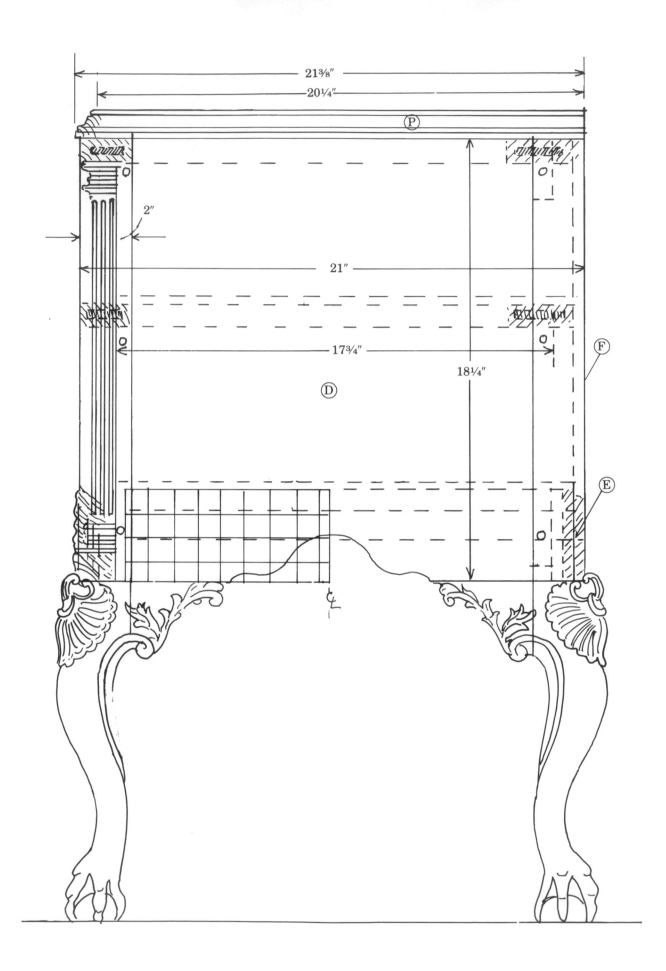

Legs

Start with the legs. First, enlarge the squared drawing and create the pattern for the cabriole leg. The leg post (A) runs from the floor to the underside of the base unit top. Glue a 1-inch-thick block on both front edges to create the thickness needed. Then glue the wing pieces (B) in place as well, to create the heavy stock needed for cutting out the cabriole leg shapes.

Mark the carving outline for the top part of the cabriole leg and include the profile when cutting the leg on a band saw. This will save a lot of rough carving for the relief work on the top of the legs. Carve the cabriole legs. Next, cut away the center block portion (on the upper leg post) for the front leg columns (C). Note that this can be rough-cut using a table or radial arm saw set to the proper depth. Stop cutting before you get to the end and finish the cut with chisels. Sand as smooth as possible.

The back legs are shaped in the same manner as the front legs, except that there are no fluted columns. So the back-leg posts are left whole.

Cut mortises in the legs for the web-frame drawer supports (G-J; see web-frame mortise detail).

Make grooves in the front-leg posts for the side (D) tenons and mortises for the bottom apron (L). Cut grooves in the back-leg posts for the side tenons and cut stopped rabbets the length of the sides in the back edges for the back piece. Cut mortises for the back apron (E) and bore the holes for the mortise-and-tenon pins.

Fluted Columns

The fluted front-leg columns (C) are quarter turnings. Enlarge the squared drawing and turn a full-sized column to shape. Make the turning block by gluing together four pieces of stock with newspaper between each piece. Turn the stock to the pattern and sand smooth. Then, while the turning is still in the lathe, use a jig to hold a router or hand grinder to cut the flutes. Or, you can use the Craftsman Router-Crafter. Once the flutes have been cut, use a wide chisel to tap apart the four turned sections.

Glue the quarter turnings in place in the notches cut in the front legs. You can also add screws from the back if you want to provide additional holding power.

Sides

Glue up the side pieces (D) from solid stock, then enlarge the squared drawings and cut the bottom shapes. Cut the tenons on each end of the side pieces and drill the pin holes in each.

Back

Saw the bottom back apron (E) from solid stock and cut the tenons on each end, as well as bore the pin

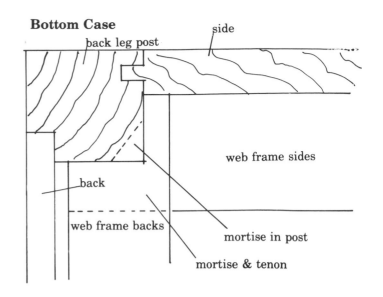

Bottom Case

side
back leg post
web frame sides
back
web frame backs
mortise in post
mortise & tenon

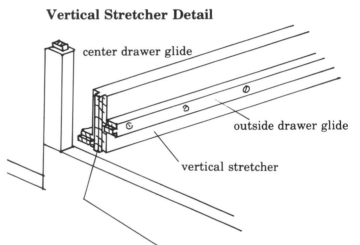

Vertical Stretcher Detail

center drawer glide
outside drawer glide
vertical stretcher
tenons to fit in mortises in lower apron

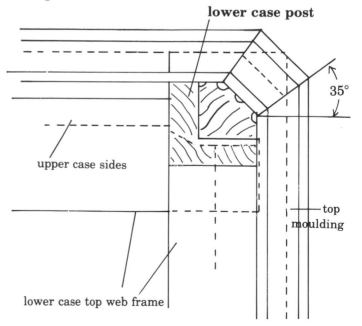

Top View of Bottom Case

lower case post
35°
upper case sides
top moulding
lower case top web frame

holes. Make a rabbet in its top edge for the back piece (F). Then cut the ⅜-inch plywood back piece to fit between the rabbets in the bottom apron and the inside back edges of the back-leg posts.

Bottom Front Apron

Cut the bottom front apron (L) to size from 1-inch-thick stock. Make tenons on each end and bore pin dowel holes in them. Cut mortises in the apron's upper edge for the vertical facer pieces (K). Transfer the carving pattern to the apron and carve the relief carvings.

Web Frame/Facer

Make up the web frame/facer assemblies (G-J) as show in the detail drawing. Use mortise-and-tenon joints for all pieces. Use hardwood to match the rest of the case for the front facer pieces (G) and softwood for the rest of the web frame pieces. Cut the pieces to shape, glue them together, and make sure they are all exactly the same size and that they are perfectly square.

Then fasten the drawer guide strips (M) on top of the inside front-to-back with glue and small brads. Fasten the side drawer glides (O) to the two lower frames with glue and screws.

Case Assembly

Place glue on the tenons of the bottom front apron (L) and fit it between the two front-leg posts. Position the vertical facers (K) on top of the front apron; then install the center web frame face assembly on the vertical facer tenons and in the front-leg mortises. Do the same for the top web frame/facer section.

Fit the back bottom apron (E) between the two back legs and then place the sides (D) in the back-leg grooves. Fasten the back assembly to the front assembly by fitting side tenons, web frames, and vertical facer/stretcher (N) in the appropriate grooves. Place the unit on a smooth, flat surface. Make sure it doesn't rock and that all four legs rest evenly on the surface. Then clamp the unit together tightly and drive the matching hardwood mortise-and-tenon holding pins (dowels) in place. Cut them off with a chisel, remove any glue that might have been squeezed out, and allow the glue to set.

After the glue has set, you can strengthen the unit by fastening the side web frame pieces to the sides with screws. Attach the front and back lower web frame to the front and back aprons with countersunk wood screws.

Drawers

The drawers shouldn't be made until the case is finished. Then hand-fit each drawer to the case, allowing about ⅟₁₆-inch clearance around each side of the drawer.

The drawers are standard dovetail construction. The top edges of the sides are rounded and the bottom is set in dadoes in the front, sides and back. The back has a small notch cut in the center of its bottom edge to allow it to fit down over the drawer slides.

The fronts of the drawers (R-T) are fitted with cock beading. If you want to add a really elegant touch, veneer the drawer fronts in book-matched, figured veneers to match the rest of the case. The bottom center drawer (R), however, has a deep carving, and you will note that it is 1¼ inches thick. After all drawers have been assembled and fitted in place, attach the back (F) with glue and screws.

Sand, stain, and finish the piece. Then add the drawer pulls.

Top Unit

Although it appears quite complicated, the top unit is constructed in a series of very distinct steps that can be taken one at a time. The basic structure of the case itself is simple. It consists of a basic box and front posts inset with quarter turnings.

Web Frame Mortise Detail (Bottom Case)

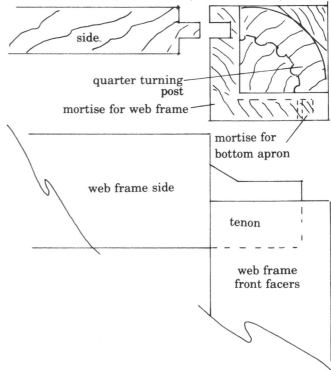

Drawer Detail

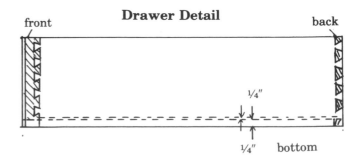

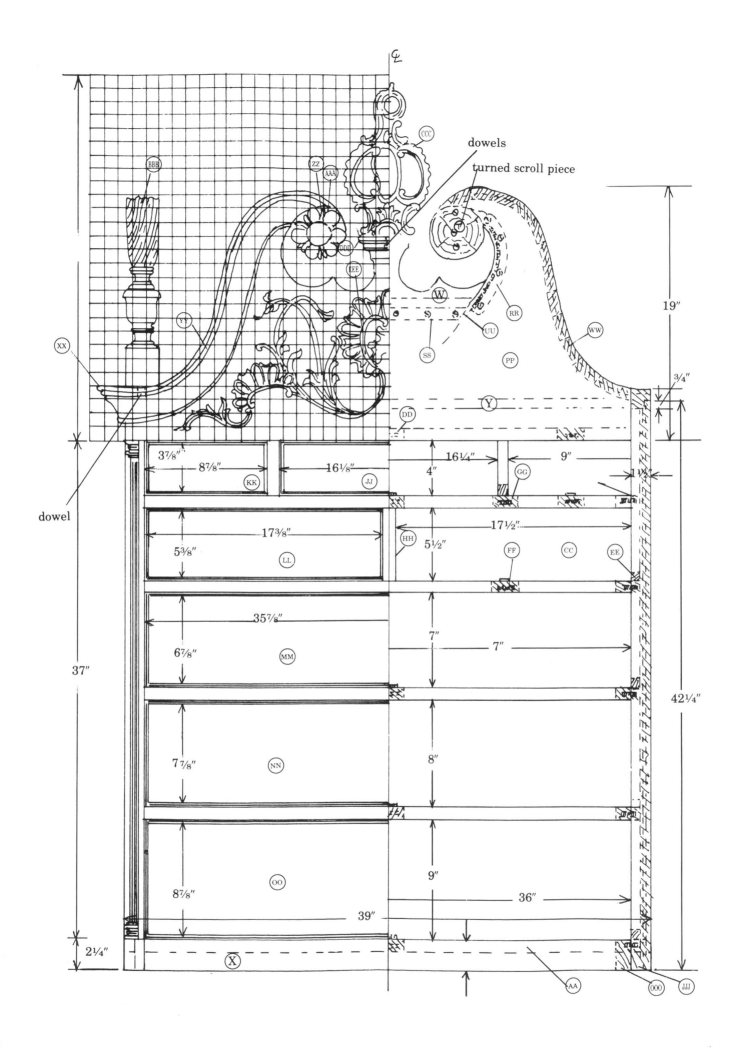

dowels

turned scroll piece

19"

3/4"

BBB

CCC

ZZ

AAA

DDD

EEE

W

RR

WW

XX

YY

UU

SS

PP

Y

DD

dowel

3⅞"

8⅞"

16⅛"

16¼"

9"

1½"

KK

JJ

4"

GG

17⅜"

17½"

HH

5⅜"

LL

5½"

FF

CC

EE

35⅞"

7"

6⅞"

MM

7"

37"

8"

7⅞"

NN

42¼"

9"

8⅞"

OO

36"

39"

2¼"

X

AA

OOO

JJJ

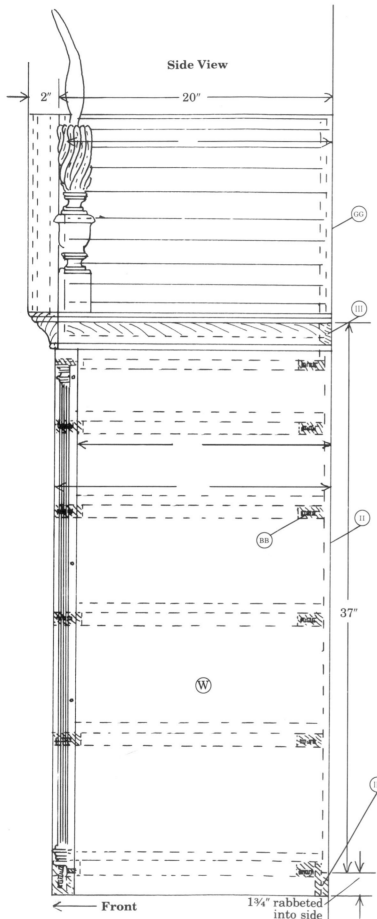

Side View

2" ← 20" →

GG

III

BB

W

II

37"

III

← **Front**

1¾" rabbeted into side

Front Posts

First make up the front posts (U). Note that these can be made by laminating two pieces together to create the L-shape. Then make up the fluted quarter turnings (V) in the same way as the bottom turnings (C). Glue and fasten them in place to the posts. Make mortises in the inside front of the post assembly for the web frames (Z-CC); then cut a stopped dado in the back of the posts for the side tenons. Cut the groove at the top for the top front board (PP) tongues and at the bottom for lower front facer (X).

Sides

Make up the sides from solid stock, or use hardwood-faced ¾-inch plywood if you prefer. Cut a tenon on each front edge to fit into the front post dado. Then cut rabbets in the back edges of the sides for the plywood back (II). Cut mortises for the back bottom and top stretcher pieces. Then cut a rabbet across the top inside edges for the top (Y).

Back

Saw the bottom back stretcher (III) to size and cut the rabbet on its back edge for the back. Make the end rabbets to mate with the rabbets at the back of the sides (W). Then enlarge the squared drawing for the top back board (QQ) and cut it to shape on a band saw. Make the shaped rabbet all around its inside top edge for the scroll top pieces (WW). Then cut the rabbet or half-lap joint on its bottom edge so it can fit down over the case top and into the back rabbets of the side (see top back board detail). Note that you will also have to make a stopped rabbet on the bottom inside face of both sides of the top back board to accommodate the rabbets for the side (as shown in the detail). Saw the back to size from ⅜- or ½-inch plywood.

Web Frame Assembly

Make up the web frame assemblies in the same way as you did for the bottom case. Use hardwood for the facers and softwood for the inside frame assemblies. Assemble with mortise-and-tenon joints. Cut mortises in the front facer pieces (Z) for the vertical facers (GG,HH). Cut these to shape and make tenons on them to fit into the front facer boards. Cut mortises in top front and back boards for the upper drawer tilt strips (DD).

Case Assembly

With these pieces cut and the web frames assembled, the next step is to assemble the case. Start by placing glue on the side (W) tongues and fitting them in the front post (U) grooves. Then put the web frame units between the two front post assemblies with glue in all of the mortises. Fit the vertical facers (GG,HH) in place at the same time.

Install the top (Y) in the rabbets in the top edge of the side pieces and attach the lower back stretcher (III).

Make sure the entire unit is square and then clamp securely to allow the glue to set. While the glue is setting, insert dowel pins into holes in the side tongues and grooves to hold them securely together.

Fasten the web-frame side pieces to the case sides with screws driven from the inside of the web frames. Fasten the upper drawer slides (EE) with glue and screws to the sides and down into the web frames. Then add the center drawer guides (FF), with glue and small brads. Fasten the bottom cleats (OOO) in place to the underside of the bottom drawer web frame.

Scroll Case

After the case has set, remove it from the clamps and saw the top front board (PP) to size following the squared drawing. Cut it to shape on a band saw, then make the back rabbet on a shaper or with a router. Cut stopped tongues on each end that fit down into the front post grooves (see top front board detail). Then enlarge the squared drawing for the

Top Front Board Detail

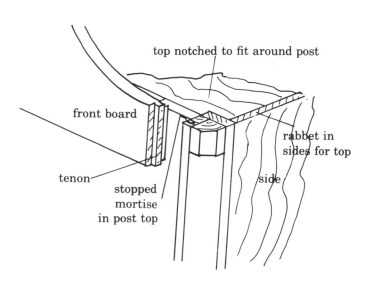

Back Corner

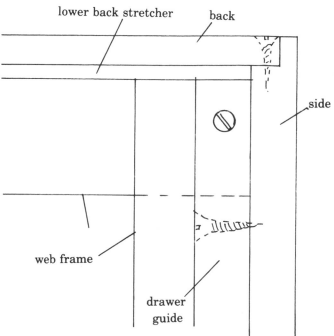

Upper Case

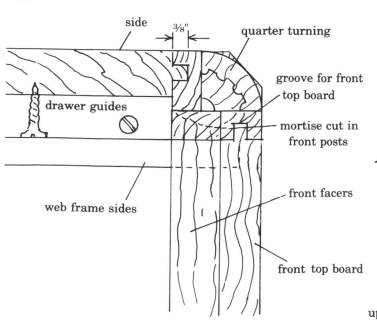

Top Back Board Detail

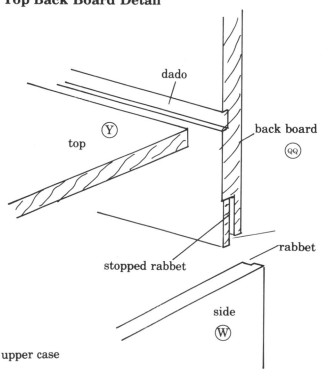

relief carving and carve to the pattern. You could, of course, use applied carvings, but they wouldn't be as authentic, and there is a chance they will loosen with time.

Cut the inside holding cleats (RR,SS) and fasten them to the inside edges of both front (PP) and back (QQ) boards. Cleats (RR) should be set back ⅛ inch from the edge. They will provide the mounting for stock used to face the inner curve of the scroll top.

Scroll Turning
There are large turned dowels (TT) that fit between the front and back top boards. They are turned on a lathe.

Scroll Case Assembly
With the front and back boards and the turned scroll pieces cut to size, the next step is to start assembly of the top unit. Do this by placing the front top board (PP) in place with its tongues in the grooves in the front posts (U). Then position the back board (QQ) down over the case top and into the rabbets in the back of the sides (W). Fasten it in place with glue and screws. Put the turned scroll blocks between the two pieces and attach with glue and screws. Install the thin inside scroll pieces (UU) below the turned scroll block and against the inside cleats (RR) on both the left and right sides of the top unit. Fasten the bottom pieces of the inside scroll to the bottom cleats (SS). Install the top board (VV) fastening in place to the cleats on the front and back boards.

Once the inside scroll pieces are installed, you're ready to apply the scroll top pieces (WW). These are cut to fit into the rabbets in the front and back boards and fastened in place with glue and screws through the front and back of the top boards into their ends. It takes quite a bit of hand fitting to get the scroll top board edges evenly joined. This is done by hand planing the edges of each succeeding board to fit to the preceding one. After the final assembly is completed, a hand-held belt sander can be used to further smooth up the top of the scroll case.

Moulding
After the basic case has been assembled, cut the top moulding. The side moulding pieces (XX) are shaped by making successive passes on a shaper or with a router. You can even use one or two pieces to make up the thick stock if necessary.

The curved front moulding (YY) is cut in basically the same way, except that the first step is to bandsaw the underside profile of the moulding. Leave the stock full size for ease of handling. Shape the curved moulding on a shaper, using a guide-pin system. Once you have the moulding shaped properly, cut it away from the stock on the top profile. This gives you the curved moulding pieces. Fasten them to the top of the arched case and to the sides with dowels

and glue. Cut a 45-degree mitre joint at the corners. Clamp the moulding in place until the glue sets.

Carve the front rosettes (AAA) for the top ends of each scroll turning (TT) and glue them in place to the front. Note that there is an "under" piece (ZZ) turned to match the profile of the turning that is first attached to the front of the front board; then the rosette is added to the top of that.

Rosette Detail

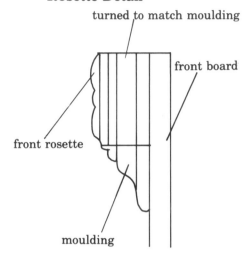

Pediments
Turn the side pediments (BBB) to rough shape and then finish-carve the upper flame portion. The top center pediment (CCC) is a filigree-carved piece. First cut it to size and shape from solid stock using a scroll saw. Then carve to shape.

Cut the rope carvings (DDD) and other mouldings (EEE) for the pediment and install on the front board.

Drawers
Assemble the drawers (JJ-OO) in the same manner as for the bottom case, then install. Make sure they fit properly. Finally, install the plywood back (II) with glue and screws.

Final Assembly of Units
The upper and lower cases are joined by fastening the lower inside frame cleats (JJJ) of the upper case to the top inside web frame of the lower case. Drive down from the inside. If at any time you need to disassemble the piece to move it, merely take out the drawer and remove the screws.

After the top piece has been carefully positioned and fastened in place, cut the trim moulding (P,Q) that goes around the outside edge to conceal the joint. Note that it is joined at the corners with two joints (see top view of bottom case). Join with glue and splines, then position it around the top of the case. Anchor the bottom case with screws from the inside.

Materials List

Base Unit

A—Legs—$3 \times 3 \times 32\frac{1}{2}''$, 4 req'd.

B—Leg wings—$2 \times 3 \times 4''$, 8 req'd.

C—Front-leg columns—$1\frac{1}{2} \times 1\frac{1}{2} \times 16''$, cut into quarters from one piece, 2 req'd.

D—Sides—$\frac{3}{4} \times 17\frac{3}{4} \times 18\frac{1}{4}''$, 2 req'd.

E—Back bottom apron—$\frac{3}{4} \times 3\frac{3}{4} \times 36''$, 1 req'd.

F—Back—$\frac{3}{8}''$ plywood $\times 14\frac{3}{4} \times 37''$, 1 req'd.

Web Frame/Facer Assemblies

G—Upper web frame/facers—$\frac{7}{8} \times 2 \times 37''$, 2 req'd.

H—Web frame backs—$\frac{7}{8} \times 1\frac{1}{2} \times 37''$, 2 req'd.

I—Web frame sides—$\frac{7}{8} \times 2 \times 20''$, 4 req'd.

J—Web frame cross-pieces—$\frac{7}{8} \times 2 \times 20''$, 4 req'd.

K—Vertical facers—$\frac{3}{4} \times \frac{7}{8} \times 6\frac{3}{4}''$, 2 req'd.

L—Bottom front apron—$1 \times 7 \times 37''$, 1 req'd.

M—Bottom drawer stretchers—$\frac{7}{8} \times 2 \times 19\frac{1}{2}''$, 8 req'd.

N—Bottom vertical facer/stretchers—$\frac{7}{8} \times 2 \times 19\frac{1}{2}''$, 2 req'd.

O—Drawer glides—$\frac{3}{4} \times 1\frac{1}{4} \times 17''$, 4 req'd.

P—Top side moulding—$\frac{7}{8} \times 1\frac{1}{8} \times 22''$, cut to length, 2 req'd.

Q—Top front moulding—$\frac{7}{8} \times 1\frac{1}{8} \times 42''$, cut to length, 1 req'd.

R—Bottom drawer

    Front—$1\frac{1}{4} \times 8\frac{1}{4} \times 12''$, 1 req'd.

    Sides—$\frac{1}{2} \times 8\frac{1}{4} \times 20\frac{1}{2}''$, 2 req'd.

    Back—$\frac{1}{2} \times 8\frac{1}{4} \times 12''$, 1 req'd.

    Bottom—$\frac{1}{4} \times 11\frac{1}{2} \times 20''$, 1 req'd.

    Slide—$\frac{3}{16} \times \frac{3}{4} \times 18''$, 1 req'd.

S—Bottom side drawer

    Fronts—$\frac{3}{4} \times 6\frac{5}{8} \times 10\frac{7}{8}''$, 2 req'd.

    Sides—$\frac{1}{2} \times 6\frac{5}{8} \times 20\frac{1}{2}''$, 4 req'd.

    Backs—$\frac{1}{2} \times 6\frac{5}{8} \times 10\frac{7}{8}''$, 2 req'd.

    Bottoms—$\frac{1}{4} \times 10\frac{3}{8} \times 20''$, 2 req'd.

    Slide—$\frac{3}{16} \times \frac{3}{4} \times 18''$, 1 req'd.

T—Top drawer

    Front—$\frac{3}{4} \times 5\frac{3}{4} \times 35\frac{7}{8}''$, 1 req'd.

    Sides—$\frac{1}{2} \times 5\frac{3}{4} \times 20\frac{1}{2}''$, 2 req'd.

    Back—$\frac{1}{2} \times 5\frac{3}{4} \times 35\frac{7}{8}''$, 1 req'd.

    Bottom—$\frac{1}{4} \times 20 \times 34\frac{3}{8}''$, 1 req'd.

    Slide—$\frac{3}{16} \times \frac{3}{4} \times 18''$, 1 req'd.

Top Unit

U—Front posts—$1\frac{1}{2} \times 1\frac{1}{2} \times 42\frac{1}{4}''$, 2 req'd.

V—Fluted quarter-columns—$1 \times 1 \times 37''$, 2 req'd.

W—Sides—$\frac{3}{4} \times 19 \times 42\frac{1}{4}''$, 2 req'd.

X—Lower front facer—$\frac{3}{4} \times 2\frac{1}{4}'' \times 37''$, 1 req'd.

Y—Top—$\frac{3}{4} \times 19 \times 38''$, 1 req'd.

Web Frame Assemblies

Z—Web frame facers—$\frac{7}{8} \times 1\frac{1}{2} \times 37\frac{1}{2}''$, 4 req'd.

AA—Inside bottom web frame facer—$\frac{3}{4} \times \frac{3}{4} \times 37\frac{1}{2}''$, 1 req'd.

BB—Web frame back—$\frac{7}{8} \times 2 \times 37\frac{1}{2}''$, 5 req'd.

CC—Web frame stretchers—$\frac{3}{4} \times 2 \times 18\frac{3}{4}''$, 20 req'd.

DD—Upper drawer tilt strips—$\frac{3}{4} \times 2 \times 19''$, cut to length, 3 req'd.

EE—Drawer slides—$\frac{3}{4} \times \frac{3}{4} \times 18\frac{1}{4}''$, 10 req'd.

FF—Drawer guides—$\frac{1}{4} \times 1 \times 19''$, 8 req'd.

GG—Vertical facers—$\frac{7}{8} \times 1\frac{1}{2} \times 5''$, 2 req'd.

HH—Vertical facer—$\frac{7}{8} \times 1\frac{1}{2} \times 6\frac{1}{2}''$, 1 req'd.

II—Back—$\frac{3}{8}''$ plywood $\times 38 \times 39''$, 1 req'd.

III—Bottom back stretcher—$\frac{3}{4} \times 2 \times 38\frac{1}{2}''$, 1 req'd.

JJJ—Lower inside frame cleats—$\frac{3}{4} \times 1\frac{1}{2} \times 18''$, 2 req'd.

JJ—Top center drawer

    Front—$\frac{3}{4} \times 3\frac{7}{8} \times 16\frac{1}{8}''$, 1 req'd.

    Sides—$\frac{1}{2} \times 3\frac{7}{8} \times 19\frac{1}{4}''$, 2 req'd.

    Back—$\frac{1}{2} \times 3\frac{7}{8} \times 16\frac{1}{8}''$, 1 req'd.

    Bottom—$\frac{1}{4} \times 15\frac{5}{8} \times 18\frac{3}{4}''$, 1 req'd.

KK—Outside top drawers

    Fronts—$\frac{3}{4} \times 3\frac{7}{8} \times 8\frac{7}{8}''$, 2 req'd.

    Sides—$\frac{1}{2} \times 3\frac{7}{8} \times 19\frac{1}{4}''$, 4 req'd.

    Backs—$\frac{1}{2} \times 3\frac{7}{8} \times 8\frac{7}{8}''$, 2 req'd.

    Bottoms—$\frac{1}{4} \times 8\frac{3}{8} \times 18\frac{3}{4}''$, 2 req'd.

LL—Drawer

    Fronts—$\frac{3}{4} \times 5\frac{3}{8} \times 17\frac{3}{8}''$, 2 req'd.

    Sides—$\frac{1}{2} \times 5\frac{3}{8} \times 19\frac{1}{4}''$, 4 req'd.

    Backs—$\frac{1}{2} \times 5\frac{3}{8} \times 17\frac{3}{8}''$, 2 req'd.

    Bottoms—$\frac{1}{4} \times 16\frac{7}{8} \times 18\frac{3}{4}''$, 2 req'd.

MM—Drawer

    Front—$\frac{3}{4} \times 6\frac{7}{8} \times 35\frac{7}{8}''$, 1 req'd.

    Sides—$\frac{1}{2} \times 6\frac{7}{8} \times 19\frac{1}{4}''$, 2 req'd.

    Back—$\frac{1}{2} \times 6\frac{7}{8} \times 35\frac{7}{8}''$, 1 req'd.

    Bottom—$\frac{1}{4} \times 18\frac{3}{4} \times 35\frac{3}{8}''$, 1 req'd.

NN—Drawer

    Front—$\frac{3}{4} \times 7\frac{7}{8} \times 35\frac{7}{8}''$, 1 req'd.

    Sides—$\frac{1}{2} \times 7\frac{7}{8} \times 19\frac{1}{4}''$, 2 req'd.

    Back—$\frac{1}{2} \times 7\frac{7}{8} \times 35\frac{7}{8}''$, 1 req'd.

    Bottom—$\frac{1}{4} \times 18\frac{3}{4} \times 35\frac{3}{8}''$, 1 req'd.

OO—Drawer

    Front—$\frac{3}{4} \times 8\frac{7}{8} \times 35\frac{7}{8}''$, 1 req'd.

    Sides—$\frac{1}{2} \times 8\frac{7}{8} \times 19\frac{1}{4}''$, 2 req'd.

    Back—$\frac{1}{2} \times 8\frac{7}{8} \times 35\frac{7}{8}''$, 1 req'd.

    Bottom—$\frac{1}{4} \times 18\frac{3}{4} \times 35\frac{3}{8}''$, 1 req'd.

OOO—Bottom side cleats—¾ × 1 × 18″, 2 req'd.

Scroll Case

PP—Front board—1 × 18½ × 39″, cut to fit, 1 req'd.

QQ—Back board—1 × 18½ × 39″, cut to fit, 1 req'd.

RR—Inside cleats—¾ × 3 × 8″, 4 req'd.

SS—Inside cleats—¾ × 1 × 12″, 2 req'd.

TT—Scroll turnings—4 × 4 × 18¾″, 2 req'd.

UU—Inside scroll pieces—⅛ × 8 × 18¾″, 2 req'd.

VV—Upper top piece—½ × 12 × 18¾″, cut to fit, 1 req'd.

WW—Scroll top pieces—¾ × 2¼ × 19¼″, cut to fit, 30 req'd.

XX—Side mouldings—2¼ × 2¾ × 24″, cut to fit, 2 req'd.

YY—Front mouldings—2¼ × 10 × 24″, cut to fit, 2 req'd.

ZZ—Front rosette mouldings—1 × 4 × 4″, 2 req'd.

AAA—Front rosettes—¾ × 4 × 4″, 2 req'd.

BBB—Side pediments—2½ × 2½ × 14″, 2 req'd.

CCC—Top pediment—2 × 7 × 11½″, 1 req'd.

DDD—Pediment moulding—¾ × ¾ × 10″, cut to fit, 1 req'd.

EEE—Pediment moulding—¾ × ¾ × 10″, cut to fit, 1 req'd.

Metric Equivalents

INCHES TO MILLIMETRES AND CENTIMETRES

MM—millimetres　　*CM—centimetres*

Inches	MM	CM	Inches	CM	Inches	CM
⅛	3	0.3	9	22.9	30	76.2
¼	6	0.6	10	25.4	31	78.7
⅜	10	1.0	11	27.9	32	81.3
½	13	1.3	12	30.5	33	83.8
⅝	16	1.6	13	33.0	34	86.4
¾	19	1.9	14	35.6	35	88.9
⅞	22	2.2	15	38.1	36	91.4
1	25	2.5	16	40.6	37	94.0
1¼	32	3.2	17	43.2	38	96.5
1½	38	3.8	18	45.7	39	99.1
1¾	44	4.4	19	48.3	40	101.6
2	51	5.1	20	50.8	41	104.1
2½	64	6.4	21	53.3	42	106.7
3	76	7.6	22	55.9	43	109.2
3½	89	8.9	23	58.4	44	111.8
4	102	10.2	24	61.0	45	114.3
4½	114	11.4	25	63.5	46	116.8
5	127	12.7	26	66.0	47	119.4
6	152	15.2	27	68.6	48	121.9
7	178	17.8	28	71.1	49	124.5
8	203	20.3	29	73.7	50	127.0

Index